The Politics and Economics of Power

This edited collection looks at the emerging relationship between politics and economics. The analysis of power relations – traditionally the focus of political science – is becoming increasingly important in enabling economists to understand concepts such as the 'contested nature' of market exchanges. These papers examine power relations in the firm and the market-place and offer an economic perspective on political relations. The book is divided into three sections:

- politics and power in economic organizations
- the economic analysis of political organizations
- politics, economics and social change

The final section considers how a combination of economic and political tools can be used effectively to analyse social change. Presenting some original and thought-provoking views on important issues, this volume will be of great interest to students and researchers in political economy and related areas.

Samuel Bowles is Professor of Economics at the University of Massachusetts at Amherst. **Maurizio Franzini** and **Ugo Pagano** are both Professors of Economics at Siena University.

Routledge Siena Studies in Political Economy

The Siena Summer School hosts lectures by distinguished scholars on topics characterized by a lively research activity. The lectures collected in this series offer a clear account of the alternative research paths that characterize a certain field. Former workshops of the School were printed by different publishers. They include:

Macroeconomics: a survey of research strategies
Edited by Alessandro Vercelli and Nicola Dimitri
Oxford University Press, 1992

International problems of economic interdependence
Edited by Massimo Di Matteo, Mario Baldassarri and Robert Mundell
Macmillan, 1994

Ethics, rationality and economic behaviour
Edited by Francesco Farina, Frank Hahn and Stefano Vannucci
Clarendon Press, 1996

New theories in growth and development
Edited by Fabrizio Coricelli, Massimo Di Matteo and Frank Hahn
Macmillan, 1998

Forthcoming:

The evolution of economic diversity
Edited by Antonio Nicita and Ugo Pagano
Routledge, 1999

The Routledge Siena Studies in Political Economy Series gives a comprehensive access to the publications of the School, which emphasizes the common methodology employed in organizing the different workshops.

The Politics and Economics of Power

Edited by Samuel Bowles, Maurizio Franzini and Ugo Pagano

London and New York

First published 1999
by Routledge
11 New Fetter Lane, London EC4P 4EE

Simultaneously published in the USA and Canada
by Routledge
29 West 35th Street, New York, NY 10001

Typeset in Times by J&L Composition Ltd, Filey, North Yorkshire
Printed and bound in Great Britain by Clays Ltd, St Ives PLC

British Library Cataloguing in Publication Data
A catalogue record for this book is available
from the British Library

Library of Congress Cataloging in Publication Data
The politics and economics of power/[edited by] S. Bowles, M.
Franzini, and U. Pagano.
p. cm.
Includes bibliographical references.
1. Political science–Economic aspects. 2. Economics–Political
aspects. 3. Power (Social sciences) I. Bowles, Samuel.
II. Franzini, M. (Maurizio), 1945– . III. Pagano, Ugo, 1951– .
JA77.P67 1999
320'.01'1–dc21   98–35367
                                                           CIP

ISBN 0-415-18542-4

Contents

List of contributors   vii

1   **Introduction: trespassing the boundaries of politics
    and economics**   1
    SAMUEL BOWLES, MAURIZIO FRANZINI, AND UGO PAGANO

PART I
Politics and power in economic organizations   11

2   **Power in competitive exchange**   13
    SAMUEL BOWLES AND HERBERT GINTIS

3   **Adaptation and opportunism in political and economic
    markets**   31
    MAURIZIO FRANZINI

4   **The internal politics of the firm**   46
    PAUL MILGROM AND JOHN ROBERTS

5   **Is power an economic good? Notes on social scarcity and
    the economics of positional goods**   63
    UGO PAGANO

6   **How politics limits markets: power, legitimacy, choice**   85
    JOHN DUNN

PART II
The economic analysis of political organizations   101

7   **Modeling politics as a competitive endeavor**   103
    ALBERT BRETON

8   **Political parties and representative democracy**   129
    GIANLUIGI GALEOTTI

9 **Constitutionally constrained and safeguarded competition in markets and politics: with reference to a European constitution**   141
   VIKTOR VANBERG

10 **Political parties, pressure groups, and democracy: a transaction cost theory of political institutions**   167
   DONALD WITTMAN

PART III
The 'contamination' between economic and political factors in institutional change   177

11 **The coming of nationalism, and its interpretation: the myths of nation and class**   179
   ERNEST GELLNER

12 **Norms of exclusion**   225
   RUSSELL HARDIN

13 **From expressionism and futurism to kitsch: ethnic and intergenerational conflict, political inaction, and the rise of dictatorship**   260
   RONALD WINTROBE

14 **Multiple equilibria, critical masses, and institutional change: the *coup d'état* problem**   286
   ULRICH WITT

   Index   300

Contributors

Samuel Bowles, Department of Economics, University of Massachusetts at Amherst, USA

Albert Breton, Department of Economics, University of Toronto, Canada

John Dunn, King's College, Cambridge, UK

Maurizio Franzini, Department of Political Economy, University of Siena, Italy

Gianluigi Galeotti, University of Rome 'La Sapienza', Italy

Ernest Gellner (deceased), formerly of Cambridge University, UK

Herbert Gintis, Department of Economics, University of Massachusetts at Amherst, USA

Russell Hardin, Department of Politics, New York University, USA

Paul Milgrom, Department of Economics, Stanford University, USA

Ugo Pagano, Department of Political Economy, University of Siena, Italy

John Roberts, Graduate School of Business, Stanford University, USA

Viktor Vanberg, University of Freiburg, Germany

Ronald Wintrobe, Department of Economics, University of Western Ontario, Canada

Ulrich Witt, Max-Planck-Institute for Research into Economic Systems, Evolutionary Economics Unit, Jena, Gemany

Donald Wittman, Economics Department, University of California, Santa Cruz, USA

1   Introduction

Trespassing the boundaries of politics and economics[1]

Samuel Bowles, Maurizio Franzini, and Ugo Pagano

The traditional division between economics and politics is collapsing. The analysis of power relations, which used to be the focus of political science, is becoming very important to understand the 'contested nature' of market exchanges; moreover, opening the 'black boxes' by which firms used to be characterized in economic theory has focussed the attention of economists on the internal politics of the firm. At the same time politics has been increasingly characterized as an exchange between utility-maximizing voters and vote-maximizing politicians.

This book is divided into three parts that focus on these stimulating developments of the relationship between economics and politics. The essays contained in the first part examine the internal politics characterizing such traditional economic organizations as firms and the power relations existing in the most classic economic institution: the marketplace. The second part considers the 'market exchange' and, in general, the economic view of political relations; the working of democracy and the rationale for constitutional constraints are examined within this framework. Finally, the last part shows that the analysis of social change can successfully exploit the two-way 'contamination processes' that have been examined in the first two parts. Nationalism, exclusion of minorities, the rise of dictatorship, and in general social change require a joint and interrelated analysis of economic and political factors.

We will briefly consider in the final three sections of this introduction how each paper contained in this book contributes to overcoming the traditional fences that used to separate economics and politics. In the next section we will give a brief account of the reasons that motivated the erection of those protective fences and the factors that made the social scientists feel increasingly uncomfortable about the fields they intended to enclose.

The demise and rebirth of political economy

Social scientists and political philosophers commonly represent human interactions as exchanges; the terms social contract, electoral marketplace, exchange of favors, marriage contract, marketplace of ideas, and linguistic exchange attest to the ample scope of the market metaphor. 'Interaction between persons is an exchange of goods, material and non-material,' wrote the sociologist George Homans (1958: 597), a founder of the theory of social exchange. But if economic analogies have been widely used in the contemporary social sciences and in political philosophy since Hobbes, modern economists have seen little need for cross-disciplinary boundaries in order to understand the economy.

John Stuart Mill famously sought to distinguish between allocational matters, the subject of economic analysis, on the one hand, and distribution, the province of politics and ethics on the other. A generation later, Leon Walras (1954), in laying out the precepts of the then-young neoclassical paradigm, sharply distinguished his contributions from the social economics of the classical founders of the discipline and from his contemporaries in the German historical school and Marxian political economy. He sought a 'pure science' of economics as 'a relationship among things,' not 'people.' The flourishing of theoretical work during the century following him did much to realize this objective. Significantly, political economy dropped the adjective, becoming simply economics. Thus, the neoclassical paradigm at its zenith borrowed its metaphors from the physical sciences, particularly physics: the exchange of goods is more like a heat exchange than an exchange of greetings.

And so when Abba Lerner (1972: 259) told the American Economics Association over a quarter of a century ago that 'An economic transaction is a solved political problem. Economics has gained the title Queen of the Social Sciences by choosing solved political problems as its domain,' it was the prose that caught one's attention; the substantive claim was uncontroversial. Economists happily interpreted Mill's separation of the allocative from the distributional aspects of economics as a prescription to leave to someone else the analysis of politics, the structure of government, and the etiology of economic policy.

A methodological schizophrenia thus emerged: economists assumed that economic actors pursued the self-regarding and outcome-based preferences of the textbook *Homo economicus*, while naïvely trusting civil servants and politicians to implement faithfully the wills of the citizenry in conformance to the dictates of an idealized *Homo civicus*. Economists trained their sights on market failures, while exempting public-policy and governmental structure from any sustained investigation of possible discrepancies between individual incentives and social objectives. Whence the hubris of mid-century welfare economics: many economists came to advocate governmental interventions to correct market failures as a kind of *deus ex machina*.

The result was a double hiatus between economic and political reasoning: political analysis had nothing to say about the functioning of the economy, while economic analysis was rarely deployed to understand politics in its recognized domain, the state. This hiatus has provided the conceptual foundation for the disciplinary boundaries which came to divide economics from the other social and behavioral sciences. At its simplest, the under- lying conception of society is one characterized by a remarkable degree of specialization among institutions: governments govern and economic institutions allocate resources, while families and religious institutions transmit culture and yet other institutions carry out other specialized functions.

Of course nobody believes this literally: historians, anthropologists, political scientists, and sociologists, often borrowing extensively from economics, routinely recognize the political consequences of economic organization.

The historian E. P. Thompson (1971) described markets more as politically charged meeting places than as the anonymous interactions of neoclassical economic theory:

> In eighteenth-century Britain or France . . . the market remained a social as well as an economic nexus. It was the place where one hundred and one social and personal transactions went on; where news was passed, rumor and gossip flew around, politics was (if ever) discussed in the inns or wine shops round the market square. The market was the place where the people, because they were numer- ous, felt for a moment that they were strong.
>
> (134–5)

For anthropologists, the exchange process, whether deemed a market or not, underpins the entire social structure. Bronislaw Malinowski, writing of the Trobriand Islanders early in this century, found that:

> the whole tribal life is permeated by a constant give and take; that every ceremony; every legal and customary act is done to the accom- paniment of material gift and counter gift; that wealth, given and taken is one of the main instruments of social organization, of the power of the chief, of the bonds of kinship, and of relationships in law.
>
> (1922: 167)

According to Marshall Sahlins (1974: 186–7) the allocational role of what he calls primitive exchange is secondary to providing social cohesion in a society in which politics cannot be confined to the state for the simple reason that there is none:

> The indicative condition of primitive society is the absence of a public and sovereign power: persons and (especially) groups confront each other not merely as distinct interests but with the possible inclination and certain right to physically prosecute these interests.

Force is decentralized . . . the social compact has yet to be drawn, the state non-existent. So peacemaking is not a sporadic intersocietal event, it is a continuous process going on within society itself.

And Gayle Rubin's 'traffic in women' (1975: 174), based on the work of Claude Levi-Straus (1969), suggests that the exchange process has political as well as allocational consequences:

The marriage ceremonies recorded in the ethnographic literature are moments in a ceaseless and ordered procession in which women, children, shells, words, cattle, names, fish, ancestors, whales teeth, pigs, yams, spells, dances, mats, etc. pass from hand to hand leaving as their tracks the ties that bind.

Nor are these assessments confined to the primitive and the past: Charles E. Lindblom (1977: 171–2) describes capitalism as a system in which significant powers little different in kind from those exercised by governments are delegated to owners and exercised at least in part through competitive markets:

Corporate executives . . . decide a nation's industrial technology, the pattern of work organization, the location of industry, market structure, resource allocation, and, of course, executive compensation and status. . . . In short in any private enterprise system, a large category of major decisions is turned over to business men both small and large.

Not surprisingly, legal theorists have found it difficult to draw coherent boundaries between state and economy, finding little grounds for restricting law to state-enforced commands. H. L. Hart (1961) refers to:

the original conception of law as consisting of orders backed by threats of sanctions which are to be exacted when the orders are disobeyed.

(36)

Within the territory of each country there may be many different persons or bodies of persons giving general orders backed by threats and receiving habitual obedience.

(24)

Relatedly L. L. Fuller's celebrated *The morality of law* (1969: 129) asserts the broad dispersal throughout society of the 'authority to enact rules and to reach decisions that will be regarded as properly binding on those affected by them,' going on to comment that 'the intellectual climate of the late eighteenth century was such as to obscure a recognition of the centers of authority created when men form voluntary associations.'

The intellectual climate of late twentieth century made the politics of voluntary exchange more difficult to ignore; the rise of the large firm attracted the attention of Edward Hastings Chamberlain (1933), Joan Robinson (1933), and others and introduced market power to the economists' lexicon. But of more lasting importance was the representation of the internal organization of the firm as a mini command economy developed by Ronald Coase (1937). According to Coase allocation by authoritative fiat within the firm has efficiency advantages over the use of markets, and the balance between the costs of each mode of allocation – exchange and command – determines the boundaries of the firm. These ideas were subsequently developed and extended by Herbert Simon (1951), Armen Alchian and Harold Demsetz (1972), Stephen Marglin (1974), Richard Edwards (1979), Herbert Gintis (1976), Harry Braverman (1974), Oliver Williamson (1985), Karl Shapiro and Joseph Stiglitz (1984), and others.

The politics of exchange

The key theoretical development that allowed economists to extend the reasoning of Coase is the recognition that contracts are frequently either incomplete – failing to specify in full the terms of the exchange, as in most employment contracts – or unenforceable – as is the promise to repay a loan by a borrower who may be bankrupt when the loan is due. By contrast to the incomplete contracting situation which Coase investigated, where contracts are complete there is nothing for power to be about, as the entire content of the exchange is fully determined at the moment of signing. 'What does it mean,' Oliver Hart (1995) asks rhetorically, 'to put someone "in charge" of an action or decision if all actions can be specified in a contract?' Moreover, suppose (whatever it means) someone was 'in charge' of a 'subordinate': what would motivate obedience if markets cleared and thus all parties to transaction could opt for their next best transaction at zero cost?

Transaction cost theory and the theory of incomplete contracts had asked questions that could only be answered by allowing some exercise of power within markets and firms. While the economic paradigm and the theory of political exchanges had already allowed economists to jump rather easily into the political field, the fence had also been broken to allow traffic in the opposite way: the analysis power, which was supposed to be enclosed in the political field, was bound to penetrate the very roots of the analysis blossoming in the economic field.

The theory of incomplete contracts provided not only a motive for power – enforcement of non-contractual aspects of an exchange – but as we will see in the essay below by Bowles and Gintis, a means to exercise power, that is to secure obedience to commands. Incomplete contracting and the resulting bargaining costs and possibilities for opportunistic behavior also form the basis of the contributions of Maurizio Franzini, and Paul Milgrom and John Roberts.

The latter paper makes the political structure of the firm an endogenous response to the problem of influence seeking and influences costs. Franzini's analysis of the structure of economic organizations, drawing on Albert Hirschman's trilogy – exit, loyalty, and voice – introduces the trade-off between an organization's capacity to adapt to exogenous changes and to address the problem of opportunism on the part of its members.

Ugo Pagano analyzes power as a positional good in his essay, again drawing attention to the implications of contractual incompleteness. However, in this case the analysis refers to the welfare consequences of power. In contrast to Bowles and Gintis, who find that the exercise of power is Pareto efficiency enhancing, however, Pagano's analysis makes power a case polar to that of public goods: one may well experience being subjected to the power of another as a welfare loss. Indeed, goods like power and status entail that some individual must suffer the 'negative consumption' of these goods when somebody is consuming positive amounts of them. Thus, while in the case of public goods the typical free-rider problem arises from the impossibility of excluding others from their consumption, in the case of power and other positional goods the externality problems arise from the unavoidable inclusion of others in the consumption of 'negative' amounts of the good.

The economics of power

If the first aspect of the double hiatus between politics and economics to come under attack was the apolitical conception of the economy, doubts about the schizophrenic assumptions underpinning the government servant as *Homo civicus* soon followed. Less than a decade after Coase's essay on the firm as a command economy, Frederich Hayek's (1945) attack on the informational foundations of the theory of state intervention captured the attention of economists. Optimism concerning government intervention to attenuate market failures had been unduly fostered, Hayek wrote, by the assumption that the appropriate government servants possessed, or could possess, the information necessary to implement allocations improving on those provided by markets.

Before another decade was through Kenneth Arrow (1951) had demonstrated the impossibility of a democratic aggregation of preferences consistent with a set of axioms apparently reflecting a minimalist version of the philosophical commitments of liberalism. The result was to throw into question the presumption that the state could implement citizen preferences where these conflicted with market outcomes, even if the information problems raised by Hayek were not decisive.

Anthony Downs' *An economic theory of democracy* (1957), James Buchanan and Gordon Tullock's *Calculus of consent* (1962), and Mancur

Olsen's *Logic of collective action* (1965) further extended the model of self-interested individual action to the political sphere. These and subsequent contributions of public choice theory by Gary Becker (1983) and others brought governments and markets under the same lens: outcomes in both spheres were now understood as manifestations of the interplay of intentional actors, both governmental and private.

Neither the rational actor view of politics nor the political interpretation of economic institutions was entirely new. The model of political behavior as intentional action goes back at least to Nicolò Machiavelli, and the representation of markets, firms, and other economic institutions as political arenas was amply developed by Karl Marx. What the recent trespassing across the boundaries of politics and economics has done, however, is not simply to rediscover old truths (or to recycle dubious claims), but rather to embed the older themes of political economy in a general model of individual interaction and generalized competition in electoral arenas no less than in markets.

Thus Donald Wittman's essay invokes the founding principle of public choice economics – that 'understanding . . . political organizations should be based on the same economic principles that are used to explain economic organization' – with the innovation that the key concept used – transactions costs – is one foreign to the conventional neoclassical paradigm.

Albert Breton argues for a neo-Madisonian alternative to the public choice, public economics, and welfare economics accounts of what governments actually do. Gianluigi Galeotti and Viktor Vanberg develop the analogies between political and economic competition and explore the associated dilemmas of accountability and efficiency of governmental outcomes. Building on these and related themes John Dunn argues for the development of an integrated political economy as a common field of study.

The expanding domain of economics

While the resulting work has obliterated the methodological boundary between politics and economics and has installed *Homo economicus* in the leading role among the *dramatis personae* of social science, the result has been not only an 'expansion of the domain of economics' in Armen Alchian's words, but a reconsideration of some of its usual practices. Among these two are striking.

First, as the rational actor model has been applied to the political arena the deficiencies of the standard assumption of self-regarding and outcome-oriented preferences as a behavioral model have become apparent. Forms of political behavior – even the most rudimentary such as voting – often escape explanation within the terms of the standard rational actor model. Thus understanding ethnic identity, the politics of exclusion, and nationalism requires a broadening of the notion of preferences and a more searching inquiry into their provenance.

The papers by Russell Hardin on norms of exclusion, by Ronald Wintrobe on ethnic capital, and the late Ernest Gellner on nationalism reflect these new interests. Hardin points out that 'solving' collective action problems may be undesirable where the results are exclusive or hostile towards others. Wintrobe explains why there may be an 'overinvestment' in ethnic capital, leading to high levels of ethnic identity and interethnic tensions. Gellner offers a sweeping interpretation of the interaction between the geographic extension of the division of labor, the development of modern 'exo-educational' institutions, and the rise of nationalism.

Gellner's theory of nationalism parallels and anticipates many topics typical of the new institutional literature (Pagano 1996): markets need a homogeneous culture requiring ethnic-specific investments that can be greatly enhanced by the political safeguards supplied by the national state. In an academic division of labor where economists (with few exceptions such as Albert Breton's (1964) contribution) were not concerned with such important issues, Gellner provided a famous and convincing explanation of nationalism. It is rather ironic that, whereas his theory appeared to many non-economists a brilliant economic interpretation of this phenomenon, some leading economists believed (and even told him) that his theory had little or nothing to do with economics: the proper 'economic' (and definitive) theory of nationalism was that individuals had a preference for it.

Second, the economic analysis of politics and of institutions generally has revealed the frequent coexistence of sharply contrasting institutional arrangements, even in highly competitive environments. As Ugo Pagano (1993) and Robert Boyer (1991) have shown, the organization of firms and labor relations contrasts sharply between Japan, Northern Europe, and the USA for example, with little apparent tendency for a single dominant form to emerge. Thus economists and other social scientists have begun to model social systems with multiple equilibria, thus rejecting the canonical economic practice of assuming a single equilibrium. Ulrich Witt's contribution applies this reasoning to the problem of institutional change, and the role of the *coup d'état*.

We dedicate these pages to the memory of Ernest Gellner, an artful trespasser across the boundaries of politics, history, anthropology, and economics. His essay, below, sadly is his last.

References

Alchain, Armen A. and Demsetz, Harold (1972) 'Production, information costs, and economic organization,' *American Economic Review* December: 777–95.

Arrow, Kenneth, J. (1951) *Social choice and individual values*, New York: John Wiley

Becker, Gary (1983) 'A theory of competition among pressure groups for political influence,' *Quarterly Journal of Economics* 98(3): 371–400.

Boyer, Robert (1991) 'Capital labour relation and wage formation: continuities and changes of national trajectories,' in T. Mizoguchi (ed.) *Making Economies More Efficient and More Equitable*, Tokyo: Oxford University Press, pp. 297–340.

Braverman, Harry (1974) *Labor and monopoly capital: the degradation of work in the twentieth century*, New York: Monthly Review Press.

Breton, Albert (1964) 'The economics of nationalism,' *Journal of Political Economy* 72(4): 376–86.

Buchanan, James M. and Tullock, Gordon (1962) *The calculus of consent: logical foundations of constitutional democracy*, Ann Arbor, MI: University of Michigan Press.

Chamberlin, Edward Hastings (1933) *The theory of monopolistic competition*, Cambridge, MA: Harvard University Press.

Coase, Ronald H. (1937) 'The nature of the firm,' *Economica*, New Series, 4: 387–405.

Downs, Anthony (1957) *An economic theory of democracy*, New York: Harper.

Edwards, Richard C. (1979) *Contested Terrain: The Transformation of the Workplace in the Twentieth Century*, New York: Basic Books.

Fuller, L. L. (1969) *The Morality of Law*, New Haven, CT: Yale University Press.

Gintis, Herbert (1976) 'The nature of the labor exchange and the theory of capitalist production,' *Reviews of Radical Political Economics* 8(2): 36–54.

Hart, H. L. A. (1961) *The Concept of Law*, Oxford: Oxford University Press.

Hart, Oliver (1995) *Firms, Contracts, and Financial Structure*, Oxford: Clarendon Press.

Hayek, Friedrich A. (1945) 'The use of knowledge in society,' *American Economic Review* XXXV(4): 518–30.

Homans, George C. (1958) 'Social behavior as exchange,' *The American Journal of Sociology* 65(6): 597–606.

Lerner, Abba (1972) 'The economics and politics of consumer sovereignty,' *American Economics Review* Vol. 62.

Levi-Strauss, Claude (1969) *The Elementary Structures of Kinship*, London: Eyre & Spottiswoode.

Lindblom, Charles E. (1977) *Politics and Markets: The World's Political-Economic Systems*, New York: Basic Books.

Malinowski, Bronislaw (1922) *Argonauts of the Western Pacific: An Account of Native Enterprise and Adventure in the Archipelagoes of Melanesian New Guinea*, London: Routledge.

Marglin, Stephen (1974) 'What do bosses do?', *Review of Radical Political Economics* 6(2): 60–112.

Olson, Mancur (1965) *The logic of collective action: public goods and the theory of groups*, Cambridge, MA: Harvard University Press.

Pagano, Ugo (1993) 'Organizational equilibria and institutional stability,' in S.

Bowles, H. Gintis, and B. Gustafsson (eds) *Markets and Democracy: Participation, Accountability and Efficiency*, Cambridge: Cambridge University Press.

Pagano, Ugo (1996) 'Can economics explain nationalism?,' in A. Breton *et al.* (eds) *Nationalism and Rationality*, Cambridge: Cambridge University Press, pp. 173–204.

Robinson, Joan (1933) *The economics of imperfect competition*, London: Macmillan.

Rubin, Gayle (1975) 'The traffic in women: notes on the "political economy" of sex,' in Rayna Reiter (ed.) *Towards an Anthropology of Women*, New York: Monthly Review Press, pp. 157–210.

Sahlins, Marshall (1974) *Stone Age Economics*, Chicago: Aldine.

Shapiro, Carl and Stiglitz, Joseph E. (1984) 'Unemployment as a worker discipline device,' *American Economic Review* 74(3): 433–44.

Simon, Herbert A. (1951) 'A formal theory of the employment relation,' *Econometrica* 19: 293–305.

Thompson, E. P. (1971) 'The moral economy of the English crowd in the eighteenth century,' *Past and Present* 50: 76–136.

Walras, Leon (1954) *Elements of Pure Economics or the Theory of Social Wealth*, London: George Allen and Unwin.

Williamson, Oliver (1985) *The Economic Institutions of Capitalism*, New York: Free Press.

Part I
Politics and power in economic organizations

2　Power in competitive exchange

*Samuel Bowles and Herbert Gintis**

Introduction

In the standard Walrasian model of general economic equilibrium, competitively determined allocations maximize each agent's utility subject to that agent's wealth constraint, and prices simultaneously eliminate excess demand or supply in all markets. In competitive equilibrium, moreover, conditions of unimpeded entry and exit ensure that for each commodity (including such factors of production as labor and capital) there is a selling price such that each buyer faces a large number of sellers offering this commodity at this price, and no seller offers the commodity at a lower price; similarly there is an offer price such that each seller faces a large number of buyers offering to buy at this price, and no buyer offering to buy at a higher price.

It follows that in equilibrium, if agents A and B engage in an exchange, B's gain exactly equals the gain from his or her next best alternative. Were this not the case, competition would imply that a third agent consigned to such an alternative could have offered A a contract superior to B's, in which case A's contract with B would not have been accepted. Because in equilibrium the cost to B of foregoing an exchange with A is zero, A cannot affect B's well-being by terminating the exchange, and hence has no power over B.[1] In Walrasian competitive equilibrium of non-colluding agents, sanctions cannot be imposed.

Because each economic agent can refuse any exchange at no cost, power must be absent in an equilibrium of a competitive economy. Hence political and moral questions concerning the distribution of power and the presence of coercion in exchange relations do not arise.[2] David Gauthier expresses this view with considerable clarity:

> the operation of market cannot in itself raise any evaluative issues . . . the presumption of free activity ensures that no one is subject to any form of compulsion or to any type of limitation not already affecting her own actions as a solitary individual.[3]

It is precisely this putative lack of compulsion in voluntary exchange which allows Robert Nozick to distinguish between taxation and profits on the grounds that the former is 'on a par with forced labor' while the latter is not.[4] Less transparently, the claimed absence of coercion in voluntary exchange motivates John Rawls' concept of justice: 'These principles presuppose that the social structure can be divided into two more or less distinct parts . . . those . . . that define and secure the equal liberties of citizenship and those that specify and establish social and economic inequalities.' In the former sphere, political liberty – meaning 'the right to vote and to be eligible for public office' – should obtain. In the latter, by contrast, 'positions of authority and offices of command need not be subject to democratic election, but rather 'must be accessible to all.'[5]

But as we will see, Gauthier's claim that compulsion is absent in the market is mistaken. Rather, the exercise of power is a characteristic of voluntary exchange under quite general conditions.[6] For agent A to have power over agent B it is sufficient that, by imposing or threatening to impose sanctions on B, A is capable of affecting B's actions in ways which further A's interests, while B lacks this capacity with respect to A.[7] While this conception of power is not exhaustive (we present a sufficient condition only) to regard the application of sanctions to further one's interests as an exercise of power is uncontroversial. Thus Harold Lasswell and Abraham Kaplan make the expectation of 'severe sanctions . . . to sustain a policy against opposition' a defining characteristic of a power relationship.[8] And Talcott Parsons makes 'the presumption of enforcement by negative sanctions . . . in case of recalcitrance . . .' a necessary condition for the exercise of power.[9] By a 'competitive capitalist economy' we mean one in which productive assets are privately owned, production is carried out by employees, and all markets are characterized by free entry and large numbers of buyers and sellers. We will show that in such an economy, voluntary market exchange engenders a structure of power relations among economic agents in equilibrium.

The assertion that the capitalist economy exhibits a system of power relations has typically been motivated by reference to such deviations from competitive conditions as to pervasiveness of monopoly,[10] the autonomy of management,[11] corporate influence over government policy and consumer demand,[12] and the ubiquity of disequilibrium.[13] Whatever their attractions, none of these approaches offers an adequate response to the fundamental claim of the Walrasian model: that capitalism is a system of generalized choice in which the extensive opportunities to walk away from any transaction preclude the private use of sanctions in the absence of collusion. Even where empirical deviations from the competitive ideal are admitted the presumed prescription is to restore competition, a not altogether utopian remedy in the highly competitive global economy of the late twentieth century.

For this reason approaches to economic power that fail to challenge the

Walrasian logic can reasonably be accused of grounding what is ostensibly a fundamental aspect of economic life, power, on an ephemeral deviation of economic reality from the conditions of competitive equilibrium. It is thus not surprising that economists have traditionally banished 'power' from their lexicon in analyzing market behavior. Like other phenomena inconsistent with competitive equilibrium, the real-world exercise of economic power in the sense we have indicated is thus thought to be an anomalous and unimportant feature of modern capitalism.[14]

Among economic theorists, however, the Walrasian paradigm has come under serious criticism. Contemporary developments in microeconomic theory, particularly transactions cost analysis and the theory of principal–agent relationships, have suggested major revisions.[15] Far from representing a general analysis of informed, self-interested economic behavior, it is now clear that the Walrasian model is in fact a limiting case based on an arbitrary truncation of the concept of rational action. The Walrasian model allows agents to optimize when they shop for groceries but not, for instance, when they decide how hard to work for their employer or whether to default on a loan they have secured.[16]

We will explore the implications of what might be termed post-Walrasian microeconomic theory for the study of the competitive economy as a political entity, demonstrating in particular that even in competitive equilibrium, a market economy sustains a system of power relations.[17] We demonstrate the existence of economic power by relaxing one of the more implausible assumptions of the Walrasian model: the *exogenous enforcement axiom*, which holds that exchanges between agents in the economy can be enforced by a third party (e.g. the judicial system) at no cost to the exchanging parties. Neither the contract between employer and employee, nor that between owner and manager, nor that between lender and borrower, nor that between parties to international exchanges, is sufficiently subject to third-party enforcement to render the Walrasian account of these exchange relationships even remotely acceptable.[18]

In cases where third-party enforcement is infeasible or excessively costly, the exchanging agents must themselves enforce their agreements. In the presence of endogenous enforcement, the terms of exchange are continually subject to *de facto* respecification by the exchanging parties. The threat of coercive sanction, the defining instrument of the state as third-party enforcer, is thus but one among several stratagems invoked by economic agents in the protection of their claims. Privately imposed sanctions, we will see, are essential to the workings of the key exchanges of a capitalist economy: those involving capital and labor. The neat division of society into an arena characterized by sanction (the state), and a sphere of voluntary exchange devoid of political content (the economy), thus collapses.

The puzzle of obedience

Ronald Coase (1937) famously distinguished the firm from relationships among individual contractors by the ability of one of the parties in the labor exchange – the employer – to command the other – the employee – with the expectation of obedience. The distinction was not new. D. H. Robertson (1930) had earlier referred to firms as 'islands of conscious power in this ocean of unconscious cooperation like lumps of butter coagulating in a pail of buttermilk' (p. 85). Well before him Marx had made the distinction between the celebrated freedom of market exchange and the workplace domination of the worker by the owner a fulcrum of this theory of exploitation.

Oliver Williamson subsequently used this distinction to erect the 'markets and hierarchies' approach to the firm. The firm is thus represented as a mini-command economy, circumscribed by the market arena which is by contrast characterized by the absence of authority relationships. But this neat distinction between market and hierarchy begs a key question, one that remarkably neither Coase nor Williamson thought to ask, namely, why should the employee obey the command of the employer? Noticing the lack of a good answer, Armen Alchian and Harold Demsetz (1972) challenged the idea that the firm is a command economy, suggesting that the labor market is not different in this respect from other markets.

> The firm . . . has no power of fiat, no authority, no disciplinary action any different in the slightest degree from ordinary market contracting between any two people. . . . Wherein then is the relationship between a grocer and his employee different from that between a grocer and his customer?

Their well-known theory of the structure of the 'classical capitalist' firm shows how hierarchy (in the person of a monitor possessing both control rights – the right to fire – and residual claimancy rights) might emerge from the unanimous decisions of a work team of equal members seeking to advance their well-being by controlling shirking. The analogy to the Hobbesian account of the genesis of an authoritarian government from a 'free and equal' state of nature can hardly have been accidental. Their account hinges on the key but unmotivated assumption that monitoring itself is relatively difficult to monitor: otherwise it would not be clear why workers should not be the residual claimants and monitor their employer. But this drawback did not deter the ready acceptance of this account of 'hierachy without power'.

Recently, Oliver Hart and co-authors (Grossman and Hart 1986, Hart and Moore 1990, Hart 1989, Hart 1995) have developed a theory of the firm using the distinction between control and residual claimancy rights as aspects of property. In their account, power does matter: ownership entails possession of residual control rights, namely the right to make decisions about what is not contractually delegated to others. Thus 'firms arise in situations where people cannot write good contracts and where the allocation of power or control is therefore important' (1995: 1). Hart observes that 'control over non-human assets leads to control over human assets' (1995: 58), and notes the affinity of this view to 'Marxian theories of the capitalist–worker relationship' (1995: 5).

Hart offers the following response to Alchian and Demsetz:

> the reason that an employee is likely to be more responsive to what his employer wants than a grocer is that the employer . . . can deprive the employee of the assets he works with and hire another employee to work with these assets, while the customer can only deprive the grocer of his customer and as long as the customer is small, it is presumably not very difficult for the grocer to find another customer.
>
> (1989: 1771)

This is not entirely satisfactory. We are to presume that, unlike for the grocer, for the employee it is 'very difficult' to find other assets to work with, namely to find another job. Apparently the difference between the grocer's current transaction (with this customer) and the next best transaction ('another customer') is ignorably small, while for the employee the analogous statement is false. The question is, why?

Hart explains the difference between the two by the special assumption that the employee needs access not just to a job (and hence some assets), but to this particular employer's assets. This might be the case due to a complementarity between the two (the employee may have made an investment in training which is of value only when combined with this particular asset, for example). While transaction-specific investments of this type undoubtedly explain some authority relationships – for some professional jobs and managers, for example – the explanation seems insufficiently general to provide an adequate explanation of the entire authority structure of the firm. Lacking a compelling general answer to the question posed by Alchian and Demsetz, most economists appear to have accepted the view that the apparent power of those in charge of firms is apparent only.

A possible answer to the question 'why should the commanded obey?' is that they promised to do so when they entered into the contract. But this explanation must strike the reader as both quaint and *ad hoc*: the subjects of economic theory cannot schizophrenically switch from the undersocialized *Homo economicus* of the marketplace (to use Mark Granovetter's apt term) to an oversocialized *Homo sociologicus* just by shaking hands or crossing the threshold of the workplace, or to quote Granovetter (1985: 485), like Thomas Hobbes' 'unfortunate denizens of the state of nature' who 'cheerfully surrender all their rights to an authoritarian power and subsequently behave in a docile and honorable manner; by the artifice of a social contract they lurch directly from an undersocialized to an over-socialized state.'

A less *ad hoc* answer to the puzzle of obedience to command would be welcome. In providing one we will see that, contrary to the markets and hierarchies approach, a hierarchical organizational structure is neither necessary nor sufficient for the exercise of power. What is crucial is that some important markets, even perfectly competitive ones, fail to clear in equilibrium, creating a key asymmetry between those on the short and long side of the market. The exercise of power is thus not something taking place outside of markets, but rather is critically dependent on how competitive markets work when contracts are incomplete.

To review: Contractual incompleteness provides not only an object of power – something for power to be about – but a means of power, the basis of obedience. Furthermore, the enforcement of claims of private parties is not sufficiently distinct from the enforcement of commands by the state to support the liberal distinction between private and public spheres.

Contested exchange

Consider agent A who purchases a good or service from agent B. We call the exchange *contested* when B's good or service possesses an attribute which is valuable to A, is costly for B to provide, yet is not fully specified in an enforceable contract. Exogenous enforcement is absent when there is no relevant third-party enforcer (as when A and B are sovereign states), when the contested attribute can be measured only imperfectly or at considerable cost (work effort, for example, or the degree of risk assumed by a firm's management), when the relevant evidence is not admissible in a court of law (such as an agent's eye-witness but unsubstantiated experience), when there is no possible means of redress (e.g. when the liable party is bankrupt), or when the number of contingencies concerning future states of the world relevant to the exchange preclude writing a fully specified contract.

In such cases the *ex post* terms of exchange are determined by the monitoring and sanctioning mechanisms instituted by A to induce B to provide the desired level of the contested attribute.[19] In the next section we analyze one important endogenous enforcement mechanism: *contingent renewal*. Contingent renewal obtains when A elicits performance from B by promising to renew the contract in future periods if satisfied, and to terminate the contract if not. For instance, a manager may promise an employee re-employment contingent upon satisfactory performance, or a lender may offer a borrower a loan, promising to renew the loan if the borrower displays prudent business behavior. We will take the labor market as a case in point.

An employment relationship is established when, in return for a wage, the worker agrees to submit to the authority of the employer for a specified period of time.[20] While the employer's promise to pay the wage is legally enforceable, the worker's promise to bestow an adequate level of effort and care upon the tasks assigned, even if offered, is not. At the level of effort expected by management, work is subjectively costly for the worker to provide, valuable to the employer, and costly to measure. The manager–worker relationship thus is a contested exchange. The endogenous enforcement mechanisms of the enterprise, not the state, are thus responsible for ensuring the delivery of any particular level of labor services per hour of labor time supplied.[21]

Let e represent the level of work effort provided by employee B. We assume effort is costly for B to provide above some minimal level e_{min}. B's employer A knows that B will choose e in response to both the cost of supplying effort and the penalty which employer A imposes if dissatisfied with B's performance. For simplicity we assume the penalty A will impose is the non-renewal of the employment relationship, dismissing the worker. Of course the employer may choose not to terminate the worker if the cost associated with the termination (demoralization or ill-will among fellow workers, a work-to-rule slowdown, a strike, or simply the search and training costs of replacement) is excessive.

In choosing a level of work intensity, the employee must consider both short- and long-term costs and benefits; working less hard now, for example, means more on-the-job leisure now, and a probability of no job and hence less income later. To take into account this time dimension we will consider the worker's job as an asset, the value of which depends in part on the worker's effort level.

We define the *value of employment* $v(w)$ as the discounted present value of the worker's future utility taking account of the probability that the worker will be dismissed; for obvious reasons it is an increasing function of the current wage rate w. We define the employee's *fallback position* z as the present value of future utility for a person whose job is terminated – perhaps the present value of a future stream of unemployment benefits, or the present value of some other job, or more likely a sequence of the two. A's threat of dismissal is costly to B if $v(w) > z$. We call $v(w) - z$, the difference between the value of employment and the fallback position z, the *employment rent*,[22] or the cost of job loss. Employment rents accorded to workers in labor markets are a particularly important case of the more general category, enforcement rents, which arise in all cases of competitively determined contested exchange under conditions of contingent renewal.

Let w_{min} be the wage which equates $v(w)$ and z. This wage rate implies a zero employment rent, and hence induces the worker's freely chosen effort level e_{min}. We term w_{min} the *reservation wage* corresponding to the fallback position z; at any wage less than w_{min} the worker will refuse employment, or will quit if employed. Its level obviously depends on the worker's relative enjoyment of leisure and work, the level and coverage of unemployment benefits, the expected duration of unemployment for a terminated worker, the loss of seniority associated with moving to a new job, and the availability of other income. In the Walrasian model the equilibrium wage w must equal the reservation wage w_{min}. For if w were greater than w_{min}, then an employed worker would prefer his or her present employment to the next-best alternative, which is impossible in a clearing labor market.[23]

We assume A has a monitoring system such that B's performance will be found adequate with a probability f which depends positively on B's level of effort.[24] If this effort level is found to be inadequate, B is dismissed; it is the link between effort and the likelihood of job retention that induces B to provide effort above e_{min}.[25]

To elicit greater effort than e_{min}, A is obliged to offer a wage greater than fallback wage w_{min}, balancing the cost of paying the larger wage against the benefits associated with B's greater effort induced by a higher cost of job loss. For any given wage, the worker will determine how hard to work by trading off the marginal disutility of additional effort against the effect that additional effort has on the probability of retaining the job and thus continuing to receive the employment rent. Noting that the fallback position z is exogenous to the exchange, we may write B's best response to w, which we call the *labor extraction function*, simply as $e = e(w)$. In the neighborhood of the competitive equilibrium e increases with w, though at a diminishing rate.[26]

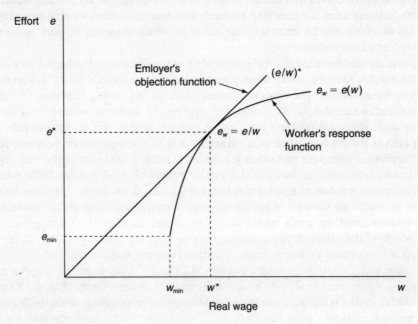

Figure 2.1 Optimal wages and labor intensity

The equilibrium wage and effort level is determined as follows. Agent A knows B's best response schedule $e(w)$. Thus once A selects the wage, the level of effort that will be performed is known. The employer thus chooses the wage w to maximize e/w (i.e. work done per unit of wage expended), subject to the worker's best response schedule $e = e(w)$. The solution to A's optimum problem is to set w such that $e_w = e/w$, or the marginal effect of a wage increase on effort equals the average effort provided per unit of wage cost. This solution yields the equilibrium effort level e^* and wage w^*, shown in Figure 2.1. The ray $(e/w)^*$ is one of the employer's iso-labor cost loci; its slope is e^*/w^*. Steeper rays are obviously preferred, while the employer is indifferent to any point on a given ray, as each entails an identical labor cost.

The equilibrium effort/wage configuration (e^*, w^*) in this contested exchange results from A optimizing *given the response schedule of B*.[27] Two important results are apparent. First, $e^* > e_{min}$, so B provides a level of effort greater than would have been the case in the absence of the enforcement rent and the employer's monitoring system; and second, $w^* > w_{min}$, so B receives a wage greater than the reservation wage. The first result indicates that A's enforcement strategy is effective; the second indicates that the labor market does not clear in competitive equilibrium: workers holding jobs are not indifferent to losing time, since $w^* > w_{min}$ implies $v(w^*) > z$, and there are identical workers either involuntarily unemployed, or employed in less desirable positions.

Both results are of course at variance with the Walrasian model, which is a limiting case of contested exchange obtaining either in the absence of a conflict of interest between employer and employee over effort, or when effort is exogenously enforceable.[28] The first of these conditions can be represented in Figure 2.1 by assuming that workers will freely choose to work increasingly hard, thus increasing e_{min}, the level of effort B supplied independently of the wage; at some point $e_{min}/w_{min} > e_w$, implying that the optimal solution for A is simply to pay w_{min} and accept the effort level e_{min}.[29] The second may be illustrated by assuming the employer has an effective enforcement strategy other than contingent renewal, such that the level of effort does not vary significantly with the enforcement rent, thus 'flattening out' the best response schedule $e(w)$. At some point we again arrive at the corner solution at (e_{min}, w_{min}), implying the Walrasian result: the employer offers a wage equal to the reservation wage w_{min}, abandons the attempt to apply enforcement rent sanctions to the emloyee, and accepts the effort level e_{min}.

Short-side power and political theory

Does employer A have power over worker B? As we have seen, in equilibrium there will exist unemployed workers identical to B who would prefer to be employed. Thus A's threat to dismiss B is credible and dismissal is costly to B. Hence A can apply sanctions to B. In addition, A can use these sanctions to elicit a preferred level of effort from B, and thus to further A's interests. Finally, while B may be capable of applying sanctions to A (e.g. B may be capable of burning down A's factory), B cannot use this capacity to induce A to choose a different wage, or to refrain from dismissing B should A desire to do so. Should B make A a take-it-or-leave-it offer to work at a higher than equilibrium wage, or should B threaten to apply sanctions unless A offers a higher wage, A would simply reject the offer and hire another worker. Thus A has power over B.

This model can be extended to include many agents and many firms in a system of general economic equilibrium.[30] This system will exhibit non-clearing markets. In particular, because such an equilibrium exhibits positive enforcement rents, it entails, by definition, involuntary unemployment as well. The existence of agents without employment (or with less desirable employment than B) follows from the strict inequality $v(w^*) > z$. This unemployment persists in equilibrium and is not derived from an aggregate demand failure, as in the Keynesian model; it is a simple inference from the fact that if B enjoys an employment rent, then there must be another otherwise identical agent, C, who would be willing to fill B's position at the going, or even a lower, wage.[31]

Moreover, should C promise A to work as hard as B for a lower wage, the promise will rightly be disbelieved and hence rejected by A. The reason is that other than their employment status, B and C are identical, so A knows exactly how much effort is forthcoming for a given employment rent, and has already selected a cost-minimizing wage. Agent C is thus involuntarily unemployed in equilibrium, so A's threat to replace B is credible.[32]

Models of non-clearing markets have traditionally been viewed as dis-equilibrium models.[33] In the contested exchange model, however, non-clearing markets are characteristic of competitive equilibrium defined in the standard manner: actors are incapable of improving their position by altering variables over which they have control. Employers have no desire to change the wage offered, employed workers have no interest in changing the level of effort supplied, and workers in search of a position can do nothing but await an offer at the equilibrium wage.

The manager's power is thus related to his or her favorable position in a non-clearing market. We say that the employer A, who can purchase any desired amount of labor and hence is not quantity constrained, is on the *short side* of the market. Where excess supply exists – as in the labour market – the demand side is the short side, and conversely.[34] Suppliers of labor are on the *long side* of the market. When contingent renewal is operative, the principle of *short-side power* holds: agents on the short side of the market have power over agents on the long side with whom they transact.[35] Long-side agents are of two types: those such as B who succeed in finding an employer and receive a rent which constrains them to accept the employer's authority, and those such as C who fail to make a transaction and hence are rationed out of the market.

Three aspects of this result deserve to be noted. First, it might appear that A has expressed a preference for power and has simply traded away some money, the enforcement rent, to gain power. But this is false: A is assumed to be indifferent to the nature of the authority relationship *per se* and is simply maximizing profits.

Second, it might be thought that A has intentionally generated the unemployment necessary for the maintenance of his or her short-side power. It is true that the employer's profit-maximizing strategy, when adopted by all other employers, results in the existence of unemployed workers, and that other wage-setting rules would not have this result. But we have assumed that the employer treats the level of unemployment (which figures in the determination of the workers' fallback position, z) as exogenous, for the simple reason that no employer acting singly can determine the level of aggregate employment.[36]

Third, it may be argued that B has power over A in the sense that B has the capacity to induce A to offer an employment rent over and above the amount needed to induce B to enter into the transation. We believe this argument confuses the *costs of exercising power* with the *location* of power. This position is supported by Harsanyi, in whose framework enforcement rents would be considered elements of 'the costs of A's power over B,' rather than a form of power that B has over A.[37] In particular, the fact that B receives a rent, while certainly conferring a distributional advantage to B as compared to a no-rent alternative, does not involve 'power' in the sense of a capacity that can be strategically deployed towards furthering one's interests. To see this, note that A's power to dismiss B is a credible threat, while B cannot credibly threaten A at all.

The exercise of short-side power would be of little interest if the sanctions based on the enforcement rent were insubstantial. But this is not the case. The time-series estimates in Schor and Bowles (1987), and more recent estimates by Farber (1997), indicate that those displaced from work are unemployed or underemployed for a substantial period and are re-employed at significantly lower earnings. Farber finds for example that the re-employment wage of those displaced by plant closings is 11 percent less than the initial wage. Other components of the cost of job loss – its psychological toll, associated loss of medical insurance for example, and the costs of job search – would substantially increase this estimate.

Despite the clear disparity in the positions of A and B in this case, both parties gain from A's exercise of power over B. Short-side power is not a zero-sum game, since if A did not exercise this power, the best mutual agreement would involve the wage/effort pair (e_{min}, w_{min}), which is strictly inferior to (e^*, w^*) for both parties. Short-side power thus is not purely distributive; it is also productive.[38] Thus entering a power relationship (one in which A has power over B) may be Pareto improving.

It should be noted in passing that the equilibrium wage and effort levels, while Pareto superior to (e_{min}, w_{min}), are not Pareto optimal: there exist other (e, w) pairs Pareto superior to (e^*, w^*), all of them involving a higher wage and greater effort levels.[39]

Our concept of power bears a close affinity to the standard analytical conception of power offered by Dahl, French and Raven, Harsanyi, March, and Simon.[40] Following Robert Dahl, we may describe the 'base' of short-side power as economic sanctions, the 'means' of its exercise as contingent renewal, and its 'scope' as the contested attributes of exchange (e.g. work intensity). Following John Harsanyi, we may take the 'cost' of exercising power as the enforcement rent A offers to B.

We note one important difference between our and Dahl's approach. According to Dahl's well-known definition, 'A has power over B to the extent that he can get B to do something that B would not otherwise do.'[41] Purchasing power has precisely this capacity in the Walrasian model: by paying money A can induce others to provide the goods and services A desires which would otherwise not have been provided. Yet according to our conception, this is not 'power over' these other agents who, by the implementation of their optimal equilibrium-defining programs, are on the margin indifferent to exactly which services they provide, or to whom they are provided. Furthermore, within Dahl's framework it might be considered that employee B has 'power over' employer A, because by working hard B can induce A not to terminate the employment relationship.[42]

We do not consider the contested exchange model to be a general model of the exercise of power in market economies. Economic power may flow, in addition, from such widely recognized sources as influence over public policy and the control of the means of persuasion. Even in these cases, however, the concept of short-side power may be illuminating. Consider, for example, the disproportionate influence of the wealthy on state policy. This derives in important measure from the fact that their decisions to invest or to withhold investment determine the availability of jobs in the future. But if employment rents were absent (as would be predicted by the Walrasian model) workers would be indifferent between holding their current job and the next-best alternative, and thus would be indifferent on the margin to the expansion or contraction of employment.

While our primary example has been the employment relationship and labor market power, contested exchange is ubiquitous, occurring where the claims arising from an exchange are not enforceable at zero cost to the exchanging parties. Typically endogenous enforcement arises as a result of asymmetric information in an exchange, one party but not the other being privy to valuable information concerning the good or service to be exchanged. Examples include exchanges of goods whose quality is variable but difficult to model and the credit market, in which the borrower's intended use of funds may be unknown to the lender.

Conclusion: the incoherence of the liberal partitions of society

If competitive price determination and resource allocation supports a system of power relations among economic agents, the distinction in liberal political philosophy between private and public spheres of society must be false, for this distinction is based on the absence of coercion in voluntary private exchanges. But the liberal demarcation of private and public realms cannot be conveniently jettisoned without compromising the foundations of liberalism. The reason is that the public–private partition forms the basis of the distinctly liberal conception of democracy: while liberal precepts of choice apply in both state and economy, the democratic precept of accountability of power applies only to the state. This inference is the basis of the liberal critique of economic democracy as an incoherent ideal based on the false premise that owners and managers wield unaccountable power in a capitalist economy. The manner in which economic democracy might abolish short-side power or render it democratically accountable is, however, the subject of another investigation.[43]

Notes and references

* We would like to thank P. Bardhan, M. Burawoy, G. D. Cohen, J. Cohen, G. Dymski, D. Fairris, E. McCrate, B. Miconi, C. Offe, U. Pagano, A. Przeworski, J. Rebitzer, J. Roemer, R. Sobel, and E. Wright for helpful comments, and the MacArthur Foundation for financial support.
1 In fact, A may be capable of affecting B's well-being through some non-market channel (e.g. by inflicting physical harm upon B). However, assuming the state enforces property and personal rights (an admittedly strong assumption in many cases), A cannot use this capacity to influence B's actions. Hence A's capacity to inflict harm upon B does not give A power over B in our sense of the term.
2 Basic contributions to this theory include Kenneth J. Arrow, 'An extension of the basic theorems of classical welfare economics,' in J. Neyman (ed.) *Proceedings of the Second Berkeley Symposium on Mathematical Statistics and Probability* (Berkeley, CA: University of California Press, 1951); 507–32, Gerard Debreu, *Theory of Value* (New York: John Wiley, 1959), Kenneth J. Arrow and Frank H. Hahn, *General Competitive Analysis* (San Francisco: Holden-Day, 1971), and Andreu Mas-Collel, *The Theory of General Economic Equilibrium: A Differentiable Approach* (Cambridge: Cambridge University Press, 1985). The Walrasian model is the basis not only of professional, but of textbook economics as well. It provides the reasoning which, for example, locates market equilibrium at the intersection of a supply and a demand curve.
3 David Gauthier, *Morals by Agreement* (Oxford: Clarendon Press, 1986): 95–6.
4 Robert Nozick, *Anarchy, State and Utopia* (New York: Basic Books, 1974): 169.
5 John Rawls, *A Theory of Justice* (Cambridge, MA: Harvard University Press, 1971): 61.
6 Our approach may be distinguished from that of Bruno Miconi. For Miconi, a coerced choice is one for which the alternative is death (or more generally some other exceptionally dire consequence) whereas for us the asymmetrical capacity to invoke sanctions is sufficient.
7 We do not claim ours to be a necessary condition for the exercise of power, since there may be forms of power that operate without the application of sanctions

(e.g. persuasion or purchasing power). See Steven Lukes, *Power: A Radical View* (London: Macmillan, 1974).

8 Harold Lasswell and Abraham Kaplan, *Power and Society: A Framework for Political Enquiry* (New Haven, CT: Yale University Press, 1950): 74–5.

9 Talcott Parsons, 'On the concept of political power,' in *Sociological Theory and Modern Society* (New York: Free Press, 1967): 308.

10 See Paul Baran and Paul Sweezy, *Monopoly Capital* (Harmondsworth: Penguin, 1966), John Kenneth Galbraith, *The New Industrial State* (Boston: Houghton Mifflin, 1967), and Max Weber, *Economy and Society*, ed. G. Roth and C. Wittich (Berkeley, CA: University of California Press, 1978).

11 See Adolph A. Berle and Gardiner C. Means, *The Modern Corporation and Private Property* (New York: Macmillan, 1932).

12 See Galbraith, *The New Industrial State.*

13 See Jean-Pascal Benassy, *The Economics of Market Disequilibrium* (Orlando, FL: Academic Press, 1982).

14 Of course, if economic conditions in advanced capitalist countries deviated sufficiently from the norms of free entry and exit to account of the observed incidence of economic power, the need for an alternative account would be unnecesssary. We do not believe this is the case.

15 For interpretation and bibliographic references, see George Akerlof, *An Economic Theorist's Book of Tales* (Cambridge: Cambridge University Press, 1984), Samuel Bowles and Herbert Gintis, 'Contested exchange: political economy and modern economic theory,' *American Economic Review* 78, 2 (May, 1988): 145–50, Samuel Bowles and Herbert Gintis, 'The revenge of *Homo economicus*: contested exchange and the revival of political economy,' *Journal of Economics Perspectives* (Winter, 1993), Joseph Stiglitz, 'The causes and consequences of the dependence of quality on price,' *Journal of Economic Literature* 25 (March, 1987): 1–48, and Oliver E. Williamson, *The Economic Institutions of Capitalism* (New York, Free Press, 1985).

16 Even this is not strictly true, since an otpimizing shopper will steal, when the chance of detection is very small, and it may not be cost effective for the firm to use the courts as the only anti-theft strategy. There are more subtle and important issues here as well. See Herbert Gintis, 'The power to switch: on the political economy of consumer sovereignty,' in Samuel Bowles, Richard C. Edwards, and William G. Shepherd (eds.) *Unconventional Wisdom: Essays in Honor of John Kenneth Galbraith* (New York: Houghton-Mifflin, 1989).

17 For related treatments, see Adam Przeworski, *The State and the Economy under Capitalism* (New York: Harwell, 1990) and Pranab Bardhan, 'Some reflections on the use of the concept of power in economics,' University of California at Berkeley, 1988.

18 See Armen Alchian and Harold Demsetz, 'Production, information costs, and economic organization,' *American Economic Review* 62 (December, 1972): 777–95, Herbert Gintis, 'The nature of the labor exchange and the theory of capitalist production,' *Review of Radical Political Economics* 8 (1976): 36–54, Samuel Bowles, 'The production process in a competitive economy: Walrasian, Marxian and Neo-Hobbesian models,' *American Economic Review* 75, 1 (March, 1985): 16–36, George Akerlof and Janet Yellen (eds) *Efficiency Wage Models of the Labor Market* (Cambridge: Cambridge University Press, 1986), Stiglitz, 'The dependence of quality on price,' and Bowles and Gintis, 'Contested exchange.' Yet many working within a post-Walrasian framework have reaffirmed the Walrasian conclusion that power is absent in competitive exchange. See Alchian and Demsetz, 'Production, information costs, and economic organization,' Bengt Holmstrom and Jean Tirole, 'The theory of the firm,' in *Handbook of Industrial Organization*, ed. R. Schmalensee and R.

Willig (Amsterdam: North-Holland: 1988), and Williamson, *The Economic Insitutions of Capitalism.*

19 Our analysis is limited to the case where enforcement problems are present on only one side of the exchange. By addressing cases in which one side of the exchange provides a monetary payment (the costs of monitoring of which are assumed to be zero), we set aside the more general problem of 'bilateral endogenous enforcement,' in which both parties to the exchange exercise strategic power. See Masahiko Aoki, *The Co-operative Game Theory of the Firm* (London: Clarendon, 1984). We discuss the applicability of our analysis to this broader framework in the concluding section.

20 This definition conforms to neoclassical (Ronald Coase, 'The nature of the firm,' *Economica* NS4 (November, 1937)), as well as to Marxian (Karl Marx, *Capital* I (Harmondsworth: Penguin, 1976)), (Original German edition, 1868), neo-Marxian (Gintis, 'The nature of the labor exchange'), and organization-theoretic (Herbert Simon, 'A formal theory of the employment relationship,' *Econometrica* 19 (1951): 293–305) approaches.

21 The analysis presented in this section is developed in Gintis, 'The nature of the labor exchange,' Bowles, 'The production process in a competitive economy,' and Herbert Gintis and Tsuneo Ishikawa, 'Wages, work discipline, and unemployment,' *Journal of Japanese and International Economies* 1 (1987): 195–228. Related models have been developed by Guillermo Calvo, 'Quasi-Walrasian theories of unemployment,' *American Economic Review* 69, 2 (May, 1979): 102–7, and Carl Shapiro and Joseph E. Stiglitz, 'Unemployment as a worker discipline device,' *American Economic Review* 74, 3 (June, 1984) 433–44. Our model includes only those aspects of work and production necessary to demonstrate the exercise of power. In particular, we model a bilateral relationship between an employer and a single member of a team of employees, thus setting aside relationships among workers as an important aspect of the labor exchange (Akerlof, *An Economic Theorist's Book of Tales*, S. R. G. Jones, *The Economics of Conformism* (Oxford: Basil Blackwell, 1984), and James Buchanan, 'Rent seeking and profit seeking,' in James Buchanan, Robert Tollison, and Gordon Tullock (eds) *Toward a Theory of the Rent-seeking Society* (College Station, TX: Texas A&M University Press, 1980).

22 We term this a 'rent' as it represents a payment above and beyond the income of an identical employee without the job. It is thus similar to the rents in the theory of rent-seeking behavior (Buchanan, Tollison, and Tullock, 1980, and Anne Krueger, 'The political economy of the rent seeking society,' *American Economic Review* 64 (June, 1974: 291–303), except that contested exchange rents arise through the lack of effective state intervention, while rent-seeking literature focusses on state intervention as the source of rents.

23 Note that while w_{min} is the only wage compatible with full employment, it is in no sense a 'market-clearing wage'. Indeed, in general there is no market-clearing wage in a contested exchange model, since supply and demand curves for labor simply do not intersect.

24 It is assumed that B knows A's criteria of dismissal, or B at least has a subjective assessment of the probability of dismissal associated with each level of effort.

25 More complete models allow an endogenous selection by A of an optimal schedule $f(e)$, an optimal choice of the level of surveillance (Bowles, 'The production process in a competitive economy,' and Gintis and Ishikawa, 'Wages, work discipline, and unemployment'), and the choice of production technologies as an aspect of endogenous enforcement (Samuel Bowles, 'Capitalist technology: endogenous claim enforcement and the choice of technique,' University of Massachusetts Working Paper, 1989). We lose little, however, by assuming that the probability of detection is exogenously given as a function of effort,

and that the worker detected providing substandard effort is dismissed, and that the production technology is exogenously determined.

26 For a complete mathematical exposition, see Bowles and Gintis (Samuel Bowles and Herbert Gintis, 'The democratic firm: an agency-theoretic evaluation,' in Samuel Bowles, Herbert Gintis, and Bo Gustafsson (eds) *Democracy and Markets: Participation, Accountability, and Efficiency* (Cambridge: Cambridge University Press, 1993).

27 A complication arises if there is more than one type of worker (e.g. high productivity and low productivity), and the employer cannot distinguish among types. This problem of asymmetric information and heterogeneous labor renders the analysis more complex, but does not change the result. In particular, the imperfect information available to the employer may raise the employment rent offered to a worker, but will not eliminate the power relationship.

28 This limiting case rarely obtains. When worker output is exogenously enforceable, contracts normally take the form of a business hiring an independent agent rather than an employee, such as a firm hiring an electrical contractor to deliver specific services (Coase, 'The nature of the firm'). When employees are paid piece-rate, ostensibly the best case for the Walrasian model of labor, there are still usually strong non-contractual elements to employee productivity (e.g. employee reliability, interaction with co-workers, treatment of tools and materials).

29 A similar result obtains if the reservation wage w_{min} is decreased sufficiently, provided $e_{min} > 0$. In both cases we must assume $e(w)$ does not have infinite slope at $w = w_{min}$.

30 The proof of the existence of equilibrium for this model, and conditions for its uniqueness, are given in Gintis and Ishikawa, 'Wages, work discipline, and unemployment.'

31 Such agents, rather than being unemployed, may simply prefer B's position to their own at the going wage. The point is that they are quantity constrained: they would prefer to sell more of their services at the going rate but are unable to (unless B is dismissed).

32 Does A have power over C? The negative sanction which A may impose on B (withdrawal of the employment rent) is exactly equal to a positive sanction which A might offer or refuse to extend to C. If A refuses to hire C in order to maintain a racially homogeneous workplace, for instance, we might say that A has furthered his or her interests (gratification of racial prejudice) and has sanctioned C (refused to offer the employment rent). However, by contrast to the relationship of A to B, the sanction is not imposed to affect C's behavior and thus is incidental to the furthering of A's interests. Thus A does not have power over C in the sense defined here.

33 Jean-Pascal Benassy, *The Economics of Market Disequilibrium* (Orlando, FL: Academic Press, 1982).

34 More generally, the short side of an exchange is located where the total amount of desired transactions is least; the demand side if there is excess supply and the supply side if there is excess demand (Benassy, *The Economics of Market Disequilibrium*).

35 Note that the power conferred upon an agent holding a short-side position need not be exercised instrumentally or consciously by the agent. For instance, consumers may be short siders facing demand-constrained sellers. Such consumers ensure the delivery of proper produce quality by switching suppliers when dissatisfied. They thus have power in our sense of the term, yet each consumer's purchase is typically too small, and collective action by consumers too difficult to organize, to render the strategic exercise of this power infeasible. See Gintis, 'The power to switch.'

36 If employers act collectively, of course, a quite different picture emerges, as the

contested exchange model demonstrates the interests of employers in the existence of unemployment and suggests that they might use their influence on the state to foster macroeconomic policies to maintain adequate levels of unemployment. An interpretation of recent US macroeconomic policy along these lines is presented in David Gordon Bowles and Thomas E. Weisskopf, 'Business ascendancy and economic impasse: a structural retrospective on conservative economics, 1979–1987,' *Journal of Economic Perspectives* 3, 1 (Winter, 1989): 107–34. A parallel treatment of the collective action of workers is presented in Samuel Bowles and Robert Boyer, 'Labor market flexibility and decentralization as barriers to high employment? Notes on employer collusion, centralized wage bargaining and aggregate employment,' in Renato Brunetta and Carlo Dell'Aringa (eds) *Labour Relations and Economic Performance* (London: Macmillan, 1990).

37 John C. Harsanyi, 'Measurement of social power, opportunity costs, and the theory of two-person bargaining games,' *Behavioral Science* 7 (1962): 67–81. The quote is from page 68. Harsanyi assumes agents can enter into binding agreements, and hence employs a cooperative game-theoretic model of power. In our model, the endogenous enforcement assumption precludes such binding agreements, so a non-cooperative Stackelberg leadership model is more appropriate. Our 'enforcement rents' are thus only roughly analogous to Harsanyi's 'costs of exercising power.' See also Jack H. Nagel, 'Some questions about the concept of power,' *Behavioral Science* 13, 2 (March, 1968): 129–37.

38 Also for Parsons, 'On the concept of political power,' power is a non-zero-sum phenomenon. Parsons infers from its non-zero-sum character that power is a functional 'system resource' that does not in principle confer differential advantage upon those who possess it. The structure and distribution of short-side power, however, despite its non-zero-sum character, is not an efficient solution to production and exchange problems even in competitive equilibrium. We suggest elsewhere (Bowles and Gintis, 'New microfoundations of political economy') that A's power does not entail a Pareto-efficient allocation of resources, and the deviations from efficiency can be explained in terms of the distributional advantages A enjoys by virtue of the exercise of power.

39 Gauthier (p. 93) insightfully distinguishes cases in which 'maximizing one's utility given the actions of others would fail to maximize it given the utilities of others' and cases in which the two are equivalent. The latter support Pareto-optimal equilibria, while the former do not. The Pareto suboptimality of the competitive equilibrium arises in the employment relationship case because the employer is maximizing subject to the worker's reaction function $e(w)$ rather than the worker's objective function $v(e,w)$, as would be the case if the constraint that $v \geq z$ were binding.

40 Robert A. Dahl, 'The concept of power,' *Behavioral Science* 2 (1957): 201–15, J. R. P. French, Jr and B. Raven, 'The bases of social power,' in D. Cartwright (ed.) *Studies in Social Power* (Ann Arbor, MI: University of Michigan Press, 1959): 150–67, John C. Harsanyi, 'Measurement of social power in n-person reciprocal power situations,' *Behavioral Science* 7 (1962): 81–91, J. G. March, 'Measurement concepts in the theory of influence,' *Journal of Politics* 19 (1957): 202–26, and Herbert Simon, *Models of Man: Social and Rational* (New York, John Wiley, 1957). This approach has been criticized by Peter Bachrach and Morton Baratz, *Power and Poverty: Theory and Practice* (New York: Oxford University Press, 1970), for focussing too closely upon the *actions* involved in exercising power, rather than the *structural context* which frames such acts. Our stress on the structure of general economic equilibrium exempts us, we believe, from this charge. Lukes, *Power: A Radical View*, further suggests that, by taking agents' objectives as exogenously given, the

behavioral approach overlooks the most effective form of power: the capacity
to influence the *preferences* of others. We believe that contested exchange, far
from being hostile to Lukes' concern, may contribute significantly to a theory
of 'persuasion' in a competitive market economy. We have elsewhere argued
(Bowles and Gintis, 'The revenge of *Homo economicus*') that in contested
markets exchange is non-anonymous, social, and durable. Thus those with
power in our sense (i.e. those with the opportunity to engage in persuasion)
have the motivation to do so.

41 Dahl, 'The concept of power,' pp. 202–3.

42 This ambiguity may represent a defect in the behavioral conception of power
not shared by interest-centered approaches, of which ours is an example. See
Alvin I. Goldman, 'Towards a theory of social power,' *Philosophical Studies* 23,
4 (1972): 221–68.

43 Samuel Bowles and Herbert Gintis, 'An economic and political case for the
democratic firm,' in David Copp, Jean Hampton, and John Roemer (eds) *The
Idea of Democracy* (Cambridge: Cambridge University Press, 1993).

Bibliography

Alchian A. and Demsetz, H. 'Production, information costs, and economic organization,' *American Economic Review* 62 (1972): 777–95.

Coase, R. 'The nature of the firm,' *Economica* NS4 (1937).

Farber, H. 'The changing face of job loss in the United States, 1981–1995,' (working
paper of Princeton University, May 1997).

Granovetter, M. 'Economic action and social structure: The problem of embedd-
edness,' *American Journal of Sociology* 91 (3) (1985): 481–510.

Grossman, S. and Hart, O. 'The costs and benefits of ownership: A theory of
vertical and lateral integration,' *Journal of Political Economy* 94 (4) (1986):
691–719.

Hart, O. 'An economist's perspective on the theory of the firm,' *Columbia Law
Review* 89 (7) (1989): 1757–74.

Hart O. *Firms, Contracts, and Financial Structure* (Oxford: Clarendon Press, 1995).

Hart, O. and Moore, J. 'Property rights and the nature of the firm,' *Journal of
Political Economy* 98 (6) (1990): 1119–58.

Robertson, D. H. *Control of Industry*, (New York: Harcourt and Brace, 1930).

Schor, J. and Bowles, S. 'Employment rents and the incidence of strikes,' *Review of
Economics and Statistics* 64 (4) (1987): 584–91.

Williamson, O. E. *Markets and Hierarchies: Analysis and Antitrust Implications*
(New York: Free Press, 1975).

Williamson, O. E. *The Economic Institutions of Capitalism: Firm, Markets, Relational Contracting* (New York: Free Press, 1975).

3 Adaptation and opportunism in political and economic markets

Maurizio Franzini

Introduction

According to a largely held view, in political markets, unlike economic markets, it is very easy to gain rents. This conclusion stems from the assumption that competition in political markets is actually quite weak and from the fact that perfect competition markets of the ideal type proposed by economists in which rents cannot be created are taken as a benchmark. In such markets, as Williamson (1991: 17) so aptly put it: 'individual buyers and sellers bear no dependency relation to each other. Instead, each party can go its own way at negligible cost to another.'

Therefore it seems that in competitive markets it is possible to exit from economic relations without suffering relevant costs. The absence of these penalties demonstrates that rents – or, to state it more precisely, quasi-rents[1] – do not exist. In fact, if the continuance of a relation allows the benefit of rents, at least from one side, it is evident that its interruption must generate losses or costs.

The absence of rents – and, therefore, of those losses derived from the interruption of the relation – means that a sanctioning mechanism is necessary in the case of opportunistic behaviour. If this situation did not exist, opportunists – even when a counterpart exits – would not sustain losses and would not have any reason to refrain from breaking contractual agreements.

A simple solution to this problem can be seen in the imposition of sanctions by a body, such as a court of law, acting outside of the economic process. Nevertheless, as is well known, this solution is difficult to implement given the imperfections that characterise the judicial system.

Many scholars believe that an alternative solution for sanctioning the opportunists is represented by the ability of exit itself. Along these general lines, which date back to the 'invisible hand' proposed by Adam Smith, the opportunist can be sanctioned by his or her counterpart if the latter has access, without relevant costs, to other alternatives and if there is no asymmetric information. More explicitly, if the seller violates a contract, the buyer can turn to another supplier, therefore choosing exit and inflicting on the former a sanction that consists of less revenues. If many buyers act in this manner the sanction can mean the expulsion of the seller from the market due to his or her business failing.

In order for this mechanism of endogenous sanctioning to function, the non-opportunistic agent must be able to turn to other suppliers without excessive costs, and the opportunist, because of the absence of asymmetric information, must be unable to find new buyers for his or her products or services. And so in general it can be said that exit – thanks to the high level of competition – should not exact too high a cost from the non-opportunistic agent, while it should cause sufficient damage to the opportunist. Only in this case can competition become effective in assuring respect of contracts and deter opportunistic behaviour.

In the past decade, many economists belonging to diverse theoretical schools – from new institutional economics and contested exchange economics to contract theory – have illustrated numerous cases in which the conditions just mentioned are not satisfied. Both because of the considerable costs of access to alternatives on the part of the non-opportunistic agents and because of the existence of important asymmetric information, competitive markets are not a barrier to opportunism. This is one of the reasons why more complex contracts must be created which allow rents or quasi-rents to be gained so as to prevent opportunism. The most notable example is probably that of efficiency wage models for workers who may try to shirk work (Shapiro and Stiglitz 1984).

It is not correct, therefore, to represent economic markets as mechanisms capable of preventing both the formation of rents and opportunistic behaviour. If it is true, as North affirms, that competition serves to reduce enforcement costs (North 1990: 362), then it is also essential to recognise that competition in the economic sphere is often not sufficient to reduce these costs significantly and prevent opportunism as well.

Developing this consideration some authors – like Wittman (1995) – have maintained that the differences between political and economic markets are much less acute than is normally assumed. With reference to the problem that most interests us, we can say that exit within the economic sphere is not as effective as believed and that competition also exists in the political sphere and that opportunists can also be sanctioned in that realm, even if in an imperfect way.

Given this formulation, economic and political markets are not radically different from the point of view of their capacity to prevent opportunism. The differences pertain to degree and not quality. All this seems convincing, yet there is a more general question that must be addressed. The difficulties encountered by both economic and political markets – even if to different degrees – when dealing with opportunism prompt us to recommend changes so that the efficacy of sanctions can be increased. There seems to be a broad consensus on the advisability of introducing such changes, but the question of whether a stronger system of sanctions is always desirable and whether it can have negative features must also be addressed.

The main purpose of this essay is to show that if opportunism is not the sole reason for worsening performances, then exit can have undesirable consequences. In particular, if organisations also face problems of adaptation to environmental changes, exit can prevent efficient organisations from successfully adjusting to the new conditions.

The details of the paper are as follows: in the next section I will briefly recall Hirschman's famous criticism of exit and put forward my own interpretation of his advocacy of voice. In the following section, by generalising Hirschman's analysis, I will introduce what I will denote as the 'wrong reaction' problem and argue that it is more fruitful to tackle such a problem by means of dyad sanctioning/recontracting than by means of Hirschman's exit/voice. In the third section, a simple model of the 'wrong reaction' dilemma will be proposed, which, amongst other things, gives a more thorough understanding of exit as a sanctioning system. In the final section I will summarise the main results of this paper and the implications for the comparative analysis of political and economic markets.

Hirschman's advocacy of voice. An interpretation

In numerous writings (1970, 1982, 1986), Hirschman has maintained that if clients (or members) of an organisation react by exit to a decline in the quality of service of that self-same organisation the result can be very negative.[2] In contrast to the prevailing position, Hirschman appears to be critical of exit and argues that voice is better. Voice is defined as follows: 'any attempt to change, rather than escape from, an objectionable state of affairs' (Hirschman 1970: 30).

It is not easy to summarise the many lines of argument developed by Hirschman in a few statements. My interpretation of Hirshman's preference for voice rests on the following points:

1   The principal cause of an organisation's decline as seen by Hirschman is not opportunism by those who manage the organisation, but what I call 'problems of adaptation of organisations to changes in environmental conditions'. Consider the following quotation :

   The performance of a firm or an organisation is assumed to be subject to deterioration for unspecified, random causes which are neither so compelling nor so durable as to prevent a return to performance levels, provided managers direct their attention and energy to that task.
                                                              (Hirschman, 1970: 3–4)

   So, Hirschman examines cases of 'recuperable deterioration' (see also Hirschman 1993) caused by factors not imputable to a rational management strategy. In order to correct the situation, managers must, as seen in the quotation, direct their attention and energy to those factors, and not receive sanctions.

2   Since the cause of the problem is the difficulty in adapting, sanctions – even in the form of exit – can be not only inefficient but even damaging. For example, if clients were to leave the firm quickly, the latter would not have the time to remedy its mistakes. Therefore, exit seems inadvisable precisely because, contrary to the fears expressed by many economists, it risks being too effective and ultimately too punitive as an instrument of sanctioning. It can easily condemn to expulsion organisations that are vital and that can promise their clients or members a high level of well-being given a reasonable remit of time.

3   In the case of problems of adaptation, the best answer on the part of the clients is more co-operative behaviour. Voice, according to Hirschman, has this characteristic: it not only allows management to acquire vital information but also gives it enough time to make necessary adjustments. The members (or clients) of organisations must not simply wait; a more active and co-operative form of behaviour is asked of them. In this way voice is different from inertia.

Following this line of reasoning one reaches the conclusion that a kind of behaviour different from exit – for example, voice – is preferable. Hirschman adds that the organisation's clients may not find voice convenient. In particular, he maintains that recourse to voice in the economic sphere is limited by the ease with which one can opt for exit. In this regard, Hirschman, in *Exit, Voice and Loyalty* (1970), affirms that facility of exit can atrophy voice[3] and that resort to voice should be encouraged. In some later works, Hirschman appears to be even more convinced of the correctness of this position; for example, referring to one of his statements from 1970, he writes:

> in some situations, the proper balance of institutional incentives ought to be adjusted so as to strengthen voice in relation to exit. I now find that my advocacy of voice was not exagerrated, but, on the contrary, be too timid.
>
> (Hirschman 1981: 214)

I suggest that Hirschman's position can be summarised as follows: voice is necessary when an organisation declines because of adaptation problems, but convenience can induce clients to chose exit. Hirschman, therefore, raises a problem which could generally be called 'wrong reaction to an organisation's decline'. This problem is very important and deserves to be analysed in depth; furthermore, such analysis will allow us to understand more thoroughly the limits and characteristics of exit as a sanctioning mechanism.

The wrong reaction problem

In the foregoing interpretation of Hirschman's position, the problem of 'wrong reaction' manifests itself only in the form of exit being chosen when voice would be required. This is the result of two assumptions: first, that the only causes of decline are what have been called 'problems of adaptation' and, second, that clients will not choose inertia as a reaction. If management can act opportunistically and if, moreover, clients can select inertia, the problem of 'wrong reaction' becomes more interesting and complex.

In broad terms, we can state that sanction is the correct reaction in the case of opportunism. When adaptation problems arise, however, the best response is to transmit all useful information to management and to be ready to accept a new definition of one's rights and duties – in short, a more co-operative attitude. I shall call this attitude 'readiness to recontract'.

Exit and voice are not synonymous with sanction and recontracting, respectively.[4] Exit is not the only possible form of sanction, nor is it always a sanction. Hirschman himself offers an example in this respect: when the most politically responsible citizens leave a non-democratic country, the ruling class will not be hurt; rather, it will enjoy an advantage (Hirschman 1993).

Voice, on its part, does not necessarily involve a co-operative attitude. It can also be employed to inflict damage. In this case it is more appropriate to view voice as a kind of sanction or at least a threat of sanction. For example, Hirschman considers both suing in court and harassment[5] as manifestations of voice. If we assume that voice as a sanction can perform a useful function, this means that we are referring to a situation in which there are problems of opportunism.

In the political sphere, exit is often not accessible and consequently voice can be both sanction (this is the case of public demonstrations in favour of a change in political leadership) and co-operation (e.g. when dialogue with management is demanded to improve the quality of public utilities). In order to understand how political leaders will behave it is important to know which kind of voice will be triggered in each case: voice as sanction or as co-operation.

The point is that the distinction between exit and voice rests on either abandoning or remaining within the organisation, while this element is inadequate for distinguishing between sanctioning and recontracting. Therefore it is preferable to use the latter concepts. We will see, however, that when the sanction is exit peculiar problems arise.

On the basis of our hypothesis, clients' reactions will be correct if they choose to sanction in the case of opportunism and to recontract in the case of adaptation problems. Any deviation from this pattern creates undesirable effects. On one hand, organisations which suffer from recuperable adaptation problems may be sanctioned and also pushed out of the market;

on the other hand, opportunism would be encouraged if the organisation which tries to cheat its clients were not sanctioned. It is not easy, however, to design an institutional setting conducive to this correct reaction.

The first difficulty arises from the lack of perfect information: clients simply cannot know the reason for the worsening of the organisation's performance. Another difficulty is represented by free riding. Hirschman draws our attention to this problem and argues in particular that it can hamper the use of voice.[6] Indeed, if exit is costly and the organisation can change its behaviour after a number of clients have left, then exit can also be vulnerable to free riding.

In the following sections, I will assume that asymmetric information and free riding are not a problem. My aim is to show that 'wrong reaction' can originate even if the information is correct and nobody free-rides. The point is that clients can find it convenient to react in the wrong way; in particular, they can select inertia which, as Barry (1974) pointed out many years ago, has not been sufficiently analysed by Hirschman.

In order to emphasise the particular features of exit as a sanction I will tackle the problem in two stages. To start with, my initial hypothesis will be that the clients cannot have access to alternative organisations; in other words the sanction is not of the exit type. Subsequently, I will introduce exit and shed light on one negative aspect which Hirschman detected but which is usually neglected, that is the possibility of exit sanctioning vital organisations to the point of their exclusion from the market.

A simple model

The problem of reactions to the worsening performance of an organisation will now be analysed on the basis of a rather simplified model.

The quality of goods or services as supplied by an organisation can assume three values: q^*, q' and q_0, with $q^* > q' > q_0$. The best rival competitor is able to supply a service of quality q, which is intermediate between q^* and q'.

The quality of the service depends both on the organisation's effort, which can be either low or high, and on an exogenous variable, which can be either favourable or unfavourable. More precisely our technology is as follows:

	low effort	*high effort*
Unfavourable environment	q_0	q'
Favourable environment	q'	q^*

Quality q', differently from the other two, can be the result of two separate circumstances which have already been extensively commented upon:[7]

1   An opportunistic attitude by the organisation which induces it to select a low effort.
2   An unfavourable exogenous event to which the organisation cannot adapt instantaneously. The organisation can, however, react to this event and return to producing quality q^* in an appropriate time span.

In such a framework – if organisations are vital in the sense of the definition which will be given later – the efficient solution requires that the organisation refrain from opportunism and be able to adapt to unfavourable external circumstances.

The correct reaction

Bad performance can be reacted to in a number of ways. Recontracting is needed to overcome adaptation problems (the assumption is that inertia is not sufficient to return the organisation to high-quality levels). On the other hand, opportunism must be tackled by sanctions which are effective if they inflict a loss that is greater than the benefit expected by the opportunistic action. If $B(q' - q^*)$ is the benefit that opportunism yields the organisation, the sanction will be effective if it cannot be avoided by the opportunists and if it corresponds to a penalty PY, such that

$$B(q' - q^*) < PY$$

Hypotheses on sanctions

To illuminate the specific features of exit, I will assume initially that the sanction allows the clients to obtain a level of utility which corresponds to the quality of the service offered by the best rival. This hypothesis gives me the chance to evaluate the consequences of a kind of sanction which, from the clients' point of view, is as good as exit but – unlike it – is applied solely in the case of opportunism.

The clients

The clients choose their reaction on the basis of a calculation of convenience which takes into account both the costs and results of alternative strategies. Clients are strictly self-interested and aim at maximising their own intertemporal well-being. Therefore loyalty to the organisation is not a factor in their utility function.

My other hypotheses, a number of which have already been introduced, are the following:

(i)   The clients know the reason for the decline and they also know what effects their reaction will have on the organisation. In other words, there is no asymmetric information.

(ii) The clients are not in conflict among themselves, rather they share the same preferences and do not free ride. Therefore it is possible to treat the entire set of clients as if they were in fact simply one client.

(iii) Both sanctioning and recontracting give rise to costs which I will denote as c_s and c_r respectively. Such costs can be interpreted as the lowest costs one has to bear to have either an effective sanction or a timely adaptation.

(iv) The clients expect to use the organisation's service for $n + 1$ time periods. Periods are measured in such a way that adaptation to the unfavourable exogenous event will take place in precisely one period.

(v)   The clients have no intertemporal preferences, so their rate of discount is equal to zero. The clients evaluate the service quality according to a monetary utility function, U. The following relations hold:

$$U(q^*) > U(q') > U(q)$$

We can also define the following two variables:

$$D = U - U' \tag{1}$$

$$CA = U^* - U \tag{2}$$

D represents the difference in terms of utility between the quality supplied by the best rival and the quality corresponding to the bad performance by the original organisation. CA represents the advantage over the best rival that the organisation can ensure in case of good performance.

Payoffs of the three strategies

The clients will select that strategy which carries the highest payoff. Let us calculate the payoff associated with each alternative strategy, separately analysing opportunism and adaptation.

Independently of the reason for the decline, the clients can always choose to wait passively without bearing any costs. Recalling that the organisation's performance will not change if the clients just wait, the payoff of inertia (or waiting) is

$$P(W) = (n + 1)U'$$

Taking into account equation (1), the preceding equation can be rewritten as follows:

$$P(W) = (n + 1) U - (n + 1)D$$

In the case of opportunism the clients will choose between inertia and sanctioning; recontracting is surely a worse alternative. The payoff of sanctioning which, as is already known, lets the clients enjoy a utility equal to the one they would get from the best rival over $n + 1$ periods, is the following:

$$P(S) = (n + 1)U - c_s$$

In the case of adaptation, it is by assumption impossible to have recourse to sanctioning; therefore the choice is between inertia and recontracting. The payoff of the latter, assuming that it allows best quality to be recovered after just one period, is the following:

$$P(R) = U' + nU^* - c_r$$

Recalling equations (1) and (2) we come to the following:

$$P(R) = (n + 1)U + nCA - c_r - D$$

The reaction in the case of opportunism

Here clients will choose sanctioning if

$$P(S) \geq P(W)$$

that is to say, if

$$(n + 1)D \geq c_s$$

Given the costs of sanctioning, the choice depends exclusively on the magnitude of D. Therefore we can define the level of D at which the clients become indifferent to either inertia or sanctioning. Let us call such a level D''.

$$D'' = \frac{c_s}{(n + 1)}$$

Therefore if $D < D''$ inertia will be chosen, whereas if $D > D''$ sanctioning will be preferred. All this can be represented by means of a simple diagram (Figure 3.1).

Vital organisations

Before examining the case of adaptation we need to define 'vital organisations'. An organisation is vital if after returning to the capacity of being able to produce quality q^* it ensures a competitive advantage to its clients which is greater than the loss they suffered; in other words $nCA \geq D$. According to this definition, vital organisations are, for example, those which do not take a long time to remedy their bad performance. In an efficient institutional setting non-vital organisations should not be allowed to adapt. This is the reason why I will focus only on the cases in which $nCA \geq D$. If CA and n are given, the vitality condition implies that D cannot be greater than nCA.

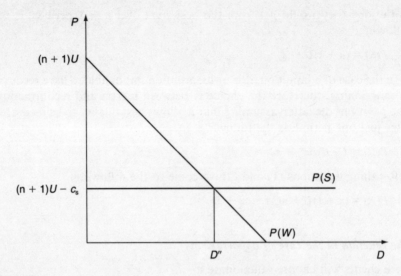

Figure 3.1

Reaction in the case of non-instantaneous adaptation

In this case the choice is between recontracting and inertia. Recontracting would be better if

$$P(R) > P(W)$$

that is to say, if

$$nCA - c_r \geq D$$

Again in this case we can determine the level of D (called D^*) which exactly balances the two alternatives:

$$D^* = \frac{c_r}{n} - CA$$

If $D < D^*$ inertia will be chosen, while if $D > D^*$ recontracting will take place. We need to distinguish between two scenarios. In the first, represented in Figure 3.2, the following condition holds:

$$\frac{c_r}{n} < CA$$

Since the stated condition implies that $D^* < 0$, recontracting is always a better choice than inertia.

The second scenario occurs when

$$\frac{c_r}{n} > CA$$

If the organisation is vital (i.e. $D < nCA$) D^* is now located between 0 and

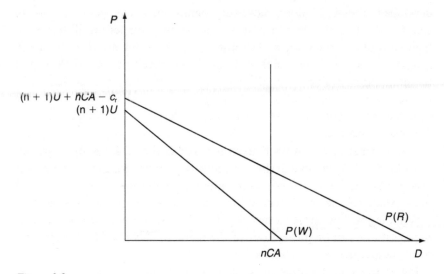

Figure 3.2

CA. As a consequence, losses less than D^* will be tolerated (inertia will prevail). At the same time, recontracting will permit vital organisations to adapt when $D > D^*$. This situation is depicted in Figure 3.3.

Exit as a sanctioning mechanism

Now let us assume that the clients do have access to alternative suppliers. This circumstance does not alter the analysis of the case of opportunism as

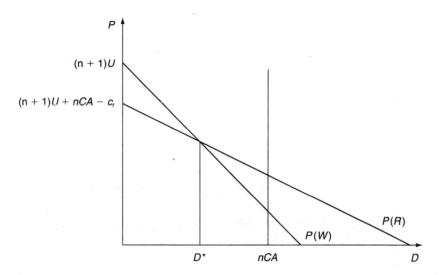

Figure 3.3

developed above. It does, however, significantly change reactions to adaptation. The clients can now switch to the competitor if this is to their advantage, even when the problem arises from non-instantaneous adaptation. More to the point, exit may: (a) reduce tolerance with respect to adaptation problems, replacing inertia with exit; (b) decrease the possibility that organisations will adapt to external changes, replacing recontracting with exit. As I will show, these two consequences can also occur together.

If recontracting is always better than inertia (i.e. if $D^* < 0$), organisations hit by a recoverable decline can now be sanctioned. Figure 3.4 makes it clear that under the previous assumption adaptation would have taken place whatever the magnitude of D, whereas now that exit is accessible, sanctioning will be chosen when $D > D''$. If the sanction is too severe, vital organisations can be pushed out of the market. This provides an example of the consequences which have been labelled (a).

Let us consider the other possibility in which the $P(R)$ and $P(W)$ curves intersect at a value of D which is greater than 0 but less than nCA. Exit can now have two different effects as shown in Figure 3.5: assuming that the cost of exit is quite low, it reduces from D^* to D'' the loss which would have been tolerated; but it also completely eliminates the possibility of adaptation when D is greater than D^*. Therefore both (a) and (b) occur simultaneously in this case.

It is easy to see that if the costs of exit are higher – and the $P(S)$ curve therefore shifts downwards – only consequence (b) will take place.

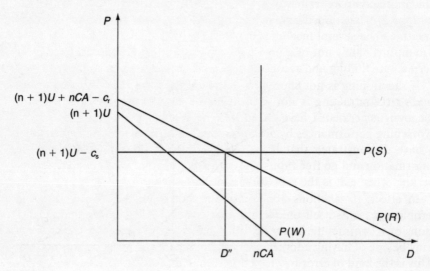

Figure 3.4

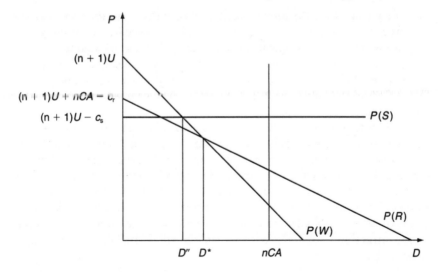

Figure 3.5

Conclusions

Economists have traditionally advocated exit on the basis of the often implicit assumption that opportunism is the sole problem; Hirschman, on the other hand, has a predilection for a more co-operative attitude on the part of an organisation's clients because he seems to assume that the main problem is adaptation to outside changes.

In this paper I have hypothesised that both kinds of problem exist. In this more complex framework, efficiency will be achieved if opportunistic actions are sanctioned and if adaptations are eased by means of recontracting. The several meanings conferred by Hirschman on exit and voice are unfortunately not of a univocal nature and the more general and clear terms, sanctioning and recontracting, have therefore been employed.

If sanctioning is not chosen as the reaction in the case of opportunism and/or recontracting is not applied in the case of adaptation, an inefficiency is generated. I have called this the problem of 'wrong reaction' to worsening performances by organisations. With the help of a simple model I have demonstrated that it can emerge even if there is no asymmetric information and no free riding and, furthermore, that it can be particularly serious when exit is the sanctioning mechanism.

In effect, if sanctions are not of the exit type, the 'wrong reaction' problem presents itself uniquely as inertia being selected in place of sanctions or recontracting. If, on the other hand, exit is accessible the problem may be one of having adopted sanctioning when recontracting was needed. This is the kind of error to which Hirschman draws our attention and it can be a very serious fault indeed; it can be seen as a peculiar negative feature of exit as a sanction. As already seen, exit can also have the probably less serious consequence of reducing the zone of tolerance by sanctioning vital organisations which find themselves in a chronic crisis of adaptation.

When sanctions differ from exit there is a simple solution to the 'wrong reaction' problem: the costs of both sanctions and recontracting must be lowered so as to make inertia less appealing. The exit option, on the other hand, complicates the situation.

If the costs of exit are lowered, the system is less exposed to the risk of opportunism but its capacity to solve adaptation problems is weaker. If, alternatively, those costs are raised, there are disadvantages in terms of opportunism but benefits in terms of adaptation. Changing the costs of exit therefore exerts contrasting influences on the two reasons for decline; a trade-off between preventing opportunism and facilitating adaptation seems to arise in this case. In order to overcome these difficulties the costs of recontracting should be reduced unless exit is replaced with another sanctioning mechanism.

A general yet definitive assessment of exit should take into account not only positive aspects such as those related to freedom of choice, but also the negative implications for adaptation. In particular, exit can be a factor in determining not easily visible losses like the disappearance of large numbers of efficient organisations.

The aforesaid conclusion has implications for a well-balanced comparison of the workings of the economic and political spheres. In the latter, exit is often either not available or ineffective as a sanction and both recontracting and sanctioning occur without abandoning the organisation. The arguments I have developed in this paper may help to mitigate the prevailing tendency to see the lack of exit in political markets as an entirely negative phenomenon.

Notes

1 According to the definition given by Milgrom and Roberts (1992: 269) a quasi-rent 'is the portion of earnings in excess of the minimum amount needed to prevent a worker from quitting his or her job or a producer from exiting its industry'.
2 The organisation we refer to is not necessarily a firm. It may be a private club, a political party or a public body. Therefore the service it supplies does not always generate market exchange. If such an exchange is involved the assumption is that the price of the service is equal to that of rival competitors. In this paper I will use the term 'clients' to mean both clients and members.
3 The idea that the exit is the enemy of the voice has been reconsidered by Hirschman, outlining – in diverse circumstances – more complex relations between the two options (Hirschman 1993).
4 In Williamson (1976), however, there seems to be an interpretation of voice as recontracting.
5 A clear example of voice as harassment can be found in Hirschman (1986).
6 The importance Hirschman attaches to free riding when analysing the limited recourse to voice is, however, not easy to reconcile with the arguments he uses

elsewhere to dismiss the relevance of the phenomenon (Hirschman 1981: 214, 1982: ch. 5).

7 In what follows the assumption is that low effort and unfavourable environment cannot occur together, so quality q_0 never materialises.

References

Barry, B. (1974) 'Exit, voice, and loyalty', *British Journal of Political Science*, 4: 79–107; reprinted in Barry, B. (1991) *Democracy and Power*, Oxford, Clarendon Press.

Hirschman, A. O. (1970) *Exit, Voice and Loyalty*, Cambridge, MA: Harvard University Press.

Hirschman, A. O. (1981) *Essays in Trespassing. Economics to Politics and Beyond*, Cambridge, Cambridge University Press.

Hirschman, A. O. (1982) *Shifting Involvements. Private Interest and Public Action*, Princeton, NJ: Princeton University Press.

Hirschman, A. O. (1986) 'Exit and voice: an expanding sphere of influence', in A. O. Hirschman (ed.) *Rival Views of Market Society and Other Recent Essays*, New York: Elizabeth Sifton Books.

Hirschman, A. O. (1993) 'Exit, voice, and the fate of the German Democratic Republic', *World Politics* 45: 173–202; reprinted in A. O. Hirschman (1995) *A Propensity to Self-Subversion*, Cambridge, MA: Harvard University Press.

Milgrom, P. and Roberts, J. (1992) *Economics, Organization and Management*, Englewood Cliffs, NJ, Prentice Hall.

North, D. C. (1990) 'A transaction cost theory of politics', *Journal of Theoretical Politics* 2: 355–67.

Shapiro, C. and Stiglitz, J. E. (1984) 'Unemployment as a worker discipline device', *American Economic Review* 74: 433–44.

Williamson, O. E. (1976) 'The economics of internal organization: exit and voice in relation to markets and hierarchies', *American Economic Review, Papers and Proceedings* 66: 369–77.

Williamson, O. E. (1991) 'Comparative economic organization: the analysis of discrete structural alternatives', *Administrative Science Quarterly* 36: 269–96.

Wittman, D. (1995) *The Myth of Democratic Failure*, Chicago: University of Chicago Press.

4   The internal politics of the firm

Paul Milgrom and John Roberts

Political activity in society at large arises inevitably from the twin facts that individuals and groups have varying interests and that the institutions of societal decision making provide channels through which to pursue those interests. Political activity within the firm has similar roots. Workers and managers, lenders and stockholders, suppliers, customers, and local communities are all potentially affected in varying ways by a firm's decisions, and all have means to influence many of those decisions. As in the public sector, groups often organize to advance the group members' shared interests. Workers may be represented by unions, stockholders by a board of directors, customers by users groups, lenders by creditors' committees, local communities by their governments and regulatory bodies, and so on. All parties have access to the courts in case of contract disputes.

The vast scope of political behavior in the firm and writings about it would make a comprehensive review of the literature unwieldy. The upsurge in corporate takeovers during the 1980s and 1990s and the associated corporate governance issues has spawned a huge literature by itself, some of which is quickly becoming obsolete as the legal and institutional climate changes. In response to the threats of hostile takeovers, managers and boards of directors have sought legislation to thwart hostile bidders. That is just one example of the kind of business–government relations that is omitted in this survey. To keep our subject manageable, we focus primarily on the *internal* politics of the firm.

We divide the relevant literature into four general parts. The first part, reviewed in the first section, treats the institutions of the firm as *exogenous* and inquires into the behavior of individuals and groups pursuing their interests within those given institutions. The remaining three parts allow the possibility that the institutions themselves are chosen or adapted to attenuate the most harmful effects of politicking. In the second section, we discuss *value-maximizing* institutions, mostly using a very special framework in which total value is a meaningful measure of economic efficiency.[1] The third section gives special coverage to the subject of *influence costs* and their effects on how decision making is organized in firms. The value-maximizing institutions studied in these latter two sections may also be *market equilibrium* institutions, that is the institutions that would evolve or emerge under the pressures of a market economy. As we shall see later, there is no assurance that even Pareto-efficient institutions are always value maximizing. The final part of the literature considers the additional insights that emerge when market equilibrium institutions may not be value maximizing.

Exogenous institutions

In the standard neoclassical model of economics, there is little room for politics inside firms, because firms' decisions have few distributional consequences. For example, if a qualified worker is passed over for a promotion in a firm then, according to the neoclassical competitive model, that worker does not suffer because he or she can find an equivalent job at the same competitive wage at another firm. Moreover, the firm would never have any reason to promote an unqualified worker, because doing so merely reduces its profits. Similarly, when a purchasing agent chooses among qualified suppliers, the winning supplier does not enjoy rents, because the neoclassical model supposes that the firm can find as many customers as it likes if it charges the competitive price for its product, and can find no customers if it charges more.

To study the internal politics of the firm, the neoclassical model has to be extended to establish the possibility that the outcomes of the firm's decisions create winners and losers. Winners enjoy *rents* or *quasi-rents*. For employees, quasi-rents are payments or perquisites beyond those that they could expect to get by quitting and taking another job. Rents are payments or perquisites beyond those required to attract them to take the job in the first place. Quasi-rents may arise after employment if an employee makes some specific investment to prepare for a job. For example, the employee may incur moving costs. They may also arise from random events. For example, an employer may offer low wages but secure employment in a combination just sufficient to attract an employee to a job. Employment then entails no rents for the employee, but it may entail quasi-rents if general economic trends cause the employee's outside options to deteriorate. Until the last section of this paper, it will not be important to distinguish quasi-rents from rents, and we shall simply use the term 'rents' for both.

Like employees, suppliers, customers, and others may enjoy rents from their dealings with a firm. In the models discussed below, attempts to capture a larger share of the total rents turn out to be costly, because they disrupt the smooth functioning of the firm. The first step of the theory, therefore, is to justify the foundational assumption that rents in firms do exist.

Sources of rents and quasi-rents

Consider the case of employees. Why would decisions in the firm ever affect the rents they enjoy? The issue arises because any decisions that might potentially affect employee welfare, such as deciding who gets the corner office, which reporter gets to work on the juicy story, or who will be forced to work overtime, could, in principle, be fully compensated by cash payments. Firms do sometimes make compensating payments to workers. There are premiums for working late night shifts, doing hazardous jobs, working overtime, and so on, but these rarely add up to full compensation for all the variations in day-to-day decisions.

Milgrom (1988) explains why full compensation is so rare. One major reason is that pay policy serves various purposes besides eliminating rents, and the two kinds of functions are almost always incompatible. Pay policy can be used to provide incentives for loyalty and hard work, to insure workers against fluctuations in working conditions or outside market conditions, to reduce turnover, to attract a high-quality labor pool, and so on. We shall study one such example in detail below, but any of these can be used to explain the absence of compensating payments. A second reason not to use compensating payments is the sheer difficulty of assessing the appropriate cash compensation amount. Any procedure for determining the cash compensation would not only be administratively costly, it would likely become a lightning rod for the very internal politics it seeks to avoid.

We formalize one source of rents using a simple variant of a model of Becker and Stigler (1974), in which high wages are used to encourage hard work. The model is one in which a worker decides whether to be diligent and work hard or whether instead to shirk. Suppose that a shirker is detected with probability p, that the wage is w, and that the opportunity wage – equivalent to what the worker expects to get after being fired – is $\bar{w}$. Suppose the model is stationary and the worker's discount factor is δ ($0 < \delta < 1$), including both time preference and an allowance for the probability of separation. Such a worker stands to lose $(w - \bar{w})/(1 - \delta)$ if fired, and to gain some amount s by shirking, where s is the value to the worker of not having to work so hard. In this case, shirking is worthwhile exactly if $s \leq p(w - \bar{w})/(1 - \delta)$. The firm is forced to pay a wage of $w \geq \bar{w} + (1 - \delta)s/p$ to prevent shirking. The amount $(1 - \delta)s/p$ is a rent enjoyed by the employee.

Rent seeking in the firm

Bowles (1985) observed that, in this model, the firm's minimum payment can be reduced by increasing the probability p with which shirking is detected. This presumably requires costly expenditures on monitoring, which could be avoided if the firm were run in the interests of the workers and was not so concerned about 'exploiting' workers in the sense of capturing the rents workers would otherwise enjoy.

Bowles' analysis reveals what economists call a *technical* inefficiency of the capitalist firm. More intensive monitoring allows the firm to elicit the same level of diligence with a lower wage, but it does not create any extra output. Monitoring serves only to redistribute income away from workers and toward the capitalists/managers.

At this point, it may be helpful to reiterate the distinction between *Pareto* efficiency and *technical* efficiency. A production plan is technically efficient if it lies on the *production possibility frontier*; that is, if there is no alternative way to produce the same or larger amounts of each output while using less of some input and no more of any other input. Monitoring in the Bowles model leads to technical inefficiency because it entails an avoidable expenditure of real supervisory resources to produce the same quantity of goods with the same labor input. Despite this technical ineffi- ciency, it is still possible that the outcome with monitoring is Pareto efficient; that is, there may not exist any alternative allocation of resources that makes the workers better off without making the capitalist/owners worse off. The possibility that a production plan is Pareto efficient but not technically efficient turns out to play an important role in several modern theories of the firm. In a neoclassical world where resources can be freely transferred among individuals, Pareto efficiency always entails technical efficiency. Only in that too simple model do the attractions of each effi- ciency concept lend support for the other.

Ironically, Ordover and Shapiro (1984) used an argument much like Bowles' to reach a contrary conclusion – that labor's political power is a source of inefficiency. They argued that workers will be led to resist pro- ductivity-enhancing technological improvements if those same enhance- ments also improve the firm's ability to monitor workers, because the better monitoring would lead to lower wages. For example, craftspersons may resist the introduction of technically more efficient production line methods for this reason.

The Ordover–Shapiro argument differs from Bowles' argument in two important respects. First, it assumes a peculiar power structure in the firm, in which workers might affect the technology that will be used but, given the technology, management establishes the wages in its own interest. This variation in the structure leads to a second variation, this time in the conclusion: successful resistance by workers is not only technically ineffi- cient, it is *Pareto inefficient* as well. The reason is that if workers were fully in control of the firm's decisions, they would be able to implement the technology without reducing their own wages – a Pareto-improving change. This describes a political advantage of labor ownership of the firm: employees of such firms are less likely to resist new technologies. As we shall see, there may be offsetting political disadvantages as well.

Additional interest groups

So far, we have considered capital and labor as the only two interest groups, but there is no need to stop there. Edlin and Stiglitz (1993) treat the management of a firm as yet another interest group and study how they might be led to distort the firm's investments and selection of projects to entrench themselves; that is, to make themselves so valuable to a firm that the board of directors would not be tempted to replace them even if more able management could be found. They do this, of course, because management jobs entail rents.

There are various ways in which managers might entrench themselves. They might invest excessively in projects that are highly complementary to their particular skills. They might devote too much effort and too many resources to acquire private information about the value of the firm. These latter investments would give them an advantage in any competition to acquire control of the firm. The results of all these efforts are, first, that the board of directors would be forced to keep management control intact even when performance has been poor and superior managers might have been found and, second, that the firm is paying to achieve this end in the form of inappropriate investments in projects and private information.

Just as the interests of capital and its hired managers are distinct, the interests of workers and union officials can be distinct as well. An example of this is found in a study by Golden (1992) of the mass workforce reductions that were announced in 1980 at British Leyland and at Fiat. Both of these companies were thought to have militant unions, which were ready to make large wage and benefit demands and to sponsor long strikes to force concessions from the firms' managements. Nevertheless, the two unions responded quite differently to the threatened workforce reduction: while the union at Fiat responded aggressively, the union at British Leyland did not. What might account for the difference? Golden argues that the layoffs at British Leyland – unlike those at Fiat – did not threaten the shop stewards or union officials, so it was not in the interest of union activists and leaders to call a strike. Similarly, the long strikes in the Japanese coal mining industry in 1953 and 1960 were provoked by the company (Mitsui) laying off union activists (Golden 1993). The same union acquiesced in workforce reductions in the interim period between these two strikes, because during that interim it had a contractual right to select who would be laid off, allowing it to protect union activists.

Public versus private sector politics

Are the politics of the firm distinguishable from those of governments and public sector institutions? Do the same principles apply in both arenas? The extensive literature on *rent-seeking* behavior, begun by Tullock (1967) and Krueger (1974), has characterized the costs of much political behavior in very much the same terms that we have used to describe it in the firm. This literature emphasizes that government grants of monopoly lead people to waste resources in an attempt to capture the rents.

According to Buchanan (1980), the losses from rent-seeking behavior occur at three different levels: direct attempts to capture monopoly rents, attempts by bureaucrats to occupy positions where they can receive bribes for distributing rents, and attempts by various parties to secure the legislation that creates the rents. Each of these attempts lead to wasteful expenditures of resources. It would seem that analogous costs could be incurred in the private sector, but Buchanan has resisted that comparison, asserting that '[t]he unintended results of competitive attempts to capture monopoly rents are "good" because entry is possible; comparable results of attempts to capture artificially contrived advantageous positions under governmentally enforced monopoly are "bad" because entry is not possible.'

If there is one common theme in these papers that all the authors seem to agree on, it is that politics is just another form of wasteful rent-seeking behavior. Whether in the government or in the firm, attempts by individuals and groups to enjoy benefits at others' expense or to defend rents that are already being earned consume resources that could be put to more productive use. In the models of exogenous institutions, the emphasis is on the costs of political activity and the reasons that even well-intentioned governmental interventions in the economy so often work out badly.

Value-maximizing institutions

The next group of papers take a sharply different perspective on the role of politics in private sector organizations like firms, focussing on how institutions, processes, and routines are designed to attenuate the costs of politicking. A few of the papers also recognize the benefits of politicized decision processes as ways to take account of the information and preferences of people affected by some decision. This is an important difference. Its theoretical consequence is that the optimal design of decision routines becomes a subject of benefit–cost analysis, where the benefits of effective decision making are balanced against *influence costs* – the value destroyed as people try to capture or defend a share of the rents that the process distributes. For reasons discussed below, we expect the solutions of the optimum problem to be an important predictor of the actual design of the institutions and routines for decision making in private firms.

Will the same benefit–cost principle also predict the structure of public sector decision making? Probably, the predictive power of the principle will be attenuated by the pervasive effects of political power, ideology, and social policy in public sector deliberations. To illustrate the public versus private sector comparison, consider the selection of suppliers by a firm in private industry. This is a straightforward exercise, at least conceptually.

Qualified bidders are identified and bids solicited. Bids are made and a possibly complex bid evaluation process ensues. A supplier is chosen, the final contract details are negotiated, and the needed product is ordered. The objective all along is relatively clear: to maximize the net value added for the firm. Government procurement objectives are typically much more complicated. A large order may be spread among different political districts, for example, to broaden the political support for continuing the underlying project. Or, public policy arguments may be invoked to justify buying from an inferior domestic supplier in order to encourage the development of domestic industry. In US government procurement, firms that lose at the bidding stage of procurement can often appeal to courts and regulators to object to the contract award decision, for example on the grounds that the product specification gives an unfair advantage to the design of one particular supplier or that the bid preparation time was too short. During the appeals, purchases of the needed equipment may have to be postponed. In one recent case, it took the US governement five years to approve orders for new desktop computers, by which time the technology described in the government's original bid specification had become obsolete. Losses to the United States from its inadequate and aging computer systems have been estimated to be in the tens of billions of dollars.[2] A private firm would hardly tolerate losses of this magnitude merely to ensure due process and fair treatment of suppliers.

Why do governments give such weight to issues like fairness and due process? No doubt part of the answer lies in political ideology: the very legitimacy of a government may depend on citizens' perceptions that it operates fairly. Another part lies in the fact that governments are shielded from many forms of competition, so that they may continue to survive and grow despite highly inefficient practices that would sink a private firm, and especially one operating in a highly competitive market. Whatever the reasons, these differences do result in greater opportunities for rent seeking in the public sector than in the private sector.

Why expect value maximization?

In much economic analysis of the firm, one important hypothesis is that the institutions, rules, procedures, and routines found in the private sector are devised to be value maximizing. The first question to ask, therefore, is: why should we ever expect value-maximizing institutions to emerge? One possible answer lies in the motives of the founder of the firm or institution. Suppose the founder is one who designs the organization, establishes its legal structure, internal organization, product offerings, and so on, and then sells it in whole or in parts to outsiders. A self-interested founder would want to design the organization to maximize the price he or she can command from the eventual buyer. The founder would design decision-making procedures and institutions not simply to minimize efforts wasted in politicking, but rather to maximize the net benefits of the decision procedures, taking into account all the costs and benefits that decision making entails.

Partly, this story of the value-maximizing founder is a parable. For an entrepreneur who founds a firm and plans eventually to sell shares to outsiders, or to sell out entirely to someone seeking to enter that business, or to transfer the busines to heirs, increasing the value of the business is likely to be an important objective, but there may be other objectives as well.

There are instances, however, where this story becomes a plausible account of the actual process. One such instance is the development of the condominium association, which is the organization that governs a condominium. Typically, the founder is a real estate developer who acquires the property, plans and builds the condominium, and then sells the units to residents who will either live there (in a residential condominium) or conduct business there (in a commercial condominium). Barzel and Sass (1990) studied condominium associations in the US state of New Mexico, where the founder/developer of a condominium is required to file a declaration specifying the assessment rules and voting rules that will apply. The assessment rules specify how the members may tax themselves for projects adopted by the condominium, such as improvements to the common areas or building a swimming pool. Assessments in their sample were all conducted in one of three ways: equal amounts per residence or business unit, equal amounts per unit of area (floor space), or equal amounts per unit of initial value. Similarly, the voting rules specify the weights accorded to various voters and the majorities that apply for various kinds of issues. For example, votes in the association may be assigned as one vote per unit or they may be allocated based on area or value and the rules may specify a supermajority such as two-thirds or three-quarters for capital improvements that require a special assessment. Finally, the developer can seek to remove some decisions about amenities from the association's decision-making process by including them with the initial building.

This is an example in which the founder explicitly chooses the rules of governance. It certainly makes sense that the developer would want to select the rules that maximize the total amount buyers are willing to pay for their units, since that is the only thing the developer receives from the deal.

Notice that this formulation of the problem supposes that there really are benefits as well as costs to political decision making. A condominium association may have perfectly good reasons to make decisions about renovating its entry area, building a playground or swimming pool, or hiring a security guard. If the initial constitution of the condominium allows those decisions to be made only by unanimous consent and using voluntary contributions, then a free-rider problem could result in the failure of the group to undertake even highly beneficial projects. Allowing the condominium association to assess members equally for their shares of capital projects, with the choice of projects made by majority rule, may improve project selection. Such a rule would make it more valuable to own a unit of the condominium, and the developer who adopted such a rule would receive a higher price.

Giving such powers to the condominium association also incurs potential influence costs, depending on the differences in interests among the members. If votes are distributed equally, for example, but assessments are assigned according to the area or value of the units, then owners of the small or low-value units might approve self-serving projects to be paid for by owners of the large or high-value units. If there is a proposal to add central air conditioning to a building, those who favor it may be located differently from those who oppose – for example, they may have a sunnier exposure or be on a higher floor of the building. The use of supermajority rules limits influence costs without much limiting the association's ability to adopt projects of general value.

Using data on condominia, Barzel and Sass have tested some specific hypotheses about efficient governance. They predict that to limit influence costs, votes and assessment shares will be distributed in the same proportion.[3] They argue plausibly that if a group that bears a minority of the cost commands a majority of the votes, that would encourage rent-seeking behavior. They argue further that when votes are not so distributed, that will reflect a desire to economize on the costs of tabulating votes, so the deviation will be to a rule of one-unit–one-vote. The data strongly supports that prediction. They also predict that greater heterogeneity among units implies a greater likelihood of conflicting interests, leading to more supermajority rules and more amenities decided initially by the developer, but the evidence on these matters appears ambiguous.

Implications of influence cost theory

The first prediction of influence cost models, developed in intuitive terms by Milgrom and Roberts (1990a) and formally modeled by Milgrom (1988), is based on the benefit–cost framework we have already described. The benefits of a wide open decision-making process with plenty of opportunity for comment by employees lies in the usefulness of the information for making better decisions. The cost lies in increased opportunities for rent seeking and therefore higher influence costs. The intuitive comparative statics, largely verified in the formal model, are as follows. A high value of information in the decision favors an open process. A large redistributive component favors a closed process with few opportunities to provide information.

These predictions accord well with the actual decision processes found in many organizations. For example, the determination of annual raises within a firm tends to use a closed and centralized process with limited and highly structured access by the employees whose pay is being determined. Once raises have been decided, they are generally not subject to appeal, and not considered again until the next regularly scheduled salary review. The theory explains this kind of process as a consequence of the large distributive aspect of the salary-setting decision. In contrast, product-pricing decisions, which often have virtually no redistributive aspect, are commonly delegated to lower-level managers, who may not follow any highly structured process for arriving at the pricing decision, and who may be quick to offer sales or reduce the price if the sales volume appears to be too low.

Benefit–cost analyses also seem to be effective for explaining the procedures applied to internal decision making in public and quasi-public organizations. One example is the use of quorum rules. Recently, the American Economic Association instituted a 1 percent quorum rule for new initiatives proposed at its annual meeting, in order to prevent small organized groups from introducing and passing resolutions that would not be favored by the majority of members. As another example, at Stanford University, office allocations for the new economics building were made on the basis of seniority. It is hard to imagine any important efficiency differences among alternative office allocations, so the system is designed to minimize politicking.[4] It is interesting to contrast this with other departmental decisions. Course content, with virtually no distributive consequences (at least for faculty), is delegated to individual faculty members. Senior faculty appointments, which affect different faculty members differently but require the expert judgment of individual faculty, are carried out in a way that is designed both to obtain useful information and to close the matter once a vote has been taken. All of this seems consistent with the benefit–cost analysis of decision processes.

A second implication of the theory is that there will be a greater emphasis on equity in units of the firm where cooperative decision making is desired, in order to homogenize interests and minimize influence costs (Milgrom and Roberts 1990b). Notice that this is a conditional prediction. Firms may sometimes seek to promote competition among their units, but then they should arrange that the units are largely independent of one another and that performance can be objectively measured (hence not vulnerable to rent-seeking manipulations). These points are closely related to Lazear's (1989) observation that reducing rent differentials tends to mitigate destructive forms of competition ('backstabbing') among employees and Itoh's (1991) that strong incentives based on a comparative performance assessment tend to undermine mutual helping activities, and are undesirable when such activities are important.

In a similar vein, Hansman (1988, 1990) has argued that ownership patterns of the firm are explained by the desire to homogenize interests and minimize influence costs. Shared control by capital and labor, he argues, would lead to costly politicking, and labor management is quite unusual except in firms where the labor pool itself is quite homogeneous, such as law firms and medical practices. Even in those cases, it is only one class of laborers that exercises control, for otherwise too many resources would be wasted in political battles for the organization to be viable.

Yet another example of organization design to minimize influence costs arises in connection with firm's divestiture decisions. Meyer *et al.* (1992) have argued that attempts by employees in declining divisions of a firm to save their jobs provides a potent reason for spinoffs and sales of poorly performing units. Divesting a unit makes it clear to the unit managers and employees that their futures are tied to the unit's performance, helping to engender a single-minded dedication to improving performance. As part of a larger firm, the same people might devote more of their energies to obtaining transfers to other units or getting extra resources for the unit.

McAfee and McMillan (1992) have argued that influence costs multiply with the number of layers in an organization, using that to explain 'organizational diseconomies of scale.' They also argue that such costs are lower in more competitive industries, because such firms have fewer rents to distribute. This provides an interesting connection between influence costs and Leibenstein's notion of X-inefficiency.

Both the McAfee and McMillan work and our own (Milgrom and Roberts 1990a) use influence costs to explain the theoretical limits on the size of an efficient firm. The theoretical problem is that by placing two organizations under common control and intervening in their operations only selectively – for example, when there are opportunities for improved coordination, or ways to exploit scale economies, or opportunities to reassign resources more productively – it would seem that the integrated firm could always be more productive than the separate ones (Williamson 1985). However, according to our theories, the very act of making these extra issues subject to administrative decision may raise influence costs, because the new issues become exposed to the politics of the decision-making process. For example, a lawyer in one law firm cannot expect to be assigned to a case being handled by another law firm, regardless of how much political effort the lawyer devotes to the matter. If the two firms were merged, however, the opportunities for influence would be increased. The merger increases influence costs.

A final prediction concerns the balance between different ways of limiting influence costs by discouraging employees from devoting excessive efforts to politicking. One way to accomplish that is to modify wage policies, introducing performance bonuses or arranging to equalize the distribution of rents as we have already discussed. An alternative, discussed earlier, is to modify the way decisions are made. What we shall argue below is that modifications to the organization are sometimes the primary way to control influence costs. The trade-offs involved between the alternative instruments are subtle enough, however, that it is useful to explore them in a formal model. We use a variant of the model introduced in Milgrom and Roberts (1990b).

Influencing a job assignment: a model

Suppose there are two kinds of jobs. In the low-level job, employees will remain without quitting only if the periodic wage is at least $\bar{w}_L$. An employee promoted to the higher-level job receives special training that increases his or her value to outside employers. To prevent the employee from quitting that job, the wage must be at least $\bar{w}_H > \bar{w}_L$. We assume that the need to train replacements for workers who quit is sufficiently costly that the firm will pay workers at least these amounts. In addition, the firm may choose to pay a bonus of $b \geq 0$ to an employee who performs especially well.

The firm wishes to learn which of two employees is better qualified for promotion to the high-level job. To determine that, the firm offers a test. Each employee's score on the test depends on his or her inherent ability and any effort expended in preparing for the test. Moreover, effort expended preparing for the test may eliminate some random differences in preparation for the test and make the test a better indicator of future performance in the high-level job. However, efforts spent in preparation for the test are costly to the firm because that much less effort is available for directly productive activities. To model this, we suppose that the employee has $\bar{e}$ units of effort that he or she supplies inelastically, of which some amount e is devoted to test preparation.

If promotion is based on the test, then the probability that employee i will be promoted over employee j is the probability of performing better on the test: $F_T(e_i - e_j)$. If performance is the basis of promotion, then the probability is $F_P[(\bar{e} - e_i) - (\bar{e} - e_j)] = F_P(e_j - e_i)$. The probability of being evaluated highly and earning the bonus b as a function of i's time devoted to producing output is $F_B(\bar{e} - e_i)$. Let π be the probability that promotion will be based on the test and $1 - \pi$ the probability that it will be based on performance. The firm's instruments are the probability π, the wages w_H and w_L, and the bonus b. Given these, employee i chooses $e_i \in [0, \bar{e}]$ to maximize

$$w_L + [\pi F_T(e_i - e_j) + (1 - \pi)F_P(e_j - e_i)](w_H - w_L) + bF_B(\bar{e} - e_i) \qquad (1)$$

We assume that the employee's objective is concave in e_i.

In the absence of influence costs, the firm would set $\pi = 1$, $b = 0$, $w_H = \bar{w}_H$, and $w_L = \bar{w}_L$, paying as little as possible and assigning the high-level job on the basis of tests of suitability. The problem is that this objective function of the employee is then globally increasing in e_i, that is the employee would be induced to devote all his or her efforts to test preparation and none to producing output. We have not yet said anything about the firm's objective, but this outcome will not generally be the one most desired by the firm.

Suppose the firm wishes to induce a level of effort that is somewhere in the interior of the interval $[0,\bar{e}]$. Assuming a symmetric equilibrium of the effort choice game between the two employees, we may differentiate (1) with respect to e_i and then substitute the equilibrium condition $e_i = e_j = e^*$ to obtain

$$0 = (w_H - w_L)[\pi F'_T(0) - (1 - \pi)F'_p(0)] - bF'_B(\bar{e} - e^*) \qquad (2)$$

Equation (2) shows how the firm can use its instruments to control e^*. One alternative is to set $b = 0$ and to fix π so that $[\pi F'_T(0) - (1 - \pi)F'_p(0)] = 0$. With these choices, the employees would be willing to set any level of e^* suggested by the firm. For higher levels of π, the firm will be forced to set $b > 0$ and to raise w_L toward w_H. A positive bonus for successful performance provides a countervailing incentive so that there is some payoff for production-related effort, while increasing w_L to w_H eliminates the pay differential associated with the high-level job and so eliminates the motive for influencing the promotion decision.

Let us suppose that, after the fact, the firm learns the value or importance I of assigning the right employee to the high-level job. The value I is distributed according to a cumulative distribution $G: [0,\bar{I}] \to [0, 1]$ with a strictly positive density G' and associated mean μ. Let $A(e^*) \geq \frac{1}{2}$ denote the accuracy of the test, that is the probability that the test accurately identifies the best candidate for promotion, when each employee prepares with effort e^*. Then, the loss of value to the firm from promoting the most productive worker, rather than the one who tests best for the job, is $A(e^*)L(\pi)$, where

$$L(\pi) = \frac{1}{2} \int_0^{G^{-1}(1 - \pi)} x \, dx = \frac{1}{4} [G^{-1}(1 - \pi)]^2 \qquad (3)$$

The firm's objective is to maximize

$$\Omega(\pi, w_L, w_H, b, e^*) = P(e^*) + A(e^*) [\mu - L(\pi)] - w_H - w_L - 2bF_B(\bar{e} - e^*)(4)$$

subject to $w_H \geq \bar{w}_H, w_L \geq \bar{w}_L, b \geq 0, \pi \in [0, 1]$, and the incentive constraint (2). Without additional assumptions, we cannot identify the optimum, but we can make some progress toward characterizing the optimum by following the suggestion of Grossman and Hart (1983), identifying the least-cost way to implement any given proposed allocation of effort e^*.

It is apparent from (4) that the partial derivatives $\partial\Omega/\partial b$, $\partial\Omega/\partial w_L$, and $\partial\Omega/\partial w_H$ are all negative, but $\partial\Omega/\partial\pi = 0$ at $\pi = 1$,[5] that is the cost of using the instrument π to provide incentives is a second-order cost. Also, each of these instruments has a first-order effectiveness in providing incentives, that is satisfying (2). These facts allow us to draw some conclusions about how incentives for e^* will be implemented, independently of the actual optimal value of e^*. First, the firm's optimum will always entail a distortion of the promotion rule away from first best. At the optimum, $\pi < 1$. Furthermore, if the maximum gain $\bar{I}$ from a proper job assignment is not too large, then the optimum entails setting $b = 0$, $w_H = \bar{w}_H$, $w_L = \bar{w}_L$, and $\pi < 1$. This means that, in some cases, the only adjustment that will be optimally made to provide incentives is to distort the decision rule. Wage policy, which is already carrying the weight of preventing turnover, will not be further distorted in an attempt to mitigate rent seeking.

Other equilibrium institutions

The value maximization framework provides a convenient way to convert organization design problems into ones of benefit–cost analysis. For example, we have argued that salary-setting processes are highly formalized and closed because the influence costs of a more open-ended process would be high while the additional benefits, if any, would be slight. The problem with this approach is that while it properly evaluates the issues of distribution and value creation after the decision routines are in place, it assumes that the routines themselves are chosen purely on grounds of value maximization, which is the institutional version of technical efficiency.

The model developed in the previous section incorporates this feature. The desire to prevent quits in that model leads the firm to pay higher wages than it otherwise would, and its preference to modify its promotion policy even at the cost of decreased efficiency of job assignments rather than to introduce performance bonuses or raise the wage w_L paid in the low-level job is a consequence of the way the costs and benefits are shared.

Other papers in the economics literature that incorporate similar features are mostly concerned with matters besides decision-making institutions. We review a few papers below only to show how much the perspective changes once the possibility of 'technically inefficient' equilibrium is admitted.

Rotemberg (1991) argues that a firm might integrate vertically to supply itself with goods even when there is a technically more efficient supplier. The reason is that, just as in the Becker–Stigler model, the firm might have to pay a rent to the supplier to maintain high quality. Even if the cost of manufacture was lower for the supplier, the price, consisting of the sum of the cost plus the supplier's rent, might be higher than the cost plus rent that would need to be paid to a unit within the firm.

Dow (1993) shows that even if labor-run firms create more total value than capital-run firms, a competitive equilibrium might still drive labor-run firms out of business. The reason is that the laborers may have insufficient wealth to start a firm on their own. Without surrendering control rights to the capitalists over the use of their equipment, the laborers may be unable to commit credibly to provide a minimum rate of return on capital. This conclusion contrasts sharply with the arguments made by Williamson (1985), which rely on an implicit assumption that there are no effective wealth constraints.

Yet another variant is the argument made by Perotti and Spier (1993) and Wells (1992) that firms may incorporate too much debt in their capital structure (relative to the value-maximizing level), in order to strengthen their bargaining position in labor negotiations. Here, too, it is the limited capital of one party that links the distribution of benefits to the value that can be created. The capital structure decision reduces total value, but increases the value that can be captured by the representatives of capital in their negotiations with labor.

These models surveyed here might be regarded as power-based alternatives to the value-maximizing theories described earlier. In addition to these two, there is one more possible obvious category of explanations that is omitted because we know of no formal models in the category. This is the category of history-based explanations. Instead of imagining that whole systems of institutions are created by perfectly rational founders, this alternative approach looks for *equilibrium* patterns of institutions, where each part of the system supports the others and no part can be changed alone in a way that increases value. Pagano (1993) reports such a model, in which complementarities between the assignment of property rights and the choice of technology create the possibility of multiple equilibria. Inefficient combinations in this theory may persist simply because it is too difficult to identify better ones. Although such arrangements are vulnerable to entry, they may nevertheless persist if the more efficient institutions differ from familiar arrangements in so many respects that they remain undiscovered.

Conclusion

There is ample reason to suppose that decision making in firms affects the distribution of rents, and is therefore subject to politicking. We have seen several examples of that and of how institutions can be and sometimes are designed to garner the advantages of the political process – acquiring useful information – while controlling the influence costs it creates. Despite its youth, the theory of the firm as a political organization has already been quite successful at lending insight into some aspects of organization.

Notes

1 See Milgrom and Roberts (1992), especially ch. 2, for an extensive discussion and critique of the conditions involved.
2 'Computer Morass Hobbles U.S.,' *San Jose Mercury News*, March 16, 1993, page 1A.
3 See also Grossman and Hart (1988) and Harris and Raviv (1988), who make a similar argument for the one-share–one-vote rule in corporate shares.
4 In this case, the cost of politicking would have been born in large part by the department chairman, who is also the one who structured this decision process.
5 $\partial \Omega / \partial \pi = - \frac{1}{2} A(e^*) G^{-1}(1 - \pi) / G'[G^{-1}(1 - \pi)] = 0$ at $\pi = 1$, because $G^{-1}(0) = 0$.

References

Barzel, Yoram and Sass, Tim R. (1990) 'The allocation of resources by voting,' *Quarterly Journal of Economics* 105: 745–71.

Becker, Gary and Stigler, George (1974) 'Law enforcement, malfeasance, and compensation of enforcers,' *Journal of Legal Studies* 3(1): 1–18.

Bowles, Samuel (1985) 'The production process in a competitive economy,' *American Economic Review* 75: 16–36.

Buchanan, James (1980) 'Rent seeking and profit seeking,' in James Buchanan, Robert Tollison, and Gordon Tullock (eds) *Toward a Theory of the Rent-Seeking Society*, College Station, TX: Texas A&M University Press, pp. 3–15.

Dow, Gregory (1993) 'Why capital hires labor: a bargaining perspective,' *American Economic Review* 83(1): 118–34.

Edlin, Aaron and Stiglitz, Joseph (1993) 'Discouraging rivals: managerial rent seeking and economic inefficiencies,' CEPR Discussion Paper No. 304, Stanford University.

Golden, Miriam (1992) 'The politics of job loss,' *American Journal of Political Science* 36(2): 408–30.

Golden, Miriam (1993) 'Workforce reductions and industrial conflict in postwar Japan: a comparative analysis,' UCLA Institute of Industrial Relations, Working Paper No. 245.

Grossman, Sanford and Hart, Oliver (1983) 'An analysis of the principal-agent problem,' *Econometrica* 51: 7–45.

Grossman, Sanford and Hart, Oliver (1988) 'One-share one-vote and the market for corporate control,' *Journal of Financial Economics* 20 (January/March): 175–202.

Hansman, Henry (1988) 'The ownership of the firm,' *Journal of Law, Economics and Organization* 4: 267–304.

Hansman, Henry (1990) 'When does worker ownership work? ESOPs, law firms, codetermination, and economic democracy,' *Yale Law Journal* 99(8): 1749–1816.

Harris, Milton and Raviv, Artur (1988) 'Corporate governance: voting rights and majority rules,' *Journal of Financial Economics* 20 (January/March): 203–35.

Itoh, Hideshi (1991) 'Incentives to help in multi-agent situations,' *Econometrica* 59(3): 611–36.

Krueger, Anne (1974) 'The political economy of the rent-seeking society,' *American Economic Review* 64: 291–303.

Lazear, Edward (1989) 'Pay equality and industrial politics,' *Journal of Political Economy* 97: 561–80.

McAfee, Preston and McMillan, John (1992) 'Organizational diseconomies of scale,' Working paper, May.

Meyer, Margaret, Milgrom, Paul and Roberts, John (1992) 'Organizational prospects, influence costs and ownership changes,' *Journal of Economics and Management Strategy* 1(1): 9–35.

Milgrom, Paul (1988) 'Employment contracts, influence activities and efficient organization design,' *Journal of Political Economy* 96(1): 42–60.

Milgrom, Paul and Roberts, John (1990a) 'Bargaining costs, influence costs and the organization of economic activity,' in James E. Alt and Kenneth A. Shepsle (eds) *Perspectives on Positive Political Economy*, Cambridge: Cambridge University Press, pp. 57–89.

Milgrom, Paul and Roberts, John (1990b) 'The efficiency of equity in organizational decision processes,' *American Economic Review Papers and Proceedings* May: 154–9.

Milgrom, Paul and Roberts, John (1992) *Economics, Organization and Management*, Englewood Cliffs, NJ: Prentice Hall.

Ordover, Janusz and Shapiro, Carl (1984) 'Advances in supervision technology and economic welfare: a general equilibrium analysis,' *Journal of Public Economics* 25: 371–89.

Pagano, Ugo (1993) 'Organizational equilibria and institutional stability,' in Samuel Bowles, Herbert Gintis, and Bo Gustafsson (eds) *Markets and Democracy: Participation, Accountability and Efficiency*, Cambridge: Cambridge University Press.

Perotti, Enrico C. and Spier, Kathryn (1993) 'Capital structure as a bargaining tool: the role of leverage in contract renegotiation,' *American Economic Review* 83(5): 1131–41.

Rotemberg, Julio (1991) 'A theory of inefficient intrafirm transactions,' *American Economic Review* 81(1): 191–209.

Tullock, Gordon (1967) 'The welfare cost of tariffs, monopoly and theft,' *Western Economic Journal* 5: 224–32.

Wells, Robin (1992) 'Strategic debt,' Draft, University of Southampton.

Williamson, Oliver (1985) *The Economic Institutions of Capitalism: Firms, Markets, Relational Contracting*, New York: Free Press.

5 Is power an economic good?

Notes on social scarcity and the economics of positional goods

Ugo Pagano

Introduction

In a recent textbook of sociology there is the following statement:

> In nearly all societies the good things of life, the things that people
> desire are unequally distributed; some have more, others less. When we
> ask – what good things? – the answers that sociologists have given,
> since Max Weber, is that they are thought of under three main heads;
> wealth, prestige and power.[1]

Out of these three heads economists, since Smith's *Wealth of Nations*, have
concentrated on wealth. The purpose of this paper is to examine a possible
way of integrating the analysis of goods such as prestige and power in
economic theory. This will be done by introducing a new type of good –
positional goods – which will be defined as having the opposite characteristics to public goods.

Consider a two-person economy. Current economic theories usually
consider two types of goods and their intermediate combination. The first
type of good is defined by the fact that if an individual i consumes a
quantity x_i of x, the second agent consumes no units of x_i. This defines
a private good. The second type of good is defined by the fact that, if an
individual i consumes a quantity x_i of x, the second agent also consumes
the same amount of x_i. This defines a public good. The purpose of this
paper is to argue, following Fred Hirsch's[2] analysis, that there is a third
category of good which has been almost ignored by economists but which
is as important as the other two for understanding economic systems. This
good is defined, in our two-person economy, by the fact that, if an individual i consumes x_i, the second individual must consume an equal but
negative quantity $-x_i$. Thus, these types of goods are zero-sum goods.
Following Hirsch, I will call this type of good a positional good.[3]

Positional goods have characteristics polar to those of public goods. In
the case of public goods, other individuals cannot be excluded from consuming a positive amount of the goods equal to that consumed by the

individual supplying the good. In the case of positional goods, other individuals are necessarily included in consuming a negative amount of the good equal, in absolute value, to that consumed by the individual supplying the good.

Why are goods like prestige and power positional goods? In our two-person economy, it will be impossible for individual i to exert or consume a positive amount of power[4] if individual j does not consume negative amounts of it. It is impossible for one individual i to dominate if the other individual, j, is not dominated. Or, to put it in another way, a person who consumes power is able to command more activity than they can execute. In our two-person economy this is possible for one individual only if the other individual consumes negative power; that is, he or she executes more actions than he or she commands. Thus power is a zero-sum or positional good.

Consider now status or prestige. Individual i consumes social status when he or she is superior to individual j according to a system of evaluation shared by both individuals. Thus consuming status is consuming a shared feeling of superiority – the consumption of which is only possible if the other individual consumes negative status or a shared feeling of inferiority. Thus status and prestige are also zero-sum or positional goods.

Pure types of positional goods may be rather important. Still, as in the case of public goods, intermediate cases (i.e. semi-positional goods) such as status-yielding luxury cars may well exist and are important in everyday life. Indeed, for our two-person economy we can define our goods as a straight line; each point on the line below shows the amount of x which the individual j will consume when individual i consumes x_i:

$$-x_i \qquad\qquad 0 \qquad\qquad +x_i$$

The extreme points of this line define x as a positional good ($-x_i$) and a public good ($+x_i$), whereas 0 units of x_i will define x as a private good. Moreover, the segments $-x_i,0$ and $0,x_i$ will respectively define semi-positional and semi-public goods.

In our two-person economy two undesirable characteristics of positional goods can be immediately observed.

The first concerns inequality. It is possible to consume a positional good only if it is unequally consumed: for, its consumption implies the joint consumption of positive and negative quantities. Only zero consumption of the positional good is compatible with its egalitarian consumption.[5] This is immediately derived from the fact that in a two-person economy the total consumption of positional goods is zero by definition. Whereas we must consume equal amounts of public goods and we can consume equal amounts of private goods, we must consume unequal quantities of positional goods.

The second concerns growth. It is impossible to have a growth of total consumption of positional goods. A growth in positive consumption will be matched by a growth in negative consumption. In our two-person economy the rate of growth of a positional good can be positive only for one individual. The other will suffer a corresponding negative rate of growth in his or her consumption of the positional good. Thus the rate of growth of positional goods is necessarily equal to zero.[6]

The purpose of this paper is to investigate the welfare implications of positional goods and some applications of their analysis.

In the first section of this paper the definitions given above are extended to the case of an *n*-person economy. Here, positional goods are distinguished in bi-positional, multi-positional and pan-positional good. In the second section we extend the analysis of the conditions necessary for maximum welfare to this extended range of possible type of goods. We also examine the performance of a market without personalised goods for dealing with externalities and the consequences of this arrangement for positional goods. The third section examines some applications of the theory of positional goods. The applications examined are: national security; education; the capitalist firm and the workers co-operative; *social* classes; status, fashions and advertising; and 'shifting involvements'.

Finally, the last section contrasts the traditional concept of economic scarcity with the concept of social scarcity which is implied by the present analysis of positional goods.

Positional goods as a case polar to public goods

If we consider an economy of *n* individuals, three cases of 'pure' positional goods can be distinguished. In the first case the consumption by an individual of a positive amount of a positional good involves the consumption of an equal negative amount by one (and only one) other individual. This good will be called a bi-positional good. In the second case the consumption by an individual of a positive amount of a positional good involves the consumption of an equal negative amount by more than one (but not all) other individual. This good will be called a multi-positional good. In the third case, the consumption by an individual of a positive amount of a positional good involves the consumption of an equal negative quantity by all the other $n - 1$ individuals existing in the economy. This good will be called a pan-positional good. Power can be either a bi-positional good if it involves the domination of one individual over the other or a pan-positional good if it involves the domination of one particular individual over all the other individuals. It can also be a multi-positional good in the intermediate cases.

Other intermediate cases are also possible. It would be desirable to have a clear idea of the intermediate cases among the three cases of positional goods mentioned above and the traditional 'private' and 'public' goods. Consider the consequences for the other individuals h $(h \neq i)$ following from the fact that individual i consumes a positive amount x_i of a good x:

(a)   All other individuals also consume x_i. This defines x as a public good.
(b)   All individuals other than i consume 0 units of x_i. This defines x as a private good.
(c.1) Only one individual j consumes $-x_j$; all individuals other than i and j consume 0 units of x_i. This defines x as a bi-positional good.
(c.2) Some individuals, s, consume $-x_j$ $(1 < s < n - 1)$; all individuals other than i and s consume 0 units of x_i. This defines x as a multi-positional good.
(c.3) All individuals other than i consume $-x_i$. This defines x as a pan-positional good.

Let us now define t_{hi} as the fraction of x_i which is consumed by individual h when individual i consumes x_i and let us also assume that t_{ii} is equal to 1 for individual i. From the definitions given above, the following five 'pure' cases can be derived:

(a) $t_{hi} = 1$, $\forall h \neq i$, defines a public good.
(b) $t_{hi} = 0$, $\forall h \neq i$, defines a private good.
(c.1) $t_{ji} = -1$, $t_{hi} = 0$, $\forall h \neq j$ and $\forall h \neq i$, defines a bi-positional good.
(c.2) $t_{si} = -1$, $\forall s \neq i$: $-1 < s < -(n - 1)$, and $t_{hi} = 0$, $\forall h \neq s$ and $\forall h \neq i$ defines a multi-positional good.
(c.3) $t_{hi} = -1$, $\forall h \neq i$, defines a pan-positional good.

Moreover, semi-public and semi-positional goods can be easily defined in the following way:

- $0 \leq t_{hi} \leq 1$, $\forall h \neq i$, and $0 < t_{ji} < 1$ for at least one $j \neq i$ defines a semi-public good;
- $0 \geq t_{hi} \geq -1$, $\forall h \neq i$, and $0 > t_{ji} > -1$ for at least one $j \neq i$ defines a semi-positional good.

In other words, changes of t_{hi} in the interval $[-1, +1]$ define all the possible intermediate cases.[7] Goods having public good characteristics are the 'opposite' of goods having positional characteristics. In the first case, an individual consuming x will make other individuals consume positive fractions of it. In the second case, an individual consuming x will make other individuals consume negative fractions of it.

Social welfare and markets in an economy with power and status as positional goods

The purpose of this section is to generalise the conditions for maximum social welfare and the conditions defining a market equilibrium in such a way that they can be easily extended to the case of positional goods.

Restating the optimality conditions

We assume that there are two goods in the economy. One good, y, is a priori defined as a private good. The second good, x, will have many a posteriori definitions according to the values which the fractions t_{ih} defined in the section above are assumed to take. In general, we assume that an individual i consumes y_i of the private good and quantities $t_{ih}x_h$ of good x. We assume that $t_{ii} = 1$, $\forall i$. Let us denote by μ the weight given to the utility function of individual i in the social welfare function and by $T(x,y)$ the social transformation function by which units of each good can be transformed into units of the other good.

The maximisation problem for society taken as a whole will then be as follows:

Maximise $w = \mu_i\ U_i(y_i,\ t_{i1}x_1 + t_{i2}x_2 + \ldots + t_{ii}x_i + \ldots + t_{in}x_n) +$

$$\sum_{\substack{h=1 \\ h \neq i}}^{n} \mu_h\ U_h(y_h,\ t_{h1}x_1 + t_{h2}x_2 + \ldots + t_{hi}x_h + \ldots + t_{hh}x_h + \ldots + t_{hn}x_n)$$

subject to $T(x,y) = 0$

This maximisation to problem gives us the following necessary conditions for optimality (see the first section of the Appendix):

$$\frac{\partial U_i/\partial x_i}{\partial U_i/\partial y_i} + \sum_{\substack{h=1 \\ h \neq i}}^{n} t_{hi}\ \frac{\partial U_h/\partial t_{h1}x_i}{\partial U/\partial y_h} = \frac{\partial T/\partial x}{\partial T/\partial y}$$

which using conventional notation can be rewritten as

$$\text{MRS}^i_{x_iy_i} + \sum_{\substack{h=1 \\ h \neq i}}^{n} t_{hi}\ \text{MRS}^h_{t_{hi}x_iy_h} = \text{MRT}_{x,y}, \quad i = 1 \ldots n \tag{1}$$

These conditions become, in the five pure cases described above:

(a) public good:

$$\text{MRS}^i_{x_iy_i} + \sum_{\substack{h=1 \\ h \neq i}}^{n} \text{MRS}^h_{x_iy_h} = \text{MRT}_{x,y}$$

(b) private good:

$$\text{MRS}^i_{x_iy_i} = \text{MRT}_{x,y}$$

(c.1) bi-positional good:

$$\text{MRS}^i_{x_iy_i} - \text{MRS}^j_{-x_iy_j} = \text{MRS}_{x,y}$$

(c.2) multi-positional good:

$$\mathrm{MRS}^{i}_{x_i y_i} - \sum_{s \neq i} \mathrm{MRS}^{s}_{-x_i y_s} = \mathrm{MRT}_{x,y}$$

(c.3) pan-positional good:

$$\mathrm{MRS}^{i}_{x_i y_i} - \sum_{\substack{h = 1 \\ h \neq i}}^{n} \mathrm{MRS}^{h}_{-x_i y_h} = \mathrm{MRT}_{x,y}$$

Conditions (1) also describe the intermediate cases (i.e. semi-positional and semi-public goods) when the corresponding value is given to t_{hi}. Observe that the 'polar' nature of goods having positional and public character is found again in the optimality conditions. In the case of a public good, the rate of substitution of other individuals has to be added to the rate of substitution of the agent consuming i; by contrast, in the case of positional goods, the rate of substitution of other individuals has to be subtracted from the rate of substitution of the individual consuming i.

Opposite market failures

Suppose that each individual i is endowed with a certain amount of the private good and that the individual can choose to transform units of the private good into units of the good x (to be defined according to the value of t_{hi}). Suppose also that each individual can transform his or her endowment $\bar{Y}_i$ of the private good y_i into units of the good x according to a ratio p; p can be conceived as the price of x in terms of y according to which each individual can buy it on an international market and/or as the constant rate of transformation according to which each individual can transform units of the good y into units of the good x. We assume therefore that:

(assumption 1) $\mathrm{MRT}_{x,y} = p$

A question may now be asked with reference to good x. If each individual i chooses independently to buy or produce units of x sacrificing units of y, will we obtain the conditions necessary for obtaining maximum social welfare?

In this case, each individual i will maximise

$U_i(y_i, t_{i1}x_1 + t_{i2}x_2 + \ldots + t_{ih}x_h + \ldots + t_{ii}x_i + t_{in}x_n)$
s. t. $px + y = \bar{Y}_i$

This implies the following necessary condition:

$$\frac{\partial U_i / \partial x_i}{\partial U_i / \partial y_i} = p$$

Using conventional notation and assumption 1 the expression above can be written as

$$\text{MRS}^i_{x_iy} = \text{MRT} \tag{2}$$

A comparison with conditions (1) shows that conditions (2) describe an efficient allocation only when x is a private good. If x is a public good, it will be undersupplied because the positive effects of its production on the individuals other than i will be ignored by individual i. By contrast, if x is a positional good, it will be oversupplied because the negative effects of its production on the individuals other than i will be ignored by individual i. In general, if $t_{hi} > 0$ (for at least one individual h), x will be undersupplied because x has (at least) a semi-public character, and if $t_{hi} < 0$, x will be undersupplied because x has (at least) a semi-positional character. The market is only efficient when $t_{hi} = 0$ for all individuals other than i, a circumstance which implies that x is a private good.

The pricing of positional goods

Public and semi-public goods can be regarded as goods having a positive externality, defined in units of the good itself and from which other people cannot be excluded. Positional and semi-positional goods can be regarded as goods having a negative externality defined in units of the good itself, and in which other people have to be necessarily included. Introducing a market for externalities implies that the market could, in principle, efficiently allocate public goods. The purpose of this section is to examine the possibility of a similar solution for positional goods.

Define p_{ih} as the price to be paid by individual i to individual h for consuming the fraction t_{ih} of the amount x_h of good x supplied by individual h. Each individual i will pay to each individual h supplying x_h an amount $p_{ih}t_{ih}x_h$ and will receive a payment $p_{hi}t_{hi}x_i$ from each individual h who consumes a fraction, t_{hi}, of the quantity x_i of the good x which he or she has bought or produced.

In this case, the maximisation problem of each individual i may be rewritten as

Maximise $U_i(y_i, t_{i1}x_1 + t_{i2}x_2 + \ldots + t_{ih}x_h + \ldots + t_{ii}x_i + \ldots + t_{in}x_n)$

subject to $px_i + y_i + \sum_{\substack{h=1 \\ h \neq i}}^{n} p_{ih}\, t_{ih}x_h \leq \tilde{Y}_i + \sum_{\substack{h=1 \\ h \neq i}}^{n} p_{hi}t_{hi}x_i, \quad i = 1 \ldots n, h = 1 \ldots n$

This gives us the following necessary conditions for each individual i (see the second section of the Appendix):

$$\frac{\partial U_i/\partial x_i}{\partial U_i/\partial y_i} = p - \sum_{\substack{h=1 \\ h \neq i}}^{n} p_{hi} t_{hi}$$

which, using the usual conventional notation, can be rewritten as

$$MRS^i_{x_i y_i} = p - \sum_{\substack{h=1 \\ h \neq i}}^{n} p_{hi} t_{hi} \tag{3}$$

This condition describes the general condition which will hold for each individual i in a situation where markets for externalities exist. This condition becomes equivalent to the following conditions in the usual 'pure' cases:

(a)   public good:

$$MRS^i_{x_i y_i} = p - \sum_{\substack{h=1 \\ h \neq i}}^{n} p_{hi}$$

(b)   private good:

$$MRS^i_{x_i y_i} = p$$

(c.1) bi-positional good:

$$MRS^i_{x_i y_i} = p + p_{ji}$$

(c.2) multi-positional good:

$$MRS^i_{x_i y_i} = p + \sum_{s}^{n} p_{si}$$

(c.3) pan-positional good:

$$MRS^i_{x_i y_i} = p + \sum_{\substack{h=1 \\ h \neq i}}^{n} p_{hi}$$

The optimality of conditions (3) is shown in the third section of the Appendix. It can be intuitively seen as the double-indexed prices compensate for the marginal (dis)utility which the consumption of the good by an individual brings to other individuals. But does this redefined market represent a feasible allocation mechanism?

In the case of a bi-positional good, the individual has not only to pay the 'price of production' p of the positional good but also to pay a price p_{ji} of the individual j who has to consume a negative quantity of x.[8] The case of pan-positional (multi-positional) goods is more complex. In these cases, an individual i has to pay not only the production price but also, to all the other (some other) individuals, a price p_{hi} because they consume a negative quantity equal in absolute amount to the positive quantity consumed by i. In general, although all the individuals other than i will consume the same negative quantity of x (i.e. $-x_i$), each individual should be charged a different price because the marginal rate of substitution of $-x_i$ into y can easily differ from that of the other individuals.

This situation closely resembles a Lindahl equilibrium for collective goods.[9] The difficulties or even the (im)possibility of the existence of such competitive markets are very much the same. The existence, enforcement or, even, the definition of property rights is as hard in the case of positional goods as it is for the case of public goods. However, the consequences of the failure to establish property rights have opposite signs. In the case of public (or semi-public) goods, the consequence of this failure implies that the agent consuming the public good does not get paid for other people's consumption; in the case of positional (or semi-positional) goods, the equivalent failure implies that the agent consuming positive amounts is not charged for the negative consumption of other agents' consumption. Moreover, in both cases, even if we do not consider property rights problems, it is hard to think of any force driving the price to its optimal level. In the case of positional goods, a price should be paid by the person consuming a positive amount of it to the person consuming the corresponding negative amount. But this implies that for this transaction only one possible buyer and only one possible seller may exist, a situation which may well move us from the 'optimal' world of competitive markets to the wasteful world of bilateral monopoly.

Although the difficulties of establishing a market for (semi-)positional goods are very much the same as the difficulties that can arise in the case of (semi-)public goods, one additional difficulty may arise *ex post* in the case of positional goods. The consumption of positional goods, occurring after that market contract has been agreed, is likely to be conflictual because the agents involved in this transaction will have to consume jointly amounts of goods having opposite signs. This may imply that even if the transactions concerning positional goods were carried out in a competitive economy characterised by large numbers of buyers and sellers, their joint consumption may be characterised by a limited number of individuals having competing interests – an *ex post* conflict of interests which competitive markets are often unable to solve *ex ante*. This conflictual consumption is a characteristic which distinguishes the consumption of positional goods from public and private goods. In the case of public and private goods consumption is either an individual activity or a collective activity characterised by non-competing consumption claims, whereas in the case of positional goods consumption is characterised by incongruence and conflict of individual goals. Of course, this *ex post* problem may have a negative feedback on the *ex ante* desirability of having market transactions for positional goods.

However, in spite of these difficulties, the possibility of a market for semi-positional goods cannot be a priori excluded. If our economy can be 'replicated', then we can imagine that the double-indexed prices p_{ij} do not represent a price to be paid by an individual i to an individual j but a price paid by many individuals of type *i* to many individuals of type *j*. The existence of many identical individuals competing against each other could ensure the existence of a competitive market. So, the issue of the (im)possibility of the existence of markets for positional goods remains an open issue which has to be solved by looking at particular (semi-)positional goods. This is what we are going to do in the next section.

Real economies and positional goods

In this section we consider some possible applications of the theory of positional goods. Some applications (national security; education; and status, fashions and advertising) are characterised by the absence of a market for positional goods. In contrast one application (the capitalist firm) is characterised by the existence of a market for positional goods. Finally, the last two applications (social classes and shifting involvements) use the theory to make economic sense of aspects of society which are usually outside the realm of orthodox economic theory.

National security

National security is usually considered the classic example of a pure public good. However, for the individuals of the 'enemy' country any expense in national security by the other country generates a negative consumption of national security, or a consumption of national insecurity. When both countries are taken into account national security becomes a positional good. In the case of national security, a 'market' deal is impossible because few countries would accept being paid a price to consume national insecurity. (Here, the *ex post* difficulties involved in the joint consumption of a positional good arising after the market contract are particularly clear *ex ante*.) Two results are therefore possible: the first is the oversupply of the positional good by both countries, which in this case takes the dramatic form of an arms race. The second is an agreement by which both countries agree not to consume national security at the expense of insecurity of the other country. In this case the consumption of the positional good is eliminated by both countries. A third possibility and also other similar possibilities such as the elimination of the countries themselves are clearly not to be considered in the present context and, hopefully, in no future context.[10]

Education

Fred Hirsch has maintained that the recent 'inflation' of education titles can be explained by referring to the positional character of the jobs which require these titles. Education is an input in the production of social power and status. The positional character of these goods may explain the increase in the demand for education and the devaluation of education titles.

Education enriches and produces human skills; these skills may be regarded as private and public goods. Thanks to them we can master nature and improve human relations. In this respect, education produces semi-public goods. But education also gives to the more educated more social status and power; the more educated get better jobs, learn skills by which they can rule over and dominate other people, and enjoy higher status. Thus, education is used in the production of both semi-positional and semi-public goods. This brings about contradictory conclusions about the amount of education which is offered by a market economy. If one refers only to the semi-public goods produced by education, one can easily maintain that education is undersupplied. By contrast, if one only takes into account the semi-positional character of the outputs of education, then one can argue that education may be oversupplied.

For instance, assume that education is only used in the production of semi-positional goods and that more education does simply mean more power and status. Application of the theory of positional goods developed in the preceding section implies that optimality conditions require that an individual should invest in education up to the point that its production cost in terms of forgone units of the private good equals the difference between its marginal 'benefit' and the marginal 'damage' incurred by the other individuals which see their education yielding less social power and status. If markets for these externalities existed, then the individual investing in education should pay for the negative externalities due to the negative outputs of his or her education process. Different prices should be paid to different individuals even if they incur the same decrease in value of the social power and status of their education. But these personalised commodities are not likely to exist owing to the problems of property rights and free competition examined in the preceding section. Thus, education may be oversupplied because a person who increases their social power and status by education does not pay for the corresponding decrease incurred by other people. Each person acting independently may find that other people's education has devalued their own education; additional education may be an individual answer to this problem, but if everyone has the same reaction then everyone has to educate themselves for a longer time to obtain the same result. This may be one possible explanation for the fact that the value of education has been recently inflated. A Ph.D becomes necessary where previously it was only necessary to have a BA and a BA becomes necessary for jobs which did not require any university education. Wouldn't it be desirable to find some ways to decrease the positional outputs of education and increase the public goods which it certainly also produces?

Status, fashions and advertising

We often say that some consumption goods are 'status symbols'; that is, that their utility derives more from the status which they yield to their consumers than from their private consumption. Status is a positional good; in a two-person economy, positive consumption of status by one individual implies a negative consumption of status by the other individual. In an n-person economy status is likely to become a semi-multi-positional good and the positive consumption of status by somebody involves some negative consumptions by more than one individual.

Consider an economy where a status symbol commodity can be produced and consumed. Suppose that the social optimum solution implies that the status symbol commodity should be produced because a group of 'status-seeking consumers' derive a welfare gain from the consumption of it which is greater than the welfare loss incurred by the other consumers. In theory, if a market for externalities existed, when consuming the status symbol commodity, the status-seeking consumers should pay for its production costs and for the welfare loss due to the fall in status of the other consumers.

But suppose that only a market for the physical commodity exists whereas a market for the status associated to this commodity does not exist. Then, at first, the status-yielding commodity may be overproduced for the status-seeking consumers because they do not pay for the loss in status of the other consumers. After that, it may be overproduced for the status-reduced consumers because they do not pay for the disruption of positive status of the first consumers. In other words, the commodity is 'fashionable' at the beginning because it is associated with some positive consumption of status by some consumers; when and if the other consumers react to the corresponding negative consumption of status by joining the fashion, then the positive consumption of status associated with it is destroyed and the commodity stops being fashionable. That is the time for a new fashion.

Advertising often attempts to help producers sell more by exploiting the fashion mechanism; this can be done by introducing a system of shared values which associate a physical commodity with status. Such an association could exist independently of advertising but advertising certainly helps it, and, in this way, it also helps a great potential source of market failure.

The capitalist firm and workers' co-operatives

The capitalist firm is an institution based on the employment contract. Such a contract involves the employer acquiring (against the payment of a wage) the power of allocating workers to various tasks for a certain length of time.[11] Thus the employment contract involves the exchange of a positional good – power – which will be consumed (or, better, experienced) as a positive amount by the employer and as a corresponding negative amount by the employee. The positional character of the employment relationship is consistent with some well-known characteristics of the labour market. In this market, problems in defining property rights may easily arise because the object of the exchange – the power given by the employee to the employer – will have to be jointly consumed, in negative and positive quantities, by these two agents. Moreover, perfect competition is an unlikely event in this market. The power exchanged on this market is a semi-positional good – this involves the possibility that, as for the other markets for externalities, a situation of bilateral monopoly may easily occur.

However, even if the exchange of power is carried out *ex ante* in a classical competitive framework characterised by many buyers and sellers and well-defined property rights, its *ex post* consumption will be characterised by goal incongruence and small-number relationships. For, once the employment contract has been signed and a wage and other terms of the contract have been agreed upon, the employer (the employee) can increase consumption of positive (negative) power only at the expense of the employee (employer). Thus, this joint consumption is characterised by goal incongruence. It is also characterised by small-number relationships because only the parties who have signed the contract are involved in this joint consumption and the costs of breaking the contract isolate them from market forces.[12]

In the employment contract the employer acquires the power to assign a certain 'area' of tasks to workers. The limits of this 'area' may be used to define the consumption of power occurring in the employment relationship: the employers consume more positive power and the employees a corresponding negative additional amount whenever the employers are able to enlarge the 'area' of tasks performed by the employees. Consuming more power increases the utility of the employers because it increases their profits and may decrease the utility of the employees who may be commanded to do more new, unpleasant tasks.

The power consumed within the factory can be considered to be a multipositional good;[13] for, if some workers agree to have their own 'area' of tasks enlarged this puts pressure on the other workers to do the same, otherwise the other workers can acquire the reputation of being troublemakers and suffer the consequences of this reputation. By contrast, if some workers refuse to have their own area of tasks enlarged this gives the other workers the possibility of achieving the same result by simply claiming that they are not fairly treated. For this reason under certain circumstances (excluding, for instance, where the employer uses 'divide and conquer' strategies to increase its power) an employer is likely to consume the same amount of positive power with respects to all its workers. An increase of power will see an equal increase of negative power of all the employees. Thus, this defines the power consumed in each firm as a multi-positional good.[14] But this implies that the power consumed by the employer is likely to be excessive. The employer can easily violate market agreements if the workers do not solve the free-rider problem which exists, as for each individual worker it may be convenient to let the other workers fight for a decrease of the consumption of negative power.

The formation of unions and other forms of worker solidarity are required to solve this problem. But let us assume that the workers are not able to solve this problem and that it takes time for any reputation effect to work. Then, it is possible to produce more output from the same amount of labour power. In this situation firms violating the optimality conditions are able to squeeze out of the industry firms which respect the terms of the contract. Only the existence of national unions might prevent this from happening. In other words, in the absence of trade unions, the capitalist firms may be an inefficient form of organisation which expands itself very efficiently.

We may contrast this analysis of capitalist firms with that of workers' co-operatives. Workers' co-operatives do not involve the exchange of negative power and time against a wage. Here, the workers may agree to co-operate to produce output, following certain social norms and rules.[15] However, free riding on these norms and rules is also possible. The benefit to a selfish free rider may well be higher than its cost if the other individuals continue to observe the social norm which the free rider has broken.

Workers' inability to solve the free-rider problem can be an important source of inefficiency for both the capitalist firm and the workers' co-operative. But the consequences of this same inefficiency are very different in each case. In the capitalist firm it implies the overconsumption of a positional good (the power of the employers). In the workers' co-operative it implies the underproduction of a public good (the output of the co-operative). For the capitalist firm it increases labour productivity whereas in the co-operative it decreases it. It allows the former to squeeze out other firms in the industry whereas it makes it very difficult for the latter to stay in business. It is no wonder then that a market economy, where both inefficiencies are very likely to exist, tends to generate capitalism instead of market socialism.[16]

Social classes

In the preceding sections it was assumed that each individual was initially endowed with an amount of private good equal to $\bar{Y}_i$. Assume that the individuals have different initial endowments of the private good. The individuals can, then, be ranked according to their initial endowments of the private good y_i and be grouped into property classes according to some arbitrary rule.

I wish to argue in this section that this grouping into property classes is quite unsatisfactory for defining social class and that a definition of social classes can only be given in terms of a positional good existing in the economy.

Some examples of social classes are slave owners and slaves, feudal lords and serfs, capitalists and proletarians. Notice that the definition of a social class is usually given in terms of the social role of one class relative to another class and it usually also implies that one class dominates the other class.[17] In other words, hidden in the definition of social class, there is the concept of a class relationship which links together the roles of the two social classes in a relationship of domination. The class of slaves only makes sense if a class of slave owners exist and a similar case can be made for the feudal lords and their serfs or for the capitalists and the proletarians.

In general, we may say that class membership involves the joint consumption (or the joint experience) of a class relationship by individuals belonging to two different classes.

This joint consumption of a class relationship is impossible in an economy where only public and private goods exist. Joint consumption of a public good is, of course, possible but the joint consumption, which necessarily characterises these goods, does not have to entail a division of the individuals into classes; for, each individual consumes the same amount of the public good. In contrast, joint consumption of private goods is impossible since, by definition, the consumption of a private good affects the welfare of only one individual.

The existence of positional goods makes the joint consumption of a class relationship possible and also clarifies the nature of this relationship. Positional goods are characterised by the fact that the individuals jointly consume the same absolute amount in either positive or negative quantities. This joint consumption divides the individuals into two classes: that of the positive and that of the negative consumers of the positional good. And indeed the examples of the class relationships considered above involve the 'joint but opposite' consumption of a different type of power, power being a pure positional good. Thus, being a slave master involves the consumption of absolute power by the slave master himself, to which there corresponds a dramatic joint negative consumption of power by the slave.

Private wealth cannot by itself determine social class membership, and it may have little or even no weight in the determination of social classes under certain social systems. But it can be very important in determining social class membership under capitalism. Consider the case of a capitalist society in which the only positional good is power and where the only way of acquiring power is by employing people under your command at a market wage. Assume that all individuals have the same tastes. Then, the amount of the positional good (power) which they buy or sell will only depend on their initial endowments of private goods. In this case wealth is the only cause of the class membership of the individuals.[18]

However, this simple relation between wealth and class membership (and between property and social class) will be unlikely to characterise modern capitalist societies for several reasons. First, under capitalism (and, indeed, under any social system) more than one positional good may determine class membership. For instance, under capitalism status may be another positional good determining class structure. Second, under capitalism, (and, again, perhaps, under any social system) there are other assets besides private wealth and other mechanisms besides the market through which positional goods can be acquired. Education, innate skills, family background and willingness to conform to powerful people's wishes may be alternative means of acquiring the positional goods defining class membership under capitalism. They may also be the main way through which positional goods are acquired under other social systems.[19] And even, if under an idealised model of capitalism, wealth is the only asset and the market the only mechanism by which positional goods are acquired, these other means of acquisition have great importance under capitalism in reality. Third, since power is a positional good, its market allocation can be inefficient and is sometimes impossible; for this reason, much of the allocation of power (especially 'public' or pan-positional power) is not done by the market mechanism and cannot be bought by private wealth. Finally, if the individuals have different tastes, not only their wealth but also their preferences will have a role in determining class membership. Such a role should not be exaggerated but it cannot be completely ruled out.

Shifting involvements

Periods of massive public participation are often followed by periods in which people retire to private activities and vice versa. Hirschman[20] has tried to explain these cycles by illustrating the delusions of private and public life. The problem with what are called *private* life and *private* consumption is that they contain much *positional* life and *positional* consumption. Indeed, the delusion that characterises private–positional life is that when other people carry out their apparently private plans we are worse off. Such a delusion can be contrasted with the delusion which characterises public life and consumption. Here we realise that if other people do not carry out plans similar to our own and using the same degree of effort, then our benefits will not be commensurate with our efforts. This double delusion can well generate a cycle characterised by shifting involvements. Is there a way out?

Conclusion

Orthodox economists regard economics as a science which studies the phenomenon of scarcity. Scarcity is usually linked to the idea of natural scarcity. The existence of positional goods implies that social scarcity may be an equally relevant phenomenon which is formally and substantially different from natural scarcity.

At a formal level, whereas natural scarcity is defined by the fact that some goods are in fixed supply, social scarcity is defined by the fact that the production and the consumption of certain goods by some individuals involves the production and the consumption of negative amounts of the same goods by other individuals. Their availability (and their scarcity) for the positive consumers is related to the willingness of other people to consume negative amounts of the same good.

At a substantial level, whereas natural scarcity emphasises a problem which is common to all societies and changes only with the change of the relationship between people and nature, social scarcity stresses a problem which differs widely from one society to the other and is strictly related to changes in social relations.

This paper has examined one possible, simple way through which positional goods and social scarcity can be integrated into the body of orthodox economic theory. The aim of this paper was to show that this integration is possible and profitable. However, a serious limitation of this approach should be noted. If the consumption and the production of positional goods is limited by the willingness of other people to consume negative amounts of them, it may well be that the most appealing way of expanding their positive consumption is by manipulating other people's preferences and increasing their willingness to consume the corresponding negative amount. Similarly, a reduction of the consumption of positional goods (and less a conflictual society) may, perhaps, be achieved only by diminishing individuals' taste for these goods – a task which implies also a change in people's preferences. However, studying these two problems does really involve a departure from the traditional domain of economics which takes preferences to be given. Preference formation has usually been the object of the other social sciences and changing preferences (by education and greater 'internalisation' in our utility function of the utility of people affected by our consumption of positional goods) raises questions of moral and political philosophy. A collaboration with other social scientists and philosophers seems very fruitful.[21]

Appendix

Denoting by λ the Lagrangian multiplier associated with $T(x, y)$, we obtain the following necessary conditions:

$$\mu_i \frac{\partial U_i}{\partial y_i} = \lambda \frac{\partial T}{\partial y} \tag{A.1}$$

$$\mu_h \frac{\partial U}{\partial y_h} = \lambda \frac{\partial T}{\partial y}, \quad h \neq i \tag{A.2}$$

$$\mu_i \frac{\partial U_i}{\partial x_i} + \sum_{\substack{h \\ h \neq i}} \mu_h t_{hi} \frac{\partial U_h}{\partial t_{hi} x_i} = \lambda \frac{\partial T}{\partial x} \tag{A.3}$$

Substituting (A.1) and (A.2) into (A.3) yields

$$\lambda \frac{\partial T}{\partial y} \frac{\partial U_i/\partial x_i}{\partial U_i/\partial y_i} + \sum_{\substack{h=1 \\ h \neq i}}^{n} \lambda \frac{\partial T}{\partial y} \frac{t_{hi} \partial U_h/\partial t_{hi} x_i}{\partial U_h/\partial y_h} = \lambda \frac{\partial T}{\partial x}$$

Eliminating λ and dividing both sides by $\partial T/\partial y$ we obtain

$$\frac{\partial U_i/\partial x_i}{\partial U_i/\partial y_i} + \sum_{\substack{h=1 \\ h \neq i}}^{n} t_{hi} \frac{\partial U_h/\partial t_{hi} x_i}{\partial U/\partial y_h} = \frac{\partial T/\partial x}{\partial T/\partial y}$$

Denoting by λ_i the Lagrangian multiplier associated with the constraint, we obtain the following necessary conditions for optimality:

$$t_{ih} \frac{\partial U_i}{\partial t_{ih} x_h} = \lambda_i p_{ih} t_{ih} \tag{A.4}$$

$$t_{hi} \frac{\partial U_h}{\partial t_{hi} x_i} = \lambda_h p_{hi} t_{hi} \tag{A.5}$$

$$\frac{\partial U_i}{\partial x_i} = \lambda_i \left(p - \sum_{\substack{h=1 \\ h \neq i}}^{n} p_{hi} t_{hi} \right) \tag{A.6}$$

$$\frac{\partial U_i}{\partial y_i} = \lambda_i \tag{A.7}$$

$$\frac{\partial U_h}{\partial y_h} = \lambda_h \tag{A.8}$$

Substituting (A.7) into (A.6), we obtain

$$\frac{\partial U_i/\partial x_i}{\partial U_i/\partial y_i} = p - \sum_{\substack{h=1 \\ h \neq i}}^{n} p_{hi} t_{hi}$$

The optimality of conditions (3) can be easily shown in the following way. From (A.5), we obtain

$$p_{hi} = \frac{1}{\lambda_h} \frac{\partial U_h}{\partial t_{hi} x_i}$$

Substituting this expression in condition (3), we obtain

$$\mathrm{MRS}^i_{x_i y_i} = p - \sum_{\substack{h=1 \\ h \neq i}}^{n} t_{hi} \frac{1}{\lambda_h} \frac{\partial U_h}{\partial t_{hi} x_i}$$

which using (A.8) can be rewritten as

$$\mathrm{MRS}^i_{x_i y_i} = p - \frac{\sum_{\substack{h=1 \\ h \neq i}}^{n} t_{hi} \partial U_h / \partial t_{hi} x_i}{\partial U_h/\partial y_h}$$

which, using conventional notation and assumption 1 of the second section, becomes equivalent to conditions (1) showing the optimality of conditions (3) achieved by an individual agent in a market with externality markets.

Notes

1 Goldthorpe (1985: 140).
2 Hirsch (1977). As the title of the book suggests, Hirsch's analysis is mainly concerned with the social, rather than the natural, limits of growth; these are not the focus of the present analysis. A good review of Hirsch's book is provided by Harcourt (1981). The importance of positional goods in evaluating the welfare implications of the 'profit motive' is very well outlined by Sen (1983).
3 Indeed, my definition of positional goods is more restrictive than Hirsch's definition. Hirsch also includes under this heading goods whose total supply is fixed (such as land for leisure). In my definition, this latter characteristic is irrelevant. In his review of Hirsch's book, Matthews appropriately points out the difference between the two categories of goods which are included in Hirsch's definition of positional goods (one involving externalities and the other fixed supply). Matthews is also right in observing that Hirsch's definition implies that 'in a static primitive society everything is positional' (Matthews 1977: 575). However, this statement does not hold true for my definition. Nor does it hold for the definition given by Frank (1985) where positional goods are defined as goods determining the social rank of individuals. In a static economy positional goods can exist in the same way that public and private goods do.
4 This characteristic of power is well illustrated by Plant (1983).
5 The characteristics of a society where individuals maximised honour (a positional good) is put forward by Moses Finley in his book *The World of Odysseus*: 'When everyone attains equal honour, then there is no honour for anyone. Of necessity, therefore the world of Odysseus was fiercely competitive, as each hero strove to outdo the others' Finley (1954: 137). Equality (and peace) are impossible in this society because they would imply the disappearance of the good desired by individuals.
6 The consequences of this characteristic of positional goods are convincingly explored in Hirsch (1977). This justifies Hirsch's inclusion of goods in fixed supply under the label of positional goods because also for these goods the rate of growth is necessarily zero. Observe that this characteristic arises in the two cases for different reasons. In one case consumption is constrained by the existence of a fixed stock of the good. In the other (positive) consumption is constrained by the fact that it involves the existence of negative consumption of the same good. In the case of distribution this difference is decisive. Whereas an equal distribution of quantities (different from zero) of a good in fixed supply is possible, this is impossible for a positional good.
7 Some goods can be (semi-)positional and (semi-)public at the same time. For instance, t_{hi} might be equal to 1 for some individuals h and t_{ji} equal to -1 for some individuals j. National security is a good example of this situation when the consumption by individuals of the enemy country (i.e. individuals j) is also considered. National security is usually considered a pure public-good because only the individuals of the country that supplies national defence (i.e. individuals i) are taken into account. On national security (and insecurity) see the next section.
8 I am assuming a system of property rights in which the 'negative' consumer of the positional good owns the right of accepting or refusing to consume any amount of the positional good. Property rights could also be defined in the opposite way and this would not make any difference to the efficiency of the allocation of positional goods. On this point see Coase (1960).
9 On the concept and the properties of a Lindhal equilibrium see Roberts (1974) and Dasgupta and Heal (1979).
10 More in general, national status and reputation is also a positional good and

can be one of the factors explaining the 'oversupply' of nationalism. An account of the 'economics of nationalism' can be found in Pagano (1995).

11 This definition of the employment contract is well underlined in Coase (1937) and Simon (1957). A summary of this literature is provided in Pagano (1985).

12 On this point see Williamson (1985).

13 The capitalist economy, being based on the employment contract, is not based only on the consumption of private goods. The firm also has a positional good aspect (i.e. the capitalist–worker relationship) and a public good aspect (the relationship among the workers). On this point see Bowles and Gintis (1983).

14 On this point see Elster (1985) and Olson (1971). A limitation of Olson's analysis is that it only considers selfish behaviour. On this point see Collard (1978).

15 The objective function of workers' co-operatives is likely to be different from that of the capitalist employer. The workers' co-operatives internalise in their objective function the preferences of the workers for different task mixes and their intensity. This may make the organisation of work and the techniques of production chosen by a co-operative more socially desirable than those chosen by a profit-maximising firm. On this point see Pagano (1984, 1985).

16 However, I do not believe in a mono-causal explanation for the weak diffusion of co-operatives under the market system. For instance, imperfect credit markets may also be another explanation. The explanation, provided in this paper, may be contrasted to that offered by Alchian and Demsetz (1972). The existence of the free-rider problem is used there to explain why workers would spontaneously choose to become the employees of a capitalist firm instead of forming workers' co-operatives. The weaknesses of this explanation are quite obvious. The free-rider problem may be an argument in favour of workers employing supervisors. But it cannot be used for maintaining that supervisors–capitalists have necessarily to employ workers. Even if employing supervisors may be advantageous for the workers, giving all the monitoring power or all the 'residual claim' to them is clearly disadvantageous. For, it implies that the workers may, then, suffer the capitalist inefficiency outlined in this section. A related criticism of Alchian and Demsetz is put forward in Aoki (1984).

17 Bob Rowthorn (1974) has argued that the main deficiency of conventional neoclassical analysis lies in its right neglect of the related concepts of class relations and the mode of production. I am tempted to argue that this deficiency may be related to the absence of positional goods (such as power) from this analysis. I hope that the remaining part of this section will justify this claim.

18 This point is clearly related to and inspired by Roemer's derivation of social classes from initial endowments (Roemer 1982). However, one advantage of the present approach may lie in the fact that people enter different social classes only if they relate to each other (i.e. they jointly consume the positional good through which social class is defined). Roemer's exploitation is a proxy for inequality in initial assets and occurs independently of the fact that real-life individuals relate to each other. Thus classes are defined independently of the interaction, among individuals. By contrast, here, the very nature of social classes depends on the nature of the positional good which can be consumed in the economy. One individual may be wealthier than another independently of their interaction. But one can dominate the other only if they interact. For instance, a market for some form of power could exist whereby one individual can trade his or her greater wealth against the negative consumption of power by the other individual. On the other hand, some of the weaknesses of a definition of classes based on domination instead of an exploitation are well outlined in Erik Olin Wright (1986).

19 For instance, family background and blood links are the main way of distributing positional goods under feudalism.
20 See Hirschman (1977). As Hirschman points out, his book is something in between a (very good) work of social science and (an acute) biography of many individuals.
21 Of course, this does not imply that economists cannot themselves investigate sociological and philosophical questions related to this problem. Good examples are Collard (1978), Matthews (1981), Sen (1983) and Hodgson (1998).

References

Alchian, A. and Demsetz, H. (1972) 'Production information costs and economic organisation', *American Economic Review* 62: 777–95.
Aoki, M. (1984) *The Co-operative Game Theory of the Firm*, Oxford: Oxford University Press.
Bowles, S. and Gintis, H. (1983) 'The power of capital: on the inadequacy of the conception of the capitalist economy as private', *Philosophical Forum* 14: 225–45.
Coase, R. H. (1937) 'The nature of the firm', *Economica* IV(November): 386–405.
Coase, R. H. (1960) 'The problem of social cost', *Journal of Law and Economics* III: 1.
Collard, D. (1978) *Altruism and Economy. A Study in Non-Selfish Economics*, Oxford: Martin Robertson.
Dasgupta, P. S. and Heal, G. M. (1979) *Economic theory and Exhaustible Resources*, Cambridge: Cambridge University Press.
Elster, J. (1985) *Making Sense of Marx*, Maison des Sciences de l'homme and Cambridge University Press.
Finley, M.I. (1954) *The World of Odysseus*, Harmondsworth: Penguin.
Frank, R. H. (1985) 'The demands for unobservable and other non-positional goods', *American Economic Review* 75: 101–16.
Goldthorpe, J. E. (1985) *An Introduction of Sociology*, Cambridge: Cambridge University Press.
Harcourt, G. C. (1981) 'Notes on the social limits to growth', *Economic forum* Summer: 1–3; reprinted in *Controversies in Political Economy. Selected Essays of G.C. Harcourt*, ed. O. F. Hamouda (Brighton: Wheatsheaf, 1986).
Hirsch, F. (1977) *Social Limits to Growth*, London: Routledge & Kegan Paul.
Hirschman, A. O. (1977) *Shifting Involvements. Private Interest and Public Action*, Oxford: Martin Robertson.
Hodgson, G. M. (1998) 'The approach of institutional economies', *Journal of Economic Literature* 36: 116–92.
Matthews, R. C. O. (1977) 'Review of Hirsch (1977)', *Economic Journal* 87: 574–634.
Matthews, R. C. O. (1981) 'Morality, competition and efficiency', *Manchester School* 49(4): 289–309.
Olin Wright, E. (1986) 'What is middle about the middle class?' in J. Roemer (ed.) *Analytical Marxism*, Cambridge: Cambridge University Press.
Olson, M. (1971) *The Logic of Collective Action*, Cambridge, MA: Harvard University Press.
Pagano, U. (1984) 'Welfare productivity and self-management', *Economic Notes* No. 3: 5–21.
Pagano, U. (1985) *Work and Welfare in Economic Theory*, Oxford and New York: Basil Blackwell.

Pagano, U. (1995) 'Can economics explain nationalism?' in A. Breton, G. Galeotti, P. Salmon and R. Wintrobe (eds) *Nationalism and Rationality*, Cambridge: Cambridge University Press.

Plant, R. (1983) 'Hirsh, Hayek, and Habermas: dilemmas of distribution', in A. Ellis and K. Kumar (eds) *Dilemmas of Liberal Democracies – Studies in Fred Hirsch's Social Limits to Growth*, London and New York: Tavistock.

Roberts, D. S. (1974) 'The Lindahl solution for economies with public goods', *Journal of Public Economics* No. 3: 23–42.

Roemer, J. (1982) *A General Theory of Exploitation and Class*, Cambridge, MA, and London: Harvard University Press.

Rowthorn, R. (1974) 'Neo-classicism, neo-Ricardianism and Marxism', *New Left Review* 86: 63–82.

Sen, A. K. (1983) 'The profit motive', *Lloyds Bank Review* No. 147, January: 1–20.

Simon, H. A. (1957) *Models of Man*, New York: John Wiley, chs 10 and 11.

Williamson, O. E. (1975) *Markets and Hierarchies*, New York: Free Press.

Williamson, O. E. (1985) *The Economic Institutions of Capitalism*, New York: Free Press.

6 How politics limits markets

Power, legitimacy, choice

John Dunn

Political economy is an extremely important intellectual and practical preoccupation. But, except at a very trivial level, it is not happily thought of as a determinate academic discipline, with definite analytical procedures and clear epistemic commitments (or even widely shared intellectual habits). What makes it practically important can be distinguished quite readily from what makes it intellectually important. Its intrinsic intellectual importance is relatively narrow, above all to a particular audience. It is intellectually important to those whose profession it happens to be to attempt to comprehend the causal dynamics of modern polities and the contests over the significance of different governmental projects and performances today, as it is for those who seek to comprehend the causal dynamics of modern economies or the systematic normative criteria by which the performance of such economies can most reasonably and illuminatingly be assessed.

Its practical importance, however, could hardly be less narrow (Dunn 1990b: Introduction and ch. 5), extending to virtually every human being now alive and to any who come to be born in the concretely imaginable future. Despite the comprehensive scope of this relevance, however, it is clear that political economy bears practically upon the individual members of modern populations in very different ways: as rulers or would-be rulers, as citizens or aspirants to citizenship, as direct subjects at almost every moment of time of governmental authority (the point is essentially Jean-Jacques Rousseau's, but compare also Joseph de Maistre: 'The people who command are different from the people who obey' – Dunn 1993(a): ch. 1, 1992b), as advisers or aspirant advisers to governments. In the first place, it is impossible to rule coherently today without espousing some form of official political economy (Dunn 1985: ch. 7, 1990a: ch. 12): a conception of prevailing economic causality and desirable or defensible economic outcomes that serve to explain and justify the choice of governmental policies over taxation, labour regulation, welfare provisions, internal and external regulation of trade conditions, investment flows, and the operation of industry, agriculture and services. In the second place, in conditions of routine politics today (if not in those of internal or foreign warfare) no aspect of governmental performance affects the lives of most subjects as profoundly as the choice and implementation of governmental economic policies.

Because of these two prominent, if complex, facts about the world today no modern citizen who hopes even to select an effective representative, still less any modern citizen who hopes to modify the exercise of governmental power more ambitiously by pressure or persuasion and in a beneficial manner, can do without an amateur political economy of their own which identifies the consequences it is reasonable to expect (and, on morally more ambitious conceptions, the consequences which it is permissible to welcome or to risk) from the courses of conduct under consideration. The politics of all modern states, accordingly, turns largely on the perman- ent, unstable and bafflingly opaque interaction between official, amateur and professional versions of political economy, none of which can readily (or justifiably) be eliminated from them, but all of which at any point in time are likely to be more or less saturated with disinformation, analytical confusion, and more or less massively inept causal misjudgement. At any particular point in time there is likely to be at least one especially promin- ent nexus of intense disagreement: over the scale and distribution of the costs and benefits of trade liberalization or extensions of managed trade (raised tariffs, anti-dumping measures (Haus 1992), bilateral deals), over alleged trade-offs between unemployment and inflation, over the degree to which and the time span over which international price competitivity within a domestic industry or firm or a national economy can reasonably be seen as (or be effectively converted into) a public good, over the overall significance of agricultural subsidies, over the workings of national, supra- national or even global monetary regimes.

It could, of course, be true that the causal component of each or any of these might be uniquely and validly understood within the economics profession, opening up the possibility of a genuinely apolitical or supra- political economy. But although there are sometimes massive swings of judgement (and, indeed, of sentiment) inside that profession over particular issues, and although it is reasonable to presume some degree of cognitive advance since the days of Thomas Mun or Sir William Petty, the prospect of effective and durable consensus on justified true beliefs about any aspect of economic judgement which is of real practical consequence is scarcely imminent. One might attempt to explain this untoward state of affairs from a variety of angles: by detailed contextual history of the development of economic thought, by analysing the social and political forces which come into conflict over particular policy issues, by a priori epistemic assessment of the conditions for identifying justified true beliefs about anything, by relatively strict analogy with the history and philosophy of other sciences, or by more programmatic and adventurous excursions into the sociology of knowledge. Each of these approaches would have its merits. But we may, for present purposes, take as a fundamental clue (on which all would be well advised to draw sooner or later) the obvious point that any attempt to ascertain the causal dynamics of a modern economy, however politically innocent (or ingenuous) it might be in its conscious motives, could hardly prove politically as innocent in its outcome, if it attained any real success in ascertaining these dynamics. In virtually all large-scale distributive struggles in the modern world there will be major participants to whose interests few things could be as immediately and brutally inimical as the clear identification of some relevant sets of justified true beliefs. Political economy may not be a determinate academic discipline. It may lack definite analytical procedures or clear epistemic commitments (perhaps, for the moment, even widely shared intellectual habits). But there are good reasons to believe that it is here to stay. It may not be the palpable intellectual solution to anything. But at the very least it is an ineliminable part of a bewildering array of modern problems.

If this judgement is correct, it is enough by itself to establish (and in some measure, if in the broadest of outlines, even to explain) the practical importance of political economy to the wide range of modern roles for which it matters so deeply. But it offers less aid in bringing into focus the potential *intellectual* significance of political economy. One possible suspicion, perhaps especially attractive to professional students of either economy or politics, would be that the purely intellectual significance of political economy may be merely a *pis aller*, a regrettable accommodation to culpably weak intellectual boundary maintenance, or a purely contingent infirmity of professional purpose in the two contending academic disciplines in question, and thus potentially soluble at any point by sterner and clearer thought or by stouter will. An interesting possibility (to which I revert later) is that this suspicion may be more pertinent, and more susceptible of coherent intellectual defence, in the case of the professional study of economies than it can ever hope to prove in that of polities.

If we take the subject matter of political economy, unexactingly, as the mutual causal interaction of economy and polity, at least in the modern world, and, more exactly, as the human significance of that mutual causal interaction (a topic which could scarcely be extruded from the study of politics (Taylor 1985) and which the more important economists have proved consistently reluctant to exclude from the purview of economics), its practical importance can scarcely be missed. The scale of that importance is sufficient in itself to stake a claim on the intellectual attention of any student of economy or polity. But it does nothing to vindicate either the intellectual prudence or the heuristic promise of attempting to endogenize the relevant analytical externality within the analytical field of either discipline. The proof of the pudding in this latter case must remain firmly in the eating. How far can one in fact understand either economies or polities better by thinking of both as a single continuous causal field?

I have tried to argue elsewhere (Dunn 1984, 1990b) that the practical importance of the causal dynamics of modern economies, the very evident impact of governmental policy decisions (for worse or for better) upon these dynamics, and the still more evident impact of these dynamics on individual life chances, make it strategically essential to any serious understanding of modern politics to construe these through a coherent conception of the economic constraints on political possibilities. It is not unreasonable to hypothesize (though it may be a little hasty to conclude) that the secular global political project of the modern Left has effectively disintegrated in the course of the last decade as a result of a quite dismaying discovery of this character (Nove 1983, Brus and Laski 1989, Dunn 1993b), even though it has emphatically yet to be supplanted by a comparable and more causally coherent global political project of the modern Right (Dunn 1992b, 1993a: Conclusion). In this sense, it is reasonable to conclude that a focus on the economic limits to modern politics is analytically optional only in the most austerely metaphysical of senses. No doubt it is true that human beings cannot be compelled by extra- or suprahuman realities to conceive or analyse other than as they choose (Rorty 1979). But, if they wish to understand what is happening to them, they would be exceedingly ill-advised to ignore the causes of their behaviour. I take the intellectual importance of political economy for understanding modern politics to be central and peremptory. But what of its intellectual importance for understanding modern economies? Or, more manageably, and since I myself have only the haziest and most metaphorical comprehension of contemporary economics, what of its intellectual importance for understanding the ways in which modern economies do or do not function effectively (which are presumably, at least for the present, the privileged analytical object of contemporary economics)?

In the case of modern politics it is essential, I argue, to analyse this, however else also, at least through the conception of economic limits upon it. It is certainly not for a non-economist to seek to answer the question of whether the converse is true of modern economies. But whether or not political economy is analytically indispensable to modern economics (a matter on which I have no clear and settled intuitions), it must be at least pertinent, as well as of some potential intellectual importance, to ask how politics limits economic options, and how political forces shape or modify economic processes, today as always in the past. It is important initially to underline that it is by no means obvious that the most important political limits on economic options or the fiercest impacts of political forces on economic structures or processes concern the pressure of either on the operations of markets in particular. While the initial Austrian critique of the socialist project of a rationally planned economy was rigorously economic in form (Lavoie 1985), however explicitly political in inspiration, the cumulative inductive impact of the experience of command economies in practice (Ellman 1979, Nove 1983, Kornai 1986, Brus and Laski 1989) came as much from political insights into the situational motivation of agents as it did from strictly economic insistence on the necessary unavailability of information of the requisite type, quantity, accuracy and timeliness. The political critique of command planning draws its force not merely from the latter's blatantly parlous relation to the avowed goals of socialism, its palpably faltering practical performance, and the intensely frustrating lessons of consecutive efforts to reform it, but also from the profoundly unconvincing representation which it required of the incentive structures facing, and the strategic and practical preoccupations haunting, the cadres of the planning apparatus, from top virtually to bottom. A preference for operating under soft budget constraints and with an expansive schedule of managerial privileges is closer to being a precept of rationality than it is to being a distinctive deformation of the cadres of socialist economic bureaucracies. What distinguished the major industrial enterprises that comprised the core of most planned soi-disant socialist economies from even larger capitalist enterprises was less any discrepancy in intrinsic managerial motivation in the two cases, or the comparatively transnational focus of the latter, than it was the increasingly apparent forlornness of any attempt to eliminate soft budget constraints (and a wide variety of other impediments to efficiency) from the ecology within which the former were obliged to operate. Similarly, peasant desertion or non-cooperation (Hyden 1980, Nolan 1988) could limit the consolidation of a state-centred, if putatively socialist, planned agrarian economy at least as readily as it could challenge the assault on its forms of life, its sense of value and its subsistence needs that was posed by the erratic rhythms of an expanding market economy (Scott 1976). In many societies, even today, the limits which politics imposes on the operation of markets are probably still of less practical consequence than the limits which it imposes on non-market means for coordinating and implementing production.

But in a society like Italy or the United Kingdom, and in a wide variety of other types of setting across the world, it is certainly an extremely important issue just how far and just why politics does limit or constrain the operations of markets. This issue arises with every sovereign or quasi-sovereign political unit (even, for example, Myanmar or Khmer Rouge Kampuchea prior to the Vietnamese invasion) in relation to the formulation, political maintenance and practical implementation of virtually all governmental economic policies, whether over taxation, domestic and international trade, industry, agriculture, services, health, education, environmental pollution, physical subsistence, capital flight or inflows, domestic inflation or deflation, and international exchange rates. It arises equally in the extraordinarily complicated, intense and bafflingly opaque tussle between the major transnational institutions for coordinating the capitalist world economy and the wide variety of more or less 'reformed' or 'recidivist' quasi-dependent national economies which these institutions are permanently attempting to discipline (Haggard and Kaufman 1992). It arises, equally, in the more sporadic (if sometimes protracted) episodes of attempted coordination of international trading or monetary regimes, from Bretton Woods to the irritable endgame of the Uruguay Round (Keohane 1984, Gilpin 1987, Winham 1986). It arises all too prominently in the erratic and even more quarrelsome struggle over the pace and means and eventual degree to which the previously at least quasi-command economies of the erstwhile 'socialist' states (as of some which for the present very much remain 'socialist' in their public self-descriptions and political legitimations) are to be remodelled on more comprehensively capitalist lines, and over the even more vexatious issue of how the costs and benefits of such transformation as does occur are to be allocated. In this last case it is obvious that the degree to which marketization will favour or preclude democratization, over a variety of time frames from the very short to the almost infinitely extended, is impossible to distinguish at all sharply from its natural concomitant, the question of whether democratization will favour or preclude marketization over just the same set of time frames. Anyone with real intellectual ambition to undertstand either modern politics or modern economics would be attracted by the idea of attempting to construct a framework of analysis that can do justice to all of these markedly disparate phenomena, treating them in the last instance as components of a single continuous causal field. Indeed I take it that economists, by and large, would be more reluctant than their political scientist *confrères* might be in the case of politics to acknowledge that as a profession (operating through an increasingly skilled and assiduous division of labour) they have now abandoned, or may shortly be forced to abandon, the attempt to understand economic phenomena, if very much in the last instance, in essentially such a framework. But in present intellectual circumstances it would not be helpful to set out from a (very possibly fantastical) cognitive ideal of this character. As of now, we still have our work cut out even to formulate reasonably clear questions about these relations, let alone to answer them with cogency and assurance.

As of now, both economics and political science dispose of a range of essentially expository techniques for expressing analytical intuitions about these relations, some of them (notably game theory) no doubt carrying a modest capacity for additional illumination in themselves. But the mastery of these techniques, an increasingly large component of professional formation in either discipline, patently fails to ensure any dependable intellectual additivity to the products of their utilization. Those who learn the techniques learn to understand some of the properties of the techniques themselves, and they learn in some measure to understand one another. But it is, quite consistently, far less clear how far they thereby learn a superior understanding of the economic or political world. I do not, of course, mean to suggest (as the late Joan Robinson used perhaps, to an incautious listener, sometimes to appear to be suggesting) that a grasp of analytical technique of any kind can in itself impair comprehension of either the economic or the political world, however mystificatory the uses to which such techniques may sometimes be put. (Elementary arithmetic, in the hands of a skilled fraudster, can be used to mystify every bit as readily as neoclassical or Marxist economics.) I simply wish to emphasize that no analytical techniques thus far invented ensure an accurate comprehension of either economic or political causality, and I would cheerfully wager that none invented in the remainder of my academic lifetime will do so either.

I do not have either the gall or the intellectual nerve to propose a favoured political economy of my own, an approach to all these questions which even hints at how they can be dragooned analytically into some clear relation to one another (though I see no clear reason why this might not eventually be achieved). But I should like to suggest the potential utility of distinguishing a number of discrete ways in which political forces or processes might and do regularly limit the operations of markets. Insofar as these ways can eventually be expressed more clearly, I take them to be on balance more user-friendly to economists than they can possibly hope to be to political scientists. (It is difficult to exaggerate the degree to which the hope of devising a systematic understanding of political causality in modern intellectual history has been parasitic on the presumption of already enjoying the good fortune to possess a systematic understanding of economic causality (Dunn 1990b).) If the impress of political forces, processes or structures upon markets sets a less than amenable limit to the scope of the types of model which economists have learnt how to operate with real analytical control, this will not be a salutary lesson in intellectual modesty, so much as a brusque demonstration of how rudimentary the analytical resources available to them, after two and a half thousand years of cumulative effort, still obstinately remain.

Markets, very crudely considered, subsist between free agents, buying or selling according to choice, on the basis of current resources, tastes and needs, and of anticipated resources, tastes and needs. They are at their most ideologically engaging where large numbers of relatively prosperous buyers (buyers with wide allocative discretion) confront appreciable numbers of competing sellers, within an effectively shared framework of property law and civil order. Where there are substantial elements of oligopoly or even monopoly in how a market operates, or where the buyers are acutely impoverished and compelled to purchase to meet their minimal subsistence needs, the ideological appeals of markets are less obvious. In limiting cases, such as famine (Sen 1981, Hont and Ignatieff 1983: Introduction), where recognized entitlements are insufficient on the food market to furnish subsistence, both exponents of classical natural jurisprudence as discrepant as Aquinas and Hobbes, and modern development economists, have confidently assumed that the normative status of the existing property order lapses, and with it any possible normative grounds for respecting market outcomes. Since the days of medieval just price theory market imperfections have always been a focus for moral and political suspicion and criticism, but the sharpest challenge to the legitimacy of market processes has always centred on the justifiability (or otherwise) of the initial resource endowments with which particular buyers or sellers enter a given market. For fairly evident reasons this challenge has been a potential source of more or less acute discomfort throughout the history of medieval and modern Europe, and it has certainly not become less discomfiting as the markets in question have become more intractably global, and the disparities in initial resources of those who buy or sell upon them have become even starker. No minimally plausible modern theory of justice in acquisition or distribution has contrived to present either the distribution of initial resources across the world economy at any point in time, or the property rights through which that distribution is articulated, or the subsequent workings of the world economy, as meeting the standards of justice (Rawls 1972, Waldron 1988, Barry 1989, Dunn 1985: ch. 10, 1992a, cf. Scott 1976). But what the world market (considered as a whole) has always lacked in legitimacy, it has long more than made up in power, in sheer causal force. Sceptical interpreters of modern history, accordingly, may well doubt whether legitimacy does in any analytically coherent sense constitute a limit to or a constraint upon markets. But such scepticism is in the end overstrained, relying, as it has to, on the presumption that human action is always prompted in the last instance not by sentiment or normative belief but only by reasonably accurately apprehended prudential rationality.

Social scientists have quarrelled about this question in a wide variety of intellectual and practical settings: over the idiosyncrasy (or otherwise) of peasant folkways (Scott 1976, Popkin 1979), through the analytical dispensability of culture to a Marxist understanding of history (Thompson 1963, 1975, 1978, Anderson 1980), to disputes over the respective scope and limits of structure and agency in the explanation of social revolutions (Skocpol 1979, Dunn 1985: ch. 4, Moore 1978), the centrality of the activities of self-understanding and evaluative choice to the understanding of human experience (Taylor 1985, 1989), or the dispensability or eliminability of mental predicates from the explanation of human behaviour (Davidson 1980). No one can claim to have subjected this bewilderingly wide range of considerations to a single convincing analytical paradigm. But for the present it seems safe to insist that the case for eliminating legitimacy from the explanatory field of politics is wholly unproven, and that a decision categorically to reject its relevance is not merely *parti pris* in an ancient quarrel about the illusory (or reality-grounded) character of human values – moral realism – but also abrasively committed to inductively implausible views about either the behavioural inconsequence of human emotions or the motivational irrelevance for human beings of perceptions of what is offensive or unjust. Neither of these strategic judgements is readily compatible with even desultory acquaintance with the nursery (to say nothing of academic committee meetings).

But if it is at best analytically imprudent to conclude that the subjective (or objective?) perception of legitimacy will seldom or never affect the operations of a market, how (if at all) is it possible to relate such considerations in a controlled manner to a causal understanding of the scope and dynamics of markets? This is not a field in which either scholars or political or economic agents have established any very clear or convincing approaches (despite its prominence in the work of Max Weber, and the massive subsequent impact of Weber's writings, especially on professional sociologists). But one important type of experience to which there is every reason to presume that it must be relevant is in episodes of governmental or popular action designed to cancel or subvert *en bloc* the set of property relations on which existing market relations are predicated. The appropriate *explicandum* here can range from governmental decisions to expropriate foreign investors (perhaps usually better modelled in the first instance purely through the rationally anticipated costs and benefits to the agent concerned – Dunn 1990a: ch. 7) to mass popular uprisings aimed at the overthrow of what are seen as quisling regimes, committed culturally, politically and economically to the interests of foreign powers over against most of their own subjects. In the case of the more massive breaches in routine politics or economics, it would be hard to deny the causal pertinence of what occurs in such episodes to an understanding of where and when markets do in fact operate. But such revolutionary disruptions are relatively unusual; it may be impossible in principle to articulate them with analytical approaches that prove serviceable under more normal conditions, and it may well therefore be deftest to think of them more as boundary conditions for other types of explanatory paradigm, rather than logical extensions under particular conditions of the implications of such paradigms.

However it may be best explained, expropriation is certainly not a market transaction. The effective destruction of an entire property order is as crisp a limit to market power as could readily be imagined. If legitimacy is explanatorily important for the causation of revolutions (Dunn 1985: ch. 4), it is certainly pertinent to an understanding of one type of possible limit to markets. But it is unattractive to presume that legitimacy (or more broadly, human sentiments and evaluative beliefs) is relevant for an understanding of some types of major political crises but irrelevant to understanding human conduct in more routine settings. This is hardly a view that could be derived from listening to (or even observing) routine political contention at any level from the most domestic to the most unctuously ecumenical. It is little more plausible as a gloss on disputes, whether bilateral or in a multilateral forum like the GATT, about the criteria for fair trade (cf. Gilpin 1987, Lawrence and Schultze 1990) than it would be as a verdict on quarrels over the justice of different approaches towards the division of domestic labour. I do not myself know if there are fields of professional economic analysis in which a systematic attempt has yet been made to incorporate perceptions of justice or injustice (whether culturally idiosyncratic or presumptively universal) into a causal analysis of economic behaviour. But I would imagine that the likeliest setting for a sustained analysis of this kind would be in the field of labour economics and in the systematic relation, if any, between the study of wage bargaining and work practices within this field and more explicitly sociological attempts to analyse industrial conflict and cooperation in their entirety.

What should be noted is that of the three categories I have chosen to consider for identifying how politics might and does limit markets – power, legitimacy and choice – it is legitimacy which offers the strongest temptation to see the issue of understanding primarily as a contest between types of explanatory model to annex explanatory domains at each other's expense: a contest, to use somewhat archaic terms, between economic, sociological and political explanation, or at its most reductive between explanation in terms of instrumental rationality, cultural subjugation and the richer and more disorderly imaginative inventories to which students of politics have long been accustomed to help themselves. I do not wish to argue that this is necessarily the best way to see the matter. The characteristic blowsiness of political explanation is motivated by more edifying pressures than mere intellectual indolence or confusion. But it is hardly in itself an intellectual merit. A more promising approach would be to attempt not to replace a political preoccupation with the causal importance of legitimacy by a more inert sociological conception of what culture in fact consists in, or with sparer economic models which dispense with the presumption that culture is in itself a locus of causation at all, but instead to insert some of the causal insight over political and cultural factors into the relatively disciplined framework of economic models. I take it that if this can be done at all, it would have to be so by attributing to (or recognizing in) the agents modelled a richer and more reflexive decision structure.

A more important and insistent issue for anyone attempting to understand modern politics, and, I would suspect, also for anyone attempting to think at all practically about the operations of modern economies, or about the well-advised or ill-advised choice of governmental economic policies, is how exactly to see the categories of power and choice as placing limits upon markets.

The case for seeing them in this light is pretty evident. All market processes depend, whatever else, upon the initial holdings of those who participate in them. (They also depend, of course, on the freedom of manoeuvre available to, and on the opportunity costs faced by, these participants; cf. Milgrom, this volume.) It is not merely a conventional political and legal presumption but a reasonably accurate analytical judgement to see such holdings as dependent upon prior political performances: on more or less institutionalized patterns of coercion and persuasion (see e.g. Cohen 1978). It may be tautologically true that every such pattern rests causally on immediately antecedent choice by varying numbers of agents (a methodological individualist explanatory axiom). But it is more economical to consider (and to attempt to explain) their presence in brisker and more holistic terms. If the explicandum is effectively enforced law over ownership, and practical control over the terms on which labour is deployed in production or exchange, then it is reasonable to conceive the explanatory problem as a problem of power, of the causal determination of outcomes in a single causal field, and therefore reasonable to regard prior states of this field as setting at any particular point in time the limits of an operating market.

For economists in their strictly professional work this could be simply the selection of a setting for their analysis, a purely contingent (and voluntary) matter of self-conscious orientation. But in their less strictly professional work, as when offering advice to governments or transnational agencies, or militating civically in favour of some lines of conduct and against others, the relation between epistemically responsible professional cognition and the (in itself, permissibly whimsical and perhaps necessarily amateur) choice of the setting for such analysis will inevitably prove more implicating. In politics, it is always of the greatest importance what is taken as given, and how whatever is taken as given is envisaged: what exactly is taken as having given it. (Consider the recent history of Bosnia, or, for that matter, of Kuwait. For the depth of political significance carried by this point see, for instance, Shklar 1990.) Rationally, agents must always take the past as given (as so much blood under the bridge). But that does not dictate (or perhaps even provide pertinent guidance over) how that past is to be envisaged, how far its implications are taken to leak into and stain the future. (Compare, in relation to personal agency, Nozick 1993.) In the case of ownership (or the origins of inequality amongst women and men) a tacit choice of historical framework for analysing market processes is no more of an escape from politics than the explicit choice of a normative criterion would be. Time itself is analytically neutral, but the temporal framework cannot on its own determine whether the past is to be taken as a normative baseline or as a clear ground for rectification (cf. Nozick 1964).

One reason why political economy is politically so important today is that the relations between social and political conflict and economic activity, both nationally and internationally for every society in the world, are too taut for the consequences of one to be distinguished with any confidence from the consequences of the other. The distribution of economic opportunities across a population at any time depends quite largely on political power. The structure of political power within a given society depends quite largely on the prior economic opportunities that have been open to the different components of its population. There is every reason to think of particular national societies (and of the globe as a whole) as integrated fields of causality in which any ultimate distinction between the economic and the political is either conventional and inherently transitory, or adopted purely for analytical convenience (which may well prove to be even more fugitive). The claims of analytical convenience are, of course, pressing. Even if the human world is happily thought of (ontologically) as a single field of power, there is every reason to doubt that it will ever prove analytically tractable, when considered as such. Thus far, when political economists have attempted to develop testable causal models of political processes, they have selected relatively narrow explicanda and attempted to explain these by deploying extremely simple (and often intuitively implausible) analytical hypotheses. (The study of political business cycles is an important example; cf. e.g. Hibbs 1987.) The ontological appeals of treating economics and politics as a single causal continuum have yet, thus far, to be matched by any concomitant methodological advantages.

To think of choice (on the part of governments, economic bureaucrats or advisers, citizens, or even consumers) as the key mechanism through which politics limits markets is ontologically no more perturbing than thinking of power as setting such limits. (On one methodological presumption, the latter view must be analytically equivalent to the former for it even to be coherent.) But if we think of choice as what crucially limits markets, we are committed even in the first instance to acknowledging that such limitation can and will take an endless variety of forms, and that it cannot in principle be captured by specifying and applying any single explanatory paradigm. Epistemic modesty and prudence, accordingly, are bought at the cost of heuristic vagueness, and the prospect of virtually infinite explanatory elaboration. Having learnt to think precisely about relatively manageable analytical objects, economists who allow their attention to stray to the question of how politics limits markets may reasonably feel that they are being asked to buy any resultant gain in the realism of their conception of what is going on in a modern economy at the steep price of accepting an endless proliferation of inherently imprecise and open-ended analytical afterthoughts.

From their own point of view, economists may be quite right to take this view. (That is a question for them, not for me.) But what is clear, I think, is that anyone interested in the attempt to understand modern politics could hardly take the same view. An endless proliferation of imprecise and open-ended afterthoughts will be no culture shock to any *aficionado* of politics, academic or otherwise. It is of the greatest political importance today exactly how political choice does set the limits of market operation, and however tatty the processes through which it does so, it is plain enough that there have already been, and will long continue to be, the most massive economic consequences of its impact. (Consider the economic history of the erstwhile Soviet Union or its successor Russian Republic, or that of the still extant People's Republic of China. Consider the economic history of Ghana (Killick 1978) or of the erstwhile West German state.)

The range of ways in which political choice can limit, and has limited, market operations is immense. Some of these ways have been studied closely and illuminatingly. Others as yet have not. Some (the determinants and consequences of the scale of public debt for example) have been argued over for a very long time (Hont 1993, Buchanan 1986). Others (the effects of informal trade barriers) are still the object of such fluent and furtive improvization that it is a nice question whether anyone yet really understands their consequences.

The best candidate for a common explanatory axis within this markedly heterogeneous but palpably consequential domain is the determination of government economic policy, above all on fiscal, welfare, trade and monetary questions. The consequences of governmental action may seldom be those intended. Few, if any, governments may be accurately thought of as taking integrated and clearly conceived sets of decisions over economic policy or any other matter (Dunn 1989). But consequences do not have to be intended for them to occur or matter, and however confused governmental decision making may be, it does in fact take place. Governmental economic policy making is explicitly political, in that it embodies at least a moment of sovereign choice, through public law and executive action. It is both conventional and reasonable to see a large proportion of modern politics as consisting in the attempt to shape governmental economic policy in ways presumed to be advantageous to the agents concerned.

The popularity of attempts to model the (presumed) political business cycle reflects not merely the plausibility of the assessment that such a cycle can be identified in a number of contemporary polities, but also the reasonable judgement that in so far as one can indeed be identified, it must be practically important precisely because of the real damage which it will necessarily inflict over time on the interests of at least the majority of those concerned. Some models of the cycle credit professional politicians with inordinately simple and irresponsible agendas, and voters with an equally damaging combination of greed and myopia. But in the face of the scale and political intractability of the American budget deficit (or indeed of the Italian budget deficit), it is reasonable to presume that something of the kind must indeed have been going on. (Note, however, the change in each between 1993 and 1998).

Comparable issues plainly arise if the levels and distribution of taxation are considered (with a measure of realism) as a set of choices by professional political agents with a major stake in the outcome, but also subject to a measure of intermittent restraint by the far wider public which contributes the taxes. The view that professional politicians are best understood as acting not as the selfless instruments of an intertemporal general will, but as a discrete (if quarrelsome) estate, which shares an interest in maximizing the resources of which it directly disposes (however it may choose to dispense them), and whose members confront one another in an endless zero-sum game to get their hands on and dispense, on their own behalf and to their own advantage, as much of their takings as possible, is a bit brusque as a verdict on the politics of some states. (All the world is not

Zaire.) But it has a measure of realism in relation to any state, and palpably applies all too literally to some contemporary states for long periods of time (Bayart 1993). There is certainly every reason to believe that these forms of extra-market allocation have a major impact on how national markets (or perhaps even the world trading system) do in fact operate. It is not merely (understandable) participant overexcitement which causes them to loom so very large today in political competition across the world.

References

Anderson, Perry (1980) *Arguments within English Marxism*, London: New Left Books.

Barry, Brian (1989) *Theories of Justice*, Berkeley, CA: University of California Press.

Bayart, Jean-Francois (1993) *The State in Africa; the politics of the belly*, trans. C. Harrison *et al.*, London: Longman.

Brus, Wlodzimierz and Laski, Kasimierz (1989) *From Marx to the Market*, Oxford: Oxford University Press.

Buchanan, James M. (1986) *Liberty, Market and State: Political Economy in the 1980s*, New York: New York University Press.

Cohen, G. A. (1978) *Karl Marx's Theory of History: A Defense*, Oxford: Oxford University Press.

Davidson, Donald (1980) *Essays on Actions and Events*, Oxford: Oxford University Press.

Dunn, John (1984) *The Politics of Socialism*, Cambridge: Cambridge University Press.

Dunn, John (1985) *Rethinking Modern Political Theory*, Cambridge: Cambridge University Press.

Dunn, John (1989) 'Conclusion', *Contemporary West African States*, ed. Donal Cruise O'Brien, John Dunn and Richard Rathbone, Cambridge: Cambridge University Press.

Dunn, John (1990a) *Interpreting Political Responsibility*, Cambridge: Polity.

Dunn, John (ed.) (1990b) *The Economic Limits to Modern Politics*, Cambridge: Cambridge University Press.

Dunn, John (1992a), 'Property, justice and common good after socialism', in John Hall and I. C. Jarvie (eds) *Transition to Modernity*, Cambridge: Cambridge University Press, pp. 281–96.

Dunn, John (1992b) *Democracy: the unfinished journey 508BC to 1993AD*, Oxford: Oxford University Press.

Dunn, John (1993a) *Western Political Theory in the Face of the Future*, 2nd edition, Cambridge: Cambridge University Press.

Dunn, John (1993b) 'The heritage and future of the European Left', *Economy and Society* 22(4): 516–24.

Ellman, Michael (1979) *Socialist Planning*, Cambridge: Cambridge University Press.

Gilpin, Robert (1987) *The Political Economy of International Relations*, Princeton, NJ: Princeton University Press.

Haggard, Stephen and Kaufman, Robert R. (eds) (1992) *The Politics of Economic Adjustment*, Princeton, NJ: Princeton University Press.

Haus, Leah H. (1992) *Globalizing the GATT*, Washington, DC: Brookings Institution.

Hibbs, Douglas A. Jr (1987) *The Political Economy of Industrial Democracies*, Cambridge, MA: Harvard University Press.

Hont, Istvan (1993) 'The rhapsody of public debt: David Hume and voluntary state bankruptcy', in Nicholas Phillipson and Quentin Skinner (eds) *Political Discourse in Early Modern Britain*, Cambridge: Cambridge University Press, pp. 321–48.

Hont, Istvan and Ignatieff, Michael (eds) (1983) *Wealth and Virtue*, Cambridge: Cambridge University Press.

Hyden, Goran (1980) *Beyond Ujamaa in Tanzania: Underdevelopment and an Uncaptured Peasantry*, London: Heinemann.

Keohane, Robert O. (1984) *After Hegemony*, Princeton, NJ: Princeton University Press.

Killick, Tony (1978) *Development Economics in Action*, London: Heinemann Educational Books.

Kornai, Janos (1986) 'The Hungarian economic reform process: visions, hopes and reality', *Journal of Economic Literature* 24(4): 1687–1737.

Lavoie, Don (1985) *Rivalry and Central Planning: the socialist calculation debate reconsidered*, Cambridge: Cambridge University Press.

Lawrence, Robert Z. and Shultze, Charles L. (eds) (1990) *An American Trade Strategy: Options for the 1990s*, Washington, DC: Brookings Institution.

Moore, Barrington Jr (1978) *Injustice: the social bases of obedience and revolt*, London: Macmillan.

Nolan, Peter (1988) *The Political Economy of Collective Farms: an analysis of China's post-Mao rural reforms*, Cambridge: Polity.

Nove, Alec (1983) *The Economics of Feasible Socialism*, London: Allen & Unwin.

Nozick, Robert (1964) *Anarchy, State and Utopia*, Oxford: Blackwell.

Nozick, Robert (1993) *The Nature of Rationality*, Princeton, NJ: Princeton University Press.

Popkin, Samuel L. (1979) *The Rational Peasant*, Berkeley, CA: University of California Press.

Rawls, John (1972) *A Theory of Justice*, Oxford: Oxford University Press.

Rorty, Richard (1979) *Philosophy and the Mirror of Nature*, Oxford: Blackwell.

Scott, James C. (1976) *The Moral Economy of the Peasant*, New Haven, CT: Yale University Press.

Sen, Amartya (1981) *Poverty and Famines*, Oxford: Oxford University Press.

Shklar, Judith P. (1990) *The Faces of Injustice*, New Haven, CT: Yale University Press.

Skocpol, Theda (1979) *States and Social Revolutions. A comparative analysis of France, Russia and China*, Cambridge: Cambridge University Press.

Taylor, Charles (1985) *Philosophy and the Human Sciences*, Cambridge: Cambridge University Press.

Taylor, Charles (1989) *Sources of the Self*, Cambridge, MA: Harvard University Press.

Thompson, E. P. (1963) *The Making of the English Working Class*, London: Gollancz.

Thompson, E. P. (1975) *Whigs and Hunters*, London: Allen Lane.

Thompson, E. P. (1978) *The Poverty of Theory*, London: Merlin.

Waldron, Jeremy (1988) *The Right to Private Property*, Oxford: Oxford University Press.

Winham, Gilbert R. (1986) *International Trade and the Tokyo Round Negotiation*, Princeton, NJ: Princeton University Press.

Part II

The economic analysis of political organizations

7 Modeling politics as a competitive endeavor

Albert Breton*

The literature of the now well-established and developing discipline which is indifferently called economics of politics or public choice and those of public economics, welfare economics and of political science generally house many models of government, many concepts of efficiency (in public affairs) and several different approaches to democracy. This is hardly surprising given the relative youth of public choice, the general lack of interest in government and democracy which characterizes both public economics and welfare economics and the absence of systematic theorizing which characterizes political science. In the world of scientific inquiry, such abundance is poverty. A first step in reducing this plethora of models, concepts and approaches is to recognize that it exists. Though unable to promise full coverage of this enormous variety, I will try to sketch, however briefly, those that seem to me to have the widest currency.

In what follows, I adopt a particular model of government, a specific concept of efficiency and a distinct approach to democracy. I make that choice because the selected building blocks can, without too much difficulty, be assembled to yield a theory which can shed new light on politics and, particularly, on the public finances of real-world governments. This means that what follows is intended to be primarily positive or descriptive, even though I have, twice already, made use of the essentially normative concept of efficiency. It will be easier to explain the use I make of that concept after the discussion of some of the different versions of it which one finds in the literature. At this point, let me simply note that I follow standard practice: I seek to demonstrate that certain mechanisms satisfactorily account for what we observe in the real world and, on the basis of results derived from a given theory of how these mechanisms blend to produce efficiency, conclude that the outcome is or is not efficient. I return to this question at the end of the second section.

The first section introduces five[1] different models of government and opts for one of them; the second section presents four separate concepts of efficiency and again chooses one. The third section is differently constructed: it argues, on neo-Madisonian lines, that two conditions or requisites must be satisfied if a political regime is to be identified as

democratic: first, at least one of the important centers of power (historically, the legislative and/or the executive branches) which are constitutive
of the apparatus of government must be popularly elected and, second,
checks and balances or other forms of competition must regulate the
relations of all the autonomous or quasi-autonomous centers of power
that make up the government. I will also argue that the two conditions
must be simultaneously satisfied. The third section also shows how the
model of government and the concept of efficiency I have chosen blend
with the neo-Madisonian theory of democracy. The fourth section
addresses some of the more important objections which, in earlier public
presentations of some of this material, have been levelled at it. The fifth
section concludes the paper.

Models of government

Virtually all discussions of the place and role of governments in the affairs
of human beings and of societies, whether they be directly or only tangen-
tially concerned with the subject, rest on one of two basic presuppositions,
which provide foundations to what, with only slight exaggeration, we may
call 'doctrines.' These presuppositions are often undisclosed even in the
best scholarly discussions. One of these doctrines is based on the proposition, which to give it saliency I express in polar form, that governments are
embodiments of the 'common will' and that, as such, they pursue the
'common good.'

It is easy to raise what are essentially unanswerable questions about the
definition of the two terms which I have, above, placed between quotation
marks, but I propose that we leave these aside and that, like most of those
who function under the proposition's sweep, we proceed as if the two
expressions could be rigorously and operationally defined. If we do this,
we must recognize that the 'common good' doctrine, as we may call it, has
nourished two different traditions of discourse.[2] A first one is embodied in
what can be called an 'organicist theory' of the state or of government.
That 'theory' recognizes no autonomous preferences or demands to
individuals different from those that are ascribed to the collectivity.
Historically, the organicist 'model' has had more sway whenever, through
one mechanism or another, collectivities have refused to conceive of themselves as groupings of persons, but instead have defined themselves as made
up of individuals of a particular creed, cranial specification, ethnicity,
blood type or language. The second tradition which derives from the
'common good' doctrine recognizes the preferences and demands of individual persons, but proceeds on the supposition that these can somehow be
aggregated into a collective welfare or utility function[3] which is given
expression by a body or institution – in effect, a benevolent despot – which,
it is usually further assumed, maximizes the collective function.

The two traditions are very different from each other in conception and in consequences, but they share one important element. The governments which embody the singular preferences and demands of collectivities and the governments which are in the hands of benevolent despots who have aggregated every person's preferences or demands know what is 'good' for 'their' citizens and, essentially as a matter of definition, must single-mindedly secure that 'common good.' Why? Because, for the first, there is only one 'good' – the same for all – and because that 'good' is exactly the same as the one wanted by the government; and, for the second, because governments are, by assumption, benevolent.

The second, and opposite, doctrine which provides foundations to the more or less continuous debates on the place and role of governments in society says, again expressed in the form of a polar proposition, that governments are nothing but the embodiments of the interests of those who inhabit the halls of power and/or of those with whom they collude. This doctrine has also nourished two traditions of discourse.

The first of these divides into two separate, but kindred, lines of analysis. According to one of these, the candidates and parties which represent the successful electoral coalition are captured by the bureaucratic agents that have been employed to implement the winning platform. These agents do not, however, produce and supply goods and services in the quantities and qualities cataloged in that platform, but, as good captors are wont to do, produce and supply what they want for themselves. For those who pursue that line of analysis, governments are monoliths in the hands of bureaucratic agents and elections are, in effect, mirages and illusions with no real significance.[4]

According to the second line of analysis, the representatives of the electorally successful coalition are not captured by their bureaucratic agents; instead, both representatives and agents are shanghaied by rent-seeking interest groups. In that approach, elections are also passing illusions, while political parties and bureaucratic agents are nothing but effective suppliers of rents. In full bloom, this second line of analysis holds that governments are exclusively engaged in transfering rents. When they appear to be supplying ordinary goods and services, they are, in fact, this line of reasoning asserts, engaged in creating rents for purposes of redistribution. Scholars (e.g. Landes and Posner 1975) who labor in this tradition have allocated much effort at developing arguments which purport to show that what looks like rivalry and competition between politicians, bureaucrats and others (e.g. judges) who work in governments is, when properly conceived, like elections, nothing but mirage and illusion. Governments, they argue, are really monoliths, notwithstanding the appearances.

Whatever the tradition or the line of analysis, for most but not all adherents, the self-interest doctrine of governments-as-monoliths operating solely to the benefit of politicians, bureaucrats, and/or interest groups is a doctrine based on the assumption that governments concern themselves *exclusively* with the manipulation of rents. According to that doctrine, if governments are efficient (see below for a discussion of that concept), their efficiency is entirely for the benefit of those who control them and is, therefore, an unqualified calamity for other citizens.

It is intriguing that though they are diametrically opposed in conception and though they are derived from very different methodologies, the organicist and the governments-as-monoliths traditions predict that those who are not organically incarnated in the apparatus of state for the first and those who cannot collude with the governing coterie for the second will be abused and exploited. That being said, observation reveals that organicist (in our times typically nationalist) governments are often intolerant *vis-à-vis* their 'minorities' – those who are not of the 'proper' creed, blood, ethnic background or language – and that they sometimes act to suppress them; governments-as-monoliths, however, being able to extract larger rents the more numerous and the wealthier their citizenry, will generally be more supportive of economic growth and, therefore, more tolerant of behaviors that are economically productive.

Before going on to discuss the second tradition nurtured by the doctrine that governments are inhabited by self-interested individuals, let me mention a third approach to governments which, in a way, falls between the 'common good' and the 'captured monolithic governments' models. In that approach, the idea that governments are monopolies does not rest on a notion of capture by non-elected agents; it is simply assumed that they are monopolists. It is useful to again distinguish between two traditions. In one, governments are treated as leviathans maximizing their own surplus. The burden of the analysis in that tradition is to convince that the assumption of monopoly is reasonable even though some features of governmental organization appear to be inconsistent with monopoly. In leviathan models, it is possible to assume that the governing coterie is forced to cater to the preferences and demands of citizens during a short period preceding elections, but in the most famous version of that model – that of Geoffrey Brennan and James Buchanan (1980: 6–8) – elections are denied even that capacity.

The second tradition has much in common with the first. I distinguish between the two because in the second monopoly is explicitly assumed to be over coercion or, in the words of Joseph Stiglitz (1989), over compulsion and that assumption drives the model. Those who cultivate the leviathan model have devoted considerable effort, as I have already noted, at trying to convince us that governments are really surplus-maximizing monopolies. Those who work what we may call the 'coercion model' have basically taken the monopoly assumption to be more or less obvious. Thomas Borcherding (1983) simply takes it as fact. Stiglitz (1989) argues that we all have the basic freedom to 'exit' organizations that would inflict on us things that we find unacceptable, but that we do not have the freedom to exit the state – Rousseauesque nature, in other words, is not an alternative.

That it is not possible, in some basic sense, to 'exit' the state is easily granted, but to have power the coercion model also needs the first part of the above proposition, namely that 'exit' from other coercive organizations is possible at 'reasonable' cost. The evidence points in the other direction. Families coerce (think of abused children and battered wives who do not 'exit'), churches coerce (think of the legions of Jews who, throughout history, well understood that their life and property were more secure if they converted to Christianity; and do not forget the Inquisition), labor unions coerce gently when helped by governments and violently when not, guilds coerce by forcing excessively long apprenticeships on sons who do not have the freedom to choose other crafts except those of their fathers, corporate bodies, including universities, coerce by demanding that their employees kowtow – be loyal – to the organizations in which they earn their living. The list could be easily extended. On the assumption of monopoly over coercion, Stiglitz (1989) ingeniously explains many organizational features of democratic governments – features which I will later on associate with the division of powers and with checks and balances – which, he reasons, are there to soften the blow of compulsion. If governments do not have a monopoly over coercion, however, it must be that one can explain the existence of divided powers and of checks and balances on other grounds. And so it is. In concluding this brief discussion of the coercion model, I should mention the work of Matthew Palmer (1992) who builds on the assumption that because they have an incentive to falsify their preferences for the (Samuelsonian) public goods they, however, really want, citizens will have a demand for coercion that guarantees that the public goods are effectively provided. The approach has the virtue of providing a 'democratic' rationale for coercion and as such is a real contribution to the coercion model. But Palmer also makes the assumption of monopoly of coercion by governments which, combined with the demand assumption, leads to the conclusion that there is less coercion than would obtain under competition – a most undesirable, but inevitable, conclusion which Palmer, however, does not draw.

We can now address the second tradition which the doctrine that governments are inhabited by self-interested individuals nurtures. It is a tradition associated with the idea of the separation of powers and with that of checks and balances. There is a school of thought, especially well rooted in academe, which derives from Walter Bagehot's classic *The English Constitution* (1867) and which identifies the notions of the separation or division of powers and of checks and balances with the American Congressional system of government. Bagehot (see, however, note 10) and the school of thought[5] that he inspires are simply wrong on this point. First, the idea of a separation of powers has occupied the minds of some of the best political philosophers and political scientists for more than two millennia as the superb monograph by Epaminondas Panagopoulos (1985) abundantly documents.[6] The ancients and many others closer to us were concerned with an 'optimum' separation and balance between the organs or branches[7] of government which often, though not always, were the monarchy, the aristocracy and the democracy (what was eventually called the 'citizenry'), and they worked hard at formulating principles that would guide them in designing 'good' governments. The American Constitution mechanically borrows from these principles: for monarchy read unelected President, for aristocracy read unelected Senate and for democracy read elected House of Representatives to obtain the exact design of the government contained in the 1787 Constitution. The notions of a separation of powers and of a balance between them and the derived notion of checks and balances are, therefore, not exclusively American. What is borrowed and has been experienced before (Renaissance Venice – a celebrated case among many – immediately comes to mind) cannot be exclusively one's own.

Bagehot and 'his' school are wrong for another reason. In the Westminster model of parliamentary government as it exists today in Canada (say), there is little formal[8] separation of powers and not much balance between the executive (the Cabinet) and the governing party. But who will deny that genuine separation exists between the judicial branch and the other branches of government? Who will deny that, properly empowered by a Charter of Rights and Freedoms,[9] the judiciary is capable of checking the executive and the legislative branches, and that it does so? And who will deny that opposition parties, during 'question periods' in the House of Commons, are capable of checking the governing party and do so? I conclude that it is unproductive to forego the use of empirically aposite concepts for the pretence of defending a model of Parliamentary government that was already obsolete when Bagehot published his monograph.[10]

Having said this, I wish to defend myself against the accusation too easily made that what I have just argued denies any genuine differences between Parliamentary and Congressional governments. The problem is one of the level of abstraction selected to analyze a particular problem. An example may help clarify what I have in mind. The theory of supply and demand and the derived theory of markets which economists have developed can be applied, giving proper attention to market structure, to virtually all traded goods and services. At the level of theory, in other words, an apparatus exists which is fairly general and capable of application to a broad range of institutional contexts. If, however, an economist wants to study the market for baseball players or the market for pollinating bees, he or she will have to do what Simon Rottenberg (1956) and Steven Cheung (1973) did and sift through a great amount of descriptive and institutional material. These two studies – and others that could be mentioned – show first that the same theory of markets – the same basic apparatus – can be used to organize and to guide the analysis and, second, that the markets for baseball players and that for pollinating bees are completely different from each other. If, therefore, at some level of abstraction, it is possible to analyze all governments with a general conceptual apparatus, that does not deny the possibility of genuine fundamental differences.

One of the reasons why so many students of politics and of governmental systems are unable to detect any separation of powers and any checks and balances in Parliamentary governments is that they have locked themselves in a legal–constitutional frame of mind which renders them incapable of understanding arrangements and behaviors which are governed by custom, convention and precedent. The legal–constitutional mindset has another negative consequence: it induces those so gifted to think of checks and balances as being either present or absent – the fact that they are a continuum which can be normalized to vary between zero and one seems to escape them.

How does one choose between these different models of government? All would agree, I am sure, that the selection should be governed by the degree of congruence that the models have with the 'facts.' That is more easily said than done. I have tried to bring the 'facts' in the discussion in the way I have organized my presentation of the dominant models. However, I propose that we postpone any further attention to 'facts' and that to help us along, we look at what the literature has to say about efficiency in the public sector and about democracy. These investigations should help us reach a more definite conclusion about how we should model governments to analyze the real world. That will help us appreciate that organicist governments, by definition, do not cater to the welfare of the citizens of their jurisdictions unless these are of the same creed, blood or language as they are; that benevolent despots do not exist and that even if they did would not be able to aggregate the preferences of their citizens in a meaningful way; that governments-as-monoliths, if they exist, will simply exploit their citizens; that coercive governments are not monopolies and that only competitive governments, that is governments designed in such a way that the centers of power of which they are constituted are well balanced and, thus, capable of checking each other (of competing with each other), will cater to the preferences and demands of their citizens.

Concepts of efficiency

The words efficiency and (especially) inefficiency are so often used in discussions of governmental policies – in particular, in respect of policies associated with the public finances – that one could be forgiven for thinking that the concepts these words identify are without difficulties and obscurities. To give saliency to the issue, I will, in the remainder of this section, identify four different concepts of efficiency that can be found in the literatures of public choice, public economics and welfare economics[11] and offer a brief sketch of their content – just enough to permit easy identification.

Without prejudice as to its relative importance, let me begin with what we may call 'welfare economics' efficiency, a concept which derives from theories of public goods and optimal taxation. According to these theories, public goods are efficiently supplied when, for each one of them, the sum over persons of the marginal rate of substitution between the public goods and some preselected numeraire is equal to the marginal rate of transformation between the goods and the numeraire – to the real resource cost of production. Efficiency on the tax side requires that the revenues needed to pay for the goods be collected in the most 'neutral' way possible; that is, in such a way as to minimize the excess burden of taxation. In the welfare economics image of the world, income redistribution is exogenous – it is not derived from preferences that citizens may have for redistribution, but is a reflection of the 'preferences' or moral norms or precepts held by an 'ethical observer' or 'planner' which are assumed to be embodied in a social welfare function (SWF). Levying taxes to redistribute in the way the 'planner' wants will, in general, be distortionary. Efficiency on the revenue side will, therefore, obtain when the deadweight losses of all taxes collected to pay for the public goods provided *and* for the SWF-mandated redistribution of income are minimized. A real-world revenue and expenditure system can, therefore, be more or less efficient depending on the size of the shortfall between the conditions for efficiency and the actual taxation and provision practices.

One noteworthy feature of the welfare economics conception of efficiency in respect of the public finances is the assumption that, at the level of individual citizens and, perforce, at the level of the organization of governments, there are no *behavioral* links or connections between the volume and the quality of goods and services (including redistribution) provided by governments and the taxes which they collect to pay for them, beyond the necessary accounting equality of outlays and revenues plus debt. The assumption is most clearly and succinctly stated by Stiglitz (1989: 22), who is admittedly not discussing welfare economics efficiency. Citizens, he writes, 'do not assess the value of the services provided to them by the government, and pay a commensurate amount.' In effect, it is assumed and reflected in academic curricula and in the organization of textbooks that decisions by governments in respect of revenues and expenditures are made separately. The recommendation that neutrality be one of the most – and for a group of public finance economists, the most – important criterion of tax reform derives from that conception of efficiency. I conclude this sketch by noting that this approach to the public finances and to efficiency is not anchored in a theory of how governments actually work. One could, indeed, say, with only slight exaggeration, that scholars working in that tradition take pride in a body of theory which, except for the tax laws and tax codes and the coefficients of some basic behavioral relations, is void of institutional content.

The second concept that I will consider can be called 'transaction costs' efficiency. It is altogether different from the 'welfare economics' approach to the problem. In most applications, it pays little attention to public finance problems, although it does preoccupy itself with questions of logrolling over expenditure projects, pork-barrel politics and the like. It is, therefore, for the most part, only indirectly concerned with the efficient supply of public goods and the efficient collection of taxes. Like much of the rest of transaction costs economics, it is basically preoccupied with what appears to be the failure of certain mechanisms – in public choice theory with voting, logrolling, contractual enforcement, information deficiencies and many others – and with the efficiency of the institutional responses to these failures – responses such as reputation, trust, political parties, committees, seniority and so on. In an important paper, Donald Wittman (1989) has argued that 'democratic political markets are organized to promote wealth-maximizing outcomes' and that 'the arguments claiming that economic markets are efficient apply equally well to political markets' (pp. 1395–6). In fact, Wittman has simply applied to standard 'political market failure' arguments the logic of transaction costs economics and, on the basis of that logic, argued for a presumption that institutional responses to failures of one sort or the other are efficient. As was the case with 'welfare economics' efficiency in government, 'transaction costs' efficiency recognizes that a shortfall is possible between an ideal and actual reality.

A third notion of efficiency in respect of government and public policy can be called 'constitutional' efficiency. Born of James Buchanan and Gordon Tullock's (1962) distinction between a constitutional or rule-making stage and a policy-making stage as basic elements in the political 'calculus of consent,'[12] this view states that outcomes will be efficient if unanimity or near-unanimity governs decisions at the constitution-making stage, because under this requirement the rules that will be selected will be the best possible for the individuals who have agreed to them. According to this notion of efficiency, attempts to evaluate the decisions and outcomes of the policy-making stage on the basis of exogenous criteria such as those of welfare economics efficiency (say) is fundamentally meaningless, if the decisions and outcomes are governed by unanimously or quasi-unanimously agreed-upon rules at the constitution-making stage. This does not mean that it is not possible to appraise real-world tax laws and tax codes. Indeed, in a notable contribution to tax theory, Brennan and Buchanan (1980) have derived a number of propositions about the structure of an efficient tax system that would incorporate 'in-period' tax laws generated by constitutional rules that had been unanimously or quasi-unanimously agreed upon by the individual members of the jurisdiction.

In his Nobel Lecture, Buchanan (1987) argued that the above notion of efficiency can be traced back to the work of Knut Wicksell (1896). Wicksell, as Buchanan recognizes, was making the case for unanimity or near-unanimity at the policy-making stage, but, Buchanan argues, given that unanimity or even quasi-unanimity is not achievable in practice at that stage, it is possible to salvage Wicksell's insight that social welfare will only be at a maximum if all individuals are allowed to count in political decisions, if we, as it were, transfer the requirement of unanimity or near-unanimity from the policy-making to the constitution- or rule-making stage. I do not wish to take issue with Buchanan's position nor deny the validity, in its own frame of reference, of Buchanan and Tullock's (as well as of many others) constitutional conception of efficiency in government and in politics. I simply wish to note, in anticipation of the discussion of the fourth concept of efficiency, that the empirical impossibility of in-period unanimity or quasi-unanimity, which led to a reinterpretation of Wicksell, is only a presumption or, at most, an observation of the world made without the benefit of a hypothesis or empirically relevant theory. Indeed, Wicksell, Wicksellians and anti- or non-Wicksellians alike appear to have understood Wicksell's *A New Principle of Just Taxation* (1896) as a plea for the *reorganization* of governments that would insure unanimity or approximate unanimity in respect of expenditure and revenue decisions – a state of affairs that necessarily requires simultaneity regarding these same decisions. The idea that real-world governments may, to a degree, already be organized to mimic these requirements of efficiency does not appear to have retained much of the attention of scholars. I will, later, suggest that the original Wicksellian model, *with one major amendment*, can be used to understand the organization and operation of real-world governments. It is, therefore, important to look at the conception of efficiency which underlies a 'strict' interpretation of Wicksell.

Before doing so I must insist, as Buchanan and Tullock (1962) already have, that under constitutional efficiency in politics, rules devised at the constitution-making stage will demand more than unanimity to be efficient – they will also have to be designed in a context in which 'the individual is *uncertain* as to what his own precise role will be in any one of the whole chain of later collective choices that will actually have to be made' (Buchanan and Tullock 1962: 78, italics in the original) or, put differently, they will have to be made 'behind a veil of ignorance' (Rawls 1971: 136). Buchanan and Tullock (1962: 78–9) argue that uncertainty is likely to exist at the constitution-making stage. I am willing to accept such a presumption, but must insist that a presumption is only that. I should add that the uncertainty or veil of ignorance principle implies that the rules designed at the constitution-making stage must *precede* and be *independent* of in-period policies. If it turned out that in the real world, constitutions, in effect, adjust to events that are the product of policy making or if their evolution is governed by in-period occurrences, the presumption of uncertainty or of a veil of ignorance would have to be abandoned and with it the presumption of efficiency even in the presence of near-unanimity.

The fourth and last concept of efficiency in government to be considered can be called Wicksell–Lindahl efficiency. It simply says that efficiency will be greater the 'tighter' the behavioral connection or nexus between expenditure and revenue decisions and the greater the number of persons for which this holds. To put it differently, if there are forces or mechanisms which operate to build links between the expenditure and revenue decisions of citizens, budgetary outcomes will be more efficient the 'shorter' these links and the larger the number of people for which the links are 'shorter' – the more powerful, in other words, the forces or mechanisms. As was the case with welfare economics efficiency, it is also the case with this fourth concept that inefficiency is measured as a deadweight or utility loss. Indeed it can be shown that the 'looser' or 'slacker' the connection between expenditure and revenue decisions, the larger the utility loss for each individual[13] and, consequently, once summed over the relevant set of persons, the larger for the collectivity. Put differently, if mechanisms existed that made the link between expenditure and revenue decision absolutely 'tight' for everyone in a jurisdiction, the outcome would be Pareto optimal.

We must again pose the question, as we did at the end of the last section, of how we can choose between the various concepts of efficiency. Again, the answer is that the selection must be governed by the 'facts' and, again, subject to the same *caveats*. There is, however, one additional point that can now be made: the selection of a model of government on the basis of 'facts' must be consistent with the concept of efficiency also selected on the basis of 'facts.'

As the next section will make clear, I opt for Wicksell–Lindahl efficiency. It would, therefore, be appropriate at this juncture to mention, however briefly, the various mechanisms and forces at work in *democracies*[14] which operate to forge more or less 'tight' connections or links between the expenditure and revenue decisions of citizens. That would, however, presuppose some basic agreement on the conditions that have to be satisfied if societies and governments are to be called democratic. As noted earlier, no agreement exists on the matter. It will, therefore, be necessary to pause for a moment to, if not search for a consensus, at least state the conditions that will govern the analysis for the remainder of this paper.

Requisites of democracy

In his well-known *A Preface to Democratic Theory* (1956), Robert Dahl suggests that the theory of the book's title 'is concerned with processes by which citizens exert a relatively high degree of control over leaders' (p. 3). This statement is imprecise, but it does capture something that seems to be fundamental to what we sense constitutes a democratic order, and can, therefore, serve as an introduction to the discussion of the two building blocks or, as the title to this section labels them, to the two requisites, of that kind of order. Dahl's utterance can, obviously, be read as a descriptive or as a normative proposition (or as both). I use it here for its positive content and because I wish to begin my own discussion of the subject by addressing Dahl's criticism of what he himself calls 'Madisonian democracy.'

James Madison, in *The Federalist* (1787–8) and elsewhere (see Dahl 1956: ch. 1 for references), proposes that, at a minimum, two conditions or requisites had to be simultaneously satisfied to insure the existence of a democratic order (in the sense we now give to that expression). The first of these, which has been embraced by conventional wisdom, by public choice theory – the logo on *Public Choice*, the journal, is a stylized ballot – and by a significant volume of scholarship (see e.g. Popper (1945) and his followers), is that some fraction of the population must be able to signal its preferences, needs, demands, frustrations or what not at the ballot box. For Madison, that fraction was very small; for John Stuart Mill and other nineteenth-century writers, it was considerably larger, but for most of us today, who look at the matter from the perspective of universal suffrage, all of these fractions seem to be very small indeed. The question of the size of the franchise is an important one, but from a Madisonian perspective, it is dominated by that of the *existence* of a capacity on the part of some citizens, at points in time that are not 'too far' apart, to cast a meaningful vote.

Madison did not attach much importance to whether the electoral rule in force was simple majority, plurality, proportional representation, or some blend of these, because of his profound conviction that 'factions' could just as well be inflicted on societies by minorities as by majorities whatever the electoral rule. For Madison, elections could, in other words, generate large *and* small coalitions that could become, to use his less than transparent language, 'tyrannical.' The way to control and, at the limit, to suppress the 'tyranny' of large coalitions is to divide political power – something that leads to the introduction of checks and balances inside governments and, better still, inside governmental systems.[15] As I have just noted, the meaning of the word 'tyranny' in Madison's writings is less than clear. After an exegesis of these writings and of those of his contemporaries, Dahl (1956) concluded that Madison's conception of democracy, built on some degree of popular representation achieved through elections and on checks and balances, is inconsistent with the definition of 'tyranny' which is an integral part of the Madisonian 'theory.'

To make his point, Dahl notes that a Parliamentary government such as that of Great Britain which is assumed to be devoid of any checks and balances – in which, in other words, 'all powers, legislative, executive, and judiciary [are] in the same hands' (Dahl 1956: 11), or, we could say, concentrated at a single point – is not a 'tyrannical' government. We can readily accept that the British government is not tyrannical on any meaningful definition of the word tyranny or, at least, that it has not been so for a very long time. Dahl's criticism of the Madisonian theory is, in fact, based on the conventional view of the division of powers and of checks and balances according to which, as we have already seen, these concepts apply, almost as a matter of definition, only to the American system of government. If we choose not to accept this conventional view of the matter, we are then free to follow in Madison's footsteps.

Before doing so and in view of the ambiguity surrounding Madison's and his contemporaries' conception of elections as events that would be best undertaken in a context in which political parties did not exist, it is important to stress that in the approach to democracy I am proposing, elections are competitive contests in which political parties have an essential role to play. As Galeotti and Breton (1986) have suggested, it is through the medium of political parties that the 'contractual enforcement' problems characterizing the relationship of citizens (the principals) with politicians (their agents) are resolved. In addition to this essential role, political parties, because they are more capable than individuals acting on their own to amass large sums of money and to mobilize the energies of many persons, give to electoral contests a vitality and drive which, in their absence, would be altogether lacking. In other words, because of the way they function, political parties increase the intensity of electoral competition.

This said, we can now rejoin Madison's theoretical construction. To do so we must, however, accept one implication of Dahl's (1956) analysis of 'Madisonian democracy': the idea of tyranny must be jettisoned. If we reject this idea, we must, however, put something in its place. There are, in principle, many alternatives opened to us, but one of these begs for special attention, especially in an exercise which, like this one, wants to be preeminently positive or descriptive. That alternative is *the supply of goods and services*.[16] Madison argued for elections combined with divided powers and checks and balances to control and, at the limit, expunge tyranny; I argue for the very same combination as the way to obtain an efficient supply of goods and services – where efficiency is defined on Wicksell–Lindahl lines (see the second section).

Why insist on the need for competitive electoral contests on the one hand and divided powers with the accompanying checks and balances on the other, with both in place and operating at the same time? Would not electoral contests *or* checks and balances be sufficient? To answer these questions, assume that the citizenry of a jurisdiction can be partitioned into x groups and that within each group preferences are homogeneous. Assume also that the government of that jurisdiction is constituted of n $(= x)$ autonomous centers of power that are well balanced and, therefore, in a position to check each other – to compete with each other – and that they do so. Assume finally that all centers of power, severally or in coordination with each other, are engaged in the production and delivery of goods and services. Should we, in such circumstances, expect the supply of goods and services to be efficient in the Wicksell–Lindahl sense? The answer, I believe, must be negative. Why? Because in such a structure, the incentive to cater to the preferences of citizens is, at best, weak and, more likely, non-existent. Because, by assumption, the centers of power are autonomous, powers will be divided between them and their relations will be governed by checks and balances. The checking will, however, only be a source of strife and conflict; it will only feed on itself. A good example of sterile checking behavior is that which characterizes the infighting that sometimes takes place in corporate boardrooms – it is barren because it seldom, if ever, improves the quality of products and/or reduces their cost of production.

It is only if some centers of power are elected and, therefore, forced to turn their attention to the demands of citizens that an incentive is created, not only for the elected centers but for all of them, to do the same thing. The reason for this is simple: non-elected centers of power compete with the elected ones; if the latter have to cater to the preferences of citizens to be re-elected they will, in effect, 'drag' the non-elected centers in doing the same thing. Non-elected centers, by definition, do not seek the electoral support of citizens, but they will be compelled by the centers that must seek such support to search for what we would call the 'consent' of citizens. Their refusal to do so would mean that they would lose out in their struggles with the elected centers.

The substitution of a goods and services provision concept for tyranny in the neo-Madisonian approach to democracy often meets, as I have discovered in the classroom and elsewhere, with two objections: first, that governments are not primarily preoccupied with supplying goods and services, but are mostly engaged in effecting 'transfers,' that is in redistributing income from one group of citizens to another, and, second, that there really is no competition in the public sector. The first objection, which is rooted in the doctrine of governments-as-benevolent despots on the one hand and in that of governments-as-monoliths on the other, must be addressed beyond declaring that benevolent despots do not exist and that citizens are not always systematically exploited. I will also address the second objection but only briefly because I have, elsewhere (Breton 1991a, 1991b), discussed the question at some length.

Addressing some objections

Before discussing the questions of transfers and of competition, it is necessary, because of a lingering, almost subliminal, confusion which characterizes the subject, to say a few words about the ordinary goods and services supplied by governments – those that are provided in addition to income redistribution. Some of the confusion has its origin, no doubt, in the normative–positive conundrum of conventional public economics: that some goods are but should not, while others are not but should, be supplied by governments. I am not concerned with what governments should or should not provide, but only with what they do supply. Among these one must include justice (laws, courts, legal services, police officers, prisons and so on) but also injustice (delays, brutality, false arrests, et cetera), national defense and peace but also war, employment and

unemployment, pro- and anti-abortion legislation, price stability and inflation, environmental protection and pollution. A list such as that one could
easily be extended. The point has hopefully, however, been made that in
addition to goods and services like snow removal, street lighting, refuse
collection, transportation, broadcasting, oil exploration and others like
them, governments also provide racism, discrimination, anti-semitism,
concentration camps and the like. One must recognize that the supply of
some of these goods and services is more abundant in dictatorships than in
democracies, but I must stress that when these goods and services are
supplied in democracies and they often are, it is necessary, in a model
based on a doctrine of self-interested actors and embodied in a neo-
Madisonian theory of democracy, to assume that the goods and services
supplied are arguments in the utility functions of some citizens. They are,
in other words, only supplied because they are demanded. We can now turn
our attention to redistribution and to competition, in that order.

Understanding transfers

The assumption (often tacit) that governments are exclusively engaged in
redistribution even when they appear to be busy laying sewers, censoring
movies, apprehending suspects, criminalizing abortion and auditing
taxpayers is basic to a number of widely cited economic models of politics
(as examples, I note Tullock 1967, Stigler 1971, Meltzer and Richard 1981
and Becker 1983). Scholars – like all free citizens – have the liberty to
choose and to examine the implications of any assumptions and, therefore,
to construct any models they want. The test of a model's worth is the
improvement it permits in our understanding of the real world and, for
reformers, in the guidance it provides to recommendations and action.

Even if models founded on the exploitation of fellow citizens by means
of rent seeking, capture and 'takings' – the basis of the models listed in the
last paragraph – have shed light on some aspects of politics, they have, I
submit, obscured the essential. They have done this by representing politics
as a zero or a negative sum enterprise, a view that is inescapable when
redistribution is seen as the product of rent seeking, capture and takings
and one that 'makes fools of us all' by insisting that, incapable of doing
anything about the way it is played, we all freely choose to engage in this
kind of political game decades after decades.

If, instead, we choose to think of politics as producing, on the average,
positive-sum outcomes and if, at the same time, we eschew the organicist,
despotic-but-benevolent or monolithic conceptions of government identified above, we are inevitably forced to seek a rationale for redistribution in
the preferences of citizens. Doing so denies validity, of course, to the claim,
sometimes made, that governments intervene in the distribution of income
because they want to redistribute a larger amount than citizens do,
because, *ceteris paribus*, if it is citizens and not some outside (benevolent

or malevolent) power that wills redistribution, the volume observed will be mandated by these citizens. As with ordinary goods and services the quantity or quality actually supplied may differ from that desired (see footnote 13), but that is irrelevant.

When probing the preferences of citizens for redistribution it is natural to turn one's mind to altruism or, in more technical terms, to the interdependence of utility functions of all or of a subgroup of individuals in a given context (for models based on that assumption, see, among many, Boulding 1962, Vickrey 1962 and Hochman and Rodgers 1969). Altruism is, without doubt, a powerful preferences-based rationale for income redistribution. In an exhaustive survey of the literature on the subject, Harold Hochman (1992: 9) speculates that 'distributional preferences which center on utility interdependence . . . across time and generations . . . underlie certain social concerns with environmental issues, like depletion of the ozone layer, the survival of endangered species, and global warming.' I concur and emphasize that even if we often lack a convincing test that would make it possible to distinguish behaviors that are truly altruistic from those that are essentially self-interested but camouflaged in altruism, it is still possible to put a fairly heavy burden on that concept to explain the redistribution we observe. Other preferences-based rationales, just as powerful, are available. I look at three of them and conclude that, together with altruism, they provide a strong explanation for the redistribution we observe in the world.

In *The Calculus of Consent*, Buchanan and Tullock (1962: 192–5), on the basis of commonly accepted assumptions about the preferences of citizens and about the likely cost of enforcing private contracts, argue that what looks like redistribution can be rationalized as 'income insurance' collectively provided and, in view of the assumed contractual enforcement costs of private versus public schemes, provided more efficiently. (For further development of this idea see Polinsky 1974 and Zeckhauser 1974.) Though not their avowed intention, Buchanan and Tullock's (1962) analysis provides solid microeconomic foundations for a long tradition of writings which goes back, at least, to William Beveridge's (1942, 1945) rationalization of redistribution as 'social insurance.'

Addressing an altogether different preoccupation, Gary Becker and Kevin Murphy (1988), building on some earlier work of Becker (1967), show that if the relation of parents and children is assumed to be embodied in incomplete contracts – contracts whose terms can be monitored by the contracting parties, but cannot be verified by a third party and cannot, therefore, be legally enforced – and, in addition, if it is assumed that children cannot commit to eventually compensate their parents for investment in their well-being, parents who plan to make gifts and/or to leave bequests to their children will invest optimally in their children because 'they can force even selfish children to repay them for expenditures on . . . human capital' (Becker and Murphy 1988: 5) by simply withholding all or part of the gifts and/or bequests. Poor parents do not have that option and may not, as a consequence, optimally invest in their children. An (implicit) intergenerational 'social compact,' mediated by governments, can remedy the contractual failure. In Becker and Murphy's (1988) words

> Taxes on adults help finance efficient investments in children. In return, adults receive public pensions and medical payments when old. This compact tries to achieve for poorer and middle-level families what richer families tend to achieve without government help; namely efficient levels of investment in children and support for elderly parents.

A third and last preferences-based rationale for redistribution is provided by the work of a number of scholars studying different aspects of the relationship between property rights and the distribution of income and wealth (see Johnsen 1986 and Allen 1991). Fairly recently Curtis Eaton and William White (1991) – apparently unaware of Buchanan's (1975) pioneering analysis of the same problem – have proposed an elegant game-theoretic model that nicely captures an aspect of the question. In a two-person, two-period economy in which each person can consume, plant and harvest or steal corn, Eaton and White show that the distribution of wealth or of initial endowments can be, in some circumstances, an important complement to legal enforcement mechanisms supporting property rights, where an enforcement mechanism is defined by two variables: the probability of being apprehended after a theft and the size of the sanction – the amount to be restituted if apprehended. The point is that, as their model is set up, efficiency requires that in the first period both persons plant their corn, but whether they do so depends on the cost of enforcing property rights which, in turn, depend on the distribution of wealth. At the end of their paper, Eaton and White (1991: 350) note that many students of regulation have pointed to the fact that small operators in, let us say, oil fields and the fisheries often receive 'favorable treatment' by regulators. They also note that 'the standard interpretation' of that treatment is based on 'equity concerns and political lobbying.' They then conclude by saying that while they do not rule out these possibilities, another explanation exists, 'namely that enforcement costs may be lower when small operators are given more to lose.' (Remarkably, many years before, Beveridge (1945) had placed on the title page of his report a quotation taken from Charlotte Brontë's *Shirley*, which reads 'Misery generates hate' and, no doubt, theft as a manifestation of that hatred.)

All these preferences-based rationales for redistribution imply that when redistribution is implemented it improves economic efficiency, strictly understood, just like the building of bridges, the delivery of mail, the administration of justice and the lighting of streets do. For this reason, one should use the words transfers and redistribution sparingly. For my part, I find it useful to think of the supply of income insurance, human capital, secure property rights and of other 'transfers' as being nothing but the provision of goods and services with an emphasis on the latter. Using the words goods and services, instead of transfers and redistribution, is also a reminder that if we believe that governments redistribute more than the 'non-market sector' does or, for that matter, redistribute less, it is because we think of them in organicist, despotic or monolithic terms. Replacing the language of transfers by that of goods and services is, of course, not mandatory but it does help avoid pitfalls in thinking about a very difficult subject.

Understanding competition

For many persons the concept of competition has a bad reputation. The realities which it evokes are, to them, unsavoury. In addition, in the minds of many lay persons and in a sizeable body of modern economic theorizing, competition is incompatible with, and even antithetical to, cooperation. With this as background, the idea that governmental centers of power – and in a broader frame of reference, other sources of supply such as families, churches, cooperatives, unions, clubs and so on – compete among themselves and with governments (see Breton 1989) is often thought to be impertinent and cynical. It will, therefore, be useful to examine briefly the senses in which we can say that these sources of supply compete with each other.

Early economists, such as Adam Smith (1776), borrowed the concept of competition from everyday usage. Over the years, however, refinement in economic thought has transformed the concept into something that bears virtually no relationship to its original meaning. In the main corpus of neoclassical economic theory, the concept is devoid of any identifiable behaviors. The state it purports to describe is associated with the concept of perfect markets, that is with markets in which buyers and sellers are numerous and have complete and accurate knowledge of all supply and demand prices and in which products traded are homogeneous and divisible (see Stigler 1957). Under these conditions, all market participants are price-takers. Such a concept is productive – it is one that practicing economists use daily – especially when it is recognized that in applying theoretical notions, as distinguished from developing and refining them, all that is needed are approximations to the above four conditions.

Even within the confines of neoclassical theory – albeit less rigorously construed – certain types of activities – attestations of competitive behaviors – are acknowledged. These have usually been and are still often treated, however, as 'imperfections' in competition. Among these activities, we may note the promotion by an enterprise of its goods and services through advertising, marketing and other means, the differentiation by a firm of its goods and services from those of other suppliers through design, packaging and innumerable genuine and artificial contrivances, and the location by entrepreneurs of their businesses on sites that are advantageously positioned.

Economic models of perfect and imperfect competition have for many years been applied with success to politics. I mention two applications. In the perfect competition tradition, Charles Tiebout (1956) assumed the existence of numerous local governments, supplying goods and services for which a demand exists, which were compelled by the competition of other local governments to supply these goods and services efficiently at tax prices equal to their marginal costs. Competition in this context is between local governments (the counterpart of firms) for the patronage of mobile citizens (the analog of consuming households). Competition insures that both local governments and citizens behave, at least if the costs of mobility are low, as price-takers. In the imperfect competition tradition, Anthony Downs (1957) modelled the rivalry of political parties along the lines of the locational or spatial competition theory suggested by Harold Hotelling (1929). It is not necessary to add that both the Tiebout and the Downs models have spawned an enormous literature.

The canonical models of perfect and imperfect competition are not particularly enlightening in respect of the more 'dynamic' aspects of competition. Following Breton and Wintrobe's (1982) earlier work, I wish to suggest that these canonical models have to be complemented by alternative models if we are to understand the nature of the competitive process which regulates the relations of the various sources which are engaged in the supply of goods and services. One such model was proposed by Joseph Schumpeter (1911, 1942) and other 'Austrian' economists (Carl Menger, Friedrich Hayek and Ludwig Mises) – hence the label of Austrian sometimes applied to it (see Kirzner 1973) – and which I will call the model of *entrepreneurial competition*. I insist that model is consistent with – is a complement to – the neoclassical model, a point which Schumpeter emphasized, Paul Samuelson (1943, 1982) proved and which I repeat below.

Schumpeterian entrepreneurs become and remain competitive not by originating but by activating technological, financial, commercial and organizational inventions; hence the distinction which that literature emphasizes between invention and innovation. Schumpeterian entrepreneurs innovate: they introduce new techniques of production, search for new sources of supply, devise new methods of financing their operations, initiate new on-the-job training programs, design and instate new organizational forms, originate and market new goods and services, inaugurate new promotion methods – in a word, they seek new and better ways of dealing with the whole set of problems that suppliers encounter, new ways of holding down or of reducing the unit cost of supplying existing goods and services, new ways of bringing forth less expensive and better products and new ways of achieving a better match between the volume and the quality of goods and services provided and the volume and quality desired by consumers.

Entrepreneurial innovators are followed by organizations – firms and other sources of supply – whom Schumpeter called 'imitators.' These organizations are induced to emulate the innovative entrepreneurs by the rents – the sums generated by the specific capacity to innovate – which these have created. In the process, the imitators increase the demand for labor, capital and other factors of production, thus pushing up their prices and the entire schedule of average costs. By increasing the supply of goods and services, they push down their prices. The increase in unit costs and the fall in supply prices eventually eliminate the rents of entrepreneurship and bring forth the equilibrium conditions called for by neoclassical theory. Schumpeter called the competitive process that I have just sketched one of 'creative destruction.' The expression is apposite. Competition, indeed, is a process that removes (destroys) suppliers who, for one reason or another, are not capable of innovation or of imitation and puts in their place those who are able to do these things.

If, following a wave of creative destruction, we compare the old with the new equilibrium, what are we likely to discover? We should expect that better technologies incorporating the more recent discoveries of scientists will be in place, that work will have become less irksome and leisure more abundant, that better products will have become available and, importantly from the point of view of the public finances, that, in addition to the above, the quantity and quality of the goods and services provided at given tax prices will more closely match the quantity and quality desired by citizens. In a word, that wealth will have increased and, generally, that more of the things associated with economic growth will be available.

I must stress that the entrepreneurial innovation which sets the competitive process in motion, the imitation which follows, and the creative destruction which they generate are not necessarily inconsistent with cooperative behavior on the part of all involved. It would, however, be a mistake to focus on these acts of cooperation and conceive of creative destruction as the outcome of a cooperative process. In looking for new technologies, supply sources, organizational forms, products, methods of finance, labour–management relations and other new ways of solving supply problems, entrepreneurs will consult with other people, collaborate with them on some projects, coordinate some activities and even integrate part of their operations. All these actions describe what is generally meant by cooperation. If this cooperation serves to bring forth new innovations, it only serves to foster competition. Indeed, to the extent that cooperation makes it possible for innovations to come on stream more rapidly than they would otherwise, it becomes itself a force in the process of creative destruction. As a general rule, we can say that in the absence of collusion, cooperation and competition can and will generally co-exist and also that the existence of one is not proof of the absence of the other. In particular, we can say that the observation of cooperation does not deny that the underlying determining force is competition.

One does not have to be a keen observer of the real world nor possess great imagination to 'see' entrepreneurial competition in action. In the governmental sector, the *innovative* manifestations of competition are often, but not always, identified by a name such as New Deal, Fair Deal, New Frontier, Great Society, Just Society, War on Poverty, New World Order and New Covenant. Sometimes they are associated with a theme such as full employment, social insurance, deregulation, privatization, free trade, productivity, downsizing, family values, change and many others. When successful, these innovations serve to channel rents towards the innovative entrepreneurs. These attract a bevy of *imitators*. The reader can easily document for him- or herself that some innovations are unsuccessful. It suffices to name the Meech Lake Accord and the Charlottetown Consensus as recent examples of failures in Canada.

Why are some innovations – and some innovators – unsuccessful? One can best answer this question by referring to Charles Darwin's (1859) theory of natural selection. According to that theory, selection plays two roles: it destroys and eliminates the innovational projects (organisms) that are undesirable (unfit), that are not able to satisfactorily fulfill a particular need or purpose, *and* it preserves, indeed, improves or builds up those that are desirable (fit). Selection works through the adaptation – sometimes only partial – of innovations to local and changing environments. Natural selection, therefore, governs the (evolutionary) struggle of innovations and innovators for differential success.

In a review of Edward Wilson's (1992) book, John Terborgh (1992) thrice characterizes the struggle for life through natural selection among species (a broader class than organisms) by the words 'checks and balances.' In respect of innovations and innovators, Samuelson (1981: 13, my italics) writes of 'large corporations that are subject to the *checks and balances* of other large corporations' in reference to intercorporate competition. John Kenneth Galbraith (1952) defines 'countervailing power' in terms of checking behavior as do Richard Nelson and Sidney Winter (1982) in describing what they call 'dynamic competition.'

The expression checks and balances no doubt correctly circumscribes the whole class of behaviors associated with the concepts of entrepreneurial competition, evolutionary struggle, countervailing power and dynamic competition. Much more research will, however, be needed to identify these behaviors – especially those which stare us in the face but which, for lack of a proper conceptual apparatus, we overlook – and to understand the organizing and stabilizing role which competition plays in ordering intragovernmental relations.

Conclusion

I have argued that amongst the variety of models of government that one can find in the literatures of public choice, public economics and welfare economics, the only model which is consistent with a neo-Madisonian theory of democracy is one that assumes that governments are constituted of a multiplicity of autonomous and quasi-autonomous centers of power which are balanced or, as it used to be said, are equipoised *vis-à-vis* each other and, therefore, capable of checking each other. I have rationalized this proposition in the following way. Madison's theory requires that two conditions – two requisites – be simultaneously satisfied: that at least one among all the centers of power be popularly elected and that all centers compete with each other. In Madison's original 'model,' the two conditions were required as bulwarks against tyranny – a concept which Dahl (1956) has shown to be intractable in Madison's own frame of reference. I have suggested that the Madisonian edifice can be salvaged by replacing the notion of tyranny with that of goods and services provision.

Amongst the various conceptions of efficiency which one encounters in discussions of public policies and public finances, the one which I have called the Wicksell–Lindahl conception is particularly attractive. Indeed, in the context of a neo-Madisonian theory of democracy, competition between centers of power which is structured or given a direction by the elected centers will operate to create links between the expenditure and revenue decisions of citizens. The links will not be absolutely 'tight' and, indeed, may be fairly slack for some citizens, but, as is the case in standard microeconomics, we can presume that the more intense and the more perfect the competition, the 'tighter' the links for a greater number of citizens.

Notes

* I would like to thank Gianluigi Galeotti and Ronald Wintrobe for their comments on an earlier draft of the paper. I would also like to thank the Lyne and Harry Bradley Foundation for their financial assistance.
1 As the reader will discover, five is an arbitrary number. It is easy to regroup concepts and doctrines or to subdivide them differently than I have done. What counts, in the end, is the light which a particular classification sheds on the subject under consideration. In Breton (1996), I discuss seven models of government. The present paper was written while that book was in preparation and reflects my early thinking on the subject.
2 I am concerned with doctrines. These, however, often have an influence on historical events which can be far from benign. I am not dealing here with these influences; hence the word 'discourse.'
3 I do not have in mind a collective welfare function such as the one which preoccupied Kenneth Arrow (1951), but one like that found in conventional welfare economics. (For the distinction between the two, see Samuelson 1967.)
4 The *locus classicus* of this line of analysis in public choice theory is Niskanen (1971). The assumption that elections are otiose is basic to the canonical version of this model, but has, in fact, been given more emphasis by some Niskanenites than by Niskanen himself who never liked the assumption (see Niskanen 1975).
5 Ferdinand Mount (1992: ch. 2) provides an excellent and lively discussion of the work of the greatest pillars of that school, who he calls 'the simplifiers.'

6 I do not dwell on the fundamental separation of church and state – inaugurated by the American and French revolutions – which eliminated 'the use of religion by the state to reinforce and extend its authority . . . and the use of the state by the clergy to impose their doctrines and rules on others' (Lewis 1992: 52).

7 I refer those who believe that the word 'branch' should be restricted to the American Congressional system of government to its use by Mount (1992 at, for example, p. 113) who is solely concerned with the British Parliamentary system.

8 Mount (1992) documents that it is contrary to the facts of history to suppose that the Cabinet can act as if the backbenchers of the governing party were passive. He shows that even if no formal separation of powers between the Cabinet and the governing party exists, there is an informal separation of sorts.

9 Mount (1992) makes the point that in the case of England – which is typically assumed not to possess any charter or bill of rights – 'the Magna Carta of John, the Magna Carta of Edward I, the Petition of Right, the Act of Settlement, and so on . . . were intended as a permanent record and entrenchment' of rights (p. 101).

10

> *The English Constitution* [was] first composed as a series of essays for *The Fortnightly* [and] published in book form in 1867 – the very year of Disraeli's Reform Act which abruptly and finally ended the period of classical parliamentary government it describes.
>
> (Crossman, Introduction to Bagehot's *The English Constitution*, 1963, p. 1)

11 I make no claim to completeness and, consequently, the conceptions of efficiency which are embodied in expressions like deficit reduction, duplication of functions, devolution of responsibilities and privatization – recently popular in political, financial and media circles – are not discussed. Some of them are, however, important discussions of, let us say, the efficiency of federalism.

12 The distinction was anticipated by Jean-Jacques Rousseau, as the following quotation, taken from Robert Dahl (1956: 35), documents: 'There is but one law which, from its nature, needs *unanimous* consent. This is the social contract. . . . Apart from this *primitive* contract, the vote of the majority always binds the rest' (my italics). The word *primitive* has many meanings. One of them – surely appropriate in the context – is *original* or *primary*.

13 At a given tax price, if q' is the quantity or quality of a good or service desired by a citizen and if q is the quantity or quality actually supplied, the utility loss for that citizen is $L = \frac{1}{2}(q'-q)$. The loss to a collectivity of n individuals is nL. The greater the difference between q' and q, the greater L and, therefore, nL.

14 As should become clear in the next section, efficiency along Wicksell–Lindahl lines is more likely in democracies.

15 Throughout, I use the expression 'governmental systems' to refer to the set of all governments that one finds in every society. The expression is an analog to the word industry which is used in microeconomics to encompass all firms which produce a commodity and its substitutes. It is also analogous to the word industry in being, like it, imprecise.

16 How these should be defined in the approach I am proposing is discussed later in this section and in the next.

References

Allen, Douglas W. (1991) 'Homesteading and property rights; or, "How the West was really won",' *Journal of Law and Economics* 34(1): 1–23.

Arrow, Kenneth J. (1951) *Social Choice and Individual Values*, New York: John Wiley; rev. edn, 1963.

Bagehot, Walter (1867) *The English Constitution*, with an Introduction by R. H. S. Crossman, Glasgow: Fontana/Collins.

Becker, Gary S. (1967) *Human Capital and the Personal Distribution of Income: An Analytical Approach*, Woytinski Lecture, University of Michigan. Reprinted in Becker, Gary S. (1975) *Human Capital*, 2nd edition, New York: National Bureau of Economic Research and Columbia University Press, pp. 94–144.

Becker, Gary S. (1983) 'A theory of competition among pressure groups for political influence,' *Quarterly Journal of Economics* 98(3): 371–400.

Becker, Gary S. and Murphy, Kevin M. (1988) 'The family and the state,' *Journal of Law and Economics* 31(1): 1–18.

Beveridge, William H. (1942) *Social Insurance and Allied Services*, American edition, New York: Macmillan.

Beveridge, William H. (1945) *Full Employment in a Free Society*, New York: Norton.

Borcherding, Thomas E. (1983) 'Toward a positive theory of public sector supply arrangements,' in J. Robert S. Prichard (ed.) *Crown Corporations in Canada. The Calculus of Instrument Choice*, Toronto: Butterworth, pp. 99–184.

Boulding, Kenneth E (1962) 'Notes on a theory of philanthropy,' in Frank G. Dickinson (ed.) *Philanthropy and Public Policy*, New York: National Bureau of Economic Research, pp. 57–71.

Brennan, Geoffrey and Buchanan, James M. (1980) *The Power to Tax. Analytical Foundations of a Fiscal Constitution*, New York: Cambridge University Press.

Breton, Albert (1989) 'The growth of competitive governments,' *Canadian Journal of Economics* 22(4): 717–50.

Breton, Albert (1991a) 'Checks and balances,' Mimeo.

Breton, Albert (1991b) 'The organization of competition in congressional and parliamentary governments,' in Albert Breton, Gianluigi Galeotti, Pierre Salmon and Ronald Wintrobe (eds) *The Competitive State. Villa Colombella Papers on Competitive Politics*, Dordrecht: Kluwer, pp. 13–38.

Breton, Albert (1996) *Competitive Governments. An Economic Theory of Politics and Public Finance*, New York: Cambridge University Press.

Breton, Albert and Wintrobe, Ronald (1982) *The Logic of Bureaucratic Conduct*, New York: Cambridge University Press.

Buchanan, James M. (1975) *The Limits of Liberty. Between Anarchy and Leviathan*, Chicago: University of Chicago Press.

Buchanan, James M. (1987) 'The constitution of economic policy,' *American Economic Review* 77(3): 243–50.

Buchanan, James M. and Tullock, Gordon (1962) *The Calculus of Consent. Logical Foundations of Constitutional Democracy*, Ann Arbor, MI: University of Michigan Press.

Cheung, Steven N. S. (1973) 'The fable of the bees: an economic investigation,' *Journal of Law and Economics* 16(1): 11–52.

Dahl, Robert A. (1956) *A Preface to Democratic Theory*, Chicago: University of Chicago Press.

Darwin, Charles R. (1859) *On the Origin of Species by Means of Natural Selection or the Preservation of Favored Races in the Struggle for Life*, London: John Murray; Penguin 1968.

Downs, Anthony (1957) *An Economic Theory of Democracy*, New York: Harper & Row.

Eaton, B. Curtis and White, William D. (1991) 'The distribution of wealth and the efficiency of institutions,' *Economic Inquiry* 29(2): 336–50.

Galbraith, John Kenneth (1952) *American Capitalism. The Concept of Counter-vailing Power*, Boston: Houghton Mifflin.

Galeotti, Gianluigi and Breton, Albert (1986) 'An economic theory of political parties,' *Kyklos* 39, Fasc. 1: 47–65.

Hochman, Harold M. (1992) 'Public choice interpretations of distributional preference,' Mimeo.

Hochman, Harold M. and Rodgers, James D. (1969) 'Pareto optimal redistribution,' *American Economic Review* 59(4): 542–57.

Hotelling, Harold (1929) 'Stability in competition,' *Economic Journal* 39(March): 4–57. Reprinted in George J. Stigler and Kenneth E. Boulding (eds) (1952) *Readings in Price Theory*, Homewood, IL: Irwin, pp. 467–84.

Johnsen, D. Bruce (1986) 'The formation and protection of property rights among the southern Kwakiutl Indians,' *Journal of Legal Studies* 15(1): 41–67.

Kirzner, Israel (1973) *Competition and Entrepreneurship*, Chicago: University of Chicago Press.

Landes, William M. and Posner, Richard A. (1975) 'The independent judiciary in an interest-group perspective,' *Journal of Law and Economics* 18(3): 875–901.

Lewis, Bernard (1992) 'Muslims, Christians and Jews: the dream of coexistence,' *New York Review* 39(6): 48–52.

Meltzer, Allan H. and Richard, Scott F. (1981) 'A rational theory of the size of government,' *Journal of Political Economy* 89(5): 914–27.

Mount, Ferdinand (1992) *The British Constitution Now*, London: Heinemann.

Nelson, Richard R. and Winter, Sidney G. (1982) *An Evolutionary Theory of Economic Change*, Cambridge, MA: Harvard University Press.

Niskanen, William A. Jr (1971) *Bureaucracy and Representative Government*, Chicago: Aldine-Atherton.

Niskanen, William A. Jr (1975) 'Bureaucrats and politicians,' *Journal of Law and Economics* 18(3): 617–43.

Palmer, Matthew S. R. (1992) 'The economics of organization: towards a framework of constitutional design,' Mimeo.

Panagopoulos, Epaminondas P. (1985) *Essays on the History and Meaning of Checks and Balances*, Lanham, MD: University Press of America.

Polinsky, A. Mitchell (1974) 'Imperfect capital markets, intertemporal redistribution, and progressive taxation,' in Harold M. Hochman and George E. Peterson (eds) *Redistribution Through Public Choice*, New York: Columbia University Press, pp. 229–58.

Popper, Karl A. (1945) *The Open Society and its Enemies*, Vol. 1, 5th edition, London: Routledge and Kegan Paul, Routledge Paperbacks, 1945/1966.

Rawls, John (1971) *A Theory of Justice*, Cambridge, MA: Harvard University Press.

Rottenberg, Simon (1956) 'The baseball players' labor market,' *Journal of Political Economy* 64(3): 242–58.

Samuelson, Paul A. (1943) 'Dynamics, statics, and the stationary state,' *Review of Economics and Statistics* 25(1): pp. 58–68. Reprinted in Joseph E. Stiglitz (ed.) (1966) *The Collected Scientific Papers of Paul A. Samuelson*, Vol. 1, Cambridge, MA: MIT Press, pp. 201–11.

Samuelson, Paul A. (1967) 'Arrow's mathematical politics,' in Sydney Hook (ed.) *Human Values and Economic Policy: A Symposium*, New York: New York University Press, pp. 41–52. Reprinted in Robert C. Merton (ed.) (1972) *The Collected Scientific Papers of Paul A. Samuelson*, Vol. III, Cambridge, MA: MIT Press, pp. 411–21.

Samuelson, Paul A. (1981) 'Schumpeter's *Capitalism, Socialism and Democracy*,' in Arnold Heertje (ed.) *Schumpeter's Vision: Capitalism, Socialism and Democracy After 40 Years*, London: Praeger, pp. 1–21. Reprinted in Kate Crowley (ed.) (1986) *The Collected Scientific Papers of Paul A. Samuelson*, Vol. V, Cambridge, MA: MIT Press, pp. 328–48.

Samuelson, Paul A. (1982) 'Schumpeter as an economic theorist,' in Helmut Frisch (ed.) *Schumpeterian Economics*, London: Praeger, pp. 1–27. Reprinted in Kate Crowley (ed.) (1986) *The Collected Scientific Papers of Paul A. Samuelson*, Vol. V, Cambridge, MA: MIT Press, pp. 301–27.

Schumpeter, Joseph A. (1911) *The Theory of Economic Development*, 1st German edition 1911, trans. Redvers Opie, New York: Oxford University Press, 1934/1961.

Schumpeter, Joseph A. (1942) *Capitalism, Socialism and Democracy*, New York: Harper & Row, 1942/1975.

Smith, Adam (1776) *An Inquiry Into the Nature and Causes of the Wealth of Nations*, New York: Random House, Modern Library, 1776/1937.

Stigler, George J. (1957) 'Perfect competition, historically contemplated,' *Journal of Political Economy* 65(1): 1–17. Reprinted in Stigler, J. (ed.) (1967) *Essays in the History of Economics*, Chicago: University of Chicago Press, pp. 234–67.

Stigler, George J. (1971) 'The theory of economic regulation,' *Bell Journal of Economics and Management Science* 2(1): 3–21.

Stiglitz, Joseph E. (1989) 'On the economic role of the state,' in Arnold Heertje (ed.) *The Economic Role of the State*, Oxford: Basil Blackwell, pp. 9–85.

Terborgh, John (1992) 'A matter of life and death,' *New York Review* 39(18): 3–6.

Tiebout, Charles M. (1956) 'A pure theory of local expenditures,' *Journal of Political Economy* 64(5): 416–24.

Tullock, Gordon (1967) 'The welfare costs of tariffs, monopolies and theft,' *Western Economic Journal* 5(2): 224–32.

Vickrey, William S. (1962) 'One economist's view of philanthropy,' in Frank G. Dickinson (ed.) *Philanthropy and Public Policy*, New York: National Bureau of Economic Research, pp. 31–56.

Wicksell, Knut (1964) 'A new principle of just taxation,' in Richard A. Musgrave and Alan T. Peacock (eds) *Classics in the Theory of Public Finance*, London: Macmillan, pp. 72–118. Trans. James M. Buchanan from 'Ein neues Prinzip der gerechten Besteuerung,' *Finanztheoretische Untersuchungen*, Jena, 1896), pp. iv-vi, 76–87, 101–59.

Wilson, Edward O. (1992) *The Diversity of Life*, Cambridge, MA: Harvard University Press.

Wittman, Donald (1989) 'Why democracies produce efficient results,' *Journal of Political Economy* 97(6): 1395–424.

Zeckhauser, Richard (1974) 'Risk spreading and distribution,' in Harold M. Hochman and George E. Peterson (eds) *Redistribution Through Public Choice*, New York: Columbia University Press, pp. 206–28.

8 Political parties and representative democracy

Gianluigi Galeotti

Introduction

More than a century ago John Stuart Mill (1863), reflecting on the nature of the relationship between the citizens of a jurisdiction and their elected representatives, posed a question that goes to the heart of an understanding of representative democracy: 'Ought pledges (to) be required from members of Parliament' (p. 315) to insure that they truly represent their constituents? Eighty years later, Joseph Schumpeter's (implicit) answer to Mill's question was negative, because he assumed that the competitive struggle for votes between political parties would be sufficient to keep politicians attuned to the preferences of citizens. It is perhaps for this reason that he accorded no importance to a calculus of voting, almost denying that one existed. Later on, Anthony Downs (1957) elaborated Schumpeter's ideas and was led to the conclusion that Schumpeter had taken for granted: for a rational individual, it is not worthwhile to be politically informed, active and to vote. That is most distressing because, in Downs' own words, 'the whole concept of representative government becomes rather empty if the electorate has no opinions (that are) to be represented' (pp. 245–6). In the same work, Downs also argued that, from the point of view of a rational citizen, elected representatives cannot be considered to be reliable delegates or agents, since the goals of citizens and those of representative are always at variance. Mill's question must, therefore, be considered anew, if the notion of representation in models of representative democracy is to have a sure logical foundation.

In a previous paper (Galeotti and Breton 1986) it has been shown that the organization of political parties serves as surrogate pledges which have features similar to the formal pledges that Mill had in mind. Political parties support the relations between citizens and representatives, both by enhancing the 'control' that voters can exercise over elected representatives and by strengthening the bond between representatives and otherwise footloose or shifting voters. With respect to that proposition, this paper moves one step backward – and considers in some detail the logic of political exchanges[1] – and one step forward, and suggests a number of

institutional factors that affect the nature and features of party organization. The ultimate purpose of the exercise is to stir up reflections on how
institutional factors shape party behavior in representative democracies. In
what follows, the second section recalls the main features of the economic
approach to politics and confronts the issue of what citizens and representatives trade in politics – the *quid* and the *pro quo* of political exchange. The
third section summarizes a Millian framework of analysis and the following
section clarifies the role and the working of party organization in its vertical
and horizontal dimensions. The fifth section discusses the impact on political parties of three institutional traits: centralization of the public decision
making, size of the public sector and electoral rules. The concluding section
stresses the risk of Michel's disease threatening representative institutions in
the presence of strong (horizontally oriented) political parties.

The conventional framework

It is convenient to distinguish between a general version of the economic
approach to representative democracy and a more narrow version which
expresses the Schumpeter–Downs model. There are five basic assumptions
underlying the economic approach, and the Schumpeter–Downs model
comes from placing particular interpretations on some of these assumptions.

The first assumption is that all actors are *rational* or self-interested. An
important implication of this assumption lies in the difference between
private incentives and social outcomes, a point first stressed by Adam Smith
(1776, 1937: esp. ch. 2) for economic life and developed by Schumpeter
(1942: esp. 282) in regards to political life. The second assumption is that
governing parties cater to the preferences of citizens. In other words,
governing parties and citizens are assumed to be engaged in an *exchange*
in which each gives something up in return for something else. The third is
that political parties *compete* with each other; the fourth, that both
exchange and competition take place in an *institutional framework*
characterized by elections. These elections, in turn, are discrete events
governed by given rules of representation (simple majority, proportional
representation, plurality, and so on). The fifth and last assumption is that
the processes of exchange and of competition take place in a world of
uncertainty.

With respect to the second assumption, the notion of exchange remains
vague unless three related questions are answered: (a) what is the precise
content of the exchange, that is what exactly is the *quid* and what is the *pro
quo*; (b) why are citizens motivated to take part in such exchanges; and (c)
what are the property rights which govern these exchanges and which ones
guarantee their effectiveness? The conventional answer to the first question
is that governing parties offer bundles of public policies (often public
goods) to citizens in exchange for their votes and general support; to the
second, that citizens have no ground for voting and for being politically

active; and, as a direct consequence of that response, the third is left unanswered or more exactly unasked. This follows from the fact that the standard Schumpeter–Downs interpretation imposes limits to some of the above assumptions.

A first restriction is with respect to the assumption of citizen rationality. That concept is taken to mean that 'any citizen is rational in regard to elections if his actions enable him to play his part in selecting a government efficiently' (Downs 1957: 24). In other words, the purpose of elections in a democracy is to select a government (Schumpeter 1942: 272), whose role in the social division of labor is to supply policies. A first consequence of this view of rationality is that neither the parliamentary (elected represent-atives) nor the extra-parliamentary parties (the general body of members) have any role in the political process. Schumpeter (p. 283) assumes that all members of a party – understood to be a parliamentary party – act 'in concert,' are like a 'trade association,' or like a cartel, while Downs (p. 25) achieves the same result more directly by assuming that members of a party – also a parliamentary party – are all alike, that is all have identical utility functions.

A second consequence of this particular notion of rationality is that the process of decision making in relation to public policies is not analyzed and the role of elected representatives – other than members of the Executive – is not modeled. This is particularly surprising in Downs' model, for he, more than anyone else, gives great weight to the uncertainty assumption. In such a context, it must be recognized that what is traded in politics are not policies against votes, but promises of policies – that is, promises that have to be translated into policies – against votes and support. The terms of such translations depend, in addition to the conditions that rule at the time they are effected compared to those that obtained when the promises were made, on at least two things. First, on the government's ability to elicit sufficient support in Parliament or Congress; and second, on the govern-ment's ability to conciliate possible contradictory, but surely different, promises made by different representatives to different groups. Both of these involve representatives in a direct way.

A third consequence of this view of rationality is that it is irrational for citizens to vote and, in general, to engage in political action. Why? Simply, because the probability that one will cast the decisive vote as to who will form the next government is negligible. Indeed, when rationality and exchange are restricted to the selection of a government, voting is irra-tional. Even if it is irrational, citizens do vote. Holding their noses, some scholars take that 'as fact,' and proceed to model the implied electoral competition between political parties. Irrespective of how that process is modeled, it is generally assumed that whoever wins, the median voter will have his or her preferences satisfied. But how that will be done is left unspecified. To assume that the median voter's or someone else's prefer-ences are met places on the fourth basic assumption, related to political competition, a burden it cannot carry. Indeed, elections take place at discrete intervals so that competition is also discrete. How can intermittent competition keep the governing party continuously on its toes? One consequence of modeling competition in the framework of a discrete electoral process is to raise in extreme form the question of the exploitation of minorities by the majority – a problem noted by Downs (1957) and by Stigler (1972) among others. As was observed, as long as political competition is conceived to be electoral competition, we must confront the paradox that while economic competition eliminates 'exploitation,' political competition leads to it.

Finally, in Downs' model of democracy – a model in which uncertainty occupies a large place – the roles of political parties and of a consequent meaningful citizen–representative relationship are suppressed for another reason. Early in his book, Downs recognizes that in an uncertain world, a government will want to employ agents as 'specialists in discovering, transmitting, and analyzing popular opinion' (p. 89), but he later goes on to argue that 'political parties [understood as parliamentary parties whose members are all identical] can never be the agents of rational delegation' (p. 234). Why? Because the first thing rational 'evaluative delegators' must ascertain is whether the agents they select have goals similar to their own. But, Downs goes on to argue,

> party officials are interested only in maximizing votes, never in producing any particular social state *per se*. But voters are always interested in the latter. Therefore, a rational voter who is not a party official himself cannot assume a member of any party has goals similar to his own. But without this assumption, delegation of all political decisions to someone else is irrational.
>
> (p. 232)

This argument would appear to fly in the face of the self-interest assumption and is surely inconsistent with the necessary distinction between individual motivations and social outcomes which is a hallmark of that assumption. But, it can be suggested that Downs was led to its development in reference to a market context. Suppose that a surgeon – whose goals are surely different from those of the patient – performs something else than an agreed-upon operation; what can this patient do? He or she can sue. But what can citizens do if their representative (their government) does something else than what was promised? Virtually nothing, at least until the next election, because there are no legally based property rights in the political relationship. Rationality, exchange and competition are meaningful only in a world in which property rights exist and have a meaningful foundation. This is the problem that now has to be faced.

The role of political parties in a 'Millian' framework

An atrophied view of self-interest, the consequent approach to political exchange as involving office (and a fixed bundle of policies) and votes, and the notion of competition as an event which takes place only at long time intervals lead the Schumpeter–Downs model of democracy to an impasse. In his *Considerations on Representative Government* (1863, 1910), John Stuart Mill provides a different approach, which can be used to construct a citizen–representative relation which permits a solution to many of the above problems.

Mill, when discussing the division of competence between the government and the assembly of representatives, gives two autonomous roles to the latter. First, it has to 'watch and control the government' (p. 239). Second, it has

> to be the nation's Committee of Grievances, and its *Congress of Opinions*; an arena in which not only the general opinion of the nation, but that of every section of it . . . can produce itself in full light and challenge discussion; where every person in the country may count upon finding somebody who speaks[2] his mind as well or better than he could speak it himself . . . where those whose opinion is overruled, feel satisfied that it is heard.
>
> (p. 239, italics added)

If we interpret that normative statement in positive terms, we can assume that when citizens engage in political action, they seek first to give expression and support to one or more *political opinions*, and second, to elect a government. In this way, the Millian approach conceives of the selection of a government as a by-product of the representation of people's opinions.

Let us interpret the Millian notion of 'opinions' in terms of *general points of view* or *attitudes, orientations or dispositions* toward policies,[3] that is toward current matters on which collective decision must be reached, but, just as importantly, toward matters not known, but that will arise during a government's term of office. In other words, opinions are in the nature of a general outlook against which views with respect to 'new' and to 'old' issues are formed.

Given that opinions and not policy preferences are what citizens consult in arriving at collective decisions, it must be that even if the *ultimate* concern of citizens is what the government does (i.e. the flow of public policies produced), the *proximate* concern, and the one that motivates their behavior, is that their opinions be represented – or be made present in time and space – in the process of policy formation. If we define representation as being present in Mill's Congress of Opinions, for that to happen, citizens must pay the price of representation: they must vote, provide support, write letters to newspapers and to their elected members, lobby, parade and manifest, engage in outrageous activities that will shock sufficiently to capture the attention of the media, and so on (Breton 1974). The nature of the exchange that involves citizens and representatives is not in terms of office or policies for votes and other activities, but in terms of opinions for votes and political action.

If representatives accept to represent the opinions of citizens and if citizens accept to pay 'the price of representation' through political support, that exchange can be effected only if protected by property rights. In other words, without property rights, neither representatives nor citizens would have any incentive to respect their undertakings *vis-à-vis* each other, especially when, as already noted, voters choose between the promises advanced by candidates at discrete time intervals, during which politicians are shielded from citizens.

The vertical and horizontal dimensions of party organization

The absence of easily enforceable contracts between constituent principals and representative agents gives a precise role to political parties in supporting political exchanges that make representative democracy work. More precisely, political parties 'are organizations which make it possible for citizens to exercise some control on the adherence of representatives to their promises, and allow representatives to gain some control on the consistency of support emanating from citizens' (Galeotti and Breton 1986: 54). Because a party is concerned about its long-term survival, it is motivated to control closely the opportunistic behavior of its representatives, and it is also motivated to use many devices to stimulate the active support of otherwise volatile voters; these devices include items such as rallies, canvassing, debates and public meetings. It is these activities that ensure the working of representative politics.[4]

A political party, while acting as guarantor of the *vertical* exchanges between voters and representatives, also develops *horizontal* relationships. This means that within the party, as in any organization, networks of horizontal ties and exchanges are developed which involve the cadres at various levels, and the relationship between leaders, elected representatives and top public positions. This horizontal dimension helps political activity to take place by facilitating the initiatives, agreements, fights and compromises that are everyday news. As with the vertical dimension, the larger the volume of the horizontal one – with its implications in terms of trust and reputation – the lower the cost of transacting among the leadership. We should therefore expect that the stronger these horizontal links, the more coordinated will be the behavior of leading politicians and the purer ideologically will be the political platforms of parties.

There is an important relationship between vertical and horizontal trust. In performing what it is supposed to in the social division of work – 'producing' representation and influencing public options – a party can use various combinations of vertical and horizontal inputs. The first of these 'factors of production' is used for such things as mobilizing public opinion, organizing publicity campaigns or provoking debates on new issues, while the second can be used to suppress a plank from a platform, to establish the predominance of leaders in party affairs or to promote patronage. In other terms, these two inputs can be viewed as technical substitutes in producing a given amount of representation.[5]

It can be shown that a system in which horizontal exchanges prevail over vertical ones leads to different results from those obtainable where instead the reverse occurs. In this way we are provided with an analytical framework fit to interpret a broad range of real-world situations, from the alleged 'phantom' US party to the Leninist organization of communist experience. And it is precisely the combination of these two inputs that determines the working of different political systems. Voters' monitoring and policing costs on one hand and institutional constraints on leaders' behavior on the other are the two basic factors at work. The 'independence' of leaders increases with the strength of the horizontal dimension up to the risky point of reducing the relevance of voters and of bringing about an oligarchic inversion of the logic of representation. In the following section we come to comment on the factors that reinforce the horizontal dimension to the detriment of the vertical one.

The impact of political institutions

It is a matter of empirical observation that politicians and political parties do much more than reflect the views of their supporters. They shape those views in the process of weighing popular approval against the perceived value of proposed policies to politicians themselves. The space for and the coordinates of such behavior are here interpreted in terms of the relative importance of the horizontal vs. the vertical dimension in the organization of political exchanges. Many institutional factors affect the balance of these two dimensions. We skip the most immediate ones – processes of candidates' selection, degree of centralization of party decisions, public financing channeled to national headquarters, etc. – because they simply represent the outcome of more basic influences, such as dimension and centralization of the public sector, electoral rules, parliamentary vs. presidential regimes, number and efficiency of checks and balances. In what follows, the analysis will be dedicated to the first three of these institutional factors.

Centralization and size of the public sector

Strong centralization of public decision making and big dimensions of the public sector affect the balance of vertical vs. horizontal political exchanges by requiring a greater voters' commitment to political parties:

that commitment allows greater scope for interaction between politicians, an interaction which tends to benefit politicians at the expense of voters. That granted, it should follow that public decisions in less centralized countries and involving a smaller budget reflect citizens' opinions more and politicians' wishes less than do centralized systems and bigger budgets.

To see how centralization and size of the public sector influence the bond between constituents and representatives, we have to recall the transactional role performed by political parties. That notion implies that when the number of functions of a certain level of government increases, the appeal to opinions becomes more important and the supporting role performed by political parties more crucial. At the same time, the vaguer the party platform becomes, the more costly it is to see what it implies and to check its coherent application in the compromises and adjustments that characterize political activity. As voters' monitoring and policing costs increase, the contractual role performed by political parties increases as well. Voters have to rely more on the party leadership and that allows the development of stronger horizontal ties inside the party. Alternatively, as the centralization of the public sector increases, and the link between politicians and their supporters tends to become stronger, the costs to voters of working out the views of different parties rise, so voters are likely to change their allegiances less often. This means again that politicians' degree of freedom in interpreting and applying the party ideology to everyday policy issues increases. If we regard *ideology as a political opinion strictly controlled by the party apparatus*, then it can be inferred that the centralization of political decisions favors the 'ideologization' of political platforms. The result we wish to emphasize is that increasing centralization and the size of the public sector bring about greater degrees of freedom enjoyed by politicians in managing the daily articulation of political choices.

Electoral rules

Different electoral rules can encourage either the vertical or the horizontal dimension of exchanges. The main propositions here are that more proportional rules stabilize people's choice (through the strong cultivation of voters' loyalties) and smooth out vote variations, when tranforming them into seat variations. Together these two factors reduce politicians' uncertainty on voters' reaction and combine to reinforce intraparty (horizontal) ties to the detriment of vertical attention to constituents, thus reducing both the competitiveness and the representativeness of the system.

Let us start by observing that electoral rules can magnify or reduce the impact of any vote variation, with differing effects on politicians' behavior. If under the so-called 'cube law' an aggregate variation of 10 percent of the vote induces a variation of seats three times greater, under pure proportionality we would expect fully proportionate variations. If that, by itself, helps to make politicians' lives less uncertain, it is an empirical observation that very often the real-world working of proportional rules can do more than this, by further smoothing out vote variations when transformed into seat variations. Thus, German postwar electoral results (before reunification) show that if one of the two leading parties of the Bundestag faced a loss of 10 percent of votes, it expected to lose 8.45 percent only in terms of seats. This stabilization of electoral results not only reduces the risk for party bosses, but makes the success of individual candidates dependent on the decisions of those very bosses, via the determination of the ranking of candidates on the party list.[6]

However, this is not the entire picture as proportionality helps to *reduce vote mobility* in the first instance. By favoring the contestability of the ideological market, the proportional rule fuels a competition that encourages platform differentiation. It follows that the level of substitution between the various platforms decreases with a greater political fragmentation, and voters find it more difficult to shift their vote from one party to another. As voters are boxed in by their choices, their 'demand' becomes more inelastic with a corresponding increase in the freedom of action enjoyed by politicians. When voters are entrapped, their interparty mobility – the essence of political competition – is greatly reduced. The proposition 'the more the parties, the lower the competition' is developed elsewhere (Galeotti 1991). Here we can recall that when competition is not necessarily for the same carrot (running the government), voters' choice can no longer be based on the simple grounds of efficiency, as implied by Stigler (1972).

The relative low level of vote mobility occurring under proportional rule is supported by several pieces of evidence. Let me mention two of them. First, in a systematic study of a century of European elections Bartolini and Mair (1990: 164) find – contrary to their own expectations – that 'those elections which produce extremely proportional results . . . are characterized by the lowest level of volatility.' Second, Table 8.1 reports the estimated flow of voters staying with the same party choice between two elections for three countries (the USA, the former FRG and Italy), characterized by

Table 8.1 Percentage of voters keeping the same choice between contiguous elections (out of 100 average votes)

USA (Presidential) average 1960–80		West Germany (Bundestag) average 1957–80		Italy (Camera dei Deputati) average 1958–83	
Republican	74.5	CDU	88.1	CDP	94.2
Democratic	78.8	SDP	93.4	Communist Party	95.6
Others/abstentions	89.1	Others/absentions	79.3	Others/absentions	93.7

Source: Galeotti 1991: 123

increasing levels of proportionality (and of centralization of public spending). As the data shows, the level of vote mobility is clearly lower as we move from the USA (about 81 percent of eligible voters repeat on average the same choice between two Presidential elections) to West Germany (about 87 percent) and to Italy (almost 95 percent).

There are many factors indeed that affect ideological reputation and political ties. However, as far as the electoral rules are concerned, we can conclude that proportional rule makes the use of the horizontal 'factor of production' cheaper, with less attention paid to the vertical links with voters. And that is so because, as a firm's brandname capital might allow its products to be trusted and so be less carefully scrutinized by customers, in the same way ideological commitment makes the cost of voters' retaliation (voting for another party) much higher, and this lowers the cost of politicians' shirking.

Concluding remarks: the risk of Michels' disease

In the suggested interpretation, a political party is seen as a quasi-pledge that helps to safeguard a degree of consistency between the expectations that citizens and representatives hold about their reciprocal behavior. Virtues and limits of that supporting function rest upon the combination of vertical and horizontal exchanges that characterize the backbone of party organization. Vertical exchanges materialize the essence of representative relationships between voters and representatives; horizontal exchanges flourish more vigorously when representatives feel somehow shielded from voters' pressure. Different combinations of vertical and horizontal links will give rise to different kinds of political parties. Two polar extremes are grass-root and leader-dominated parties that can be interpreted in terms of weak vs. strong party organization.

As in any organization, vertical trades are efficient from the point of view of the voter/principal, whilst horizontal ones supply a potential space for appropriations by the representative/agent (Wintrobe and Breton 1986): an overexpanded horizontal dimension can degenerate in political collusion. In other words, when horizontal exchanges come to prevail on vertical ones, voters' influence is lower, and the sufficient conditions come to be fulfilled for the formation of political rents. In such an instance, we are facing strong party structures that recall the 'Iron Law of Oligarchy' suggested by Robert Michels (1915, 1962). According to Michels, the need to organize a mass of supporters combines with the growing independence of political leadership up to the point of transforming any democratic organization into the subordination of supporters to a group of leaders.

We have seen how the centralization and the expansion of the public sector, as well as highly proportional rules of election, converge in making voters' mobility more costly and politicians less uncertain about voters' reactions, thus reducing the spur effect of political competition. The notion of weak vs. strong political parties relates to the role the government comes to play in the universe of pressures and conflicts that develops inside the competitive working of the public sector. Contrasts and conflicts among decision centers (namely, the actual working of checks and balances) can be easily mediated to a great degree inside the incumbent party, thanks to the presence of strong horizontal networks. And the ensuing internal and underhand dealings show political parties as a potentially reuniting factor of the fragmentation of power which has evolved with the democratic state.

Notes

1 On this point the exposition will follow a working paper (No. 8409, Department of Economics, University of Toronto, 1984) prepared with Albert Breton.
2 The same point is made by John R. Commons (1934: 1961: 750).
3 Why will rational citizens possess utility functions defined over opinions, instead of over policies? The reasons suggested by Galeotti and Breton (1986: 50–3) relate to the fact that the substitution of opinions for preferences is a rational response to the scarcity and costs of political information.
4 For an empirical support of the suggested interpretation, see Galeotti and Breton (1986).
5 The above analysis is further discussed and developed in Breton and Galeotti (1985).
6 Note that, in general, when moving from single- to multi-member constituencies, the pooling of votes reduces the variance of the expected share of seats.

References

Bartolini, S. and Mair, P. (1990) *Identity, Competition, and Electoral Availability*, Cambridge: Cambridge University Press.

Breton, A. (1974) *The Economic Theory of Representative Government*, Chicago: Aldine.

Breton, A. and Galeotti, G. (1985) 'Is proportional representation always the best electoral rule?', *Public Finance–Finance Publique* 40: 1–16.

Commons, J. R. (1934, 1961) *Institutional Economics: Its Place in Political Economy*, Madison, WI: University of Wisconsin Press.

Downs, A. (1957) *An Economic Theory of Democracy*, New York: Harper & Row.

Galeotti, G. (1991) 'The number of parties and political competition,' in A. Breton, G. Galeotti, P. Salmon and R. Wintrobe (eds), *The Competitive State*, Dordrecht: Kluwer, pp. 113–28.

Galeotti, G. and Breton, A. (1986) 'An economic theory of political parties,' *Kyklos* 39: 47–65.

Michels, R. (1915, 1962) *Political parties*, New York: Free Press.

Mill, J. S. (1863, 1910) *Considerations on Representative Government*, London: J. M. Dent.

Schumpeter, J. A. (1942, 1950) *Capitalism, Socialism and Democracy*, New York: Harper & Row.

Smith, Adam (1776) *An Inquiry Into the Nature and Causes of the Wealth of Nations*, Oxford: Clarendon Press, 1976.

Stigler, G. (1972) 'Economic competition and political competition,' *Public Choice* 13: 91–106.

Wintrobe, R. and Breton, A. (1986) 'Organizational structure and productivity,' *American Economic Review* 76: 530–8.

9 Constitutionally constrained and safeguarded competition in markets and politics

With reference to a European constitution

Viktor Vanberg*

Introduction

The collapse of communism and the demise of socialist central planning have refocused attention on the merits of market principles. Yet, in spite of the apparent general increase in appreciation for markets, it is not quite as obvious how widely the 1. fundamental, as well as the 2. more subtle lessons have been learned that the history of the socialist experiment has to offer. These more fundamental and subtle lessons have to do, in my view, with our understanding of the role of *competition* as an organizing principle in human social affairs. In what follows, I want to develop some thoughts on the functions that competition can serve in social organization, not only in markets but also in the realm of politics. More specifically, I want to discuss this question in a *constitutional* dimension, as an issue that pertains to the ground rules of a socio-economic–political order. After developing the general argument, I shall elaborate on some of its implications for the constitutional choices involved in the process of European integration. My argument falls into three main parts. I shall, first, review some of the familiar arguments on the role of competition in ordinary markets (the first three sections). The second part will be concerned with the role of competition as an organizing principle in politics (the next two sections). In the third and last part I shall examine some implications for European constitutional concerns (the final section).

I shall approach my theme from the perspective of *constitutional political economy*, an emerging field in economics that is primarily associated with the name of James M. Buchanan (Buchanan 1990, 1991).[1] Constitutional political economy takes its departure from a fundamental distinction between levels of choice, a distinction that can be most easily understood by analogy to ordinary games. For ordinary games we can clearly distinguish between the *rules of the game* and the *moves* that players make when playing the game within the agreed-upon rules. We can, accordingly, distinguish between the choice *among* rules and the choice among strategies *within* a given set of rules or, in other terms, between *constitutional choices* and *sub-constitutional choices*. Essentially the same distinction can be made with regard to the 'games of life,' the socio-economic–political arrangements within which persons interact, cooperate and compete.

The principal focus of constitutional political economy is on choices among rules, and on the question of how such choices affect the ways in which 'games' are played. It seeks to examine and compare the working properties of alternative rules, and it explores the question of how persons may come to play a *better game* by agreeing on *better rules*, rules that make the game more desirable for all parties involved.[2] Applied to the case of European integration, a constitutional political economy perspective would seek to examine how the ultimate 'players' in this 'game,' the citizens of Europe, may be affected by alternative constitutional ground rules for a united Europe, and how, through the adoption of suitable rules, the game might be improved for all parties involved.

Competition and markets

If one were to argue to the members of a (hypothetical) European constitutional convention why it would be in their constituents' interests to adopt a constitution that emphasizes competition as an organizing principle, what reasons could one provide in support of such argument? There are, it seems to me, three main arguments, related to three kinds of problems for which competition may provide a remedy, namely, as I shall label them, the *incentive* problem, the *power* problem, and the *knowledge* problem. I shall discuss these arguments, first, in the context in which they are most familiar, namely applied to competition in ordinary markets.

Adam Smith talked about the incentive problem when he noted, in one of his most often quoted statements, that it 'is not from the benevolence of the butcher, the brewer, or the baker, that we expect our dinner, but from their regard to their own interest' (1981: 26f.). Of course, he was very clear about the fact that it is not the butcher's, brewer's, or baker's self-interest *per se* that assures us of their services, but, instead, the constraints that competition imposes on their behavior. It is the necessity to compete for customers that induces suppliers of goods and services to seek to find out, and to satisfy, consumer wants. Competition generates responsiveness to consumer interests; it places – as Franz Böhm, one of the major figures of German Ordo-Liberalism (Vanberg 1990, 1991), has put it – 'the entrepreneur's pursuit of profit in the direct service of the consumer,'[3] or, stated more emphatically, 'competition forms the moral back-bone of a free profit-based economy' (Böhm 1982: 110).

German Ordo-Liberals, like franz Böhm and his colleague at the University of Freiburg, Walter Eucken, emphasized that, in addition to its role as an incentive mechanism, competition also works as a mechanism for limiting and dispersing power.[4] In Böhm's (1961: 22) words, 'competition is the most magnificent and most ingenious instrument for the confinement of power (*Entmachtungsinstrument*) in history.'[5] Competition means availability of alternative counterparts for trade, of alternative sources of supply, a condition that reduces the dependence of consumers on any particular supplier and, thereby, reduces the power that such dependence would provide to the latter.

The last of the three problems that I distinguished before, namely the knowledge problem, has been discussed, in particular, by F. A. Hayek who has stressed that what we may call the 'economic problem of society' is in essence a problem of knowledge: the problem of finding a method that not only best utilizes the knowledge dispersed among the individual members of society, but also best uses their abilities of discovering and exploring new ways of doing things (Hayek 1979: 190).[6] Market competition constitutes an explorative learning process in which continuously new and potentially better solutions to a wide range of problems – from supplying bread or producing computer software to organizing large corporations – are tried out and put to test, under conditions that make for responsiveness to the interests of consumers, the ultimate judges of success and failure. Market competition is, in other words, a knowledge-creating process (Kerber 1991) or a 'process of exploration' (Hayek 1978: 188); it is an open-ended evolutionary process that allows for, and provides incentives for, continuous and countless efforts to come up with better problem solutions than those that are currently available.[7] It is a process that facilitates adaptation in a world in which our knowledge and the problems we face change in ways that can never be fully anticipated, a process that, for these very reasons, by necessity 'always leads to the unknown' (Hayek 1960: 40).[8]

Constitutionally constrained competition

So far, I have left unspecified what I mean by 'competition.' Competition in the most general sense of a process in which different parties seek to obtain something that they all strive for, but that not all can have, is, to be sure, a perennial phenomenon. As long as human wants exceed the means available for their satisfaction – and ever-changing human desires prevent this discrepancy from ever disappearing – there will be competition for 'scarce goods.' This means that we cannot choose to live *without* competition. All we can do is to choose the *ways* in which competition is carried out.[9] And it is only in terms of the latter, not in the presence or absence of competition, that societies differ. In Hobbesian anarchy, 'anything goes' is the order of the day; that is, there are no effective constraints on the ways and means by which persons compete. What we call 'social order' is made possible by effective limits being put on the strategies allowed in competition. Social order means, in other words, that competition is effectively *constrained by rules*. Societies can differ greatly in the nature of these rules, or, as we may call it, in their *competitive order* (*Wettbewerbsordnung*), and these differences can affect significantly their working characteristics. What distinguishes, in this sense, a socialist economy or a mercantilist system (Ekelund and Tollison 1982) from a market economy is not the absence of competition, but the different nature of their respective competitive orders. To seek privileges (monopoly rights) from political authorities, or to stand in waiting lines, are no less methods to compete for scarce goods than is competition through the market-price mechanism. Yet, the working properties of economic systems that employ these different methods of competition will, of course, significantly differ.

When Adam Smith described market competition as 'the obvious and simple system of natural liberty,' he did not mean to imply that competition is *per se* beneficial, irrespective of the ways and means by which it is carried out. Instead, he quite explicitly argued that competition will only work beneficially when carried out within the constraints of *appropriate rules*, within what he called the 'laws of justice.'[10] In his modern restatement of the principles of classical liberalism, F. A. Hayek has equally emphasized that, to operate beneficially, competition is to be 'restrained by appropriate rules of law' (Hayek 1978: 125, 1988: 19), and he has explicitly noted that the fundamental principle of liberalism is misunderstood if it is interpreted 'as absence of state activity rather than as a policy which . . . uses the legal framework enforced by the state in order to make competition as effective and beneficial as possible' (Hayek 1948: 110). To make only the most obvious point, we could compete with each other by means of fraud, threats, and coercion, but we would hardly consider such a competitive regime a desirable social order. Market competition is *constitutionally constrained competition*, competition within rules that serve to enhance its adaptive potential and its responsiveness to consumer interests, or, more briefly, by rules that secure the essential feature of market transactions, *voluntary* trade and contracting.[11]

The German Ordo-Liberals, Walter Eucken, Franz Böhm and others, made it clear that the desirable working properties which the classical liberals had attributed to market competition can only be expected from what they called *Leistungswettbewerb*, competition according to rules which assure, as W. Röpke (1960: 31) worded it, 'that the only road to business success is through the narrow gate of better performance in service of the consumer.'[12] And they emphasized that to create and maintain an appropriate framework or '*Ordnungsrahmen*' for *Leistungswettbewerb* is a genuine and indispensible political task, a task for *Ordnungspolitik* or *constitutional politics*. In fact, they saw a critical deficiency in some of the nineteenth-century interpretations of classical liberal principles in their insufficient recognition of the role of government in maintaining a conducive legal–institutional framework for market competition.[13]

To be sure, what rules are *appropriate* for guiding competition in a desirable direction is a question that cannot be answered once and for all, but needs to be re-examined, at least in some of its aspects, as relevant circumstances change. In this regard we face, as Hayek (1960: 230) argues, a perennial 'task of gradually amending our legal system to make it more conducive to the smooth working of competition.' There is, he notes,

> ample scope for experimentation and improvement within that permanent legal framework which makes it possible for a free society to operate most efficiently. We can probably at no point be certain that we have already found the best arrangements or institutions that will make the market economy work as beneficially as it could.
>
> (ibid.: 231)[14]

Constitutionally safeguarded competition

Beneficially working market competition needs not only *appropriate constitutional constraints*. A related, yet distinguishable, requirement is that a competitive order needs to be *safeguarded* against anti-competitive interests, interests that seek to escape competitive constraints through private arrangements or through political means. Their experience with the cartel problem in the German economy of their time had focused the German Ordo-Liberals' attention mainly on the first of these alternatives, that is the problem of private power. They emphasized that a functioning competitive order not only requires the government to refrain from directly inhibiting competition, but also requires it 'to ensure that the restricting of the market by private pressure groups does not take place' (Eucken 1982: 119). It has to prevent, the Ordo-Liberals argued, that the freedom to contract which is 'obviously central to the realization of a competitive system' is used as an instrument 'to eliminate competition and to establish monopolistic positions' (ibid.: 123).[15] In this context they pointed, in particular, to the problem of distortionary indirect effects that may be caused by legislation in such areas as, for instance, trade policy or patent law.[16]

Though the German Ordo-Liberals were doubtlessly aware of the problem, they concerned themselves less with the issue of how the political process itself may be used to seek protection from competition in the form of subsidies, tax exemptions, tariffs, and import restrictions, as well as all kinds of regulations that create monopoly privileges of various sorts and degrees. To pursue this method for escaping competitive constraints means to lobby for protective legislation, like Frederik Bastiat's famous candel-makers who lobbyied for a building code disallowing windows in order to be protected from the sun's unfair competition. The use of the political 'escape route' from competition has been extensively studied in modern public choice theory under the name of *rent seeking*.[17] I shall concentrate on this part of the issue of anti-competitive strategies.

It helps in understanding the problems that are involved here to recall my earlier distinction between two levels of choice, the *constitutional* and the *sub-constitutional* level, or the choice *among* rules and the choice *within* rules. In analogy to this distinction we can distinguish between two corresponding kinds of interests, namely *constitutional* interests and *sub-constitutional* or *action* interests. The first are our interests with regard to the constitutional regime or the rules under which we would like to live, interests that inform our choices at the constitutional level, for example, when we vote on proposals for constitutional reform. The second are our interests with regard to the alternative strategy options that are available to us within the confines of a *given* constitutional–institutional framework, interests that inform our subconstitutional choices in playing the game within given rules.

The *benefits from competition* that I have discussed before under the rubric of incentive, power and knowledge problems would seem to suggest that it should be in everybody's *constitutional* interest to live in a competitive order and that, therefore, political support for a competitive framework should be easily forthcoming. Yet, this seems to be manifestly contradicted by the pervasiveness of anti-competitive, protectionist rules and regulations, of arrangements, that is, that serve to impede and restrict competition.[18] How can the economist's insight in the productivity of a competitive order and the reality of widespread anti-competitive practices be squared? At least part of the answer to this question can, as I want to suggest, be found in the distinction between *constitutional* and *action* interests.

If we would have to choose to live either in a generally competitive system or, in a system that is immobilized by pervasive anti-competitive regulations and protectionist rules, we would have good reasons to prefer the first environment because it promises to make for a much richer society. Yet, this is not how the choice between competition and protectionism is typically presented to us. And for the choices that we really face, the presence of a *constitutional* preference for a generally competitive over a generally non-competitive environment does not at all mean that we would have no incentives to seek protection against competition for our own particular business or trade. The problem lies, of course, in the fact that there is an asymmetry of interests in the sense that our direct interest is in having others compete, not in us being subject to competitive constraints. In other words, competition is clearly desirable for those who are competed for; it is less desirable for those who have to compete. Or, as Hayek (1979: 77) has noted:

> To those, with whom others compete, the fact that they have competitors is always a nuisance that prevents a quiet life; and such direct effects of competition are always much more visible than the indirect benefits which we derive from it.[19]

If it were possible, we would like to have it both ways: to have our own business or trade protected from competitive pressure, while enjoying the benefits that an otherwise competitive environment has to offer. And, conversely, we would certainly not want to be the only ones who have to compete, while all others on whose services we depend would be protected from competition.

Protectionist legislation is a discriminatory practice. It grants privileges to some, but not to others. Where such *differential treatment* or *discrimination* is practiced, where some may enjoy protection while others have to compete, we have a reason to wish to be among the former. By contrast, in a system that would not allow for any privileges, that would rule out such discriminatory treatment, and where, therefore, protectionist provisions could only be legislated as a *general principle*, granted either to each and every business or trade or to nobody at all, in such a system our preferences would be clearly different. Protection is only advantageous if one is the beneficiary of discriminatory treatment, not if it were practiced as a general rule. In other words, producer interests in protectionist privileges cannot be generalized; they are *not compatible* across the polity. A generalized protectionist system would be desirable for nobody. By contrast, what can be generalized and what is compatible across the polity are our interests as consumers. And what can be beneficially practiced as a general principle is a competitive order that serves these *consumer interests*. This can be seen as the rationale behind the concept of consumer sovereignty, a rationale that Böhm appealed to when he noted that consumer interests are 'the sole directly justifiable economic interests.'[20] To be constrained by competition is not something that we like *per se*; it is, however, a price that we would most certainly be willing to pay if it were the entrance requirement to a system where everyone else is equally subject to the discipline of competition.

That our generalized consumer interests apparently have not prevailed is due to the fact that in the world 'as it is,' the political process has allowed for discriminatory treatment, thus inviting the whole set of problems that, as I mentioned before, public choice economists have discussed under the rubric of rent-seeking (Buchanan *et al.* 1980, Buchanan 1993).[21] In such a world, to seek protection is – in the terminology of game theory – the dominant choice in a prisoners' dilemma type of setting, resulting in an overall outcome that, in the end, makes all parties – the beneficiaries of existing protection included – worse off than they could be in an open, competitive environment (Vanberg 1992b). As long as discriminatory or privileged treatment can be obtained from governments and legislators, there will be rent seeking or special–interest lobbying, and in each case explanations will be readily produced for why, in the particular instance, the public interest was served by granting the privilege in question. It is difficult to see how this problem may be remedied in any way other than depriving legislators and governments of their *authority* and their *power* to discriminate. There are two principal means by which this can be brought about. Governments can be deprived from such authority through appropriate, explicit constitutional provisions. And they can be deprived from such power through the discipline of intergovernmental competition, an issue to which I shall return later.

Constitutional choice and political process

So far I have discussed reasons why citizens of a polity may wish to rely on market competition as an organizing principle. I have discussed reasons why competition needs to be *constrained* by appropriate rules if it is to work to the general benefit of all parties involved. And I have argued why a competitive order needs constitutional *safeguards* against anti-competitive interests. In other words, I have provided reasons why competition may be a desirable organizing principle, and why it needs to be embedded in an appropriate constitutional framework or *Ordnungsrahmen*, the maintenance of which is a genuine political task.

To recognize the role of politics in creating and maintaining the institutional–constitutional framework within which markets operate means, of course, to raise another question, namely whether and, if so, under what conditions we may expect the political process to produce an 'appropriate Ordnungsrahmen,' a framework that suitably conditions and safeguards a competitive market order. The obvious starting point in examining this question is the fact that the political, rule-producing process itself operates under *rule constraints*, notably those that are specified in the 'constitution' in the standard, narrower sense of the term. Yet, the political process is subject to *competitive constraints* as well, and its working properties will clearly depend on the nature of both kinds of constraints. They determine, in particular, the extent to which the process can be expected to work to the benefit of its constituents, the citizens.

From a constitutional economics perspective, the issue at hand can be stated in terms of the following question: in drafting the constitution of a united Europe, what principles or devices might the citizens of Europe wish to include, in order to make the political process more responsive to their, the citizens', interests? In other words, what constitutional provisions would promise to make the political process operate in ways that are desirable from the citizens' perspective? There are, to be sure, many elements of the Western constitutional tradition that are relevant in this context, and that have been discussed in such more recent contributions as Harold Berman's *Law and Revolution* (1983), Erik Jones' *The European Miracle* (1987) or N. Rosenberg and I. Birdzell's *How the West Grew Rich* (1986).[22] Staying within my chosen theme, I shall concentrate on the role of *competition* in the realm of politics or, more precisely, on the role of *market-type* competition in politics.

When we speak of competition in politics we can mean two different things: namely, on the one hand, competition *for* or *within* government and, on the other hand, competition *between* governments. Competition for government is competition for votes, competition between parties and candidates to be elected into political office. As competition within government we can describe the system of checks and balances between different branches and levels of government. The rules of competition for and within government are a principal subject of constitutions in the standard sense. And it is through these rules that democratic systems of government seek to make office holders responsive to their constituents' interests. Competition between governments is competition for citizens or, more generally, for resources that governments want to attract to their jurisdiction (Sinn 1992).[23]

Competition *between* governments can be compared to ordinary market competition between firms,[24] even though, to be sure, an obvious difference lies in the *territorial nature* of governments.[25] When a dissatisfied customer of an ordinary market firm decides to take his or her business elsewhere, this has normally little impact on other parts of the customer's life. By contrast, when a dissatisfied citizen wants to 'choose' a different government – not by marking a ballot, but by his or her individual and separate choice to get out from under the authority of a particular government[26] – this citizen has to physically move from one jurisdiction to another, a transaction that can be very costly. Because such a choice typically involves significant costs, the conclusion is frequently drawn, prematurely in my view, that market-type competition cannot be of much relevance in the political realm.

It is certainly true that the costs of migrating between jurisdictions tend to be typically high, compared to the costs of moving between alternative suppliers in ordinary markets. Yet, before any conclusions concerning the effectiveness of competition between governments are drawn, a number of things ought to be considered. First of all, relevant for market-type competition between governments is not only the migration of persons–taxpayers, but also the migration of taxable resources, in particular capital. Migration costs are typically lower for resources than for persons, and the lower their migration costs are, the more governments are under competitive constraints in their treatment of these resources. Financial capital has become enormously mobile in today's world, with predictable consequences for intergovernmental competition. Governments may be able to exploit capital that has been sunk in their jurisdiction, but they can do so only at the expense of their capability to attract financial investments in the future.[27]

Second, migration costs for persons–taxpayers can vary considerably. They vary, most obviously, with the size of jurisdictions. Moving between local communities is less costly than moving between states in a federation and the latter is less costly than moving between nation–states.[28] Furthermore, they vary among citizens and, just as in ordinary markets, it is not necessary for all customers/citizens to respond to unsatisfactory performance to make competition effective. A sufficient number of 'marginal citizens,' that is of citizens for whom the choice between jurisdictions is associated with lower costs, can significantly increase the responsiveness of governments to citizens' interests, just like a sufficient number of 'marginal customers' can make firms more responsive than they would otherwise be.

Third, and most importantly, migration costs are to some extent a function of conditions that are subject to constitutional choice, that is conditions that can be influenced by political decisions. If we know, for instance, that a decentralized, federal organization tends to reduce these costs, then choosing such a constitutional arrangement can be an instrument to increase the effectiveness of intergovernmental competition and, thus, the responsiveness of governments (Lowenberg and Yu 1992). To sum up, market-type competition between governments can be – and can be made to be – a more important mechanism than may appear on first glance, an insight that hardly surprises anybody who still remembers the not so distant past when communist regimes made extraordinary efforts to keep their 'subjects' from choosing for themselves, by migrating, a different government.

There are two notes that I want to add here to my previous comments on intergovernmental competition. First, in ordinary market competition, there is a 'symmetry' between exit and entry in the sense that an alternative seller is readily available for whatever goods or services the firm from which one walks away provides. For polities such symmetry does not necessarily exist,[29] yet the option to exit is, for obvious reasons, not worth very much if one is not allowed entry into some other polity. If the right to exit is to work as an effective constraint on government, there have to be entry options available. Persons who want to adopt a constitutional framework that induces responsive governments should, therefore, have a constitutional interest in provisions that secure free exit and entry between polities, provisions that can be the subject of a federal constitution or some other contractual commitment among several polities.[30]

Second, to the extent that a federal government must be given authority and power to enforce the rules of intergovernmental competition *vis-à-vis* the member–states, the problem of how such power can be effectively controlled and limited arises, of course, anew at the federal level. While being intended to limit the power of the member – states by securing competition among them, the federal government may itself become, now on larger scale, a source of the very same problems that it is supposed to remedy with regard to the former. At the federal level these problems may even be magnified, since with increasing size of the polity the effectiveness of both voice and exit tends to decrease. It is as a safeguard against unresponsive federal government that the collective analog to individual exit, namely *secession*, may be an essential ingredient of a constitution for an effectively *limited* federal government. As an instrument to induce responsive government, the right of subunits to secede from inclusive polities would seem to be a natural complement to the individual's right to exit. This right should be of particular significance for groups that have particularly strong ties to their particular living environment, be it for cultural, ethnic, or whatever reasons. To such groups, the option to walk away from an undesired government and to move into another jurisdiction may have little appeal. The presence of such ties – they are clearly a much more significant factor in Europe than, for instance, in the United States – obviously increases exit costs and, thereby, the degree to which a government can neglect the interests of those who have these preferences. The reduced effectiveness of exit can, in such cases, be compensated by the right of territorially defined subgroups to exit from a given jurisdiction, either to join another polity or to constitute a jurisdiction of its own. Switzerland provides an example for how such a device can work in a polity that is divided into many groups with their own cultural and ethnic identities. The rules for the Swiss confederation allow for parts of cantons to split off and to form a new canton, an option that seems to have helped to pre-empt or to solve conflicts that otherwise might have become much more troublesome.[31]

Competition between governments

After having introduced the notion of intergovernmental competition I want to examine more closely the role it may play in the realm of politics. More specifically, I want to argue that *citizens* can benefit from such competition in essentially the same ways in which consumers can benefit from competition between firms in ordinary markets. In the political realm, just as in ordinary markets, competition can provide a remedy for the three types of problems that I discussed earlier: the *incentive* problem, the *power* problem, and the *knowledge* problem.

The relevance of intergovernmental competition for the incentive problem has been already pointed out in what I said before. I can, therefore, be brief here and just note that we would naturally expect governments that have to compete for citizens–taxpayers to be more responsive to their constituents' interests than governments that are not subject to the discipline of such competition. As Dye (1990: 15) summarizes:

> Competition in the private marketplace forces sellers to become sensitive to preferences of consumers. Competition among governments forces public officials to become sensitive to the preferences of citizens. Lessened competition in the marketplace results in higher prices, reduced output, and greater inefficiency in production. Lessened competition among governments results in higher taxes, poorer performance and greater inefficiencies in the public sector.

The conclusion with regard to the power problem should likewise be obvious. The lower the costs at which citizens can remove themselves and/

or their resources from any given jurisdiction, the less power the government of that jurisdiction will have over those persons. The notion that the right and the capacity of individuals to move with their resources between jurisdictions impose effective constraints on the power of governments has, for obvious reasons, been an important theme in discussions on federalism in general, and on fiscal federalism in particular (Marlow 1992, Brennan and Buchanan 1980: 168ff.). In his 1939 article on 'The economic conditions of interstate federalism' Hayek (1948: 255–72) noted that the free movements of men and capital within a federation 'limit to a great extent the scope of the economic policy of the individual states' (p. 258) and that, as a consequence, 'much of the interference with economic life to which we have become accustomed will be altogether impracticable under a federal organization' (p. 265).

This is, perhaps, a good place to add a remark on the general issue of limiting the power of government, because the emphasis on this issue may not be entirely plausible to someone whose focus is on the government's capacity to carry out its intended functions. If we look at the relation between citizens and government as a principal–agent relationship, we can certainly assume that the principals, the citizens, have an interest in a government that is powerful enough to carry out its assigned task. Yet, we can also assume that the principals–citizens will be concerned about the possibility that the power transfered to government may be used in ways that violate their interests, either in the form of direct misuse of power on the part of the agents, or by other groups who use the political process for exploitative purposes, as an instrument of rent seeking.[32] It is as a protection against such risks that constitutions are supposed to serve, and competition among governments is a provision that reinforces such protection.[33]

The third problem, the knowledge problem, has received less attention in discussion on the role of competition among governments than the other two, but it is no less important.[34] What has been said, in this regard, about the role of competition in markets can also be said about its role in the realm of politics.[35] Without the possibility of experimenting and exploration, and without competition between alternative potential solutions, we could not know what constitutional arrangements or political regimes are better equipped to serve the interests of constituents than others. To be sure, history provides us with rich evidence on what kinds of constitutional arrangements seem to have worked to the benefit of their respective constituents, and it provides us with, perhaps, even richer evidence on what has not worked. Yet, in a changing world and with changing knowledge, the need for exploration in institutional–constitutional matters has certainly not yet come to an end (Vanberg 1990, 1992a).

It should be understood, of course, that experimenting and diversity in constitutional matters is not an end in itself, just as experimenting and diversity is not *per se* an indication of good performance and responsiveness in ordinary markets. Competition can lead to a *de facto* dominance of particular kinds of problem–solutions in markets, as a result of consumer choice. The absence of visible experimenting and diversity in such cases need not at all reflect a neglect of consumer interests. In the same sense, competition between governments may well produce a *de facto* 'harmonization' of institutional–constitutional provisions in certain areas, as a consequence of citizens' revealed preferences, and in such cases the lack of experiments and diversity would not be a reason for alarm. Yet, such *ex post* 'harmonization' that is produced by a competitive process is strictly to be distinguished from legislated *ex ante* harmonization. What is essential, in both contexts, is the *possibility* for experimenting and diversity, and the absence of monopoly privileges and regulatory provisions that rule out such experimenting and diversity (Donges *et al.* 1992).

It should also be understood, that, when I speak of institutional–constutional exploration, I mean *parallel* as opposed to *consecutive* experimenting. Experimenting in ordinary markets is, in this terminology, parallel experimenting in the sense that alternative solutions to problems are tried out simultaneously, providing market participants the opportunity to, more or less directly, compare the attributes of relevant alternatives. Intergovernmental competition provides, in the political realm, a similar opportunity for parallel experimenting and diversity, and allows citizens to, more or less directly, compare the working properties of alternative institutional–constitutional arrangements. Sometimes the notion of experimenting in the political realm is also meant in the sense of what I call consecutive experimenting. Under such a label I classify the trying of alternative institutional–constitutional arrangements over time, that is consecutive changes in the 'rules of the game' that are adopted in a particular polity.[36] Even if carried out by a perfectly responsive government, consecutive experimenting cannot generate the information that would allow for a comparison among institutional–constitutional alternatives in the way that parallel experimenting does.

Competition between governments cannot only be said to help solve the same kinds of problems that market competition does; it is also subject to the same kind of qualifications as the latter. Its working properties depend, as much as the working properties of markets, on the presence of appropriate institutional–constitutional constraints. In both cases, what we mean by competition is *constitutionally constraint competition*. In markets these constraints restrict the strategies that market participants may use in their competitive efforts. In the political realm they restrict the strategies that governments are to employ in their competition for citizens–taxpayers and their resources.[37] These rules may concern such more obvious things as the exclusion of certain inhibitions or barriers to the movement of persons and resources, as well as such matters like, for instance, the use of special subsidies or the granting of special privileges to attract business investments. And they may concern, more generally, problems of externalities between jurisdictions within a federation. For intergovernmental competition to work as an inducement for responsive government, the 'rules of the game' ought to ensure *accountability* in the sense that the costs and benefits of policy choices of state and local governments are borne by the citizens–taxpayers in the respective juridiction. This principle implies that distortions of such accounting – as they are introduced, for instance, by federal transfer programs – undermine the very foundations on which the competition between jurisdictions rests.[38] It also implies, on the other hand, that *policy coordination* may be required in areas, such as environmental policies, in which positive externalities make policies profitable for more inclusive polities that would not be undertaken by smaller jurisdictions.

To provide an appropriate institutional–constitutional framework or *Ordnungsrahmen* for ordinary market competitions is, as I stated earlier, a problem that has no simple and final solution in a world in which the problems that we face and our knowledge of how to deal with these problems constantly change. It requires the continuous efforts of an adequate constititional politics or *Ordnungspolitik*. The same is true, and for the same reasons, with regard to the creation and maintenance of an appropriate institutional–constitutional framework or *Ordnungsrahmen* for intergovernmental competition. This too requires the continuous efforts of an adequate *federal Ordnungspolitik*.

Furthermore, a competitive order in the realm of politics is in need of *constitutional safeguards* against anti-competitive interests, no less so than the competitive order of the market. Politicians, like anybody else, do not like to be subject to competitive restraints, and they are no less tempted than others to seek relief from competitive pressure.[39] Competition in ordinary markets is there to benefit consumers, not to please business-people. And competition between governments is there to benefit citizens, not to please politicians. Just as consumer interests are the only directly justifiable economic interests, so citizens' interests are the only directly justifiable interests in politics. The appropriate measuring rod for the desirability of the institutional–constitutional order of markets is its effectiveness in making suppliers responsive to consumer interests or, in other words, its effectiveness in enhancing consumer sovereignty. The appropriate measuring rod for the desirability of the institutional–constitutional order of politics is its effectiveness in making governments responsive to citizens or, in other words, its effectiveness in enhancing citizen sovereignty. Competition between firms and governments is desirable because it makes for responsiveness to consumers' and citizens' interests. And it is for the sake of consumers' and citizens' interests that competition needs constitutional safeguards in both arenas against the inclinations of those who would rather do without.

A European constitution: between centralist and competitive federalism

When I speak of a European constitution I do so not in reference to a particular document but in a more general sense, refering to the set of ground rules that define the relations among, and the division of rights between, the citizens and the various levels of government in a united Europe. I want to constrast here two different paradigms that can be applied to this issue, paradigms that reflect fundamentally different concepts of what the creation of a federal Europe ought to be about, namely *centralist federalism* on the one side, and *competitive federalism* on the other (Dye 1990, Buchanan 1992). These two concepts are, to be sure, not meant to be descriptive of existing federal structures. They are, as I said, meant as *paradigms*, as principles that can be conceptually separated, even if empirically they can only be found in various kinds of mixtures. Nevertheless, their explicit conceptual separation is helpful for analytical purposes in providing a foil against which existing arrangements as well as constitutional proposals can be evaluated.

According to the centralist paradigm, to create a united federal Europe means to organize the polity 'Europe' after the model of the nation state; it means to form a federal government in the image of traditional national governments. The essence of such a process of integration would be to institute, at the federal, European level, authorities that replace their respective counterparts at the national level. In other words, in forming the union, the national governments transfer part of their authority or sovereignty to a central European agency, like, for instance, the transfer of monetary authority from national central banks to a European central bank. By contrast, according to the competitive paradigm, the principal subject of a European constitution would be the exchange of commitments among the member nations, their joint commitment to rules that serve to constrain what the national governments are permitted to do in their dealings with each other, with third parties and, most importantly, in relation to their citizens and lower-level governments. Such joint commitments would constitute what I refered to earlier as a framework or *Ordnungsrahmen* for intergovernmental competition, a competitive order or *Wettbewerbsordnung* for governments.

By contrast to its centralist counterpart, competitive federalism means that, in forming the union, the national governments retain their authority in whatever area of politics is concerned, whether monetary or otherwise, but jointly submit to certain constraining rules that define the terms under which they can compete in the respective area of activity, rules that may need to be enforced by federal agencies, like, in particular, a federal court. In the case of monetary politics this could mean, for instance, that the national governments submit to a system of competing currencies, an arrangement under which they retain their monetary authority but submit to rules that impose on them the *discipline of competition.*

As I already indicated, by drawing this distinction I do not want to suggest that a federation needs to be based either on the one or the other principle. The creation of a federal union will always include both components. My point, however, is that the *emphasis* can be more on one or the other principle, and that the nature of a federal union can be critically different, depending on where the overall weight lies. To be sure, under both principles the national governments will have to sacrifice part of their power. But this 'sacrifice' means totally different things if the one rather than the other principle is applied. Under *centralist* federalism authority is shifted from one political agency to another, from the national governments to a central government, increasing the degree of political centralization. Under *competitive* federalism the power that national governments will have to sacrifice is not shifted to some other governmental authority but is, instead, dissipated in a competitive arrangement. It returns, in effect, to the ultimate sovereigns, the individual citizens whose choice options are increased compared to the previous national constitutional arrangement.

A concern that is sometimes voiced with regard to the process of European integration is the 'loss of national sovereignty,' a notion that is fundamentally ambiguous in a way instructive for the present theme. As an example, under both arrangements, the creation of a single European central bank as well as a system of competing currencies, the power of national governments in monetary matters would be diminished. Yet, this reduction in power would come, as indicated above, in two critically different forms. While the creation of a European monetary monopoly requires a sacrifice of 'national sovereignty' (in the sense that a matter over which the national governments had control becomes subject to a federal authority), it is clearly misleading to say the same could not be said about a system of competing currencies. The latter arrangement would not involve any transfer of 'sovereignty' between political bodies. It would simply mean that national monetary politics became subject to the discipline of competition. If, for instance, the German mark were to emerge as the leading currency in a competitive arrangement, this would not mean that any other nation would have been made to yield its sovereignty in monetary matters to the German Bundesbank. Whatever leading role the German mark would be able to play would be the result of its market performance and would be strictly contingent on such continued performance. Like all other national currencies the German mark would be subject to constraints that are not imposed by any political authority but result from the choices of market participants. No transfer of national sovereignty, in any meaningful sense, would be involved. Instead, what would occur under a competitive regime is a shift of power from governments back to their citizens whose freedom of choice would be enlarged. By contrast, the creation of a single European central bank clearly requires a sacrifice and transfer of national sovereignty.

I have chosen the example of monetary organization only as an illustration of the general point that I want to make. While both principles, *centralist* and *competitive* federalism, mean a decrease in the power of national governments, the competitive variety does so to the beenfit not of some other political authority but of the individual citizens.[40] This relates to another issue that I want to mention, if only briefly. The welfare gains that a competitive federalism promises have two principal sources, the creation of a larger market due to the removal of trade barriers between the member nations, and the deregulation at the national level, induced by intergovernmental competition. In this sense, one might say that competitive federalism provides a remedy for the protectionist and regulatory ballast that rent-seeking efforts have accumulated over time at the level of the nation state, a ballast that considerably impedes economic activity. Yet, the creation of federal authorities may, of course, create new targets for rent seeking at the federal level (Vaubel 1992), and to the extent that this occurs, an emergence of protectionist or regulatory provisions at this level may be observed along with the deregulation that the federal unit induces at the national level. Whether such counteracting tendencies occur, and how quick the buildup of protectionist and regulatory provisions at the federal level may be, will depend, of course, on the authority that a federal government will command. The danger of a re-emergence of rent seeking at the European level will clearly be less if the federal constitutional structure is closer to the competitive than to the centralist end of the spectrum.

The nation state became the target for rent-seeking activities because it had and has the authority to legislate discriminatory treatment in the sense explained before, the authority to grant privileges through protection and regulation, to selectively provide protection. A reversal of this process by way of constitutional reform at the national level seems unlikely. Its reversal through intergovernmental competition in a European constitution context may be the only realistic hope. Yet, if a European government is given the same authority, it will inevitably follow the same path that the nation-states went, and any welfare gain that a European union may produce will be temporary only, until the deregulation effects at the national level will be offset by new regulations at the federal level. If the gains that a competitive federalism promises are to be permanently secured, a necessary requirement would seem to be to withhold from a European government the legislative authority that made the national governments the target of rent-seeking efforts.

Conclusion

It seems that many of the concerns that have been voiced after 'Maastricht' are concerns about dangers and problems that are immanent to a centralist federalism,[41] dangers and problems that need not at all be associated with a competitive federalism. The prospects of gains that a competitive federalism would have to offer to the citizens of Europe are considerable, while its demands on the scope and authority of a central federal government are relatively modest and, in any case, significantly less than what a centralist federalism would require. While offering all the benefits of an open competitive system, competitive federalism requires less in terms of 'national sovereignty' that the member countries would need to transfer to central authorities, and it puts lesser demands on what the parties forming the federal union would have to agree upon, a fact that would make, among other things, the integration of new members like, for instance, the new democracies in central and eastern Europe a much easier task. The essential authority that is required for a central government in a competitive federalism is the ability to enforce the constitutional commitments to the rules of a competitive order.

The fact that a competitive federalism puts lesser demands on what its members would have to agree upon is not a small advantage. What may have been lacking in the process by which European integration has been orchestrated is a sufficient appreciation of the essential differences between constitutional choice and ordinary politics, differences that concern, in particular, the much greater need for securing a broad consensus in the former as compared to the latter. Where the ground rules for the operation of a polity are to be chosen, and this is what the creation of a united Europe is ultimately about, broad agreement among the ultimate sovereigns, the citizens, is an essential prerequisite for stability and viability, a prerequisite that would seem to limit, at the same time, the constitutional framework to general principles that are genuinely agreeable.

Notes

* I am indebted to James M. Buchanan and Peter Bernholz for helpful comments on an earlier draft.
1 See also the journal *Constituional Political Economy* edited by my colleague Richard E. Wagner and myself.
2 Constitutional economics has affinities to a contractarian or 'social contract' philosophy taking the persons involved in an institutional–constitutional arrangement as the ultimate judges of what is desirable, and considering agreement among these persons as the ultimate source of legitimacy.
3 With reference to the classical liberal critique of a producer-oriented system of privileges and monopoly, F. Böhm (1982: 109) notes:

> The quest for profit ought not to operate to the detriment of a helpless consumer tied to the apron-strings of the producers. On the contrary, the consumers should be liberated and enabled to choose from among the suppliers the ones who met their requirements most thoroughly and willingly. This link between the profit motive and competition placed the entrepreneur's pursuit of profit in the direct service of the consumer. Only those with something to offer the consumers could realize a gain and this in turn became an

automatic, precise and sensitive criterion for assessing a producer's economic qualities.

4 Böhm (1980: 202): 'Daher die große Bedeutung, die dem *Wettbewerb* zukommt, der keineswegs nur ein Leistungsansporn, sondern vor allem auch ein *Entmachtungsinstrument* ist.'

5 W. Eucken (1982: 123) argued similarly: 'It is only under a competitive system that the much cited proposition applies: private property benefits not only the owner but also the non-owner.' F. A. Hayek (1978: 35) has pointed in the same direction when he notes that 'we need the general practice of competition to prevent abuse of property.'

6 Hayek (1978: 149): '[C]ompetition is the most effective discovery procedure which will lead to the finding of better ways for the pursuit of human aims.'

7 The effectiveness of functioning competitive markets in catering to consumer preferences is, as Hayek (1979: 75) points out, 'demonstrated by the difficulty of discovering opportunities for making a living by serving the customers better than is already being done.'

8 Hayek (1948: 101):

The solution of the economic problem of society is in this respect always a voyage of exploration into the unknown, an attempt to discover new ways of doing things better than they have been done before. This must always remain so as long as there are any economic problems to be solved at all, because all economic problems are created by unforeseen changes which require adaptation.

9 In A. Alchian's (1977: 127) words:

'In *every* society conflicts of interest among members of that society must be resolved. The process by which that resolution (not elimination!) occurs is known as *competition*. Since, by definition, there is no way to eliminate competition, the relevant question is what kind of competition shall be used in the resolution of the conflicts of interest.'

10 In reference to well-meant but misguided governmental interventions in the economy A. Smith (1981: 687) notes:

All systems either of preference or of restraint, therefore, being thus completely taken away, the obvious and simple system of natural liberty establishes itself of its own accord. Every man, as long as he does not violate the laws of justice, is left perfectly free to pursue his own interest his own way, and to bring both his industry and capital into competition with those of any other man, or order of men.

11 As F. Knight (1982: 449) phrased it:

A free market means simply . . . that every man as buyer or seller (or potentially one or the other) is in a position to offer terms of exchange to every other, and any pair are free to agree on the most favorable terms acceptable for both parties.

L. von Mises (1940: 261) argues similarly:

Wettbewerb äussert sich auf dem Markte in der Weise, daß die Käufer den übrigen Kauflustigen durch das Angebot höherer Preise, und daß die Verkäufer den übrigen Verkaufslustigen durch das Fordern niedrigerer Preise bei gleicher Leistung oder durch Erhöhung der Leistung bei gleicher Preisforderung zuvor-zukommen haben.'

12 A beneficially working market economy requires, as W. Röpke (1949: 76) notes, 'Maßnahmen und Institutionen, die dem Wettbewerb denjenigen Rahmen, diejenigen Spielreglen und denjenigen Apparat unparteiischer Überwachung dieser Spielregeln geben, denen der Wettbewerb so gut wie ein Wettspiel bedarf, wenn er nicht in eine wüste Schlägerei ausarten soll.'

13 Böhm (1980: 200) notes on this issue:

Denn eine rational ablaufende Marktwirtschaft kommt nich etwa dadurch zustande, daß man durch Gesetz die Gewerbefreiheit einführt und sodann die Dinge laufen läßt, wie sie laufen. Vielmehr fordert dieses sich selbst steuernde System das Vorhandensein und die dauernde Pflege und Verbesser-ung einer ganzen Reihe von politischen, rechtlichen, sozialen, zivilisatorischen Vorbedingung, das Vorhandensein einer ziemlich hochgezüchteten sozialen Parklandschaft.'

Röpke (1942: 364) had argued similarly about a 'desirable economic constitution':

Kern dieser Wirtschaftsverfassung wird . . . der freie Markt und der unver-fälschte Wettbewerb sein müssen, in dem sich unter fairen und glcichen Bedin-gungen des Wettkampfes der privatwirtschaftliche Erfolg nach der Höhe der Leistung für die Konsumenten bemißt (*Leistungswettbewerb*). Freier Markt und Leistungswettbewerb stellen sich jedoch nicht . . . von selbst als Ergebnis eines völlig passiven Verhaltens des Staates ein . . . Sie sind vielmehr ein außerordentlich gebrechliches und von vielen Bedingungen abhängiges Kunst-produkt, das . . . einen Staat voraussetzt, der . . . fortgesetzt für die Aufrech-terhaltung von Marktfreiheit und Wettbewerb sorgt, indem er das notwendige Rahmenwerk des Rechts und der Institutionen schafft.

See also Röpke (1949: 75): 'Eine lebensfähige und befriedigende Markt-wirtschaft entsteht nämlich nicht dadurch, daß wir geflissentlich nichts tun. Sie ist vielmehr ein kunstvolles Gebilde und ein Artefakt der Zivilisation.'

14 In critical reference to certain 'laissez-faire' versions of liberalism Hayek (1948: 111) has noted:

Where the traditional discussion becomes so unsatisfactory is where it is suggested that, with the recognition of the principles of private property and freedom of contract . . . all the issues were settled, as if the law of property and contract were given once and for all in its final and most appropriate form, i.e. in the form which will make the market economy work at its best. It is only after we have agreed on these principles that the real problems begin.

On a version of liberalism that he considers more appropriate Hayek (1959: 594) comments:

Der neue Liberalismus unterscheidet sich vom alten vor allem darin, daß er sich des engen wechselseitigen Zusammenhangs zwischen wirtschaftlichen und poli-tischen Institutionen bewußter ist . . . vor allem auch, daß das befriedigende Funktionieren der *Wettbewerbswirtschaft* ganz bestimmte Erfordernisse bezü-glich des rechtlichen Rahmenwerkes stelle . . . An die Stelle der irreführend gewesenen Formel 'Laissez faire' trat das ausdrückliche Bemühen um eine Gestaltung der Rechtsordnung, die der Erhaltung und dem ersprießlichen Wirken des Wettbewerbs günstig ist und das Entstehen von privaten Machtpositionen sowohl auf der Seite der Unternehmer wie der Arbeiter zu verhindern sucht.

15 Eucken (1952: 275f.): 'Vertragsfreiheit is offensichtlich eine Voraussetzung für das Zustandekommen der Konkurrenz. . . . Aber Vertragsfreiheit hat auch dazu gedient, um Konkurrenz zu beseitigen, um monopolistiche Positionen herzustellen oder auch um sie zu sichern und auszunutzen.' The Ordo-Liberals' concern with this issue is, in Eucken's (1952: 267) account, in contrast to the politics of laissez-faire, 'in der private Machtgruppen das Recht hatten, sich nicht nur zu konstituieren, sondern auch ihre Märkte mit Kampfmitteln zu schließen.'

16 Eucken (1982: 120) notes on this issue: 'In many sectors of German industry, cartels would disappear immediately if tariffs were to go. . . . Despite certain legal precautions, patent law has unexpectedly triggered powerful tendencies towards the formation of monopolies and concentration processes in industry.'

17 Despite the differences in emphasis between German Ordo-Liberals and public choice theorists, the problem of rent seeking would not have been a matter of controversy. What might have been controversial is the tendency among the latter to be much less concerned than the Ordo-Liberals with the problems of monopoly in particular, and private power in general. Hayek (1979: 73) points to the issue that is at stake here when he notes that monopoly power has to be differently judged when it is gained by serving 'customers better than anyone else, and not by preventing those who think they could do still better from trying so.' Monopoly power, Hayek (ibid.) adds, 'does not constitute a privilege so long as the inability of others to do the same is not due to their being prevented from trying.'

18 Note that I mean, of course, fundamentally different things when I talk about *constraining* competition on the one side, and *restricting* competition on the other. While the first is about the 'how' of competition, the second is about the 'how much,' and while the first must be a necessary requirement for beneficially working market competition, the second works as an inhibition on competition. I should add, though, that this distinction may be often more difficult to apply in practice than it can be stated conceptually. The difficulties that may exist in political practice reliably to distinguish provisions that *restrict* competition from those that serve to *constrain* competition invite, of course, attempts of anti-competitive interests to camouflage their intentions to restrict competition to their favor as concerns for generally desirable constraints.

19 Hayek's above quote continues:

> In particular, the direct effects will be felt by the members of the same trade who see how competition is operating, while the consumer will generally have little idea to whose actions the reduction of prices or the improvement in quality is due.
>
> (1979: 77)

Böhm (1980: 209) comments on this issue:

> Denn die Marktwirtschaft ist eine Ordnung, die den Unternehmer zum Nutzen der ganzen Gesellschaft steuert, nicht eine Ordnung, in der die Gesellschaft den undomestizierten Interessen der Unternehmer huldigt. Die Unternehmer freuen sich immer des Gewinns, was ihr gutes Recht ist; aber sie freuen sich keineswegs immer der Marktkontrollen und befinden sich bei dem Versuch, sich ihnen zu entziehen, durchaus nicht in Übereinstimmung mit der Gesellschaft.

20 Franz Böhm (1982: 107): 'The fundamental assumptions on which the teachings of the classical economists hung were that . . . the consumer's interests represented the sole directly justifiable economic interests and that in particular the producer's interests . . . rested on a *derived* economic justification.' What Böhm has in mind here is, specifically, the following passage from A. Smith's (1979: 660) *Wealth of Nations*:

> Consumption is the sole end and purpose of all production; and the interest of the producer ought to be attended to, only so far as it may be necessary for promoting that of the consumer. The maxim is so perfectly self-evident, that it would be absurd to attempt to prove it. But in the mercantile system, the interest of the consumer is almost constantly sacrificed to that of the producer; and it seems to consider production, and not consumption, as the ultimate end and object of all industry and commerce.

21 For an exemplification of this issue see G. Habermann's (1990) study of the German '*Handwerksordnung*' (Crafts Regulation Act).
22 For a brief discussion see Vanberg (1992a).
23 For a comparative discussion of the two kinds of 'competition in politics' see Vanberg and Buchanan (1991) and Vanberg (1992b: 385ff.).
24 As Dye (1990: 14) puts it:

> Competitive federalism envisions a marketplace for governments where consumer-taxpayers can voluntarily choose the public goods and services they prefer, at the cost they wish to pay, by locating in the governmental jurisdiction that best fits their policy preferences. In this model of federalism, state and local governments compete for consumer-taxpayers by offering the best array of public goods and services at the lowest possible costs.

25 Another significant difference is that for ordinary market firms there is a bottom line for bad performance, namely bankruptcy, while for polities and governments formal bankruptcy procedures do not exist. The existence of such provisions would clearly impose an effective constraint on governments, yet it is not easy to imagine how, in the political realm, a formal analog to bankruptcy in the business world could be devised.
26 As indicated here, one obvious difference between the two kinds of political competition is the fact that by casting a vote a person cannot control what government he or she gets. That vote is, of course, insignificant. The only way for a person to effectively choose his or her government is, as a rule, by his or her choice of residence.
27 The case of financial capital exemplifies the fact that, in terms of A. O. Hirschman's (1970) distinction, a viable exit option can be a valuable substitute for a lacking voice option. Though in modern democracies votes are assigned to persons (one person one vote), while capital does not carry formal voting rights, the mobility of capital certainly provides considerable protection to capital owners. In a similar way, though as hotel customers we do not have a vote in the operation of the facility, we typically do not expect that our interests will, therefore, get insufficient attention. We can count on our exit option to make for responsive service.
28 This aspect is commented on by Hayek when, in reference to *local government*, he argues that 'people can escape exploitation by voting with their feet' (1979: 16), and when he notes the classical liberal's preference for local government over central arrangements as being based on 'a hope that competition between

the different local authorities would effectively control and direct the development . . . on desirable lines' (1978: 144).

29 Jordi Baccaria drew my attention to this issue.

30 While the right to exit is, for any polity, clearly a viable constitutional provision, independent of what other polities practice, it is not so obvious whether a unilaterally granted right of entry is in the constitutional interest of the constituents of a polity, or whether it is even viable. Yet, whatever may be true for unilateral right-of-entry provisions, it should be apparent that mutual commitments between governments to allow for free entry should increase the responsiveness of these governments to citizens' interests. In such case, the 'free entry' provision could be seen as part of a social contract among the inclusive group of citizens in the participating polities.

31 On the potential relevance of secession rights for a European constitution see Buchanan (1990: 5ff.) and Bernholz (1992).

32 Röpke (1963: 22) notes on this issue:

Leveling a revolver at someone is one of the quickest but also one of the riskiest ways of getting something for nothing. Much safer and more efficient are the devices of special privilege and monopoly for they can be tricked out in ideological trappings which may make them seem not only innocuous but even beneficial to the general interest.

33 As Dye (1990: 14, 19, 32) notes:

Matching public policy to citizen preferences is the essence of responsive government. Competitive elections and political parties were designed to achieve this goal. But decentralized government is also a way to match citizen preferences with public policies . . . Democracy itself, with competing parties and periodic free elections, is a powerful inducement to policy responsiveness, at least to majority policy preferences, even in a monopoly government. But if multiple governments are both democratic and competitive, citizens have two separate mechanisms to help achieve congruence between their preferences and public policy. . . . [C]ompetitive federalism operates independently of the type of political system to encourage responsiveness. Theoretically, even authoritarian governments, if they were forced to compete with each other and if citizens could migrate to the government of their choice with little cost to themselves, would be responsive to citizen preferences.

34 Hayek points to this issue when, in his previously mentioned article, he notes that competition between the individual states in a federation forms 'a salutory check on their activities and, while leaving the door open for desirable experimentation, would keep it roughly within the appropriate limits' (Hayek 1948: 268).

35 Dye (1990: 15) notes: 'Competition in the marketplace promotes discoveries of new products. Competition among governments promotes policy innovation.'

36 In this sense of the term, even the Soviet Union was an 'experimenting' polity, but such experimenting, if carried out in a unitary, 'closed' system, cannot serve the knowledge function that parallel experimenting allows for in a decentralized open system.

37 As Kenyon and Kincaid (1991: 19) put it, to advocate competitive federalism does not mean to recommend for states 'to engage in unbridled competition, but rather to compete and cooperate within the bounds of the civil order established by the constitution and within the agreed-upon rules enforced by an overarching government (i.e. the federal government).' Dye (1990: 26) comments on this

issue: 'Competition is not anarchy; it is restrained disciplined, orderly behavior. Just as the marketplace requires rules . . . so also intergovernmental competition requires rules.' For the case of the United States Dye (ibid.: 27f.) discusses various provisions in the Constitution that 'set forth a series of basic rules of competition among the states.'

38 Dye (1990: 114f.) notes on this issue:

> Competitive federalism requires that states and communities have significant and autonomous responsibility for the welfare of people living in their jurisdictions. It requires that these governments be free to pursue a wide range of public policies. Most important, competitive federalism requires that the costs of state and local government goods and services be fully reflected in the revenues collected by these governments. Federal grants-in–aid create distortions in the relationships between the preferences of citizen-taxpayers in the states and the policies of state and local governments. On this issue see also Marlo (1992: 81), Bernholz and Faber (1988: 245), – and Holcombe (1993).

39 What Adam Smith (1981: 145) has said about the collusive inclination of private business can be assumed to apply to politicians as well: 'People of the same trade seldom meet together, even for merriment and diversion, but the conversation ends in a conspiracy against the public, or in some contrivance to raise prices.'

40 This is, unfortunately, also a reason why one can expect not only politicians at the federal level, but national politicans as well, to have a natural preference for the centralist over the competitive version, because it provides, at least, a new arena for political activity, while competitive federalism means a definite reduction in the politicized realm.

41 Critical observers have noted about the Maastricht accord that it 'is a step into the direction of strengthening reregulation over deregulation' (Kirchner 1992: 25).

References

Alchian, Armen A. (1977) *Economic Forces at Work*, Indianopolis: Liberty Press.

Bernholz, Peter (1992) 'Constitutional aspects of the European integration,' in Silvio Borner and Herbert Grubel (eds) *The European Community of 1992. Perspectives from the Outside*, Basingstoke: Macmillan, pp. 45–60.

Bernholz, Peter and Fober, Mable? (1968) 'Reflections on a normative theory of the unification of law?', in James D. Guartney and Richard E. Wagner (eds) *Public Choice and Constitutional Economics*, Greenwich, CT: JAI Press, pp. 229–49.

Böhm, Franz (1961) 'Demokratie und unternehmerische Macht,' in *Kartelle und Monopole im modernen Recht*, Vol. 1, Karlsruhe: C. F. Müller, pp. 1–24.

Böhm, Franz (1980) 'Freiheit und Ordnung in der Marktwirtschaft,' in Ernst-Joachim Mestmäcker (Hg.) *Freiheit und Ordnung in der Marktwirtschaft*, Baden-Baden: Nomos, S. 195–209.

Böhm, Franz (1982) (orig. 1933) 'The non-state ('natural') laws inherent in a competitive economy,' in W. Stuetzel *et al.* (eds) *Standard Texts on the Social Market Economy*, Stuttgart/New York: Gustav Fischer, pp. 107–13.

Brennan, Geoffrey and Buchanan, James M. (1980) *The power to tax: analytical foundations of a fiscal constitution*, Cambridge: Cambridge University Press.

Buchanan, James M. (1990) 'The domain of constitutional economics,' *Constitutional Political Economy* 1: 1–18.

Buchanan, James M. (1991) *The Economics and Ethics of Constitutional Order*, Ann Arbor, MI: University of Michigan Press.

Buchanan, James M. (1992) *An American Evaluation of Europe's Constitutional Prospects*, Center for the Study of Public Choice, George Mason University.

Buchanan, James M. (1993) 'How can constitutions be designed so that politicians who seek to serve "public interest" can survive and prosper?' *Constitutional Political Economy* 4: 1–6.

Buchanan, James M. *et al.* (eds) (1980) *Toward a Theory of the Rent-Seeking Society*, College Station, TX: Texas A&M University Press.

Donges, J. B., Engels, W., Hamm, W., Möschel, W., Neumann, M. J. and Sievert, O. (1992) *Einheit und Vielfalt in Europa – Für weniger Harmonisierung und Zentralisierung*, Frankfurt (Frankfurter Institut für wirtschaftspolitische Forschung, Schriftenreihe: Band 25).

Dye, Thomas R. (1990) *American Federalism – Competition Among Governments*, Lexington, MA: Lexington Books.

Ekelund, Rovert B. Jr and Tollison, Robert D. (1982) *Mercantilism as a Rent-Seeking Society: Economic Regulation in Historical Perspective*, College Station, TX: Texas A&M University Press.

Eucken, Walter (1952) *Grundsätze der Wirtschaftspolitik*, Tübingen: J.C.B. Mohr (Paul Siebeck).

Eucken, Walter (1982) 'A policy for establishing a system of free enterprise,' in W. Stützel *et al.* (eds) *Standard Texts on the Social Market Economy*, Stuttgart/New York: Gustav Fischer, pp. 115–31.

Habermann, Gerd (1990) 'Die deutsche Handwerksordnung als Relikt der Gewerbebindung,' *Ordo* 41: 173–93.

Hayek, Friedrich A. (1948) *Individualism and Economic Order*, Chicago: University of Chicago Press, pp. 255–72.

Hayek, Friedrich A. (1959) 'Liberalismus (I), Politischer Liberalismus,' in *Handbuch der Sozialwissenschaften* 6: 591–6.

Hayek, Friedrich A. (1960) *The Constitution of Liberty*, Chicago: University of Chicago Press.

Hayek, Friedrich A. (1978) 'Competition as a discovery process' in *New Studies in Philosophy, Politics, Economics and the History of Ideas*, Chicago: University of Chicago Press, pp. 179–90.

Hayek, Friedrich A. (1979) *The Political Order of a Free People*, Vol. 3 of *Law, Legislation, and Liberty*, London: Routledge & Kegan Paul.

Hayek, Friedrich A. (1988) *The Fatal Conceit – The Errors of Socialism*, London: Routledge.

Hirschman, Albert O. (1970) *Exit, Voice, and Loyalty – Responses to Decline in Firms, Organizations, and States*, Cambridge, MA: Harvard University Press.

Holcombe, Randall G. (1993) 'Federal funding and the cartelization of state governments,' Mimeo, Florida State University.

Kenyon, Daphne A. and Kincaid, John (1991) 'Competition among states and local governments,' in Daphne A. Kenyon and John Kincaid (eds) *Competition among states and local governments: efficiency and equity in American federalism*, Washington, DC: Urban Institute Press.

Kerber, Wolfgang (1991) 'Zur Entstehung von Wissen: Grundsätzliche Bemerkungen zu Möglichkeiten und Grenzen staatlicher Förderung der Wissenproduktion aus der Sicht der Theorie evolutionärer Marktprozesse,' in P. Oberender and M. E. Streit (Hg.) *Marktwirtschaft und Innovation*, Baden-Baden: Nomos, S. 9–52.

Kirchner, Christian (1992) 'The potential effect of EC-law on deregulation and reregulation,' Paper presented at the 19th Karl Brunner Symposium on Liberty, Analysis and Ideology, Interlaken, 8–12 June.

Knight, Frank H. (1982) (orig. 1947) *Freedom and Reform – Essays in Economics and Social Philosophy*, Indianapolis: Liberty Press.

Lowenberg, Anton D. and Yu, Ben T. (1992) 'Efficient constitution formation and maintenance,' *Constitutional Political Economy* 3: 51–72.

Marlow, Michael L. (1992) 'Intergovernmental competition, voice and exit options, and the design of fiscal structure,' *Constitutional Political Economy* 3: 73–88.

Miksch, Leonhard (1947) *Wettbewerb als Aufgabe – Grundsätze einer Wettbewerbsordnung*, 2nd Aufl. Godesberg: Verlag Helmut Küpper.

Mises, Ludwig von (1940) *Nationalökonomie – Theorie des Handelns und Wirtschaftens*, Genf: Editions Union.

Röpke, Wilhelm (1942) *Die Gesellschaftskrisis der Gegenwart* (4. Aufl.), Elenbach-Zürich: Eugen Rentsch Verlag.

Röpke, Wilhelm (1949) *Civitas Humana – Grundfragen der Gesellschafts- und Wirtschaftsreform* (3. Aufl.), Erlenbach-Zürich: Eugen Rentsch Verlag.

Röpke, Wilhelm (1960) *A Humane Economy – The Social Framework of the Free Market*, South Bend, IN: Gateway Editions.

Röpke, Wilhelm (1963) *Economics of the Free Society*, Chicago: Henry Regnery.

Sinn, Stefan (1992) 'The taming of leviathan: competition among governments,' *Constitutional Political Economy* 2: 177–96.

Smith, Adam, (1981) *An Inquiry into the Nature and Causes of the Wealth of Nations*, two volumes, Indianapolis: Liberty Classics (reprint of the 1976 Oxford University Press edition).

Vanberg, Viktor (1990) 'Vom Wettkampf der Systeme zum Wettbewerb von Ordnungen,' *Neue Zuercher Zeitung* Nr 173: 35.

Vanberg, Viktor (1991) 'Review of ORDO (Vols 40 and 41, 1989 and 1990),' in *Constitutional Political Economy* 2: 397–402.

Vanberg, Viktor (1992a) 'Innovation, cultural evolution, and economic growth,' in Ulrich Witt (ed.) *Explaining Process and Change – Approaches to Evolutionary Economics*, Ann Arbor, MI: University of Michigan Press, 105–21.

Vanberg, Viktor (1992b) 'A constitutional political economy perspective on international trade,' *Ordo* 43: 375–92.

Vanberg, Viktor and Buchanan, James M. (1991) 'Constitutional choice, rational ignorance and the limits of reason,' *Jahrbuch für Neue Politische Ökonomie*, Tübingen: J. C. B. Mohr (Paul Siebeck), Vol. 10, pp. 61–78.

Vaubel, Roland (1992) 'Die Politische Ökonomie der wirtschaftspolitischen Zentralisierung in der Europäischen Gemeinschaft,' *Jahrbuch für Neue Politische Ökonomie*, Tübingen: J.C.B. Mohr (Paul Siebeck), Vol. 11, pp. 30–65.

10 Political parties, pressure groups, and democracy

A transaction cost theory of political institutions

Donald Wittman

The economic approach to understanding social and political organization should be based on the same economic principles that are used to explain economic organization. The key concept is transaction costs. Transaction costs determine the choice between the firm and the market and influence the internal organization of the firm. Similarly, transaction costs explain how political institutions are organized.

Pressure groups and special interests

Pressure groups and special interests are singled out as the key reasons for the failure of democratic systems to provide desirable results. This view is held not only by sociologists and political scientists, but by economists as well, who should know better. After all, self-interest is usually viewed as leading to desirable outcomes in the economic sector. And more important from the viewpoint of this chapter, firms are not viewed as creating demands, but rather as low-cost methods of satisfying those demands. Pressure groups should be seen in the same light.

The ability of pressure groups to distort the political process is greatly exaggerated. As I have argued elsewhere (see Wittman 1989), voters are neither naïve nor do they have biased expectations. Even if individual voters respond only marginally to bad behavior by incumbents, the law of large numbers suggests that the majority will almost always vote against a politician who has gone against the majority's interest.

Pressure groups perform a valuable function by reducing the costs of transmitting information from individuals to politicians and vice versa. Politicians are informed of various constituencies' preferences in a relatively low-cost way. Not only are politicians provided information regarding various policies, they gain information from the existence of the lobbying activity itself. Other things being equal, politicians can infer strength of preference from the strength of lobbying efforts. The more spent on lobbying, the more important the policy is to the group. Of course, other things may not be equal. Congressmen and their constituents know that certain groups have lower organizational costs and that greater lobbying need not reflect more votes at the ballot box. In such cases, politicians take into account these biases and discount the effect of organizational advantages. Congressmen know that unorganized voters will not fly out to Washington to lobby against a bill, yet they will vote against a Congressman if the Congressman votes in favor of the legislation.

Seeing pressure groups as institutions that reduce transaction costs rather than seeing them as institutions that distort democratic decisions suggests an entirely new research agenda: discovering the optimal method of organizing information networks to elicit preferences and transmit them to politicians. Pressure groups are part of the solution. Their scope depends on the optimal division of labor and comparative advantage within the context of the political structure. Consider the following thought experiment. Suppose that you were designing a method to elicit and transmit preferences and that you had limited means to do so. Would you organize by first letter of a person's last name or by certain interests, such as job and religion? Clearly, the latter. How fine a division would you create and would the structure be parallel or overlapping? The answer depends on the span of differences and whether the added information from parallel networks overcomes the cost. Thus in the USA, Orthodox and Reform Jews are more likely to work together under one umbrella when lobbying Congress than they are in Israel when lobbying the Knesset. What would be the extent of vertical integration; that is, which information-gathering tasks would be allocated to the legislator's office staff, which would be allocated to an independent organization (such as a polling firm), and which would be allocated to externally organized groups? These are the same types of questions that one asks about the structure of economic organization. And the answers are based on similar concepts – strategic complementarity, credible commitments, and the ability to contain opportunism. The actual solutions to these and the previous questions are not determined by one person setting up the overall structure, but by individuals trying to achieve their own particular needs.

Legislatures specialize in resolving political conflict. Comparative advantage suggests that pressure groups are less effective in this role. Hence pressure groups are much more focused than would be the case if pressure groups were effective at internally resolving conflict. If pressure groups were good at aggregating diverse preferences, then we would see pressure groups representing many different people on unrelated issues. But pressure groups cannot be effective in such a mode. Instead, the role of pressure groups is to determine and represent the preferences of relatively narrowly defined interests.

Political parties

There are a host of questions that one can ask about the organization of political parties. What determines the number of parties? Why are there parties and not individual candidates? Why are parties organized along some issues and not others (e.g. why is there not a labor party in the USA)? How does a federal structure alter party organization? We will first concentrate on the following question: how do parties maintain their cohesiveness? In particular, how does a political party monitor its elected members and provide the correct incentives?

Maintaining party cohesiveness

We first consider party organization in the USA. Here parties are less centralized than in other systems (we will try to partially answer why later) and the question becomes: how do the parties maintain their cohesiveness?

Although numerous authors have argued for the declining importance of political parties in the USA, the party label provides information and has an important influence on the vote tally. Few independents win Congressional elections, indicating that the party label is a valuable commodity. In addition, we observe that party identification of the voter is the most important variable in predicting an individual's vote (Jacobson 1987: 107, 126). Even those voters who are independents may make use of the party label to infer policies of a candidate (Downs 1957, Popkin 1991). A political party that promotes unpopular policies will discover that its candidates lose more elections than otherwise.

Political parties develop reputations so that candidates do not shirk on the party's ideology. Other members of the party have strong incentives to maintain the reputation of the party since the brand name is valuable in attracting votes. Especially in legislatures, it is easy for party leaders to monitor and sanction fellow politicians' voting behavior. Those legislators who have proven to be reliable in the past are rewarded by being appointed to influential committees. Unless the person's vote is pivotal, a wayward member without party support is generally ineffectual in a system which requires a majority coalition. The political party is thus the analog to a franchise in the economic sector. The creation of the party (franchise) brand name allows the voter (consumer) to make more informed judgments about how the coalition of its members will behave. An important part of the franchise activity is to prevent shirking that might result in a diminution of the value of the franchise.

Party organization helps to make commitments credible. For example, party leaders determine committee assignments. Although Shepsle (1978) viewed appointments to committees in the US Congress as predominantly determined by individual legislator's preferences, assignments to committees are ultimately the responsibility of the political parties. The majority would not make assignments which would result in negative-sum legislation. Although rarely used, Congressmen have lost their committee chairs for not abiding by party principles. In 1971 the Democratic Caucus began allowing separate votes on individual chairs on the demand of any ten members. In 1974 the Caucus deposed the chairs of the Agriculture, Armed Services, and Banking Committees, replacing them with less senior members. 'Thereafter, no chair was deposed until 1985, because it was not necessary' (Tiefer 1989: 82). Chairs yielded to pressure from junior members and party leadership rather than losing their position.

A more important method of party control is to make transfers to major committees partially dependent on past behavior on minor committees. Those who have voted with the leadership on key votes in the past are rewarded with choice assignments. Empirical support is found in Coker and Crain (1992) who show that House members who have demonstrated more loyalty to the party leaders by voting in agreement with their positions in the past are more likely to obtain assignments on important committees. More important committees also have a greater percentage of members from the majority party, thereby controlling for the possibility of defection.

Because of seniority, committee assignments are stable. The party, however, is still able to influence the make-up of the committee by new assignments. If the present make-up of the committee is to the left of the median member of the party as a whole, the party can appoint a new member to the right of the median voter. Evidence that partially corroborates this view is found in Kiewiet and McCubbins (1988) who showed that new appointments tended to move the median committee member from outside the middle 50 percent to inside more than the reverse. If necessary, the House can alter the size of committees and/or change their composition (as it did to the Rules Committee in 1961).

Other methods of control include choosing committee membership on control committees (Rules, Appropriations, and Budget) to reflect the preferences of the median Congressman in the party, there being less potential for opportunism when the goals of the agent and the principal coincide. Cox and McCubbins (1990) show that these control committees (universal, in their terms) are more representative of Congress than special committees such as agriculture. Since agricultural appropriations ultimately have to go through the Budget and Appropriation Committees, special interests ultimately have to defer to majoritarian interests.

I have shown how party leaders control party regulars, but how are party leaders controlled by the party? Since these are elective offices, competition is the primary method of party control. There is evidence demonstrating that whips and other Congressional leaders tend to be from those districts that represent the median voter in the party. Kiewiet and McCubbins' (1988) study of House leaders showed that leaders gravitated toward the median of their caucus (Jim Wright's score made him the median Democrat). It should not be surprising that party leaders represent the interests of the median party representative since these positions are elective, and if we have a unidimensional issue space with two candidates, party leaders will converge to the median.

Another method of insuring that party leaders follow the party line is to choose leaders from safe districts. In this way they can afford to toe the party line without risk of defeat even if this runs contrary to their district's interest. Supporting evidence is found in the fact that in the USA party leaders are rarely defeated for re-election to their district. In the UK, party leaders typically face election in safe districts.

Creating coalitions

The role of parties and candidates is much more complex than the simple spatial models would suggest. It is not just moving left or right in a continuum toward the median voter. If that was the essence of democratic politics, economists and pollsters would be presidents, but they are not. Besides the aforementioned control over the party's representatives, the party must forge a winning coalition which involves convincing the participants both that they will be better off if the party's candidates win and that they have a good chance of winning. There is a constant struggle to redefine the issues so that the coalition is a winning one. Seen in this light, a party is a coalition of 'special interests.' Special interests therefore should not be viewed as outsiders who distort the will of the majority, but as the basic building blocks in forming a majority.

Political parties reduce transaction costs by facilitating trade among their members. Winning coalitions are created within the context of the party platform rather than on an *ad hoc* basis. A political party is designed to overcome shirking of its members and to take credit for universal policies (e.g. foreign policy). National political parties internalize the negative externalities that might arise from local interests trying to shift costs onto other districts.

I have argued that political parties are coalitions that create positive-sum gains for their members. But suppose that parties are weak. Then one should look for other institutions that perform such a function. For example, the President can create a cohesive policy that minimizes the possibility of too narrow a focus by the legislature. The President can also punish and reward particular members of Congress for supporting (or undermining) presidential policy. For example, the President can give public credit for individual assistance on major legislation, provide campaign appearances, or focus media attention on selected representatives.

Cross-country comparisons

Our examples of party organization have come mainly from the USA. However, the same need for control exists in other systems as well. The optimal organizational form is partially dependent on the basic political structure. In turn, the basic political structure can be viewed as an optimal institutional arrangement. We will now briefly make a cross-country comparison of the organization of political parties.

Proportional representation and majority rule systems have more centralized parties than plurality rule systems. And the two systems require different skills. In proportional representation systems, each party appeals to a narrow band of voters. The party leader provides a clear message to followers, but must negotiate successfully with people outside the party in order to be part of the ruling coalition. In contrast, under plurality rule systems, such as the US presidential election, the winner need not compromise with the loser; rather the compromise takes place with the voters (the well-known convergence to the median). Under plurality rule, parties try to create a winning electoral coalition. The latter is essentially a decentralized process as information must be elicited from a wide variety of voters and a winning coalition must be formed. As a consequence, plurality rule systems have significantly less centralized political parties.

Viewing the issue from a different perspective, one might ask why some countries have plurality and others have proportional rule. It is quite possible that proportional rule systems are much better at resolving conflict when there are more than two clear divisions in society. I believe that this is a more fruitful approach than saying that it is historical happenstance that one form was chosen over the other or saying that one form is always superior to the other.

The number of political parties

According to Riker (1982) one of the few established theoretical relations in political science is Duverger's law. Duverger's law says that majority rule systems (such as the electoral system that existed in France until recently) will have more political parties than plurality rule systems (such as the electoral system in the USA) because expected utility maximization by the voter means that the voter will not want to waste a vote for a third party under the latter system. While Duverger's law explains why there will not be more than two parties in a plurality rule system, it provides no insight as to why there are likely to be more than two parties in a majority rule system. Again organization theory is needed. Why are there not just two political parties in majority rule systems? That is, why do the compromises take place within the parliaments across parties rather than within the parties themselves? To a great extent compromises do take place within the parties, but rearranging coalition power within a majority party is much more difficult than rearranging power between a governing coalition. Votes for each separate party within the governing coalition generate a much clearer picture of relative electoral strength than internal jockeying within a majority party to influence the party's policies.

Parties in federal systems

A federal system creates federal parties. That is, there are different parties in either name or fact in and across the various federal levels. Policies in Ontario rarely have an effect on policies in British Columbia and in the Canadian federal system many of the policies regarding these two provinces are decided independently. So members of the same party in these two provinces would not negotiate to have a similar policy. That is, horizontal integration is slight. A more difficult question to answer is when are the parties on the local level at least in name related to the national party and when are they entirely different organizations? The greater the differences between jurisdictions and the less important the central government, the less likely the parties will be related across jurisdictions. Similarly, the degree of vertical integration of the parties (i.e. the relationship between the candidates who run for local, state, and national office) depends to a great extent on the overlapping interests and the ease of monitoring.

Federal systems

The last section asked about the organization of parties within a federal system. In this section, we briefly investigate the design of federal systems.

In standard public finance texts, federalism is about externalities. If an action in one jurisdiction affects a neighboring jurisdiction (as would be the case if pollution in one state crossed over into another state), then the decision regarding that action is taken at a higher government level which encompasses both jurisdictions. In this way, the externally is internalized. The externally argument is at best a partial answer. It does not say whether the 'externally' is best resolved by the central government or by direct negotiation between the states. The former method is superior only if total transaction costs are minimized.

The organizational structure that minimizes transaction costs is not always obvious and clearly depends on the task at hand. If there are many jurisdictions, then economies of scale might not be exploited. On the other hand, fewer people need be involved in forming coalitions, thereby reducing transaction costs within jurisdictions, but possibly increasing transaction costs between jurisdictions. So the key becomes which issues are best resolved on an *ad hoc* basis between states and which are resolved within the context of a central government? Consider the prime example of a public good – defense. Some political units have military alliances with each other; other political units have a much more complete merger and are called countries.

Turning to interstate relations, which state's laws should take precedence when the laws of different states are in conflict? Again, a transaction cost analysis provides the answer.

Federalism is based on territory. And in many cases, making territory the basis for rule-of-law choice minimizes information costs. Suppose, for example, that a driver from Alabama runs into a pedestrian from Florida while both are in California. Which state's rule should be operative? California is the obvious choice. If not, drivers and pedestrians would constantly be looking at license plates to determine which state law applied. Since pedestrians do not identify themselves by state, the most reasonable expectation is that the pedestrian is from California even if the stereotype is that Californians don't walk. Not surprisingly, US courts have upheld the view that place of automobile accident determines the prevailing law.

Concluding remarks

This chapter has served as an introduction to the theory of political organization. Detailed studies of other democratic institutions in other countries besides the USA should be undertaken. All systems have to control opportunism and to aggregate diverse preferences. The key to our understanding of democratic institutional design is to realize that competitive forces in democratic systems tend to minimize transaction costs. The interesting issue is not that there is opportunism, but how the political system is designed to control agency problems. A complete theory of political institutions would predict the different organizational structures based on different needs and technologies. Legislatures are not organized like political parties and principal–agent problems are resolved differently in courts and bureaucracies. The role of the economist is to show why this is the case.

References

Coker, David and Crain, W. Mark (1992) 'Legislative committees as loyalty-generating institutions,' *Papers in Political Economy*, University of Western Ontario.

Cox, Gary and McCubbins, Mathew (1990) *Parties and Committees in the House of Representatives*, Berkeley, CA: University of California Press.

Downs, Anthony (1957) *An Economic Theory of Democracy*, New York: Harper & Row.

Jacobson, Gary (1987) *The Politics of Congressional Elections*, Boston: Little Brown.

Kiewiet, Roderick and McCubbins, Mathew (1988) 'Presidential influence on Congressional appropriation decisions,' *American Journal of Political Science* 32: 713–36.

Popkin, Samuel (1991) *The Reasoning Voter*, Chicago: University of Chicago Press.

Riker, William (1982) 'The two party system and Duverger's law: an essay on the history of political science,' *American Political Science Review* 76: 753–66.

Shepsle, Kenneth A. (1978) *The Giant Jigsaw Puzzle*, Chicago: University of Chicago Press.

Tiefer, Charles (1989) *Congressional Practices and Procedure,* New York: Greenwood Press.

Wittman, Donald (1989) 'Pressure group size and the politics of income redistribution,' *Social Choice and Welfare* 6: 275–86.

Part III

The 'contamination' between economic and political factors in institutional change

11 The coming of nationalism, and its interpretation

The myths of nation and class

Ernest Gellner

This is a theoretical essay. It purports to offer a general, theoretical account and explanation of a very major social transformation, namely the coming of nationalism in the course of the nineteenth and twentieth centuries. The claims made are the following:

1 A very major and distinctive change has taken place in the social conditions of humankind. A world in which *nationalism*, the linking of state and of 'nationally' defined culture, is pervasive and normative is quite different from one in which this is relatively rare, half-hearted, unsystematised and untypical. There is an enormous difference between a world of complex, intertwined, but not neatly overlapping patterns of power and culture, and a world consisting of neat political units, systematically and proudly differentiated from each other by 'culture', and all of them striving, with a great measure of success, to impose cultural homogeneity internally. These units, linking sovereignty to culture, are known as nation states. During the two centuries following the French Revolution, the nation state became a political norm. How and why did this happen?
2 A theoretical model is available which, starting from generalisations which are eminently plausible and not seriously contested, in conjunction with available data concerning the transformation of society in the nineteenth century, does explain the phenomenon in question.
3 Most though not all of the relevant empirical material is compatible with this model.

These are strong claims. If sustained, they mean that the problem under discussion – nationalism – unlike most other major problems of historical social change, does have an explanation. Most of the other major transformations which have occurred in history have also repeatedly provoked attempts at explication. But the explanations offered only consist of specifying interesting possibilities, or provide plausible partial contributions to a final answer. They are seldom definitive and sufficient and convincing. By contrast, a cogent, persuasive explanation of nationalism is available.

The model

It is best to begin with the specification of the model. It specifies two different, very generic types of society. The argument focuses on the difference in the role of structure and culture in the two distinct types of society.

Agro-literate society

Agro-literate society is defined by a number of characteristics. It is a society based on agriculture (including pastoralism), in other words on food production and food storage.It is endowed with a fairly stable technology; though innovations and improvements can and do occur from time to time, they are not parts of some sustained process of discovery and invention. The society is free of the general idea (so pervasive and commonplace now, amongst *us*) that nature forms an intelligible system susceptible to exploration, which when successful engenders a powerful new technology. The vision on which this society was based is *not* that of an ever-increasing comprehension and mastery of nature (as ours is), justifying the expectation of perpetual improvement in the human condition. Rather, the vision presupposed a stable partnership between nature and society, in which nature not merely provides a modest but fairly constant material provision, but also somehow underwrites, justifies the social order, and mirrors its arrangements.

The consequences of the possession of a stable technology, and no more, are various. Given the relative inelasticity of the supply of food, *and* the existence of a definite and none too high, ceiling on food production, the values of the members of the society are generally directed towards coercion and hierarchy. What really matters for a member of such a society is that he or she be well placed on its hierarchical scale, rather than that he or she should *produce* copiously and efficiently; and being an effective producer is not the best way (or perhaps is not a good way at all) of enhancing one's status. A characteristic value of such a society is 'nobility', which means a conjunction of military vocation and ascribed high status.

The orientation follows from the basic logic of the situation in a society with a fairly stable productive potential: there is nothing much to be gained by attempts to increase production, but the individual, and also any sub-group, has everything to gain from a favoured position *within* society. Increased production will only benefit the privileged power holders, rather than the person responsible for the increase; but *becoming* one of the power holders does benefit the successful aspiring individual. So the individual must strive to enhance his or her power and status, and should not waste effort on increasing output.

This tendency is much reinforced by the second trait following from a stable technology – a Malthusian condition. The possibilities of increasing food production are limited, those of population growth are not. The units of which this kind of society is composed tend to value offspring, or at any rate male offspring, as a source of labour power and defence power. However, the high valuation of offspring must at last intermittently bring the total population close to the limit, or beyond the limit, of the available food supply. All this, in turn, reinforces the martial and hierarchical orientation of the society: when hunger comes, it does not strike at random. It strikes in accordance with rank. People starve in accordance with status, lower orders starving first. This is ensured by the socially controlled access to the guarded storage centres of sustenance. In North Africa, a most suggestive term for central government is in use: *Makhzen*. It has the same root as *magazine*. The government controls and *is* the storehouse.

Some of the self-maintaining mechanisms operative in this kind of society are indicated in Figure 11.1.

The consequence of this situation is that an agro-literate society constitutes a complex system of fairly stable statuses. The possession of a status, and access to its rights and privileges, are by far the most important consideration for a member of such a society. A person is their *rank*. (This is quite different for the society which was to replace it, in which a person is their *culture* and/or their bank balance, and where rank is ephemeral.)

How was the earlier system maintained? In general, there are two possibilities of maintaining order: coercion and consent. Those who would disturb the existing system of roles and modify them in their own favour are prevented from doing so, either by menaces, and possibly by the actual execution of threats, or by inner restraints, by causing them to internalise a system of ideas and convictions which then inhibits deviant conduct. In

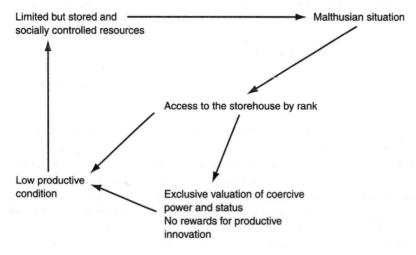

Figure 11.1

practice, each of these two mechanisms operated. The two mechanisms are not separated, but work in conjunction. They are intertwined so intimately that it becomes impossible to disentangle their contributions to the maintenance of the social order.

Which of the two factors is the more important? This is an exceedingly difficult question. There is no reason to suppose that a single answer applies to all circumstances. Marxism is most naturally interpreted as a doctrine which would ascribe the greatest influence on a social order neither to coercion nor to ideology (castigating both of these affirmations as 'Idealism'), but to *production* instead. But it is less than clear just what a direct determination of the social order by the productive system, unmediated by either coercion or ideas, could possibly mean. Tools and techniques on their own cannot make people conform to the rules of distribution: this can only be done through either coercion or consent, or a fusion of both. How does a mode of production engender its own mode of coercion? It is difficult not to suspect that Marxism owed some of its appeal and persistence to its lack of clarity on this point.

The ideological system of a society does not enhance the stability of the system only by inducing its members to perceive the system as legitimate. Ideology plays a much more pervasive and complex role: by giving the principles needed to organise and solve internal conflicts to those who make coercion – who otherwise would simply be a chaotic, badly organised and ineffective aggregation – makes coercion possible.

In addition to a more or less stable agrarian base, this kind of society shows a certain degree of literacy. Writing is a technique which makes it possible to record and select data, ideas, information, formulae and so on. The pre-literate society does not necessarily lack a technique for recording meanings and statements: even important formulae could be fixed by ritual or repetition. Yet, writing greatly enhances the ability to store and transmit ideas, statements, information and principles.

In this kind of society, writing tends to enhance status differentiation. It is an art which requires a complex and quite long process of initiation, that is known as 'education'. An agrarian society does not have the incentives or resources to promote a wide diffusion of literacy, and, more, to make it universal. This skill draws a distinction between those who have and those who lack it. In addition to being a mystery of corporative initiation, literacy becomes a mark of rank distinction. The use of written communication as a status symbol might be reinforced by means of other instruments, as for example the use of dead or special languages for written messages. In this way, the messages become distinct not only because they are written, but also because they are compiled in another language. Reverence for writings is based on mystery, not on its understanding. The cult of clearness comes later in the history of humankind, and it represents a real revolution.

The main part of the ordinary members of this kind of society acquire their own culture 'on the job': each of them stores ideas and symbols in the course of living, in the everyday exchange with relatives, neighbours, teachers and pupils. This living culture – neither coded nor frozen in written form, and lacking a rigid and formalised system of rules – is simply transmitted as a part of a 'way of life' in its becoming. Skills such as writing are not generally transmitted in this way: during prolonged and specialised training, they are inculcated not by ordinary people in the course of doing ordinary things, but by full-time specialists, dedicated to perpetuating and exemplifying superior norms.

There is a profound difference between a culture transmitted simply in the course of living, 'on the job', informally, and culture transmitted by full-time specialists, committed to doing very little else, who in so doing carry out a formal, well-defined duty, specified in some detail in normative texts, which are fixed and cannot easily be manipulated by individuals. The former is liable to be flexible, changing and regionally diversified, and very pliable, sometimes to an extreme degree. The latter can be made rigid, resistant to change, standardised over an extensive territory.[1] It can be sustained by an impressive corpus of writing and reasoning, and be possessed of theories which further legitimise its own messages. Its doctrine may contain a theory specifying the origin of important truth – 'Revelation' – which then in turn reconfirms its *other* theories. A theory of revelation is part of this creed, and the creed is vindicated by the revelation. The circle is closed and complete.

This kind of society is characterised by a tension between a high culture, transmitted by formal education, enshrined in texts, and setting up socially transcendent norms, and, on the other hand, one or more low cultures, incarnated only in living practice, and not in that disembodied form of speech known as writing, and hence incapable of rising above actual practice. So what is typical of this kind of society is a discrepancy, and sometimes conflict between a high and a low culture, which can of course assume a variety of forms: the high culture may strive to impose its norms on the low, or the members of the low may strive to assume as many of the characteristics of the high as possible, in order to enhance their own standing. The former is typical of Islam, the latter, of Hinduism. But neither endeavour is likely to be very successful. The characteristic end product is a marked cultural differentiation between 'high' and 'low' styles frequently to the point of mutual unintelligibility. The unintelligibility is functional. People can hardly strive to elevate themselves into a condition which they simply do not understand, or defy a doctrine they know to be beyond their humble comprehension. Cultural differences define positions within society, they control access to them and inhibit escape from them, far more than they define the limits of the society as a whole. It is only in the transition from agrarian to industrial society that culture ceases to be the device which defines specific social positions and allocates individuals to them, and becomes, instead, the boundary demarcation of large and internally mobile social unity, *within* which individuals have no fixed position and are rotated in the light of the requirements of production.

If this overall model of the old Agraria be accepted as valid, what are the consequences for the relationship between culture on the one hand, and political legitimacy and boundaries of states on the other? The answer must be that generally there will be *very little* such connection between the two spheres.

A society of this type is constantly given to, as it were, secreting, engendering, elaborating cultural differentiations within itself. It constitutes a system of differentiated ranks and statuses, and these need to be recognised, highlighted, externalised. That is what culture is. The Russian cultural historian Yuri Lotman reports an eighteenth-century Russian nobleman who had a different mode of address to various people in accordance with just how many 'souls' they owned. He deployed a varied repertoire of differential greetings, sensitive to various sizes of human holdings. A character in a novel by Graham Greene notes the disrespect in the tone of the bank clerk addressing him, and reflects inwardly that he would be treated better if only his overdraft were significantly larger.

This kind of acute semantic sensitivity to nuances of status and property helps eliminate ambiguity and diminish friction. No status differences without externalisation! No visible marks without status warrant! As major breaks occur in the stratification of society, culture signals those chasms by similarly dramatic discontinuities of dress, speech, comportment, consumption. Peasants are quite liable to speak a language literally different from that of gentry, burghers or bureaucracy. Notoriously, in nineteenth-century Russia, the upper strata of societies differentiated themselves from the rest by an extensive use of French. It has been claimed that at the time of Italian unification in 1861, only $2\frac{1}{2}$ per cent of the Italian population actually spoke 'proper' Italian.[2] Agrarian society engenders estates, castes, guilds, status of all kind, and these require a cultural expression. Cultural *homogeneity* by contrast has little if any function in it. On the contrary, attempts to standardise cultural bearing constitute an offence, sometimes in a perfectly literal, penal sense. To attempt to emulate the bearing of distant ranks is a violation of the protocol and of the command structure of the society. It is a form of insolence which can hardly be allowed to go unpunished. The offender is fortunate if he or she receives only informal punishment.

There is also a strong tendency towards, so to speak, lateral differentiation, in addition to functional and vertical differentiation. Not only do people tend to acquire distinctive styles so as to protect themselves against emulation from below, or to refrain from giving offence upwards; there is also a tendency for rural communities to acquire cultural distinctiveness in comparison with geographic neighbours of similar status. In illiterate peasant communities, dialects generally vary from village to village. The insulated style of life encourages a kind of cultural and linguistic drift, and divergence ensues even when it had not been present at first.

Rulers seldom have the incentive to impose cultural homogeneity on their subjects, and often, on the contrary, derive much benefit from diversity. Cultural specificity helps allocate people to their social and geographical niche, inhibits the emergence of far-flung and possibly dangerous identities and loyalties. 'Divide and rule' policies are easier to implement if culture in any case already divides the population. Rulers are interested in the taxes, tithes, rents, corvée of their subjects, but seldom in either their souls or their culture. In agrarian society, culture divides rather than unifies. Occasionally, there are tendencies towards cultural homogenisation. These may be due to an effective imperial bureaucracy or to a soteriological–universalist world religion (which insists on saving human souls *as such*, rather than ministering to social ranks or segments), or to a combination of the two. But bureaucratic centralisation, or religious universalisation and institutialism especially in that accentuated form known as a Reformation, are precisely amongst the social features which prepared or induced the passage to a post–agrarian and nationalism-prone world.

The overall conclusion must be that in such societies, shared culture is seldom a plausible basis for the formation of political units.[3] The term 'nation', if used at all, is more likely to denote a loose corporate body, the politically enfranchised gentry of a given territory, those committed to take part in politics, than literally the sum total of participants in a culture. The Polish 'nation', for instance, was once the collectivity of enfranchised gentry of the Polish republic, and included persons of Ukrainian speech, but not peasants of Polish stock and language. The term denotes a political and not a cultural category of persons.

Political units in such a society have a strong tendency to be either smaller or larger than cultural units. Tribal segments, city states, seldom exhaust the culture which they practise, but rather, they share it with a much wider area; empires, on the other hand, are circumscribed only by military resistance or by geographical obstacles, but have not the slightest inclinations to restrict themselves to some single culture. The Muslim conqueror of North Africa is said to have ridden his horse into the Atlantic to show that he could go no further – but he was unperturbed by the cultural and linguistic distance of the Berber indigenous population.

People in this kind of society have plural and nested and cross-cutting memberships and loyalties, some of them perhaps vaguely related to what later comes to be called nationality, but most of them bearing no relation to it. There is great cultural diversity, and there are complex political units and groupings, but the two sets of linkages have no clear or important relationship to each other. Political hierarchies and cultural networks simply are not mediated and united by something called 'nationality'.

Of course, linguistic and cultural differentiation may be used to mark off not merely nuances of status, but a more general membership of, say, the dominant administrative–military class. In so far as a language is then a token of the political unit controlled by that class, we may occasionally have something which, at least superficially, resembles modern nationalism. But this is not a general phenomenon, and the differences between it and genuine modern nationalism are more important than the similarities.

Advanced industrial society

A type of society now exists in the world (and is spreading fast) which is radically different from agro-literate society, as described. Its economic foundation is altogether different: it is self-consciously based on sustained, continuous innovation, and on an exponential growth in productive resources and output. It is committed to a theory of knowledge which makes nature intelligible without recourse to Revelation, and thus also renders nature effectively manipulable and a source of ever-growing affluence. At the same time, nature is no longer available as a source of legitimating principles of the social order. In fact, economic growth is the first principle of legitimacy of this kind of society: any regime which fails to attain and maintain it is in trouble. (The second principle of legitimacy is nationality, which constitutes our theme).

This society is no longer Malthusian: economic growth eventually outstrips demographic growth, which, for independent reasons, diminishes, or disappears altogether. Its culture no longer values offspring so highly, if at all: sheer labour power or brawn is of little consequence, either for authorities or for individuals, either productively or militarily. (It is true that early industrialism engenders conscription and mass peasant armies, and peasants are valued as cannon-fodder. But in the age of the Falkland and Gulf Wars, numbers count for little, whereas technological sophistication and training become decisive.) Human beings are usable only if educated, and education is expensive. Quality not quantity of personnel counts, and quality depends on the machinery of cultural production of people, in other words on 'education'. Offspring are not valued by authority for their military or productive potential, or by parents as a form of insurance. Offspring are expensive and must compete, often unsuccessfully, with other forms of satisfaction and indulgence.

The nature of work has also changed radically. In agrarian society, 'work', essential but not at all prestigious, was predominantly physical, manual labour, and in the main was connected with agricultural production. It amounted to the application of human muscle to matter, with some limited assistance from animal power, and some mechanical devices based on the utilisation of water or wind. All this changed completely in advanced industrial society. Physical work in any pure form has all but disappeared. What is still called manual labour does not involve swinging a pick-axe or heaving soil with a spade, which on the whole people only do for recreation: it generally involves controlling, managing and maintaining a machine with a fairly sophisticated control mechanism. But for most people, 'work' is even further removed from the coal-face of nature, so to speak. It involves the rapid manipulation of meanings and people through computers, or at worst, telephones and typewriters and faxes, computerised tills, and so on.

All this has profound implications for culture, for the system of symbols in use. Such rapid interchange of messages between anonymous, distant interlocutors simply cannot tolerate the dependence of meaning on local dialectal idiosyncrasy, and still less on context, let alone highly specific context. Context is erased by the very method of communication. So meaning cannot be transmitted by the body posture, identity, tone, location of the speaker, or the timing or context of delivery. Status can neither contribute to meaning, nor be reinforced by it. The medium does not convey it. All those elements – posture, tone, etc. – were, in the actual folk language, a kind of phoneme: they contributed to the determination of sense. But these were phonemes with a strictly and narrowly limited use and validity, like an unconvertible municipal currency. A universal communication system requires that only tokens endowed with a universal, standardised, context-free significance be used.

It is now essential that the meaning is carried by the message alone, and be *internal* to it. Both the emitting and the receiving centre must be trained to attend to message alone, in accordance with shared rules concerning what is and what is not part of the message. People must be able to isolate the elements which generally contribute to the determination of meaning, and to ignore local idiosyncratic context. The acquisition of such a fine and well-tuned and *standardised* sensitivity to what is and what is not relevant, is not at all an easy matter. It presupposes sustained schooling and great semantic discipline. It calls for the conceptual equivalent of military drill: finely tuned responsiveness to formalised words of command with sharply defined rules of implementation – though the range of these possible commands is immeasurably greater than the one available in the military idiom. The meaning must be clear, the range of comprehended meaning very large, probably infinite.

What all this amounts to is that, for the very first time in the history of humankind, a *high* culture becomes the pervasive, operational culture of an entire society. People can respond to the full, infinite range of meanings contained in language, instead of merely responding, like a peasant recruit, to a finite list of words of command, and those only when yelled by a person with the appropriate insignia, and in the recognised context. The implications of this are tremendous and still have not been fully appreciated and explored. The importance of universal education – presupposed by the very basic organisation of society – goes far beyond woolly and pious commendations of the broadening of cultural horizons (assuming this takes place at all). Those implications include the pervasiveness of nationalism, which is our theme. A high culture is an orderly, standardised system of ideas, serviced and imposed by a corps of clerics with the help of writing. Roughly speaking the syllogism runs: work has become semantic, and work requires impersonal, context-free communication between individuals, members of a broad mass. This can only be done if the members of that broad mass share the same rules for formulating and decoding messages. In other words, they must share the same culture, and it will be a high culture, for this standardised skill can only be acquired in formal schooling. Conclusion: the entire society msut be pervaded by one standardised high culture, if it is to work at all. Society can no longer tolerate a wild proliferation of internal subcultures, each of them context bound and severely inhibited in their mutual intercommunication. Access to the appropriate high culture, and acceptability within it, is a person's most important and valued possession: it institutes a precondition of access not merely to employment, but to legal and moral citizenship, to all kinds of social participation. So a person identifies with their high culture, and is eager that they inhabit a political unit where various bureaucracies function in that same cultural idiom. If this is not so, the person will hope that either the boundaries or their own location change, so that it should *become* so. In other words, the person is a nationalist.

There is a further factor making for the standardisation of culture. Not wealth as such, but *growing* affluence is the key validating principle. This society is based not merely on mass affluence but, above all, on economic growth. It is the anticipation of continuous improvement which has come to legitimate the social order. If once upon a time a good harvest was the mark of a good king, now it is the sustained raising of industrial productivity which signifies a sound regime. The wasteland with an impotent king is now one with a zero or negative rate of growth. The ruler's virility is expressed in expanding productivity. The idea of progress is the philosophical expression of this attitude.

The price of growth is innovation and the perpetual and continuous transformation of the occupational structure. This society simply cannot constitute a stable system of ascribed roles, as it did in the agrarian age: the important roles are positions in bureaucracies, productive and other, and the bureaucratic structures are unstable, and they must be such. (It is the stability of certain defective structures, e.g. communist hierarchies, which is a sign, and probably the cause, of their low effectiveness.) Moreover, the high level of technical skill, required for at least a significant proportion of posts (probably not the majority, but in any case, for a significant minority of them), means that these posts have to be filled 'meritocratically', by competence, rather than in the old habitual way, that is by birth and ascription, and with a view merely to the perpetuation of a stable structure and the reinforcement of its loyalties.

All this renders this society basically egalitarian: it cannot easily ascribe rank, for such permanent rank would often come into conflict with the standing entailed by the actual occupational effectiveness of the person in question. The need to fill posts in the light of performance and competence is incompatible with the old principle of filling them in terms of permanent, ascribed, deeply internalised rank. The society is egalitarian because it is mobile, and not mobile because egalitarian, and it *has* to be mobile. All this has totally reversed the long-term trend towards ever-increasing inequality, which had previously accompanied the movement towards increasing complexity of societies, prior to the coming of the industrial–scientific age.[4] The egalitarianism, which the new order displays, does not exclude, of course, tremendous inequalities in wealth, power and life chances. But a baseline egalitarianism is nonetheless accepted as the norm by the society, and it is not devoid of a certain reality. It does possess a genuine social authority and effective social meaning.

The inequalities which do exist are gradual and continuous, rather than being marked by theoretically quite uncrossable chasms between estates or castes; they are so to speak, statistical, consisting of the probabilities of success or fortune, rather than of formal, definitive exclusions or entitlements, as used to be the case; and the differences are not internalised in the souls of the beneficiaries and the victims of the inequality. They are not self-justifying, but require pragmatic justification. If excessive, they are held to be scandalous. Privileges tend to be camouflaged rather than flouted. 'The very rich are different from us', said Scott Fitzgerald to Ernest Hemingway. 'Yes, they have more money', replied Hemingway. Hemingway was not altogether wrong, even if Fitzgerald had a point. Hemingway expressed the modern vision, for which external status does not enter the soul; Fitzgerald was a romantic attached to the old world, in which it *did*. The world has moved, in large measure at least, from Fitzgerald to Hemingway, as Tocqueville had insisted. People differ in their externals not their internals.

But above all, the formal rules of operation of the society, at work and in politics, both permit and, above all, *require* members of the society to have the same culture. The flow of context-free information is required for the running of the society in all its aspects. The information network requires that anyone can be slotted in at any point: it is no longer possible to reserve positions for prespecified categories of people. The sockets of the information network are standardised for all users, and not status specific. Anyone not competent to take part in this flow of signals is an obstacle and an irritant, and provokes reactions of hostility and exclusion, and is liable to suffer humiliation.

How should one best sum up the implications of such a social organisation for the relationship of culture on the one hand, and society and polity on the other?

So this kind of society not merely permits, but positively requires homogeneity of culture. It must be a culture of a specific king, that is a 'high' culture (needless to say, the term is used here in a sociological and not in an evaluative sense). It must be standardised and disciplined. All this can only be achieved by sustained education, and this kind of society is indeed marked by the near-complete implementation of the ideal of universal education. People are no longer formed at their mother's knee, but rather in the école maternelle.

The standardised educational system which processes the totality of the human material which goes to make up the society, which turns the biological raw material into an acceptable and serviceable cultural product, is enormously large, and exceedingly expensive. A large part of its cost tends to be taken up by the state or by its local subunits. In the end, only the state, or the public sector in a slightly wider sense, can really shoulder this onerous responsibility, and only the state can perform the task of quality control in this most important of all industries, that is the production of socially acceptable, industrially operational human beings. This becomes one of its main tasks. Society must be homogenised, *gleichgeschaltet*, and the only agency capable of carrying out, supervising or protecting this operation is the central state. Given the competition of various states for overlapping catchment areas, the only way a given culture can protect itself against another one, which already has its particular protector state, is to acquire one of its own, if it does not already possess one. Just as every girl should have a husband, preferably her own, so every culture must have its state, preferably its own. The state–cultures live in competition with each other. So this is the end product: a mobile, atomised, egalitarian society with a standard culture, where the culture is a literate, 'high' one, and where its dissemination, maintenance and boundaries are protected by a state. Stated even more briefly: one culture, one state. One state, one culture.

The theory of nationalism proposed here is materialist (though by no means Marxist), in so far as it derives the phenomenon to be explained from the basic manner in which society ensures its own material self-perpetuation. The earlier society based on agricultural production and on a stable technology was more or less doomed to a military–clerical ethos, to hierarchy, dogmatism, cultural plurality, a tension between a high and a low culture, and a political system based on power structures and religious ideology, but generally indifferent to cultural similarities. It proliferated differences, related to social positions, but not to political boundaries. The new society, based on expanding technology, semantic not physical work, on pervasive impersonal and often anonymous communication by means of context-free messages, and on an unstable occupational structure, is destined for a standardised, educationally transmitted high culture, more or less completely and pervasively diffused amongst all its members. Its political or authority structures will be legitimated by two considerations: by whether they can ensure sustained economic growth, and whether they can engender, diffuse and protect the culture which is the idiom of the society in question. Polity and high culture will thus become intimately linked, and the old links between polity and faith or dynasty will be dissolved, or reduced to a merely decorative, rather than genuinely functional, status. The state is a protector of a culture and not a faith.

The argument establishing this link seems to me virtually Euclidean in its cogency. It seems to me impossible to be presented with these connections clearly and not to assent to them. Spinoza claimed that it is impossible to state a truth clearly without granting it assent. Alas this is not generally true; but in this case at least, the connection does seem to me luminously manifest. (That, at any rate, is how the matter appears to me. As a matter of regrettable fact, an astonishing number of people have failed to accept the theory even when presented with it.)

It is no doubt exceedingly presumptuous to compare oneself to Euclid, or to hope that Euclidean cogency is ever available in the social sphere. My excuse is that I make the point with irony, and more in self-criticism than in vainglory. The argumentation does seem to me to have Euclidean force, but I also note that the world we live in is only in part Euclidean. There are many cases which illustrate the argument, but there are also many which fail to support it. This requires investigation. There is something odd about an argument which is cogent but whose conclusions are (even in partial) conflict with the facts. Perhaps – though that remains to be seen – the recalcitrant facts can be explained away as corollaries of other, complicating factors, not included in the initial model, but operative and significant in the real world.

Refinement of the theory

The original formulation of our position only specified two abstract ideal types, an agrarian society which is not nationalism prone, or rather, is liable to be positively nationalism resistant, and fully industrial society, which could hardly be organised on any base other than a national one. It presupposes, within each political unit, a standardised culture (or the other way round – it presupposes that each standardised culture would strive to attain its own state). But this formulation said nothing about the *path* by which societies or polities moved from the first of these two conditions to the second. Any properly worked theory will of course need to do precisely this. It is part of the present theory that nationalism manifests itself in its most acute form not at the terminus, but at some of the points of the transition between the two social types.

One can postulate five typical stages on the path from a world of non-ethnic empires and micro-units to one of homogeneous nation states:

1   Baseline. A world exists where ethnicity is still not yet self-evidently present, and where the idea of any link between it and political legitimacy is almost entirely absent.
2   A world which has inherited and retained most of its political boundaries and structures from the previous stage, but within which ethnicity

as a political principle – in other worlds, nationalism – is beginning to operate. This is the stage of Nationalist Irredentism. The old borders and polities are under pressure from nationalist agitation.

3   National Irredentism trimphant and self-defeating. Plural empires collapse, and with them the entire dynastic–religious style of political legitimation, and it is replaced by nationalism as the main effective principle. A set of smaller states emerges, purporting to fulfil the national destiny of the ethnic group with which they are identified. This condition is self-defeating, in so far as these new units are just as minority haunted as the larger ones which had preceded them. The new units are haunted by all the weakness of their precursors, plus some additional ones of their own.

4   Nacht und Nabel. I use this term, employed by the Nazis for some of their operations in the course of the Second World War. Under cover of wartime secrecy, or in the heat of conflict and passion, or during the period of retaliatory indignation, moral standards are suspended, and the principle of nationalism, demanding compact homogeneous ethnic groups within given political–territorial units, is implemented with a new ruthlessness. It is no longer done by the older and benign method of assimilation, but by mass murder or forcible transplantation of populations.

5   High level of satiation of the nationalist requirement, plus generalised affluence, plus cultural convergence, leads to a diminution, though not the disapearance, of the virulence of nationalist revendications.

Each of these stages requires some more detailed comments.

Baseline

Europe at the eve of the French Revolution did not in fact closely resemble the ideal–typical 'steady–state' agrarian society, as described. For over a millenium, there had been economic growth, and sustained political and ideological change. There was extensive urbanisation, fairly centralised polities had to a large extent replaced feudal fragmentation, and states were endowed with an effective bureaucratic apparatus. The Reformation had profoundly altered the rules of the game of cognitive and legitimative activities, and introduced the idea of direct private appeal to a socially independent fount of authority: initially scripture and private conscience, and eventually, individual reason or experience. The scientific revolution had begun, shortly to be followed by the working out of its philosophical presuppositions and sequences. The Enlightenment had formulated a vision of the world and society which was secular, individualistic and naturalistic. The economic and even the military centre of gravity of Europe had moved to its north-west corner, where a civil society, practising the separation of powers, was well established in England and Holland.

Surprisingly, the liberal states proved to be militarily at the very least equal, or superior, to centralised, war-orientated monarchies. In the eighteenth century, the nation of shopkeepers repeatedly defeated the larger nation of military aristocrats. (The latter could prevail only when in alliance with another set of shopkeepers across the ocean.) In extensive parts of north-west Europe, the pattern of kinship and household formation was individualistic, with late marriage based on individual choice by partners, rather than committed to the perpetuation of relations between larger kin groups.[5] In many areas, literacy and its use for secular purposes was very widespread. In all these ways, and no doubt in many others, Europe had long ago begun to move in the direction of that modern world which was to emerge and become so conspicuous in the nineteenth century.

Nevertheless, when it came to the determination of political units and their boundaries, and establishing their legitimacy, the world which was challenged by the French Revolution, and which was re-established after the defeat of Napoleon, continued to be governed by dynastic principles. The position of monarchs had actually been strengthened by the aftermath of the Reformation and the Wars of Religion, by abrogating the idea of an overall interstate arbiter of legitimacy, and thus rendering the sovereignty of an independent state and ruler absolute. Much of the modernisation carried out in the eighteenth century was the work of 'enlightened' absolutist monarchs, rather than of some more broadly based movements. It is true that royal absolutism had been challenged, both in political theory and in practice: but the English, after an experiment with a commonwealth and a Restoration, in the end found their liberties best ratified by a suitably restrained monarchy, rather than by its abolition. The Dutch Republic drifted towards a personal monarchy. Republican and elective institutions were rare, few of the erstwhile city states survived, and participatory form of government was on the whole restricted to smaller and less important entities. It is true that a *new* republic also emerged, and was successfully established towards the end of the eighteenth century in defiance of one powerful west European monarchy, though aided by another – but that was on the other side of the ocean.

The majority of agrarian polities had been monarchic, but the drift towards industrial society eventually also led to a move towards democracy. The inherent impulsion of industrial society towards egalitarianism may provide part of the explanation for this. The monarchical tendency of agrarian society is probably a consequence of the general logic of power situations: in all conflicts, it is desirable for the victor to eliminate the loser for keeps so as to preclude a return match, and it makes sense for all others to seek the favours of the victor, thereby strengthening the victor further. The logic of this snowball effect is operative in most circumstances, and explains the pervasiveness of monarchy in agrarian society, though there are exceptions, such as pastoralists in open country, or peasants in mountainous terrain, or sometimes, trading communities. All of these may escape the force of this argument, and find themselves endowed with participatory and internally balanced political institutions. Pastoralists escape central domination thanks to the mobility of their wealth, and are impelled to communalism by the need to defend themselves as collectivities; mountain peasants are endowed with forts by nature; and traders need elbow-room for individual initiative if they are to be effective, and suborning them is counter-productive.

Industrialisation, on the other hand, means the dominance of wealth acquisition over power acquisition. Wealth leads to power, and the contrary process, though not absent, is less overwhelming. The snowballing of power ceases to operate, and the snowballing of wealth (contrary to Marxist predictions) does not take place. So, power and wealth tend to become far better diffused.

One may add that government in an agrarian society does not require great talents or training, nor does it often permit their deployment if they happen to be available. To put this point more simply, any fool can be a king or a baron. Some personal qualities – ruthlessness, aggressiveness, courage, cunning – may be an advantage, but the equipment required for facing the decisions which have to be taken are such as to allow the filling of these posts at random, for example by heredity, which is the simplest, and commonest, manner of filling social slots in the agrarian world. In general, one may suppose that such a principle operates unless a society is loose and devoid of structure, or unless *special* factors operate so as to ensure the filling of positions in the light of some other consideration (e.g. the need of specific suitability for the complex and highly specific tasks which are to be performed).

Roughly speaking, the agrarian world fills social roles at random, and also attributes this allocation of positions to higher, transcendent authority. The deity is often credited with the supervision of recruitment to high office. By contrast, industrial society, at least in principle, fills them in terms of efficiency and performance, and justifies the procedure by human convenience. The shift to democracy can in part at least be explained as the effect of this general tendency to the problem of the filling of high posts in society and polity. When there is, at least in principle, equal access to most posts, it is difficult and illogical to restrict participation in decisions to some special segment of the population.

The theories of accountable, participatory, limited, plural, etc., government, which anticipated, accompanied or ratified the political changes of the eighteenth and nineteenth centuries, did not possess an agreed coherent theory concerning the precise nature and limits of the *unit* which was to be endowed with government. Society was to be democratic – but just *which* society was it to be? This question was not yet at the centre of attention. That there were indeed societies was something taken for granted; the question was just how they were to be run, on what principles, under whose rule, rather than precisely how they were to be delimited.

In the course of the nineteenth century, history gave an answer to a question which had hardly been asked: what exactly are the units which are to be endowed with government? It turned out to be – *nations*. But the unit which, in the modern world, is called a 'nation' does not altogether resemble anything known previously. It is a large body of anonymous individuals, either initiated into a high culture which defines that nation, or, at the very least, initiated into a low culture which has a recognised connection with the high culture in question, which constitutes its plausible human catchment area, and which predisposes its practitioners to enter the particular high culture in question, as probationary members. Units so defined had scarcely existed before. Now, they become the norm of political propriety. All other units become anomalies.

At the beginning of the modern world, in 1815, whether they existed or not (and on the whole, as yet they did not), nations were not yet taken into consideration in the making out of the new frontiers. And yet the world was such that it was soon to become ready to listen to those who would soon preach that *this* is how the world should be run: that legitimate political units were only those which were based on the nation, whatever that might be.

Irredentism

The age of nationalism or irredentism is the period during which there is much striving on behalf of the implementation of the ideal of one culture, one state. The old world of endless cultural diversity and nuance, only very loosely connected, if indeed connected at all, with political boundaries, acquires an air of political impropriety, illegitimacy. It is to be replaced by a world in which each culture has its own political roof, and in which political units and authorities are only legitimated by the fact that they protect and express and cherish a culture. An enormously complex linguistic or cultural map of Europe of (say) 1815, within which linguistic–cultural boundaries hardly correlated at all with political ones, is to be replaced by a new map on which, by (say) 1948, the correlation, whilst not absolute, is very marked.

There are various methods by means of which this congruence *in the end* be secured.

1   People can be changed. They can acquire the culture – including the self-image fostered by that culture, and the capacity to project that image and have it accepted – even if they had started from some other culture, some other set of internalised and projected images. The base-line from which they start may be a subculture or dialect reasonably close to the, as it were, terminal culture, or it may also be distant. The process may be largely spontaneous and even barely conscious, or it may be accompanied by directions from political and educational

authority, or it may be directed by freelance, independent cultural activists, acting independently of political authorities or even in defiance of them.

2   People can be killed. Persons held unsuitable for incorporation in the desired homogeneous 'ethnic' socio-political unit can be gassed, shot, starved, etc.

3   People held unsuitable for incorporation in the unit to be established in a given territory can be moved from that territory to some other place (whether or not that other place is occupied by a political unit welcoming them). The moves in question can be wholly compulsory, as when gendarmes simply pack off people in cattletrucks or lorries, or they may be voluntary in a sense, as when populations move of their own accord under threat of danger and harassment.

4   Frontiers can be adjusted with a view to combining culturally similar populations within single political units. Given the complexity of the ethnographic map of Europe in the nineteenth century, there are limits to what can be achieved by such a method, *unless* accompanied by the use of some or all of the preceding methods.

All these methods have in fact been used, sometimes also in combination or in succession. In the age of irredentism – stretching from 1815 to 1918 – on the whole, the relatively benign methods 1 and 4 were employed. Methods 2 and 3, though not unknown, only came into their own at the later stage. One way of establishing a typology of the manner in which the world-without-nationalism has been transformed into a nationalist world, is in terms of the concrete method used for the tidying up of the ethnic–political map.

It is worth noting that irredentism, whilst strong, was far from all powerful. It made the period 1815–1914 turbulent, but nevertheless it did not succeed in making *many* changes. Eastern Europe continued to be divided between three poly-ethnic empires. In that period, irredentism succeeded in creating five or six new buffer states in the Balkans, it united Germany and Italy, and produced one change in Scandinavia and another in the Low Countries. But clearly, it did not sweep all before it – till 1918. The brutal methods were in fact not much used in this period: it was a period of assimilation, and also of counter-assimilative 'awakening', that is of nationalist agitation encouraging people to form new state–cultures on the basis of the raw material of uncodified peasant cultures, as an alternative to entering cultures *already* linked to a state apparatus. The idiom of 'awakening' was deeply characteristic of the self-perception of this movement. It insinuated the existence of permanent but somnolent 'rational' entities, requiring a waking agent. The truth of the matter is rather that these entities were being *created*, not woken.

Irredentism triumphant and self-defeating

The Great War of 1914–18 brought to an end the Age of Nationalist Irredentism – by conceding many of its demands, at any rate when made by the victors or their protégées. Given the nature of the ethnographic map of Europe, satisfying *some* demands inevitably meant thwarting others. The greatest impact of this was in what we shall call the third time zone, in the area of highly complex multi-ethnic empires. Two of them in particular disappeared by 1918, presumably for ever, as a result of the two minor Balkan wars first, and then of the First World War.

The obliterated empires were replaced by smaller political units, self-consciously defined and legitimated by the nationalist principle. Each such new state was meant to provide political protection for a 'nation', that is a culture which was to provide the crucial moral identity for those who accepted it. The state is, awkwardly, the expression and agency of a nation, rather than of the totality of its citizens.

The principle of 'national self-determination' was implemented in the course of the peace-making procedures, and was intended to provide the outcome with its legitimacy. The implementation was of course not even-handed: the victors, and the clients of victors, naturally did rather better out of it all than did the losers, or those with inadequate clout in the negotiating process. However, the unfairness of some of the new boundaries did not constitute the only weakness of the new international order. Given the complexity and ambiguity of ethnic boundaries, *any* boundaries were bound to be offensive to some, and to be unjust by some perfectly plausible criteria. Given the complexity of the ethnic map of Eastern Europe, no uncontentious, manifestly just, political map was possible.

The real weakness of the new system followed from all this. The new states were smaller and hence weaker than the empires which they had replaced. But this diminution in size and strength was not compensated by a greater homogeneity and hence greater cohesion: not at all. They were as haunted by irredentist minorities as the dismantled empires, those much-abused 'prisonhouses of nations': perhaps they in turn should have been called the provincial or county goals of minorities. And the nouveaux minoritées, so to speak, those who suddenly had minority status and hence irredentist sentiment thrust upon them, were often members of the previous culturally dominant ethnic or linguistic group, not habituated to such a lowly position, and hence more liable to resent it, and better equipped to resist it. They could find help and encouragement in their home state which was dedicated to their own culture. They at any rate did not need to reconstruct, revive or invent past national greatness: it was, only too painfully, a matter of living recollection.

So to sum up, the new order set up in the name of the Nationalist principle had all the weakness of the system it replaced, plus some additional ones of its own. Its weaknesses were soon and rapidly demonstrated.

With the consolidation of an ideocratic dictatorship in Russia, and the establishment of an overtly nationalistic one in Germany, the entire edifice crumbled with amazing speed. Polish military resistance was to be measured in weeks, Yugoslav (official) and Greek resistance in days, and the other new national states did not resist at all (with the most remarkable and successful exception of Finland). Hitler and Stalin carved up the territories which separated them, with great ease and little opposition, at any rate from the state structures.

Nacht and Nebel

What was to follow was the period in which the benign method of securing homogeneity – namely, assimilation – was replaced on a terrifying scale by two less benign methods – mass murder and forcible transplantation of populations. This had already befallen some groups much earlier, notably the Armenians, and forcible population transfers also occurred in the wake of the Turkish–Greek War in the early 1920s. But the really extensive use of these methods came to be seen – or rather, initially, hidden – during the Second World War, and in the course of the period of retaliation immediately following it. Wartime secrecy, and then indignation and temporary Victors' Licence which followed the end of the war, made possible the deployment of methods hardly thinkable in more normal circumstances.

Mass murder and then forcible deportation (accompanied by a certain amount of incidental murder) tidied up the ethnic map of large parts of Eastern Europe, though certainly not all of it. The mass extermination was directed above all at certain populations held quite specially ill-suited to inhabit a Europe destined to exemplify the nationalist ideal of homogeneous communities, joyfully celebrating a shared culture, proud and secure in the knowledge that they were under the protection of a political organisation committed, above all things, to the safeguarding and perpetuation of that culture. Dirt has been defined as matter in the wrong place: minorities, in this New Europe, were cultures in wrong places. But there were certain cultures which were in the wrong place *wherever* they may find themselves: they constituted, so to speak, a kind of universal dirt, or rather, absolute dirt, a form of pollution which cannot be purified by any relocation. They exemplified that severance from both folk roots and biological vitality which is the mark of cerebral intellectualism, individualist calculation, abstract and universalist identity and aspiration. Diaspora nations, especially when socially located in the commercial, financial and later intellectual and creative zones of society – and thereby separated from the earthy vigour of physical work directly at grips with nature – incarnated that cerebral pathogenic cunning which was, for romantic–biological communalism, deeply antithetical to health and community. This is certainly what the Nazis (of a wide variety of nationalities) felt about the Jews. They constituted an offence against the principle of nationality, against the essentially ethnic and communal nature of man, tied to blood and land, and they did so not in virtue of being in the wrong place, but simply in virtue of existing at all.

The metaphysics of this kind of mass murder is extremely interesting, and constitutes an integral and significant part of the intellectual history of Europe. The original metaphysics of romantic nationalism had been relatively gentle and benign. It claimed only that it was legitimate, or preferable, for people to find fulfilment in an idiosyncratic folk culture, in the song and dance of the village green, rather than in emulating some formal, cold rules of courtly conduct. If the folk culture was a little less disciplined than the formal model of the court, if the dance was wilder and the drink coarser and stronger, and the gastronomy less refined, this in itself was not, as yet, lethal for anyone. The newly commended folk culture was often even held to be gentler than the aristocratic style it was to replace, with its roots in a professional warrior class. But there was already an inescapable shift towards the valuation of feeling rather than reason. This expression of feeling on the part of the less powerful strata of society, deprived of access to the more powerful weaponry and devoid of extended and disciplined, centralised organisation, was, however, not yet really all that menacing.

But beware. The gentle communalism, committed to nothing more than a romantic idealisation of peasant life and the folksong, is now supplemented by a new creed which says that true humanity, real fulfilment, lies in feeling, and that cold ratiocination is deadly, corrosive, pathogenic, unhealthy. The antithesis of the healthy peasant is the urban trader, whose work consists of calculation and of manipulation, and not in healthy, physical, vigorous and co-operative action in the fields. The communal-istically inspired argument can also, by about the middle of the nineteenth century and thereafter, be reinforced by another one, drawn from Darwin-ism. Vigour, assertion and feeling are good not merely because they are parts of a beautiful ethnic culture, but because they further that competi-tion which aids the survival of the fittest, and which leads to genuine beauty. How ugly those urban traders, with their flabby bodies and shifty eyes, and how beautiful the yeoman! How repulsive the self-tormenting thinkers, how handsome the confident warriors! Significantly, these senti-ments were on occasion internalised not only by the killers, but also by some of their victims.

When anti-intellectualistic, anti-cerebral romanticism blends with the revaluation of aggression and compassion, it thereby loses its erstwhile innocuousness. And now, consider the endowment of this cluster of senti-ments and ideas with formal organisation and political clout. This is precisely what the advance of nationalism does for it.

Nationalism presents itself as the reaffirmation of the culture of the village green against the cold putative universalism of some courtly or industrial or bureaucratic language: the village against Versailles or the

Hofburg and the Viennese coffeehouse – or against Manchester. But in fact, villagers themselves seldom if ever have the confidence, the resources, the organisational or conceptual means, or even the inclination, to fight for their own culture against city, court or industrial complex. They have more earthly concerns, and if they rebel, it is seldom for a culture. The people who do organise and agitate for a culture are the atomised, anonymous members of an industrial or industrialising society, eager not to be disadvantaged in the new world by being of the 'wrong' culture, anxious that the culture in terms of which they themselves operate, and the culture defining the dominant political unit in which they live, should be one and the same, so as to give them maximum professional prospects and psychic comfort.

What form does their organisation take? The cult of action and feeling which is inherent in populist romanticism turns the sports or gymnastic association into the paradigmatic form of nationalistic club. It is the Turn-Verein (sporting club) which, above all, provides nationalism with its sacraments. Gymnastics is quite specially suitable, more so than competitive and individualistic sports. Gymnastics is the most Durkheimian of sports, providing modern society with a ritual in which the solidarity of very large, anonymous, but co-cultural societies can be celebrated. Czech nationalism, for instance, is almost synonymous with the Sokol (Falcon) organisation: to say that a man is a Sokol was equivalent to saying that he was a patriot, though, ironically, the founders were two Germans. The Czech nation worshipped itself at the *Slet* (rally). When the communists took over after the coup in 1948, they decided, wisely from their viewpoint, to take over the Sokol organisation rather than to suppress it or fight it.

So nationalism came to be an ideology which combined the erstwhile gentle cult of the life of the village green with a vitalist metaphysics of assertion and physical vigour, and with a distrust of ratiocination if not a positive hostility to it. Darwin as interpreted by Nietzsche complements Herder. Natural selection was the means towards health and excellence, whereas universalism and bloodless, cosmopolitan intellectualism and compassion were the path to ugliness and disease. It was assumed that natural selection would operate primarily not on individuals, or the human species as a whole, but on what seemed to correspond to species within the human race, namely nations. Nations were assumed to be the permanent real categories of the social world: if they had not manifested themselves politically in earlier periods, this was only because they had been 'asleep', and the nationalists saw themselves as, above all, *awakeners*. To oppose conflict and ruthlessness in the dealing between nations was to align oneself with pathogenic forces of degeneration. These values and sentiments and ideas were carried and implemented by young men trained, *encadrées*, not so much by academic schooling, as by the shared disciplined exercises of collective physical action. In that age, nationalists made rather good soldiers. The chances were that they were in good physical shape, had taken a lot of exercise, done a lot of hiking, or even rock-climbing, had a keen eye, were good shots, and were used to responding to crisp words of command. Love of nature and of communal, energetic activity were unwittingly para-military. In modern times, the parts of Europe which constitute what might be called the zone of romantic and nature-friendly populism, on the whole, did better on the battlefield than populations more committed to other and more refined styles of joy.

This virulent style of nationalism, going so far beyond that which is merely required by the need for culturally homogeneous, internally mobile socio-political unity (i.e. nation states), reflects and expresses what one might call the Poetry of Unreason. Communality, discipline, hierarchy and ruthlessness are good, and constitute the true fulfilment of human needs, not *despite* the fact that they are anti-rational, but *because* they are such. Bloodless, barren universalistic reason was in conflict with real deep springs of human conduct, if not actually at the service of pathogenic ones (roughly, Nietzsche's view). When the German Army conquered Europe around 1940, it impressed those it conquered not merely by its might, but also by its beauty. ('How beautiful they are', Sartre makes a French prisoner of war remark, as he looks at his captors, in Sartre's novel depicting the fall of France.) This endowed the conquest with a certain legitimacy. The German soldier fought well not merely because he knew that he would be shot if he did not: he was also moved by a powerful national *esprit de corps*. Romantic *Kameradschaft* complemented Prussian discipline. The achievement of Nazism and its reritualisation of politics was to endow an anonymous and industrial *Gesellschaft* with the powerful and effective illusion that it was a genuine *Gemeinschaft*. It combined the efficiency both of industrial and absolute-monarchy discipline with the (idealised) affect-saturated cohesion of the localised kin group.

So this is the scenario: a purging of the joyful cohesive communal nation state not merely of intrusive minorities, but above all of those eternal–universal minorities whose intellectualism and/or commercialism made them inherently unfit to be a member of *any* folk culture, let alone of 'ours'. So the exterminations which took place in the 1940s, though secret, were not, so to speak, shifty, underhand and opportunist. They were carried out, or ordered, to a considerable extent by people who were doing what they were doing not out of individual self-interest, but in fulfilment of a duty, for the general good, in pursuit of purification and beauty. It was indeed secret: mass murder continued to be sufficiently appalling to make it politically preferable to hide it. But if the secrecy was a means, the act itself was not. It was *wertrational*, it was the fulfilment of an end held to be inherently valuable. One of the Nazis who commented on the extermination project invoked the name of Kant, and what he said was not absurd: it was done for a principle, not from self-interest. Indeed it did not advance, but hampered, the interests of those who perpetrated it. To ignore this, or to deny or obfuscate it out of shame and embarrassment, is to distort and obscure an important point in the history of European thought and feeling.

One of the best-known commentators of twentieth-century totalitarianism, Hannah Arendt, has argued[6] that the ideology of Nazism is somehow quite discontinuous with European thought, that it has emerged unheralded and unprecedented from some dark conceptual underworld. This seems to me altogether false. The particular blending of elements – a repudiation of universalism, a valuation both of culture and cohesion and of competitive ruthlessness, of discipline and hierarchy rather than market anarchy within society, plus a few other themes – is all, of course, far from being the sum total of the European intellectual tradition, but it also does not stand outside it either. In its naturalism, it is a continuation of the Enlightenment, and in its communalism and cult of idiosyncrasy, it is part of the romantic reaction to it.

But what all this amounts to is this: the fourth stage of the development of nationalism, that of the tidying up of the ethnic map by unimaginably brutal means, was not something accidental, a chance by-product of the opportunity (under cover of wartime secrecy) to be less scrupulous and publicly well behaved than is customary when under general observation and scrutiny. On the contrary, it was something which was inscribed on the agenda, so to speak, of European thought. On the complex ethnic map of Europe, especially Central and Eastern Europe, *any* solution of the problem of political boundaries was bound to thwart *many*. The fury provided by the prolonged frustrations was now aided by a social metaphysic which commended brutal solutions anyway, and it was implemented by a temporarily victorious movement genuinely committed to that metaphysic, and in possession of the will and the means to carry out its requirements.

Diminution of intensity of ethnic sentiment

A new age began in 1945. Those who had embraced the romantic cult of aggression – and of ethnic community – had been defeated, ironically, at the very court they had themselves chosen and declared to be ultimate and valid: trial by combat. That was the negative lesson. But fairly soon, it was to be followed by a complementary positive lesson. The postwar period turned out to be one of sustained and unprecedented prosperity, the age of generalised, or at any rate very widespread, affluence. But some were to be more affluent than others: the greatest affluence came to those who had *lost* in the war, and were thereby deprived of the opportunity for further cultivation of collective aggression, and who had also been ruthlessly shorn of much territory. From the very viewpoint of success and of natural selection, the warrior ethic turned out to be rather less than commendable. But on the positive side, the commercial–productive ethic also turned out to have great charms, and success in that field was clearly seen to be independent of the possession of territory. Consumerism made greater inroads on the traditional ethos of 'honour' than commercialism alone had ever done. *Lebensraum* turns out to be an irrelevancy. So peasant landhunger came to be seen to be as antiquated as the cult of military valour. Contrary to what Marx had said, *consume* rather than *accumulate* was Moses and the Prophets of the new order.

These considerations undermine the vigour of expansionist nationalism. In so far as it was rational, or claimed to be such, it assumed that the possession of territory was the mark or the precondition of national great-ness and/or prosperity, and it had now become clear that this is not so. The non-rational elements, the high valuation of aggression and martial virtues, is also undermined by consumerist values. So much for the level of ideology. But of course the main sphere of operation and transmission of nationalist sentiment is not the ideological, but the level of ordinary, daily, personal life. People really become nationalists because they find that in their daily social intercourse, at work and at leisure, their 'ethnic' classification largely determines how they are treated, whether they encounter sympathy and respect, or contempt, derision and hostility. The root of nationalism is not ideology, but concrete daily experience. A member of culture A, involved in constant dealings with economic, political and civic bureaucracies employing culture B, is exposed to humiliations and discrimination. This member can only escape by becoming either an assimilationist or a nationalist. Often the member vacillates between both of these strategies.

It is at this level that nationalism receives diminished impetus during the later and prosperous stages of industrialism. For one thing, there is an element of truth in the 'Convergence thesis' concerning industrial societies. It may or may not apply to cultures which are very distant from each other: cultures of European and East Asian advanced industrial societies may well fail to resemble each other, even when based on similar technology, and in possession of comparable standards of living. But if the cultural baseline is reasonably similar to begin with, as for instance is the case of most or all European nations in relation to each other, then the attainment of the late industrial stage of industrial competence and affluence also brings with it a quite considerable cultural convergence. The youth culture of Atlantic societies, for instance, is remarkably similar, and incidentally it was in this very field that the Soviet Union first humbly capitulated to the West, long before beginning to do so in other spheres with the coming of Perestroika. Soviet Pepsi Cola and longing for blue jeans preceded the Soviet love affair with the idea of the market. Amongst advanced industrial nations with a reasonably close cultural starting point, differences tend to become phonetic not semantic: people have and conceive and handle the same 'things' (generally made in the same way or even in the same places), and characterise them by the same concepts, but express these with words differing only in the sounds they use, rather than in their content.

Our theory of nationalism linked its emergence to the transformation of work: shared culture becomes important when work ceases to be physical and becomes semantic. Members of the same interacting community must share one and the same standardised code, and a person is identified by the code in terms of which they can operate. But if this is so, why should nationalism diminish again when the semanticisation of work reaches its height, and why should it have been most acute when this was only in its beginnings? And why should a *universal* phenomenon manifest itself as insistence on *distinctive* ethnic units? The answer lies in the unevenness of industrialisation, which maximises inequalities and tensions in the early stages, at the points of entry into the world of semantic work. It is then that it is in the interest of somewhat later entrants to organise their own state–culture unit.[7]

So, the other factor conducive to the lessening of the intensity of ethnic sentiment in daily life is the diminution of economic distance. This must be compared with the situation which had prevailed during the period when nationalist sentiment was liable to be at its strongest, that is during the early stages of industrialisation. At that stage, economic differences between the early entrants into the system, and others more privileged, are enormous. Early migrants into the industrial workforce, inhabiting rapidly erected slums or shantytowns, deprived of virtually any material or moral or political resources, really do have nothing other than their labour power to sell, and are obliged to sell it on the worst possible terms, barely if at all above the level required for merest survival. They note the difference between their own condition and those more fortunate, and the class hatred postulated by Marxism, and also noted by ideologically more disinterested observers such as Tocqueville, does indeed emerge. But, contrary to the predictions of Marxism, it does not persist and grow, unless it is endorsed with a, so to speak, ethnic *prise*. If the unfortunates are in a position to note that the more fortunate ones are culturally distinct from themselves, say in their speech, whether or not these differences are as yet linked to some ethnonym, then powerful sentiments, duly to be labelled national ones, rapidly emerge and persist. The impoverished ones have their own condition highlighted by the existence of others who are less unfortunate, and if those others are also distinct culturally, the unfortunates soon note that those who exploit them, or at any rate surpass them economically, are also those who add insult to injury by spurning them. They can spurn them generically, if indeed there is some generic cultural *differentia* which makes it possible to identify them as a human category. So, cultural *differentiae* become significant as catalysts of social cleavages and antagonisms, *if* they more or less coalesce with the marked, but culturally unhallowed, economic differences so characteristic of early industrialism. Generic contempt and privilege then engender a new generic identity. The new hatred arises on both sides of the great barrier. For the better placed category, the culturally distinguishable poor constitute a menace, not only to the social order as a whole, but also in daily life.

They are dirty and violent, they make the city unsafe, and they constitute a kind of cultural pollution.

During the later stages of industrialism, things are quite different. There are still enormous economic inequalities, and these sometimes correlate with cultural ones, and then become septic. Cultural category A is in general better off than category B, generating resentment among the B and fear among the A. But if both categories find themselves at a relatively high level, which is generally the case under late industrialism, though in 'objective', material terms those surviving differences may still be great, subjectively they matter much much less. Hence the intensity of resentment generated is also correspondingly smaller. The difference between objectively appalling poverty and mild prosperity is something tremendous: the difference between considerable prosperity and *very* considerable prosperity is psychologically far less great. Under conditions of advanced industrialism, differences between cultural categories tend to be of the latter rather than the former kind. The only categories of persons who are then massively underprivileged tend to be not cultural, 'ethnic' ones, but, so to speak, medical or personal ones – people with serious medical handicaps, isolated persons, and so forth. But such categories do not generate a 'nationalism'. (This general point does not of course apply to late labour migrants, who tend to be both underprivileged and culturally distinguishable, and who of course do generate virulent national sentiments on both sides.)

So, although a shared, context-free, education-based high culture continues to be the precondition of moral citizenship, of effective economic and political participation, under late industrialism, it need no longer generate intense nationalism. Nationalism can now be tamed, as religion had been tamed. It is possible to move a person's ethnicity from the public sphere to the private sphere, to pretend that it is only their own business, like their sex life, and something which need not interfere in their public life, and which it is improper to drag in. But this is really a pretence, which can be indulged if one dominant culture is appropriated by all and is usable as a kind of general currency, permitting people to be bi-cultural and use another one, if they so wish, in their homes and other restricted areas.

When the process of making work semantic reaches its apogee, it also has the tendency to endow advanced industrial cultures with the *same* meanings, to promote a convergence which, jointly with generalised affluence, diminishes conflict. It is *early* industrialism which both engenders maximum economic jealousy and resentment, and promotes the social imposition of high culture, which have not yet come to resemble each other.

All kinds, as it were, of federal or cantonal arrangements now become possible in the later stage. Political boundaries become less important, less obsessional and symbolic: it is no longer a matter of deep concern that 'our' border should be on a certain river or that it should follow the crest of a certain mountain range. Bitter tears are no longer shed, nor passionate poetry written and recited, concerning the failure of the custom barrier to be located on that beautiful waterway or that dramatic mountain range, for the attainment of which our boys had bled so bravely. It now seems sufficient that mobility and access to the advantages be more or less evenly distributed among cultural categories, and that each culture has its secure home base where its perpetuation is assured by its own university, national museum, national theatre, TV network and so forth. Solutions of roughly this form seem to be attained, or close to attainment, in a number of areas – which of course does not mean that they will be attained in general or universally.

The stages here described are the, so to speak, 'natural' steps along a path from the agrarian world, in which culture underwrites hierarchy and social position, but does not define political boundaries, to the industrial world in which culture *does* define boundaries of states, but where it is standardised, and hence insensitive, non-discriminating with respect to social position. It is hard to see how the transition could follow any other trajectory. In the beginning, there were dynastic or religious units, co-existing with and superimposed on local communal ones. Then came irredentism, seeking congruence of culture and state, and bound to be frustrated in most cases, because the complexity of the ethnic map simply does not allow the fulfilment of all the ethnic aspirations at once. Nationalism is not a zero-sum game, it is a minus-sum game, because the majority of cultures–participants is *bound* to lose: there simply are too many cultures, as it were potential state-definers, for the amount of space available on this earth for viable states. So, *most* of the cultures are bound to go to the wall and fail to attain their fulfilment, that is the marriage of the culturally defined nation with its own state, which is what nationalist theory anticipates and ardently desires. But the anger and fury engendered during this process, in conjunction with the Darwinian cult of ruthlessness, the Nietzschean endorsement of deep feeling as against reason, and the widespread social dislocation, lead very naturally to the kind of murderous excess, witnessed in Europe above all in the 1940s, but not unknown at other times. Finally, with the coming of generalised affluence and the diminution of cultural distance through late industrialism and a universal market and standardised life style, there comes a certain diminution of intensity of national sentiment.

That, in brief, is the trajectory one would naturally expect, and which, in many areas, one does indeed find. But the schema is by no means universally applicable, even in Europe. It may fail to find complete fulfilment in actual history for a variety of reasons. In Europe, the underlying mechanism played itself out in different ways in various time zones, and these differences deserve to be noted.

1   Centralisation *by* the state. A political unit may exist which was established by dynastic politics in the pre-nationalist era, but which happens

to correspond – all in all, though of course never completely – to a homogeneous cultural area. The territory it occupies contains a variety of local dialects (i.e. languages without any army and navy) which are, however, close enough to the language employed by the state apparatus in question to be treated as its 'dialects'. The speakers of these dialects may come to be persuaded that the formal and standardised speech which they are now encouraged to adopt, and obliged to use in writing and in dealings with the bureaucracy, is the 'proper' variant of the speech they employ at home.[8] That is how one *should* speak. The cultural habits of such populations, and their genetically transmitted traits, are such that they can be incorporated in the 'national' self-image of the dominant high culture without contradiction and without too much strain. This kind of situation on the whole prevailed along the Western, Atlantic seaboard of Europe. Strong dynastic states based on London, Paris, Madrid and Lisbon had existed since early modern times, if not longer, and could transform themselves into homogeneous nation states (though adjustments had to be made in Ireland, and minor internal organisational changes elsewhere as well). A centralised culture is established *against* peasants, and not on the basis of their culture. Peasants have to be turned into real citizens, rather than being used for the definition of a new national culture. Hence ethnography is here irrelevant to nation building. There is no call to record that which you wish to destroy. It is only when a new national culture is being constructed on the basis of an existing unself-conscious peasant mode of life that the latter becomes of absorbing interest for nationalist scholars.

2   Immediately to the east of the zone of strong dynastic states, which only needed to 'civilise' their peasants, there is another time zone, of what one might call unificatory nation-state building. Here we find a strong, confident, self-conscious high culture (or rather, to be precise, two of them). A standardised and normative German speech existed since the collective crusading push by Teutons into Eastern Europe, or at the very latest, since the Reformation. A literary movement around the turn of the eighteenth and nineteenth century finally consolidated it. The Italians possessed a normative, standardised literary language since the late Middle Ages, the early Renaissance. Admittedly, this normative variant of the language might only be used by a minority (in Italy, it has been claimed that this minority remained tiny well into the nineteenth century), and failed to penetrate the lower orders of society or of outlying regions.

But the main problem facing such a culture was the provision of a single and shared political roof for the entire zone, in which this culture was indeed already dominant, rather than creating a new culture. Once this was achieved, the problem faced was identical with that faced by the first zone: civilise the peasant savage. But political unification had to come first, and was at the very centre of attention: high cultural diffusion or 'education' came second. In this kind of state–nation building, thinkers and poets and propagandists, though neither absent nor unimportant, were less crucial than statesmen, diplomats and soldiers. What needed to be done in this zone was to unify a patchwork of mini-states or medium states, and in some cases, expel alien rulers from key positions. Achieving all this involved altering the balance of power of Europe in some measure, and acting against some powerful vested interests. This could hardly be done without some degree of violent conflict, and this kind of unification was indeed secured by war, and greatly aided by diplomacy.

3   The next time zone further east is the one which has supplied the best-known image of 'nation building': cultures exist, or are held to exist, which neither have their own state and merely require to 'educate' the lower orders, nor merely need to unify a multiplicity of political units (possibly also needing to expel some rulers thereof): on the contrary, cultures are found which do not possess a political unit at all, and which are not endowed with their own codification, their own internal authoritative norms. Plural folk cultures need to be replaced by norm-ative high cultures *and* endowed with a political cover.

   Within this category, it is usual to distinguish between 'historic' and 'non-historic' nations. The former had once possessed a state but had lost it; the latter had never had one at all. The former require a 'rebirth' of a political unit which had once existed, but had been somehow eliminated in the course of dynastic or religious conflicts. The latter require the creation of a political unit which is to be defined in terms of culture alone, without support from history. The difference between these two types is probably not as important as is often supposed.

   What is important about this species is that it requires 'awakeners', activists–propagandists–educators, committed to reviving the glories of the past, or alternatively, to bringing the nation to consciousness simply by virtue of its cultural existence, without the blessings of previous political history. Either way, these people have to act in a freelance manner, or if organised, under the guidance of organisations not endowed with the support of the existing political authorities. They do not as yet have a state to help them do it. It is this above all which distinguishes this pattern from 'centralisation from above'.[9]

4   Finally, there is a fourth time zone. This shared the fate of the third time zone in so far as it had passed through the first two stages between 1815 and 1918, experiencing dynastic/religious politics and the irre-dentist reaction to them. In fact, in 1815, Eastern Europe was divided between three empires, and the Czarist empire seemed set for the same trajectory as the Habsburg and Ottoman empires. All three empires had for a time on the whole resisted the nationalist onslaught – the Ottoman empire less successfully than the other two – and all three of

them, notwithstanding the fact that they were on opposed sides in the war, went onto the dustheap of history in 1918.

But thereafter, the land of Orthodoxy and Autocracy followed quite a different path from the territories of the other two empires, which now went ahead under the inspiration of a varied set of ideological cocktails. Within these, nationalism was the only stable and ubiquitous ingredient. In these small successor states, nationalism was blended, variously, with populism, democracy, fascism, clericalism, modernisation, dynasty, etc. The blends were not unduly impressive, at any rate as intellectual products.

The situation was quite different in the lands of the Czar of all the Russias. Within a few years of a shattering military defeat, the empire was re-established under new management and under a new ideology, one which was no feeble and opportunist cocktail, but, on the contrary, constituted one of the most powerful and moving belief systems ever created.[10] With hindsight, it is easy to see that Marxism was tailor-made for the needs of the anguished nineteenth-century Russian soul. This soul had been crucified between the desire to emulate and catch up with the West, and the messianic–populist aspiration for a total, and yet locally rooted, fulfilment. Marxism claimed, on the one hand, to be scientific and materialistic, and thereby to embody and unmask the secret which had made the West rich and strong, and to provide a formula for a shortcut which would lead to an overtaking of the West and to even greater power and wealth. But on the other hand, it also promised an eventual total fulfilment, one wholly free of exploitation and oppression and the moral defects and the compromises and tawdriness associated with the Western form of industrialism. In this total consummation, miraculously and mysteriously, the yearnings of the human soul for community, *and* the desire for individual independence, would be satisfied all at once. Humans would be both wholly free and yet at one with their fellows. This was the manifest destiny of all humankind, and its accomplishment was only thwarted by defects of social organisation which Marxism had at long last effectively diagnosed, and which it would in the fullness of time remedy. In its form, this programme was to be implemented by a dedicated, disciplined and ruthless secular order, whose possession of the absolute truth made redundant any preoccupation with formal procedural propriety and checks. Indeed, it felt obliged to disregard the requirement of merely formed justice (which it held to be a tool of bourgeois domination) in the interests of the class credited with the mission of liberating humankind. Its possession of substantive justice meant that it had little or no need of that formal justice which had only been used to mystify and to thwart real fulfilment.

This doctrine and spirit, superimposed on a country which had in any case long been endowed with centralist and authoritarian and messianic traditions, and one faced with tremendous tasks in its struggle for modernisation and for military security, led to horrifying consequences which are well known and hardly need to be rehearsed once again. But from the viewpoint of tracing the story of the implementation of the nationalist principle in European society, a few of the salient points of this development need to be restated. First of all, the shortcut in the end proved to be quite spurious, and, far from leading to an overtaking of the West, actually led to a widening of the economic gap and to increasing retardation. The strength of the ideology and of the institutions it engendered did, however, prevent the lands of the Czar from following, for seventy years, the same path as that followed by the erstwhile lands of the Habsburgs and the Ottomans. The faith eventually evaporated, not under the impact of the terror of the Stalin years – which, evidently, it could morally accommodate – but under the impact of the squalor of the Brezhnev era of stagnation.

My own guess is that the first secular faith to become a state religion lost its hold over the faithful, not because it was secular and thereby more open to refutation by historic fact (faiths tend if anything to be strengthened by such trials), but because it oversacralised the world, and granted the faithful no retreat into a profane realm, in which they could rest during periods of diminished zeal. Through Hegel, Marxism is descended from Spinoza, and it is implicitly pantheistic and sacralises all life. It has been claimed that societies cannot live without the sacred, but the fate of Marxism shows that they cannot live without the profane either. A faith which turns the economy into a sacrament cannot easily survive a prolonged period of manifest economic squalor and sluggishness. As long as the members of the apparat only murdered each other, faith remained vibrant; but when they started bribing each other instead, faith evaporated. When a failure of international competitiveness – economic and military – obliged the system to seek to reform itself through liberalisation, it was discovered that no one believed any more. The Nazis had believed in war and were eliminated by a violent trial by combat; the Bolsheviks believed in the verdict of the economy, and were eliminated by an economic contest.

At this point, the societies caught within this system resumed the development which had been frozen seventy (or in some areas, forty) years earlier. But the development was resumed on a social base altogether different to that which had been left behind seventy years ago: although there was considerable *relative* economic failure in comparison with the West, there had also been tremendous development compared with the past. There was now near-universal literacy, extensive urbanisation, and a certain modest, but nonetheless significant, economic sufficiency, large enough at any rate for many people to have a good deal to lose.

The system could now slot itself into the development which it had not been allowed to follow at any one of the three remaining stages: it could indulge in irresponsible irredentism and the setting up of new political units (which reproduce, on a smaller and hence even more vulnerable scale, the ethnic conflicts of the disintegrating imperial unit); or it could pass to the murderous stage of *Nacht und Nebel*, with killing and forced or encouraged migration; or it could reach out to that stage of diminished ethnic hatred which, one hopes, goes with very advanced industrialism. There is clear evidence for each of these three possibilities, and it is yet too early to say which one of them will predominate; we can only say with confidence that none of them will be wholly absent. But which one will prevail – *that* is the crucial question concerning the development of the Soviet Union or its succession in the 1990s.[11]

One should add that the schema of the four time zones needs a certain modification if it is to correspond to historic reality: there is an extensive area between the Baltic, the Adriatic and the Black Sea, which belonged to the third zone in the interwar period, but was forcibly transferred to the fourth zone by the advancing Red Army in 1944–5, and remained there till 1989.

An alternative vision

The periodicisation proposed here differs significantly from that offered in the highly influential and powerfully argued and well-documented work of Miroslav Hroch.[12] As Eric Hobsbawm observes,[13] 'the work of Hroch . . . opened the new era in the analysis of the composition of national liberation movements'. Hroch represents an interesting attempt to save *both* Marxism and the nationalist vision of itself, and this constitutes part of his interest: nations really exist and express themselves through nationalist striving, instead of being engendered by it and being its creation. At the same time, the transition between the past Marxist 'modes of production' remains *the* basic event of the time, and the (autonomous?) nationalist development is plotted against the event. Hroch's outstandingly well-documented argument deserves full examination, though I disagree with him on both counts: nations do not 'really exist' (they only emerge as a special form of correlation of culture and polity under certain economic conditions); and the Marxist feudalism/capitalism transition is acceptable only if reinterpreted as the transition from the agrarian to the industrial world.

So, Hroch's typology or periodicisation is engendered by the superimposition of two sets of distinctions. One of them is defined in terms of the stages of the overall social order, the other in terms of the successive character of the national movement itself. The first distinction is binary:

it refers to the distinction between feudalism and absolutism on the one hand, and capitalism on the other. The book was written from an avowedly Marxist viewpoint, though at the time it was written and published, it could hardly have seen the light of day in Prague had it not been formulated in that way. This does not necessarily imply that the Marxism of the argument was less than sincere; that is a question which it would seem to be inappropriate to raise here. At the same time, this is obviously a part of the background of the book, and it cannot be ignored.

This use of the Marxist theory of historical stages calls for some comments. Hroch as stated combines 'feudalism' and 'absolutism' in *one* 'stage'.[14] It is no doubt possible to include both of them with a broader, generic 'feudalism': within both of them, status is linked to land. Within each, there is a sharply differentiated system of ranks, connected with unsymmetrical obligations and duties, and organised in a pyramid with a monarchical apex. In each, there is an ethos of martial valour, a low valuation of productive work, and an even lower or ambiguous valuation of commerce and trade. The terminology of rank under centralised absolutism is the same as in, and is indeed inherited from, feudalism in the narrower sense. So they do share certain important features.

But the differences are at least as great and as important as the similarities. An absolutist state relies largely on a standing and professional army, within which the nobility may serve as officers, but to which they do not normally bring their own entire social units 'in arms'. The 'regiment' of a given nobleman, or one named after him, is in fact a standard unit subject to standardised rules of equipment, organisation and command, and it is not the nobleman's household, estate and retinue reorganised for campaign, and run in terms of its own local, particularistic traditions. The absolutist monarch controls the territory over which he or she is sovereign, and legal and political authority in outlying or inaccessible regions is not delegated to nobles with a local power base. As Adam Smith noted in connection with Cameron of Lochiel, such delegation, unsanctioned by law, did in fact occur in the pre-1745 Highlands, but it is precisely this which made the Highlands untypical and exceptional in an otherwise centralised state.[15] Under absolutism, the *noblesse d'épée* is complemented and in some measure replaced by a *noblesse de robe* – in effect, a bureaucracy. Under the Tudors, a new nobility with a service ethos complemented and replaced an independent, territorially based aristocracy.

It is significant that the name of Tocqueville does not occur in Hroch's bibliography. The idea that the French Revolution completed, rather than reversed, the work of the centralising French monarchy receives no discussion. The French Revolution is in fact only mentioned once (though the generic notion of 'bourgeois revolution' occurs far more frequently and plays an important role in the argument). When the French Revolution is mentioned by name, it occurs in the context of a methodological discussion, and of an affirmation of the author's commitment to a Marxist view of history, and to seeing *class*, rather than, so to speak, surface social position, as ultimately significant.[16]

But it is hard not to suspect that at this point at least this author's indisputably most important argument suffers not from an excess, but from a lack of Marxism. The assumption of a generic (and homogeneous?) social baseline, a catch-all feudalism–absolutism, prevents one from even raising the question of the relation of the rise of nationalism to *earlier* structural changes in European society. But it clearly is, at the very least, necessary to ask the question concerning the connection between nationalism and that earlier transition from a politically fragmented, genuinely feudal society, within which bureaucracy is largely absent, or at best present in or drawn from the church, to that later 'absolutist' society, in which a secular bureaucracy is already prominent.[17] In that later social order, widespread administrative use of writing already begins to engender that linkage of a centralised polity and a literate, normative, codified high culture, which lies close to the essence of the nationalist principle. Nationalist movements did not yet emerge in this period, but it is certainly arguable that it prepared the ground for them, through the centralisation, bureaucratisation and standardisation which it practised. Whether or not this is so, it should be possible at least to ask the question. Though I subscribe to the view that, on the whole, nationalism in the form in which we know it is a phenomenon of the last two centuries, nevertheless it must be a defect of a theory of nationalism if, starting so uncompromisingly from an implicitly generic baseline of 'absolutism–feudalism', it actually inhibits the formulation of any questions concerning possible earlier roots.

There are other candidates for this role of early progenitors or harbingers of nationalism, notably the Reformation and, to a lesser extent perhaps, the Renaissance. The Protestant use of vernacular languages and the diffusion of literacy, and the direct contact of the believer with the Sacred Word (in an idiom intelligible to the believer) clearly has affinity with the social profile of nationalism. The creation of national rather than international clergies, or the diffusion of the clerkly status throughout the whole of society, cannot be irrelevant to the eventual emergence of the nationalist ideal of one culture, one state, one society. The fragmentation of the universal political system, the diffusion of sovereignty, cannot but be a significant part of the prehistory, if not the history, of nationalism. When Bernard Shaw causes his version of St Joan to be burnt as a Protestant by the church and as a nationalist by the English, was he being altogether anachronistic? The absence of the name of Jan Hus from the index of a Czech book on nationalism is also strange.

So one can repeat the point that, in a curious way, this remarkable work in part suffers not from an excess, but an insufficiency of Marxism. The major social transition to which its argument links nationalism is simply the move from absolutism–feudalism to capitalism, and it altogether ignores earlier, and possibly relevant, transitions. A person like the present writer, who does believe that nationalism is essentially linked to the coming of industrialism, cannot wholly disagree with such an approach, and does not really object to the use of 'capitalism' where 'industrialism' would be more appropriate: that is simply a part of the Marxist idiom, and made mandatory by that repudiation of the convergence-of-capitalist-and-socialist-industrialism thesis to which Marxism was committed; but one can easily carry out one's own translation of the terminology here. Nevertheless, one feels that the convention that the world began in the late eighteenth century is here carried to excess.

In this connection, it is of course also worth noting that the discussion of the implications for nationalism of the transition from capitalism to *socialism* is equally absent. Its handling would of course have been extremely delicate. Work attempting to handle the role of ethnicity in Soviet society (that of the late Yulian Bromley's) is, however, cited.

The basic logic of Hroch's approach then is to relate nationalism to a single and stark transition, namely that from pre-industrial to capitalist society. What exactly is it that is then so related to the underlying single great change in social ecology and structure?

The answer is – the phenomenology of nationalism. Here Hroch operates not with a binary, but a three-term classification, a three-stage account of the development of nationalism. Hroch distinguishes between stage A, that of scholarly interest in and exploration of the culture of a nation, stage B, of nationalist agitation – the intellectuals no longer restrict themselves to ethnography, but promote national awareness amongst the population whose national culture they investigate – and finally stage C, the emergence of a mass national movement.

This typology is inspired by and specially applicable to (as the author recognises) the emergence of 'small' nations not already endowed with, so to speak, their own and distinctive political roof. So, by implication – though the author does not formulate it in any way – the two dimensions formally introduced (traditional/capitalist, and the three stages of national awakening) are *also* related to a third dimension, along which we have the distinction large and state-endowed nations, as against small and 'oppressed' ones. In this last dichotomy, state endowment would seem to be more important than size in a literal sense, in so far as the Danes appear to be consigned to the 'large nation', which can hardly be correct in some simple numerical sense.[18] This makes the Danes a large nation, and the Ukranians a small one.

Formally speaking, this dimension or variable does not enter the argument, in so far as the official, declared subject of Hroch's enquiry is precisely nationalism amongst 'small' nations, that is nations which need to *acquire* their political unit. However, notwithstanding the fact that this – the nationalism of 'small' nations – is the formal subject matter of the book, it is I think natural, appropriate and illuminating to reinterpret the argument as a general treatise on nationalism, in which the focus on 'small oppressed' nations covers an approach which treats them as one distinctive variety of nation formation in general. The theory implied then in fact covers both species, 'great' and 'small' alike.

However, officially, at the heart of the book there is the relationship between the two-fold classification of societies, and the three-fold classification of stages of nationalism. The manner in which these two overlap with each other then leads Hroch to propose four types of nationalism.[19]

The first type he calls the 'integrated type' of development. The transition from scholarly interest to active agitation precedes the industrial and bourgeois revolutions. The completion of the 'formation of a modern nation' follows these, and is in turn followed by the emergence of a working-class movement.

The second species he calls the 'belated type': national agitators replace scholars before the coming of the bourgeois and industrial revolutions, and the emergence of a working-class movement precedes or is contemporaneous with the transition from agitation to mass nationalism, and the formation of a full modern nation only follows all the other processes considered.

The third variety he calls the 'insurrectional type': agitators replace scholars already under feudal society, and a modern nation is actually formed under feudalism: 'The national movement had already attained a mass character under the conditions of feudal society.' The nation is formed before the emergence of bourgeois society.[20]

Finally, there is the fourth species, which he calls 'disintegrated': in this variety, even the early forms of nationalist activity only follow the bourgeois and industrial revolutions, and the nationalist agitation is not necessarily replaced by a mass movement at all. The generalisation which seems to follow (and the author articulates it, though not quite in these words) is that very early industrialisation can be fatal for nationalism.

An interesting and distinctive aspect of Hroch's approach is the importance of phase A in nation formation, which he describes as follows: 'The beinning of every national revival is marked by a passionate concern on the part of a group of individuals, usually intellectuals, for the study of the language, the culture, the history of the oppressed nationality'.[21] Hroch rightly notes that these ethnic explorers are quite often not members of the ethnic group in question: the awakening does not necessarily or exclusively come, so to speak, from within. There often are vicarious awakeners.

The presence and salience of this state could usefully be made into a *variable* in a general theory of nationalism, embracing 'large' and 'small' nations alike, rather than being, as it is in Hroch's argument, a *constant* in the study of 'small' nations (by which Hroch as stated means not size, but the absence of an indigenous ruling class and state). If we adopt such an approach, we can both see that, *and why*, this stage is so prominent in some of the European time zones, and absent in others. In the westernmost time zone, national unity is forged not with, but against, the peasantry. 'Peasant' is a term of abuse, not of endearment, in such societies.[22] National unity and the sense of nationhood is formed in a 'Jacobin' spirit, around an already existing and expanding set of central institutions, and the high culture associated with it. Peasant regional idiosyncrasy is an offensive hindrance, and it is to be ironed out as quickly as possible by an educational system which holds this to be one of its most important objectives. In the second time zone, populist romanticism *is* encountered, especially in Germany: the fragmented political units preceding national unification often practised alien speech and manners in their courts, and the local culture is stressed in opposition to this alien style. Nonetheless, a sense of national unity is forged against and not in support of regional dialects and life styles, and ethnography is not the handmaiden of nationalism. When Mussolini encouraged Italians from the south and from Veneto to settle in the Val d'Aosta, he was, all at once, combating both the good French speech of the Savoyard ruling class, habituated to seek their brides in Chambery rather than in Italy, *and* the idiosyncratic local dialect of the Valdotain peasantry.

It is in the third time zone that this ethnographic 'phase' is pervasively and inherently present. Here, a national and state culture is created not in opposition to peasant idiosyncrasy, but on the basis of it. Of course, it has to be sifted and distilled and standardised, but nontheless it must first of all be investigated in its raw state, if it is ever to be streamlined and codified, and to provide the base for a new high culture around which a nation and state are to be created. The much-used distinction between historic and non-historic nations matters relatively little: it does not make too much difference whether the dialect group in question had, long ago, been linked to a political unit and its own court culture, or whether it had never had such a standing. This makes some difference to the content of national myth which is to be created: the Czechs or Lithuanians can look back to medieval glories, whereas the Estonians, Latvians, Byelorussians or Slovaks cannot. Only peasant folklore or the odd social bandit, but no monarchs or imperial exploits, can enter their mythology. But this hardly matters much.

The fourth time zone possesses features both of the first and the third zones. Ethnic exploration, in the form of Slavophil populism, not only existed, but was extremely important and prominent. But its point was not to create a national identity as a basis for a new state: a state already existed, and was linked to a national church, which seems to have done a good job in creating a national cultural identity. The celebrated 'going to the people' was concerned more with the definition or modification or re-establishment of the 'true content' of the national culture, than with its actual *creation*. Was this culture to be based on the values of peasant life style and religiosity, or on the elite or courtly orientation, with its orientation towards strong Westernising themes? Amongst the other, non-Russian ethnic groups of the empire, on the other hand, the parallel with the third zone largely prevails. This is also the part of Europe much of which, in or around 1945, so to speak, 'changed zones'. The countries forcibly converted to communism with the help of the Red Army, in the later 1940s were in the third zone till then, but were absorbed into the fourth zone thanks to communism – that is, the nationalist trajectory was interrupted between about 1945 and 1989. It expressed itself dramatically in Yugoslavia in 1991.

One can sum up all this as follows: the nation states which replaced dynastic religious ones as the European norms in the two centuries following the French Revolution could grow around pre-existing states and/or high cultures, or they could, as it were, roll their own culture out of existing folk traditions, and then form a state around that newly created normative great tradition. In the latter case, a consciousness and memory had to be created, and ethnographic exploration (in effect: codification and invention) were mandatory. This is Hroch's 'phase A'. But in the former case, folk tradition, instead of having to be endowed with memory, had to be consigned to oblivion, and be granted, not the gift of memory, but of forgetting. The great theoretician of this path of nation formation is of course Ernest Renan.[23] In the East they remember what never occurred, in the West they forget that which did occur. It was Renan who urged the French, in the interest of consistency, to abjure the political use of ethnography and ethnology: the boundaries of France never became ethnic, and they continue to invoke geopolitics and choice, rather than folk culture. It was also he who eloquently expounded the idea that the basis of national identity is not memory but amnesia: in the national Jacobin French state, French people were induced to forget their origins, in contrast to the non-national Ottoman empire, where the very bases of social organisation ensured that everyone knew their ethnic–religious origin. To this day, Ottoman legislation survives in Israel, thanks to a parliamentary balance which makes the religious vote valuable for most coalitions, and so helps ensure that a man can only marry in terms of his pre-modern, communal identity, by using its church.

So ethnographic research is relevant in some but not all European contexts of nation building: in others, its absence, or at least its political irrelevance, is just as important. Western nationalism ignores and does not explore folk diversity. So the options are created memory, or induced oblivion. The great irony occurred in the history of social anthropology: through the enormously influential work of Bronislaw Malinowski, who virtually created and defined the British and Imperial school in this discipline, the kind of cultural–holist ethnography, initially practised in the interests of culture preservation and nation building in the East, was adapted in Western science in the name of and for the sake of empiricist method.[24]

However, the main centre of Hroch's remarkable work lies not in his characteristically Central European stress on the contribution of ethnography to nationbuilding, but in his manner of relating the general story of the transformation of the European socio-economic system to the rise of nationalism. Here, in effect, he faces one of the most persistent and deep issues in this field: is it nations, or is it classes, which are the real and principal actors in history?

Admittedly, he proclaims his intention to start from Marxist principles:

> We shall not disguise the fact that the generalising procedures we use in investigating hidden class and group interests and social relations are derived from the Marxist conception of historical development.[25]

Yet interestingly, his formal position also firmly disavows any reductionism with respect to nations:

> In contrast with the subjectivist conception of the nation as the product of nationalism, the national will and spiritual forces, we posit the conception of the nation as a constituent of social reality of historical origin. We consider the origin of the modern nation as the fundamental reality and nationalism as a phenomenon derived from the existence of that nation.[26]

This affirmation could hardly be more clear or categorical. Nations or, strangely, 'the *origin* of the modern nation' (my emphasis), is part of the basic social ontology, and not merely a historical by-product of structural change, although it also appears (p. 4) that the characteristics which define a nation are not stable.

So his position in the book might be described as semi-Marxist: on the one hand, nations are granted an independent historical importance and reality, and are not reduced to a reflection of changes in class structure, but nevertheless they remain at the centre of the stage. Yet the transition from feudalism–absolutism to capitalism also retains its central position. A discussion of the subsequent transition to socialism is largely avoided – which is understandable, though in an oblique way it remains present through the importance attributed to the emergence of a military working-class movement, presumably meant to usher in a new era. It is neither affirmed nor denied that this working-class movement will eventually prevail and lead to new social formation altogether. There is nothing in the book to preclude anyone from supposing that this will happen. Given the fact that the book was written and published under a regime which was formally committed to the view that it had happened, and did not permit any public denials of such a claim, the sheer fact that there is no actual and explicit affirmation of it is not without some interest.

So the overall conclusion of the book seems to be that, on the one hand, nations do have an independent and irreducible existence, and that, nonetheless, the main historical reality remains the kind of change in class relations postulated by Marxism. History would seem to have *two* themes: class conflict *and* the reality of nations. So the emergence of modern nations must be related to this great transformation – a task the book then carries out with an unrivalled empirical and conceptual thoroughness. Neither of the two movements – the transition to industrialism (capitalism, in the book's terminology) and the other to nationalism – is said to explain the other. The book conspicuously steers clear of any reductionism: both Marxists and nationalists are granted their respective realms, but neither is allowed to claim domination of the other. By implication, the two realms are declared to be independent. This seems to me mistaken: both are in reality aspects of *one single transition*.

But in the light of the actual more concrete findings of the book, can these conclusions really be sustained? Or is it the case that these admirable analyses and documentation in fact support quite a different conclusion? Such a conclusion would, on the one hand, be far more reductionist *vis-à-vis* nations, and refrain from endorsing their ultimate reality; on the other hand, it would also take far less seriously the Marxist theory of social transition. It would be silly to be dogmatic on these complex matters, or to disagree with Hroch's contention that there is much more work to be done; nonetheless, I am inclined to argue that, even or especially in the light of evidence adduced by Hroch, the rival conclusion does seem to be borne out by the facts.

This rival conclusion could run something as follows: the pre-industrial world (feudalism–absolutism in Hroch's terminology) is endowed with a complex patchwork of cultures, and very diverse political formations. Some cultures pervade the ruling strata and the political apparatus of a state. These cultures eventually define, in his terminology, 'great nations' (though actual size in the literal sense seems to be irrelevant). Other cultures (those of 'small' nations) are not so favourably located. They do not include rulers and occupants of key political posts amongst their fellow practitioners of the same culture. They must *create* their high culture, before they could even strive for a state which would then protect it.

Hroch agrees that genuine modern nationalism does not occur in the earlier, pre-industrial stage, and that territorial movements ('Landespatriotismus') in this period should not be counted as a form of nationalism, contrary to the views of authors such as Hans Kohn.[27] The real national principle comes to operate only in a new social order, with its greatly increased social mobility and the enormously increased importance of high, literate culture. Thus far, we seem to be in agreement.

The pre-industrial world is characterised by strata which, as it were, 'know their place': in other words, estates. The industrial world by contrast is characterised by strata which do *not* know their place, in other words, by 'classes'. Their places are not frozen. If this transition is the essence of the 'bourgeois revolution', then this revolution, at any rate, really does take place. But is there any example of the series of transformation of class relations, as postulated by Marxism, actually being completed? And why should we treat it as independent of nationalism and of *its* phases?

What *has* in fact happened is that national revolutions did occur in those cases in which class and cultural differences overlapped: classes without cultural differences attained nothing, and cultural ('ethnic') differences without class differences also achieved nothing. It was only their conflation which had a true revolutionary potential. In Hroch's very own words:

> Class struggle on its own led to no revolutions, and national struggle without conflict between strata in a mobile industrial society was similarly ineffective. . . . [C]onflicts of interest between classes and groups whose members were divided at the same time by the fact that they belonged to different linguistic groups had indisputable significance for the intensification of the national movement. The polarity of material contradictions therefore ran parallel to differences of nationality, and as a result of this conflicts of interest were articulated not (or not only) at the social and political level appropriate to them but at the level of national categories and demands.
>
> (p. 185)

So, class conflict only really took off if aided by ethnic/cultural differences. But equally (pp. 185 and 186).

> where the national movement . . . was not capable of introducing into national agitation . . . the interests of specific classes and groups . . . it was not capable of attaining success.

So national movements were only effective if sustained by class rivalry. So, classes without ethnicity are blind, but ethnicities without class are powerless. Neither classes nor nations on their own engender structural changes. It is only their conflation which, in the conditions brought about by industrialism, does so.

Or again (p. 189)

> the members of the new intelligentsia of the oppressed nationality in as far as they did not assimilate – were faced with an obstacle which impeded . . . their chance of rising into a higher social position. As soon as membership of a small nation began to be interpreted . . . as a group handicap, it began to function as a source of transformation of the social antagonism into a national one. It is the presence of cultural barriers to the mobility inherent in industrial society which leads to social transformation. Industrial society leads not to class war but to the emergence of homogeneous nation states.

So, in the end, we are faced with a picture which in effect treats neither classes nor nations as given. Standardised cultures become politically significant in the new industrial world, but, of the very many available cultures, the ones selected for the new role are those which overlap with important economic cleavages, engendered by the turbulent passage to industrial society. This is precisely the theory we have been arguing.

Industrialism engenders mobile, culturally homogeneous, units. It leads to nationalist revolutions when class and cultural differences overlap. Hroch's strategy of relating these to each other, as if they were independent, is unworkable. They are politically effective if, and only if, they are *jointly* present. He himself spells this out. Class conflict on its own fails to engender revolutions. As the overwhelming majority of cultural differences also fails to find political expression, and cannot and does not find political expression, there is no case for reifying nations either. Before the event, we can only identify countless cultural differentiations, and we simply cannot tell just which will turn into 'nations'. *After* the event, we know which nation *happened* to crystallise, but this does not justify saying that the nation in question 'was there' from the start, ready to be 'awakened'. Neither national nor class ideology should be taken at face value. Both antagonistic classes and antagonistic nations are explicable, though not in Marxist fashion. They are only effective in conjunction. This is the truth of the matter.

Hroch's work is valuable not only for the outstanding and unrivalled richness of its empirical material, and the ingenious manner in which it is used for the deployment of the comparative method; it is also valuable for its underlying theoretical purpose. That aim seems to me deeply misguided, but the determined effort to implement it is valuable precisely because it enables us to see its weaknesses. What Hroch in effect tries to do is to confer scholarly respectability on two of the great myths of the nineteenth and twentieth centuries, namely Marxism and nationalism. He does this by retaining the Marxist theory of historic stages (or rather, a truncated segment thereof), and to relate it to a schema of national awakening, specially applicable to what we have called Europe's third time zone. The nationalist myth is also endorsed by attributing some kind of genuine independent and pre-existent reality to the nations which *did* succeed in 'waking up'.

This vision is in the end indefensible. History in general is *neither* the conflict of classes *nor* of nations. In general, it is rich in countless kinds of conflict, not reducible to those two alleged basic forms of conflict. Pre-industrial society is exceedingly rich in status differences, but there is nothing to support the argument that, under the surface, these are reducible to generic 'classes' defined by their selection to the means of production, and that the underlying very process, in the end governing all else, is the conflict of these 'classes'. Nor are these persistent compact 'nations' waiting for the alarm-bell. Under the impact of a certain kind of socio-economic form, best described as 'industrialism', both classes (loose and unhallowed strata in a market society) *and* nations (anonymous, self-conscious, culturally defined human categories) emerge and become politically significant, and engender changes in boundaries *when the two converge.* Economic tension signalled and underscored by cultural differences is politically potent, and it does radically reorder the map. Cultural homogeneity is imposed, and when cultural boundaries more or less converge with economic differences, related to the point of entry into industrialism, *new* boundaries emerge. Neither economic tension nor cultural difference on its own achieves anything, or at any rate, not much. Each of them is a product rather than a prime mover. The socio-economic base is decisive. That much is true in Marxism, even if its more specific propositions are false.

The genuine reality underlying the historic development seems to me to be a transition between two quite different patterns of relation between culture and power. Each of these patterns is deeply rooted in the economic bases of the social order, though not in the way specified by Marxism.[28] In the pre-industrial world, very complex patterns of culture and power were intertwined, but did not converge so as to form national–political boundaries. Under industrialism, both culture and power are standardised, and they underwrite each other and they converge. Political units acquire sharply defined boundaries, which are also the boundaries of cultures. Each culture needs its own political roof, and states legitimate themselves primarily as protectors of culture (and as guarantors of economic growth). This is the overall pattern, and we have also sketched out the manner in which its specific manifestations differently appear in various parts of Europe.

Neither classes nor nations exist as the inevitable and permanent furniture of history. This does not exclude the possibilities that, in certain specific circumstances, the dominant conflict may not occur between large anonymous groups defined by shared culture (nations), or large anonymous groups defined by their place in the productive process (classes, in the Marxist sense). What it *does* exclude is the doctrine that either classes or nations provide the units for some kind of permanent conflict which is the key to history. *Neither* in fact provides such a permanent underlying theme. Agrarian society is endowed with both complex stratification and complex cultural diversity, but neither engenders major and decisive groupings. Under industrialism, economic polarisation occurs for a time, and cultural standardisation occurs for a *longer* time. When they converge, they decisively transform the map. All in all, this theory is better compatible with Hroch's own data than is his own general theory, which, interestingly, attempts to perpetuate all at once both the 'class' and the 'nation' interpretations of history. But we have no further need of *either* of these two myths.

Notes and references

1 Cf. J. Goody, *The Logic of Writing and the Organisation of Society*, Cambridge University Press, Cambridge, 1986.
2 E. Hobsbawm, *Nations and Nationalism since 1780*, Cambridge University Press, Cambridge, 1990.
3 For the presentation of a contrary view, see A. D. Smith. *The Ethnic Origin of Nations*, Oxford, Basil Blackwell, 1986.
4 Cf. G. Lenski, *Power and Privilege: Theory of Social Stratification*, New York, 1966.
5 Cf. Alan Macfarlane, *The Origins of English Individualism*, Basil Blackwell, Oxford, 1979.
6 Hannah Arendt, *The Origins of Totalitarianism* (3rd edition), New York, Harcourt, Brace & World, 1966.
7 Cf. Roman Szporluk, *Communism and Nationalism*, Oxford University Press, Oxford, 1988.
8 Cf. E. Weber, *Peasants into Frenchmen: the modernization of rural France 1870–1914*, Stanford, CA, Stanford University Press, 1976.
9 The contrast between the second and the third zone underlies the distinction central to John Plamenatz's remarkable essay, 'Two types of nationalism', in E. Kamenka (ed.) *Nationalism. The Nature and Evolution of an Idea*, Edward Arnold, London, 1976. Plamenatz contrasts the relatively benign and liberal nationalism of nineteenth-century unificatory movements with the arduous and often brutal operations of those who had to *forge* a national culture where it did not yet exist, rather than merely endowing an existing one with its political roof.
10 The fact that some of the other ideologies were hotchpotches without much merit as intellectual constructions was not in itself necessarily a disadvantage, from the viewpoint of their social and political effectiveness and usefulness. For instance, the Kemalist aspiration to modernise and secularise Turkey was rather rigid in its scholastic secularism. It was carried out in the *ulama* spirit, so to speak, and it was deeply marked by the very thing it opposed. It reproduced some of its traits in a secular idiom, and it involved the Turkish elite in an unnecessarily painful *Kulturkampf*. Nevertheless in the end it proved superior to Marxism and more durable, precisely because it did not tie the hands of the elite in social and economic policies. Its lack of a clear social doctrine eventually proved a great advantage.
11 Please note that this paper was written at the beginning of the 1990s, and of course could not be revised by the author [eds].
12 Miroslav Hroch, *Social Preconditions of National Revival in Europe*, Cambridge University Press, Cambridge, 1985.
13 E. Hobsbawm, *Nations and Nationalism since 1780*, Cambridge University Press, Cambridge, 1990, p. 4.
14 Hroch, op. cit., pp. 10, 25. For instance, on p. 25 he refers to 'the period when the decisive feature of social conflict was the struggle against feudalism and absolutism'.
15 Cf. Adam Smith, *The Wealth of Nations*, Oxford, Clarendon Press, 1976.
16 Op. cit., p. 17.
17 Perry Anderson, *The Lineages of the Absolute State*, London, Routledge, 1974.
18 Op. cit., p. 8.
19 Op. cit., p. 27 ff.
20 The author's European orientation seems to prevent the author from considering the parallel case of nationalist sentiment in societies which are partially feudal, but still have significant tribal traits – for example, Somalis, Kurds, possibly some ethnic groups on the territory of the (former) USSR.

21 Hroch, op. cit., p. 22.

22 In Angus Wilson's insightful novel about historians, *Anglo-Saxon Attitudes*, Harmondsworth, Penguin, 1978, there is a perceptive account of the incomprehension occurring between two middle-class women, one French, the other Scandinavian. For the Frenchwoman, peasant is a pejorative notion, and she simply cannot grasp the admiring, nostalgic, romantic–populist use of the idea by the other lady.

23 Ernest Renan, *Qu'est-ce qu'une nation?*, Paris, 1882. Republished in *Ernest Renan et l'Allemagne*, ed. E. Bure, New York, 1945.

24 Cf. *Malinowski between Two Worlds*, ed. R. Ellen, E. Gellner, G. Kubica and J. Mucha, Cambridge University Press, Cambridge, 1988.

25 Hroch, op. cit., p. 17.

26 Hroch, op. cit., p. 3.

27 Kohn, op. cit. pp. 178.

28 On the Marxist ontology of nations and classes, see Roman Szporluk, *Communism and Nationalism*, Oxford University Press, New York and Oxford, 1988.

12 Norms of exclusion*

Russell Hardin

Norms of difference and universalistic norms

To understand communal norms, we can best put them into comparison with more broadly directed norms. I wish to discuss norms in two quite general categories: those that redound to the benefit of members of a more or less well-defined subgroup within a larger society, and those that seem to apply universalistically to more or less all members of a society. In general, comparison of these two classes suggest that norms of difference and exclusion are especially tractable to rational choice analysis and that universalistic norms are less tractable. This conclusion is the reverse of what may be the common view in the literature that norms of difference and exclusion – sometimes called communal norms – are especially intractable to a rational choice account, that they are perhaps primordial or, in the view of communitarians, that they are extra-rational commitments to something beyond the self or to community sources of the self.

Norms of great social interest are those that enforce something that might go otherwise. For example, an ethnic group might simply assimilate, as many have done in the USA over the past couple of centuries, or aristocrats might join the larger society. Norms for behavior against such assimilation might have a significant impact on the rate of assimilation. Subgroup norms typically reinforce individual identification with the group and enhance the separation of the group from the larger society or from another specific group in the society. They commonly work by changing the interests of marginal group members to get them to act in conformity with the interests of the core of the group. This is not to say that they are somehow 'intended' to do that, but only that they happen to do so. Universalistic norms tend to reinforce behavior that may be collectively beneficial but contrary to individual interest or even contrary to a subgroups' interests. Norms of difference and exclusion might be said to make good use of self-interest. But self-interest might also be said to make good use of norms of difference and exclusion. In either case, such norms may gain enormous force from their congruence with interests.

Many norms appear to have the strategic structure of coordination. In

David Lewis's terms, they are conventions or, rather, they govern conventional resolutions of coordination problems.[1] For example, driving on the right in North America is merely a convention. But it benefits us all to follow the convention rather than to violate it. Oddly, however, it would be wrong to claim we have that *particular* convention *because* it is in our interest. What is in our interest is merely that we have *some* convention that makes driving safe. For example, driving on the left would be as good as driving on the right, as suggested by the experience of the UK, Japan, and many other nations. What is rational for me is to follow the extant convention when I drive. Hence, it is rational for me to follow whatever convention prevails where I am – on the right in North America and on the left in Australia.

The convention of driving on the right (as in North America) or the left (as in the UK and Japan) might be seen as an ideal type of the category of universalistic norms. Having everyone in the relevant society follow that norm is beneficial to all. However, the driving convention is not a norm of great social interest in the sense above: there is very little or no need to enforce it, there is only rare need to instruct people of what they would immediately acknowledge to be erroneous, self-destructive behavior. We are apt to accuse someone of stupidity rather than of cupidity when they drive on the wrong side of the street. If we call following the convention a norm, it is a norm whose function is almost wholly epistemological rather than to affect motivations by affecting incentives.[2] I will restrict the term 'norm' to those cases that are motivational and will therefore not count the driving convention as a norm here. Still, many norms have much of the coordination quality of the driving convention. We would all be better off if all follow a certain norm just as we would all be better off if we all drive left or all drive right. Hence, we can coordinate on following that norm in preference to not following it.

The norm of truth-telling might similarly be of universal appeal, but the incentive for it is not already built into the situations in which it might be invoked, as the incentive for driving according to the local convention is built into the situation on the road. Hence, the norm of truth-telling is not always redundant, it can potentially add to the incentive for relevant behavior. Such norms are universal in a given society. I will refer to them as *universalistic norms*.

The ethnic norm that supports identification with a particular community is also not redundant. There is likely to be some mixing and intermarriage. Without the norm, there might be far more. Those who are most comfortable in their group are most likely to find their norms of community redundant for themselves but not for others. But the norm is likely to be of interest to people in the community precisely because it can be invoked against certain behaviors that are attractive to at least some members of the community. If everyone in our community shared identical interests in sticking with the community, we might not need a community norm.

Some of us benefit from having such a norm merely because the community's boundaries are not well defined; there is no clear dividing line or step function between those who identify with the community and those who do not. The functional role of community norms is typically to establish difference. Indeed, they might most instructively be called *norms of particularism, difference, or exclusion* rather than of community. The often have some variant of the content of the Vietnam-era norm expressed in the slogan 'Love it or leave it,' where 'it' was the USA.

Note that the terminology for these two classes of norms is not parallel. One might refer to universalistic norms as norms of universality or similarity, but that would be misleading. Kantians, utilitarians, egalitarians, and other universalistic moral theorists may follow their own norms of universality or similarity. But their more specific norms, such as norms of altruism, reciprocity, or veracity, are universalistic in the sense that they apply to everyone.

The central difference between the two classes, universalistic norms and norms of difference, is that the latter require a sense of group separation or even an outside, typically adversary, group to give them any value. Difference is a relative value that depends on an external referent. There is obviously no point in difference if there is no alternative to the group that is to be different. A norm of exclusion is, by implication, also a norm of inclusion for the relevant group. The ideal for norms of difference would be individual submission through acceptance of the value of identification with the group. At the fringes of the group, however, there may be people who are tempted by the alternative benefits of weaker identification with the group, even of defection from it. If the group did not react, full defection would not be necessary, but the group might react to even partial defection by excluding the defector. For an individual case, the incentive structure might be essentially prisoner's dilemma, with both the individual and the group better off with partial defection than with full defection or exclusion. But there is a strategic benefit to the group from full exclusion, which raises the costs of partial defection and therefore, plausibly, reduces its incidence. The role of the group norm is to raise these costs and thereby to reduce the size of the prisoner's dilemma fringe.

Interethnic marriage rates might suffice as a rough proxy measure of the sizes of prisoner's dilemma fringes. Some groups appear headed for mixing quickly, others only slowly. In particular, blacks in the USA may now have stronger norms of difference and a narrower prisoner's dilemma fringe than in earlier decades, while Jews may be going through a dramatic widening of their fringe and the rapid breakdown of their separateness. Among American Jews married before 1965, 9 percent had married outside the Jewish community; among those married after 1985, 52 percent married outside.[3] For eliminating the force of norms of difference between two groups, both groups must be open, perhaps because each has a very large prisoner's dilemma fringe. When enough mixing in the fringes happens, others in the groups have less to gain from difference, and they fall into a still wider fringe.

Norms of difference typically have a prisoner's dilemma fringe of more weakly identified group members. The size of the fringe is a function of the relative benefits of membership and defection. Universalistic norms typically have prisoner's dilemma strains throughout the relevant society. The function of these norms is to raise the cost of certain individually rewarding behaviors, such as lying and cheating, to reduce their incidence. But, since there is no group boundary for the universalistic norm, there is no relevant sense in which those who violate the norm are at the margins of the group. The incentive to lie or cheat may affect any member of the society, not merely fringe members. In both classes of norms, the general norm has enforcement value if it can block prisoner's dilemma incentives to defect from the relevant social order and the content of the norm itself is a matter of coordination.[4]

There are many other ways to categorize norms. For example, Edna Ullmann-Margalit lumps them into prisoner's dilemma, pure coordination, and unequal coordination categories. Ullmann-Margalit speaks of 'norms of partiality,'[5] which are norms that permanently ensconce two groups in a coordination that benefits one of them more than the other, as one might suppose it the interest of humans that some group, such as women, should specialize in procreation and rearing of the species, which just happens to redound to the special advantage of men. As it happens, a statable norm may fit one of these categories quite clearly in one period of its history, and then fit another category in a later period, or the same statement of a norm might be pure coordination in one context and unequal coordination in another. For example, the norm of truth-telling might be of generally beneficial quality in a benign community but of divisive quality in a malign society such as that in which some might hide Jewish or other refugees from a genocidal government. Many of the norms in a given society may be residual norms; they may be norms gone awry, left over from prior conditions in which they made sense and still invoked in contexts that lack the relevant strategic structure. They may be survivals past their time. Marx said that the norm of dueling was 'a relic of a past stage of culture.'[6] Others may be overgeneralized norms that cover more than they should if they were thought to have a simple strategic structure.

Norms of universality may fall into either prisoner's dilemma or nearly pure coordination strategic structures or, perhaps more typically, they may fall into a mixed strategic structure, if only because they govern ongoing relationships. Many of us might not need a norm to get us to go along with the community principle because we might see ourselves as benefiting directly from going along. Hence, application of the norm to us is little different from application of the driving 'norm.' But we might see the value of having the norm to regulate the behavior of those more nearly marginal to the community, those for whom weaker identification with the community has its more than compensating rewards.

Norms of difference

Ethnic and other groups commonly have norms that differentiate their members from the larger community in which they live, and those of the larger society may have related norms to reinforce the separation. This is most conspicuous, perhaps, in religious contexts. For example, the Jewish biblical injunction that one could lend at interest but not to a brother[7] was interpreted to mean that Jews could not lend at interest to other Jews but only to non-Jews. Although Thomas Aquinas held it sinful for a Christian to lend at interest, he conveniently supposed it not sinful to borrow at interest.[8] The separate merchants' and lenders' role for Jews in medieval and later European society was therefore the strategic implication of the combination of Jewish and Christian norms.

Why would members of a group wish to be different, to exclude non-members? Often because there might be benefits of membership. Benefits can take at least two quite different forms. First, there might be conflict of interest over limited resources that make it the interest of one group to gain control of those resources on behalf of its members. For example, land and other resources in fixed supply might not be expandable to make them more widely available. Also, jobs under the control of a group or of the state might be in relatively fixed supply in the short run. In a conflict in what is roughly a constant-sum game, at least for the short run, some subgroup or coalition can benefit its members most quickly by excluding others from access to the limited resources. Second, there may be straightforward benefits of comfort, familiarity, and easy communication in one's group. We might call these epistemological benefits, because they take the form of reducing the need for knowledge beyond what one may have just from growing up in a community or being part of it. The two kinds of benefit might often work together. For example, members of a group might have easy access to jobs through community networks of information and assistance. Dealing with an outsider who comes to a group might require more effort from group members than dealing with an insider would. For example, if I marry outside my community, my fellow community members might find my spouse to be more trouble to deal with, less predictable, and generally much less enjoyable than they find the neighbor whom I might have married. As a result, my spouse may feel relatively ill at ease in my community and we might together have far poorer opportunities for social intercourse than other couples of our age and status would have.

Not every apparent group member need share in either of the two forms of benefit to membership. Some may see better opportunities outside than inside the group. And some might bridle at the limits of the familiar. Such people are, in the discussions here, members at the fringes of their groups.

Much of what we must understand about norms of difference and exclusion will depend on the mix of people at the fringes and people in what might be called the core of relevant groups.

Universalistic norms

Universalistic norms apply indifferently to everyone. Such a norm may be held in a specific community without necessary reference to or ongoing effect on any other community. In general, such norms take one of at least two distinct forms. First, they may be theoretically deduced, as for example by Immanuel Kant, by a religious leader, or more or less by everyone through some principle of universality. Second, they may be socially constructed with, perhaps, unknown origin. Generally, norms in the second category are likely to be community specific. One might argue that all norms, even those ostensibly in the first category, are in the second category in that they are community based, although it is at least conceivable that some norm or set of norms would someday be literally universal for humans in whatever community. Because all or nearly all norms are community based, it would be misleading to refer to norms of difference and exclusion as community norms as though this were a distinguishing mark for them.

There is a class of important universalistic norms which are virtually self-enforcing in many contexts. These are norms such as those for telling the truth, keeping promises, and maintaining fidelity to spouses and friends. They are self-enforcing when they govern ongoing relationships between pairs or very small numbers of people. In brief, I will refer to these as *dyadic norms*. The enforcement of these norms comes naturally from the fact that the relationships that they govern are of value to the participants beyond the instant interaction on which someone must keep the relevant norm or violate it. These characteristics of the relationship suggest that it is an iterated prisoner's dilemma in its incentive structure. Each participant in the dyad sometimes has a short-term interest in violating the norm but a long-term interest in maintaining the relationship. If the latter is great enough, it can trump the short-term interest and make it worthwhile to forgo short-term gains in the interest of longer-term gains.

One might tell the truth out of strict moral scruples, but one also has an interest in telling the truth to one's ongoing relations. Even if you are bound by moral scruples, you may nevertheless depend on the incentives of self-interest that keep others honest enough to make dealing with them worth your while. The usual resolution of an iterated prisoner's dilemma in which one party fails to cooperate often enough is not to join that party in cheating but simply to withdraw from the relationship. If others have an interest in cooperation with you, you have better prospects from cooperating than from withdrawing or cheating. In general, you have better life prospects if those around you recognize their interest in maintaining cooperative relations with you.[9] Being cooperative loses much of its value if too few others are cooperative and it may finally even become disvalued. Similarly, truth-telling may often seem to serve perverse purposes for many relationships in a Nazi or other totalitarian society.

Typically, then, these dyadic norms are straightforwardly self-enforcing. Such a norm may govern a very large population, all of whom are involved with various others in dyadic relationships. But there is no large-number equivalent of the dyadic norms. A norm that governs relationships that are inherently large number rather than dyadic cannot be reinforced merely by the withdrawal of cooperative parties from interactions with uncooperative parties.[10] The norms of difference and exclusion discussed below govern large-number relationships of identification of a whole community and exclusion of others from it. They are self-enforcing through the mechanism implicit in their functional structure, not directly through the iterated incentive offered by the fellow group members in a large-number prisoner's dilemma. The explanation of large-number norms in general cannot turn on a rational regulation of the problem of collective action in enforcing the norm, although there may be some cases that can be regulated through somewhat unstable conventions.[11]

Incidentally, modern nationalism has often turned into the analog of a subgroup norm of difference, but, of course, at the whole-nation level. It has the function of differentiating the nation and its people from other nations and their peoples. There can be a universalistic, non-adversarial nationalism, and no doubt many nationalisms have been. For example, a particular nationalism could be directed at stimulating economic activity and productivity and artistic and other efforts, at lifting the condition of the nation's citizens without onus to anyone else. Lovers of blood sports might think such a nationalism uninteresting and might prefer the nationalism that tends to war. Nationalism that is a norm of difference often has bellicose tendencies. The general category of seemingly universalistic norms will not be extensively considered here.

Explaining norms of exclusion

Norms of exclusion and difference take many forms. For example, there can be quite local norms that elevate my town over other towns, my club over other clubs, or my company over other companies. In most societies, there are norms of dress that differentiate men and women. Some Canadians think there are norms that differentiate Canada from the USA, while other Canadians fear that no such norms survive. Two general types of norm of exclusion will be of special interest here: norms that define ethnic or racial groups and those that define social classes. In this section, I will call on many norms of the first type to explain how norms of exclusion work. Then, in the following section I will discuss an odd but uniquely important norm – the duel – that helped to maintain the definition and status of a social class that was of declining significance.

Consider an important category of non-religious norms that function to establish difference: norms for linguistic usage, especially for slang and specialized terms. Some community-specific slang may not be anything more than useful shorthand to relevant parties, as psychologists, plumbers, musicians, opinion pollsters, and others might develop terms to deal with matters of special interest to their groups. But some community-specific slang may have no such simple function; linguistically it may do no more than substitute for standard terminology. Its effective function is, rather, to distinguish its users as users, to signal their difference from those who do not use the special terminology.

For some group norms, such as that of the rapper, it is not necessary that those who most express and define the norm be of the community that adopts it. Some of the rappers, whom we might call the 'bearers of the norm' of rap, are from bourgeois backgrounds, not from inner cities. Yet it may still be true that the norm in which they participate is primarily the norm of the inner-city poor. The norm has been commercialized – that is, after all, how it was communicated with such rapidity. Anyone with the relevant commercial vision can see the benefits of bearing the norm of rap independently of whether they actually share in its values, even independently of whether they personally wish to flout the bourgeoisie for any reason other than profit. Even a convicted white racist can commercially exploit the norm as a bearer of it while posing in some of the whitest and most bourgeois of all underwear.

Among the possible terms for establishing difference and therefore special community are those that are, in the broader community, negative in their connotations, terms that are perhaps even epithets. For example, some blacks now call each other 'nigger,'[12] a term which was once despised by blacks and commonly used as an insult by white racists. While the term is still an epithet when used by whites, it has become a term of affection and community for many blacks – mostly younger blacks. Blacks now can get away with such usage while whites cannot, so that the term entails exclusion of whites from at least the language community of blacks. On his account, a white professor in Chicago once attempted to help students understand the power of racist language to do harm by saying to the only black student in his class: 'We have a nigger student here.' The student said afterwards that she couldn't move: 'I wanted to run out but was afraid I didn't have the strength to make it to the door.'[13] Yet that woman could well also have heard blacks calling their friends nigger, and she might have smiled at their communal jocularity.

That the term can so demean someone and yet also elevate may seem astonishing. Nevertheless, it may make sense to the relevant community. American blacks use many other terms that sound negative in strong positive senses. For example, a 'bad mutha' is, in some sense, especially good, a bad outfit is a great outfit, and a bad meal is one you would go out of your way to eat. When the standard terms, such as great, terrific, and so forth, have been diminished by overuse, bad sounds very good.

Even more generally, for more than a century, American blacks have been 'redefining race as an abiding source of pride rather than stigma.'[14] This move, which was discouraged and deplored by Frederick Douglass, reached its height with the slogan 'Black is beautiful.' What much of American society has treated as a stigma for many centuries has ceased to be a stigma in the vision of many blacks. It has even become a claim to special quality and a norm of exclusion.

What is in it for you? Why should you adopt the slang and manner of a group? Doing so allows you entrée to the group and what rewards it has. These may be more attractive than what you lose from adopting the odd slang and manner. Refusing to adopt the slang or abandoning it later casts doubt on your commitments and your trustworthiness, making you less attractive to other members of the community. Indeed, it may even seem to other members of the group to be a rejection of them as persons, rather than merely of their style. And if you reject them, what are they to make of your hanging around them, what motives must they impute to you?

In the early 1970s in New York, I was walking between a group of four or five young black men and a group of as many young black women. One of the men was imploring one of the women to do something with him but she repeatedly spurned him. He went up to her and put his arm around her waist, but she pushed his arm away. In disgust, he said, 'You a mother-fucker.' She slowed and turned back to look at him with a beatific smile, saying, 'No, I can't be no mother-fucker – you must be thinking of yourself.' The entire crowd laughed in appreciation of her sly put-down. Her target laughed hardest. Much of the rest of their conversation had been witty and extraordinarily overt. I would have liked to have such openness in my own community, but anyone who tried it there would have fallen out of favor and would have been spurned. The style of open-ness of much of the black community and the style of privacy and primness of much of the white community constitute norms of difference that reinforce the separateness of the two communities.[15] There may be nothing invidious in these norms, but their effects are *de facto* invidious and they virtually become norms of exclusion.

The slang and other linguistic devices of the rapper may be enhanced by the full panoply of the 'cool pose' of young black men, especially in the inner city. Janet Mancini Billson and Richard Majors interpret that pose as a response to the exclusions of white or at least prosperous American society.[16] But consider the range of plausible audiences for the pose. In addition to whites (who do not live in the ghetto), it could be directed at members of the group itself, older blacks who do not share the norm of the pose, or at young black women. It seems likely that the various behaviors are directed at different ones of these plausible audiences. The words of rap songs may have the widest audience, from the young inner-city black males themselves to whites. The pose, which is overwhelmingly visual and of therefore little effect unless it is seen, seems more likely to be directed only at an immediate, frequent audience, including the poseurs themselves, young women, and older blacks. As Billson and Majors read the pose, it is macho. Hence, its main audience could well be young black women, whose relative independence from men may provoke its swagger. Rap may be fundamentally political; the pose may not be very political at all.

Functional explanation

What makes particular slang acceptable is not that it is deliberately chosen by someone but that, however it arises, it survives as a convention. Once the convention is in place, I can most readily show my identity by following it. The norm of using it becomes functional to identification with the group. Indeed, we may give a functional explanation of the survival of the norm once it is established, as follows:

An institution or a behavioral pattern X is explained by its function F for group G if and only if:

1   F is an *effect* of X;
2   F is *beneficial* for G;
3   F maintains X by a causal *feedback* loop passing through G.[17]

In the present case, X is the norm of group slang or style; F is group identification; and G is the members of the relevant subgroup, such as certain blacks. The full explanation is as follows:

1   We might suppose that those who adopt the slang and style of the group are likely to identify more closely with the group thereafter because they will find the rewards of life in the group better than if they did not adopt the slang and style.
2   To show that group identification is beneficial for members of a group may seem difficult. But there are many reasons for this conclusion to follow (not necessarily, but contingently in many instances). Tight group affiliation can reduce the costs of requisite daily knowledge and thereby facilitate one's daily activities. It can give one access to benefits, such as jobs, controlled by the group.[18] For example, for both of these concerns, it can provide readily available networks for discovering information and making connections. It can also be directly pleasurable for the relationships it underlies and the activities it organizes.
3   Now we may see that group identification (F) maintains the norm of group slang or style (X) by a causal feedback loop passing through the members of the relevant group (G). Members who strongly identify with the group are likely to spend more of their time in it than

members who identify more loosely. They will find it more natural to indulge, and hence to develop, the slang and style of the group. Hence, that slang and style may become more extreme as time passes, not because the group intends for it to do so but because that is the individual incentive of the most identified members of the group.

A cost of becoming closely associated with some subgroup in a society may be relative exclusion from other groups, including those that have better economic and social opportunities than the subgroup has. For some people this cost could outweigh the benefits under 2 above, in which case the relevant norms of difference are not beneficial. But these costs might be imposed by an alternative group that practices its own exclusions, so that one's own group may have norms of separation without fear of aggravating the losses from exclusion by others. In North American history, the exclusion of blacks by whites has been overwhelmingly important for black lack of opportunity. Today it is conceivable that the benefits of black norms of difference are finally rivaled for some by their costs in exacerbated exclusion by whites.

The black teenager who dresses, walks, and gestures like a rapper or who adopts a cool pose may bear no costs for that style. But the later adult who has developed the language of the rapper and has adopted gestures that have since become second nature may bear substantial costs. The later adult may have to choose between cultivating a different image and language and continuing membership in the subcommunity. The costs of the transition and the uncertainties of succeeding in the larger community weigh against making the change. The costs of the transition may typically include at least some loss of camaraderie in the rejected community. Shawn Hunt, a Brooklyn 17 year old striving to get through high school and into university, says he talks to whites in 'Regular, straight up and down English.' But that would not go over well with his black friends, 'They'd be like – that's not what they're used to. They wouldn't take too good to that. They'd think I was funny.'[19] But this split may not work indefinitely. The novelist Kristin Hunter Lattany notes that 'An individual in conflict with himself is only marginally functional, and if half his loyalty lies elsewhere, his community cannot trust him.'[20]

Once, at a barbecue party, I was one of the few whites among the black friends of my neighbors. The husband was a brilliant gardener who produced miracles from a six-foot square carved out of the pavement of our back alley and who filled his house with thriving plants. Someone complimented the wife for all her plants, and she declined the praise. 'I have nothing to do with those. Jim does them all – and he tells *me* to stay away. I have a white thumb.' I laughed because the phrase was completely new to me but was wonderfully evocative. In part, I was enchanted by the phrase the way one might be on reading or hearing a figure of speech in a second language. It then comes across vividly, even though one's own language might use the equivalent figure of speech. 'Catch fire' in English is mundane to me; the first time I read it in German, it evoked an instant image of a hand reaching up to catch a ball of fire and it turned into the usual mundane meaning only after interpretation. But in the case of my neighbor's white thumb, of course, the phrase was especially powerful because it said something in a new and novel way. It was slave traders with white thumbs who killed most of the blacks shipped across the Atlantic, it was plantation owners with white thumbs who ruled over the survivors and their progeny, and white thumbs may still press heavily on black lives in America. My neighbor's 'white thumb' evoked all of that. But at my laughter one of the women in the group gave my neighbor a look of disdain. She was up to the occasion; she grinned and said to me, 'That's okay, that's just what *we* say.' Clearly, *their* phrase was apt. But the phrase was not one that could readily be shared; it was *their* phrase. There was therefore a mild jolt to both communities when my neighbor spoke her language in my presence. We might generalize the look of disdain one of her black friends gave my neighbor. Like Shaun Hunt she was expected to talk regular, straight up and down English in the presence of whites. Clearly it would be strenuous to do that if one's ordinary catch phrases are going to turn into balls of fire, so that one must constantly monitor every statement. There must be evenings, days, weeks, and even longer times, when one would rather not bother.

At the extreme of trying to fit in two communities at once is a San Francisco taxi driver who recently told me of his life as a heavy drug user. He had stopped all of the harder stuff and now consumed only marijuana. But it had taken him a couple of years to realize he would never success- fully leave the more insidious drugs behind if he did not sever contacts with his drug-using friends, who could not stand to have him around while they shot up and snorted various things if he was not going to join in. At another extreme is the case of a Serbian refugee from Sarajevo who was impressed into military service in one of the units besieging the Muslim- majority city.

> 'You stayed with the balija for eighteen months,' the commander said, using a term for Muslims that is common among Serbian soldiers. 'Okay, let's see how you feel about the balija now. You can go to the front lines and kill a balija, then maybe we'll let you go.'[21]

Eighteen months of consorting with Muslims evidently put that refugee off into the dubious fringe of the Serbian community, where the hard core of that community could not trust him.

As an aside, note that the convention of driving on the right cannot be defended with a functional explanation. Suppose F is prosperous driving, X is the convention of driving right, and G is the class of drivers. Condition 3 is simply not applicable. Prosperous driving does not maintain the norm of driving right; people drive right in order to benefit from the prevailing convention much as they drive at all in order to get where they are going.

In his definition of functional explanations, Jon Elster includes two other conditions:

(i) *F* is *unintended* by the actors producing *X*; and
(ii) *F* (or at least the causal relationship between *X* and *F*) is *unrecognized* by the actors in *G*.

In this era of the instant sociology of everything,[22] it would be surprising if the second of these conditions would hold universally for a norm that has been established for even a short while and eventually, therefore, even the first of these conditions might fail to hold. But, even though some of the supporters of the norm might fully understand its functional role and might deliberately work to maintain it, many of the followers of the norm would typically still fit Elster's conditions.[23] In fact, these two conditions are merely the extra conditions that distinguish 'latent' from 'manifest' functions. This distinction may be important, because some feedbacks that work well even when they are latent might fail once they become manifest. Other feedbacks work very well even when they are fully manifest. Indeed, organizations commonly have feedback designed in to enhance organizational effectiveness. The workings of such devices often clearly fit the model of functional explanation. For the present discussion, the important concern is that feedback is functional, not whether it is latent or manifest.[24]

It can be dysfunctional to accede to a functional relationship. We may be members of a group that has been identified by others and that has faced contrained opportunities. We might finally get better opportunities primarily by improving the status of the group, and this claim is one we could make to help motivate actions by fellow group members. But members might also benefit from having members reject aspects of the identification foisted on them by others or by having them transform those aspects into good rather than bad things. Here it could be counter-productive to argue overtly that this is why we should think these things good. We are more likely to motivate each other successfully if we can convincingly argue that somehow these things *are* good. Blacks might say black is beautiful and that might energize many blacks and lead them to be more stalwart in seeking opportunities and overcoming racial barriers. We could then fit the slogan to a functional explanation of improved black status. But blacks could not very well assert that this is all they mean when they say black is beautiful. Hence, making this particular functional relationship work may depend on keeping it unstated and latent.

Finally, also note that the form that functional feedback takes can be quite varied. It can work through biological mechanisms, through structural impacts on environment, or through effects on incentives for various behaviors. When it works through incentive effects, then functional explanation is a part of rational choice explanation. And if the feedback produces important incentive effects, functional explanation is inherently an important part of rational choice explanation. In the discussion here, the functional feedback relations all work through effects on incentives and they yield rational choice explanations of behaviors that superficially might not seem consistent with self-interest. It is only when unpacked functionally that the rational incentives for the relevant behaviors can be comprehended.

Origin and development

Note that the issue in the preceding discussion is how the norm works. But the norm here contributes to establishing or asserting identity by seemingly abasing oneself, one's ways, or one's appearance. This may seem odd. Hence, one may wish to ask the prior question of how an individual could think to do such a thing *before the establishment of such a norm in the individual's community*. If no one did so, the norm could not arise. This seems likely to be a much harder psychological trick than merely following a well-supported norm. But it is also a trick that need not be turned by very many people. After a few have done it, the norm may be on its way. For example, an early rapper might merely have accentuated gestures that are commonly used in stylized, dismissive argument, indeed, in intrafamilial, not interracial, argument. Giving the object of the rap the back of the hand, dramatically pointing at the imagined object, waving it away, dismissing it with egocentric posturing – these were all daily fare long before rap, probably in many communities other than the black inner city.

Competition in distinctiveness has the odd result of producing such extreme gestures that they become stylized and no longer distinctive from one rapper to another – any 8 year old can do them with ease. Flouting the bourgeoisie has a long tradition (*épater le bourgeois*, in France), with the cultivated belch, the up-yours swagger, the I-am-all-that-matters bearing. In the USA, being bourgeois correlates fairly strongly with being white. Flouting the bourgeoisie and flouting whites are not easily kept separate for many American blacks.

The term 'nigger' is one of the harshest racist epithets in the USA. Those who have used it may largely, as Irving Lewis Allen asserts, have used it to distinguish themselves as not black.[25] Now, however, it is used to distinguish oneself as black.[26] How does someone turn 'nigger' into a term of honor when used by blacks? Again, it is hard to answer the individual-level question before the norm is established. At that level, the move was a seemingly strange trick. But at that level there are millions of strange tricks turned daily. The basic question for us, therefore, is how this particular trick came out of the millions to become a norm. To a large extent, the issue must be roughly parallel to questions of how certain products make it in the market. Competition kills many and lets some through. In such competition, oddity or distinctiveness may be an advantage, and helps to make a slogan or product memorable. When the vocabulary and politics of race changed at the height of the Civil Rights Movement in the late 1950s and the 1960s, elderly Toms sometimes admonished the young: 'You're nothing but a nigger and don't you forget it,' just as many whites had regularly done for generations. A stump speaker might naturally appropriate this slogan, not to admonish, but to incense. 'You ain't nothin' but niggers in this country, and don't you forget it.'[27] Earlier, the term had been used, especially by white racists, to distinguish and separate off blacks to keep them 'in their place.'[28] On the political stump it was also used to distinguish blacks and to acknowledge the separation imposed on them, but then to galvanize them as a political group. The old, ugly slogan turned positive, and what was formerly derogatory had become hortatory. The step to making 'nigger' an honorific term was presumably easy after that because the ground was fully prepared for treating it as a positive identification.[29]

To establish how the convention of using nigger honorifically arose, we would have to investigate millions of actions by vast numbers of people over several years. We might have to determine not only who drifted into such usage when, but also why alternative norms did not get more widely adopted. No matter whether we are clear on how the convention specific-ally arose, however, we can still understand how that convention works as a norm. In general, the latter is the more interesting task for social scient-ific understanding. Perhaps this realization underlies or at least is taken to support theories of cultural determination. But it would be wrong to conclude from the competitive generation of norms that they are inherently irrational. They may often be no more irrational than driving on the right in North America: they often coordinate for common ends, especially common ends that are group specific. If we had an authoritative leader with many exclusive options for coordinating us, all reasonably acceptable and functional for achieving our common end, it would be merely rational for the leader to pick one and benefit from it.[30] But we can evidently sometimes also 'pick' one without the help of an authoritative leader, as we did in the original adoption of the driving convention.

There may be other instances of the elevation of a derogatory term for a group into a term of approbation and distinction that are more easily traced through. For example, during the hegemony of Spain over the Netherlands, the Dutch revolutionary movement became known as *les Gueux*, after the French word for beggars (*Geuzen* in Dutch). The term plausibly arose when one of Philip's counselors used the word *gueux* to express contempt for the group of Netherlands nobles who presented a list of political demands to the Spanish regent in April 1566. To defy the Spanish or to goad themselves or to do both, the Dutch then called themselves beggars and went on to rally themselves to rise against Spanish rule. Victory went to *les Gueux*, who were not begging but demanding. The insult became their rallying cry.[31] In the end there were beggars of many varieties, designated by region, by leadership (such as that of William of Orange, the eventual monarch), and by kind (such as the beggar navy).

Maintenance

An obvious question for the development of a norm of exclusion or difference that is to be enforced against community members is how the enforcement is done. In part it is done merely by misfit, as in the discussion of the rapper turned quasi-bourgeois. After publishing *Black Like Me*, an account of his passing for black and suffering the discriminations of southern racism,[32] John Howard Griffin was treated to shunning by many in his small hometown of Mansfield, Texas. Perhaps some of the shunning was morally or politically motivated rather than merely an expression of his misfit with the community. Many people have had the experience of returning home after going off for education or for job opportunities and of finding themselves not very welcome. Indeed, this is one of a related pair of general theses in the title of Thomas Wolfe's *You Can't Go Home Again* and throughout his work.[33] The other thesis in this pair is that one may not find the comforts of home as pleasing as they once were because one may have learned or changed too much.[34]

Wolfe clearly appreciated the benefits, the comforts of home. He characterized a town as 'coiling in a thousand fumes of homely smoke, now winking into a thousand points of friendly light its glorious small design, its aching passionate assurances of walls, warmth, comfort, food, and love.'[35] Hence, on his view, the costs of separation were real and potentially large. Nevertheless, Wolfe saw that the comforts of home may be as appealing as they are in part because of ignorance of what alternatives there are. The full story is as follows. The comforts induce staying at home, which secures ignorance by pruning vistas, which maintains tastes for the comforts of home. That is a demoralizing chain of relationships. Those like Wolfe can break that chain only at the price of permanent disquiet. Incidentally, the epistemological comforts of home feed back to reinforce themselves. But this may work for many people only if the feedback is latent, not evident. To make it evident is almost by definition to violate it. The ignorance implicit in settling for the epistemological comforts of home might be actively opposed by some if they come to understand its functional role in reinforcing belief in the goodness of their community. Most of the other norms discussed here would be effective even if they became fully manifest.

It is sometimes supposed that the costs of shunning or otherwise sanctioning those who deviate from a norm cannot be in the interest of the sanctioner, so that a norm that requires sanctioning for its enforcement cannot be rationally sustained. For some norms, this conclusion may follow. But for norms of difference and exclusion, there may be no costs to some sanctioners. They are not sanctioning *per se*; rather they are merely acting in the interests of their comfort in familiarity or whatever and excluding those who are unfamiliar. For whites in Mansfield to shun Griffin was no harder than for them to shun blacks. Both actions fit into their world of the separation of whites and blacks to the supposed advantage of whites, who controlled most of the economic and other opportunities of the community.

Furthermore, the success of a norm of exclusion must typically depend on how widely supported it is. In the American south before the Civil Rights Movement, the norm of white supremacy was apparently very widely held.[36] Yet, as soon as blacks mobilized and the laws began to change, many whites joined the cause of racial equality. Were people's views so quickly changed? Probably not. Many of them were people who might not have spoken their true feelings before because the costs of bucking the apparent norm were too great.[37] The core of those who strongly held the norm had succeeded in coordinating others behind the norm even when the others did not literally support the norm or even benefit from it. As is generally true of norms of exclusion and difference, southern racism was enforced on the – perhaps large – fringe of those whose identification with the community was weak. The Civil Rights Movement finally enabled these people to join blacks to attempt a new coordination on a norm of racial equality.[38] That norm too is enforced against those who do not share it.

How does this account of norms of difference fit the sudden efflorescence of often violent ethnic conflict in former republics of the Soviet Union? Many commentators attribute this explosion to the end of Soviet suppression of conflicts that, while suppressed, remained latent. This analysis seems to be fundamentally wrong. During the era of Soviet hegemony, the ethnic groups were not in control of opportunities, which were more nearly universalistically open to all independently of their ethnic identification.[39] There was, during that era, almost no call to suppress the conflicts because ethnic identification had little to offer besides the epistemological comforts of home. A sustained burst of economic growth that made opportunities less a matter of taking or withholding from others and more a matter of individual (not group) opportunism would similarly undermine the power of extremist ethnic groups. Alas, the transition from central control of the economy to market control entailed immediate loss of productivity and earnings, not least because it made a large fraction of the workforce (the bureaucrats and others involved in control, both in the government and in firms) irrelevant while only slowly conjuring a new class of entrepreneurs into being. Hence, at the end of the Soviet hegemony over various republics, immediate economic prospects were grim and the quickest way to hold the ground was likely by excluding others.

The duel

The duel and the vendetta seem to have similar points: vengeance and, perhaps, the defense of honor. But the explanation of the norm of dueling depends very clearly on its association with a single class, the aristocracy, in a time when aristocrats were slowly being displaced in economic and political importance by the rising bourgeoisie. The duel arose and became a remarkably powerful institution because it 'set the gentry class above all others, as possessing a courage and resolution no other could emulate, and a code of conduct none but it could live up to.'[40] Although seemingly similar to the duel in its focus on vengeance, the vendetta does not have the role of separating one group from others or of excluding other groups. It is potentially universally appealing if it appeals at all. Let us try to make sense of the greater complexity of the duel.

At its height, 'the duel was one of the most fantastical things in human annals.'[41] Sir Francis Bacon, while he was attorney general of England, asserted simply that the blemishes of honor that led to duels were too inconsequential to exact such a price as the risk of murder or death. These blemishes, after all, were merely lies and slurs of kinds that had not motivated Greeks, Romans, and others to such drastic responses.[42] As Adam Smith argued, where the law of honor was revered, it was wholly from this new notion of honor that the injury of the relevant affronts arose. He, too, acknowledged 'that formerly those actions and words which we think the greatest affront were little thought of.'[43]

It was sometimes recommended that government could stop dueling by taking over the punishment of the provocations to duel. Bacon supposed these should not be punished at all, unless they reached the level of slander or assault, for which law already existed. Against the complaint that the law provided no remedy for lying, he asserted that this was only right. He denied that there is an effect of lies and insults on honor.

> Any law-giver, if hee had beene asked the question, would have made Solons answer, *that he had not ordained any punishment for it, because he never imagined the world would have been so fantasticall as to take it so highly.*

If the gentleman's honor was so fragile as to be harmed by petty lies and contumely, it was cut from flimsy cloth.[44] To gild the lunacy, the nineteenth-century Polish poet and nationalist Adam Mickiewicz noted, 'it is the custom of men of honor, before proceeding to murder, first to exchange greetings.'[45]

Rather than punish lying and contumely, Bacon held, government should punish dueling. To do the latter, he proposed to stop the duel by responding to the thing it supposedly responded to: honor. He wished the King to banish duelers from his court and his service 'for certaine years.'

And he proposed that the law punish all the actions that are part of the organization of the duel: appointing a field, making a challenge, delivery of a challenge, accepting or returning a challenge, agreeing to be a second, leaving the country in order to duel, reviving a quarrel contrary to a proclamation by the King.[46]

In his assessment, Bacon missed the main point of the institution of dueling. What was at stake in the duel was ratification of one's status in the dueling class and of most others' exclusion from that class. Dueling over frivolous insults that could not plausibly rank in importance with the risk of killing or dying was at least as effective for this purpose as dueling over grievous assaults. Indeed, the functional account which follows is consistent with a tendency over the years to make the standards for provocation *less* grievous. The more grievous an affront is, the less dueling depends on assertion of status and the more it begins to seem fitted to the actual affront of the moment. It was frivolous duels that would balk non-aristocrats. *Therefore, it was frivolous duels that best served the function of defining aristocrats as a separate class.*

Although he failed to grasp the urge to duel, characterizing it as 'noe better then a sorcery that enchanteth the spirits of young men,' Bacon seemed to catch its core in another observation. 'Nay I should thinke,' he wrote, 'that men of birth and quality will leave the practice, when it begins to bee vilified and come so lowe as to Barbers-surgeons and Butchers, and such base mechanicall persons.'[47] Had it come so low, with aristocrats called out by any tradesman, the norm would have lost its distinguishing power.

If the dueling norm was one of setting boundaries for a group, there is the obvious question of how individuals in the group could be motivated to act by it, especially if these motivations reinforced and were reinforced by the role of the duel in excluding others from the aristocratic class. If the duel functioned as a norm of exclusion, it fit the form of functional explanation for such norms above (in 'Explaining norms of exclusion'): X is the norm of dueling, F is identification with the class of aristocrats, and G is the class of aristocrats. These fit our functional model:

1   Identification was an effect of the norm. Aristocrats held their status by acting on the norm and non-aristocrats, who could not readily be admitted to the class, also identified the aristocrats by that 'ultimate hallmark of gentility': 'the right of gentlemen to kill each other.'[48] Even non-aristocrats have often admired the apparent courage and vigor of the dueling class, although many of them might not have been willing to pay the price of membership in that class.
2   Identification as a separate class was beneficial for members of the class of aristocrats. They were rewarded with jobs by the state, jobs in government and in the officer corps of the standing armies that arose after Napoleon's havoc.

3   As with conventions, the successful following of the norm of dueling by many aristocrats raised the costs of not following it, therefore likely increasing its support. Indeed, the norm contributed to its own reinforcement in especially frivolous contexts.

Costs of not dueling

One of the first conclusions from the functional account is that, for the individual facing a situation that called for giving or accepting a challenge, the duel was rational, that is to say, *it was in the interests of the dueler*. Against this claim, V. G. Kiernan says the duel 'cannot be made to look rational in terms of the individual, but only as an institution from which a *class*, a social order, benefited.'[49] Similarly, Warren F. Schwartz, Keith Baxter, and David Ryan argue that conformity to the code of honor of which the duel was a large part in the pre-Civil-War south of the USA required the imposition of 'a moral cost on cheating.'[50] At the level of the dueler, it is not clear that Kiernan and Schwartz *et al.* are right. They assert more than argue the case and, indeed, Kiernan's rich survey of dueling in Europe commends the contrary view that dueling must commonly have been individually rational.

A century after Bacon, Montesquieu wrote of the dilemma potentially faced by a French *gentilhomme*: 'If he obeys the laws of honor, he perishes on the scaffold; if those of justice, he is banished forever from the society of men.'[51] Bacon had deplored the invocation of 'laws' outside the national law, scornfully asking whether the French and Italian manuals on dueling should be incorporated in the laws of England in order to prevent such dilemmas as Montesquieu's *gentilhomme* might face.[52] But Bacon's view did not prevail. Two centuries after him, a duelist in Scotland in 1822 was acquitted of a murder charge. The justification of his acquittal, in the tutored opinion of the celebrated Judge Cockburn, was 'the *necessity*, according to the existing law of society, of acting as he did.'[53]

The sense of the necessity to abide by a strong social norm might be spelled out in at least two ways. First, it might be something in the range from Sartrean or Nietzschean declaration of self, as it seems to be in the words of many a fictional dueler, to the mere flaunting of personal bravery or the quest for glory.[54] Second, it might be a recognition that one's life must be shattered by failure to live up to the norm and face the risk of dueling. For the second ground of necessity, the failure to take on a duel, either to deliver a challenge when requisite or to accept a challenge, would dearly cost a member of the small caste of the odd, selective society of which the duelers were part.[55] The cost of shunning or merely shaming by that society was serious to those who enjoyed the benefits of living as members of it. As Kiernan remarks, the 'penalty for rejecting a challenge was far more severe than any condemnation by the elite of its members' lapses from the morality of parsons.'[56] In his apologia before his fatal duel,

Alexander Hamilton wrote, 'The ability to be in future useful, whether in resisting mischief or effecting good, in those crises of our public affairs which seem likely to happen, would probably be inseparable from a conformity to the prejudice in this particular.'[57]

In some contexts the cost of balking at a duel could be quite explicit and even imposed by the state or by other powerful institutions. In the nineteenth-century French Army it was virtually compulsory to accept a challenge. In 1900, a Habsburg officer was demoted to the ranks 'for failing to resent an insult.' Between 1871 and 1914, when German officers had little other reason for fighting, one who balked at dueling was compelled to resign on a vote of two-thirds' majority of his regiment's fellow officers. This position was ratified as executive policy by Chancellor Prince Bernhard von Bülow in 1906. Bülow's statement, possibly an oversight in a time when he was too busy to note what was being said for him, declared that the officer corps could not tolerate in its ranks anyone too cowardly to defend his honor in a duel. In eighteenth-century England, King George II held a similar position.[58]

Costs of dueling

By comparison, consider the costs of participating in a duel. A writer in the early nineteenth century did experiments using the relatively primitive guns used for duels and found them quite inaccurate at the typical dueling distance. He tallied results of 200 duels, and estimated that about one in fourteen duelers was killed.[59] Many duels without casualties may not have been registered. In 400 duels at Leipzig in one year during the 1840s while he was a student there, Max Muller reported only two deaths. In Georges Clemenceau's reputed twenty-two duels, 'only one of his opponents seems to have been wounded at all seriously.' Hence, the costs of risking loss of life may not have overwhelmed the costs of risking loss of society. If that was true, participating honorably in the duel was merely part of the price of being in the society. Much of the practice of the duel suggests that public reputation and face-saving were centrally important. For example, the seconds at a duel were 'delegates of the class to which all concerned belonged, and whose standards of conduct all of them were taking the field to vindicate.'[60]

Finally, consider the possibility that dueling was a good for some;[61] it was perhaps a variant of current thrills such as hang-gliding, skiing down mountains that are deadly dangerous to climb, auto racing on public roads, and other reckless joys. For many people, dueling may have been more nearly a consumption good than a means. Therefore, we cannot say it was irrational merely because it failed to further someone's interests. Consuming a vacation in a ski resort also may fail to further someone's interests. But the only reason we are concerned with interests is as means to consumption and to fulfillment of various desires. Those who especially enjoyed dueling and who were good at it may have had a tendency to offer more challenges than others did. They more readily crossed the threshold of acting in their own interests. But then the stakes of interest were drastically raised for one who faced a challenge. Hence, differences in tastes for dueling may have increased the likelihood that participants were rational, contrary to the view of Kiernan noted above.

The force of the dueling norm

Superficially, dueling appears to be a decentralized device for regulating aberrant behavior, such as insulting women or, perhaps more typically, insulting a fellow aristocrat by, for example, calling him a liar or striking him during an argument. Dueling may function rather as an aberrant behavior that signifies and reinforces who is and who is not in the relevant group.[62] An aristocrat (*gentilhomme* in France) would not offer a challenge to a workman who insulted a woman but could use devices of shunning and economic exclusion to exact punishment (or might even resort to violence without the protections of a code of behavior). Nor would an aristocrat be obliged to accept a challenge from a commoner.[63] Moreover, the norms of dueling were themselves enforced by shunning and exclusion. Perhaps that would have been at least as effective for enforcing the norms that dueling regulated, since the usual incentives to violate those norms might seem to be far less compelling than the incentive to avoid a duel.

There is, however, perhaps one important way in which regulation of dueling was especially easy, and this fact might go far to explain its prevalence. Violations of the norms of dueling were on fairly conspicuous public display with well-defined actions that might not be misinterpreted. Early on, seconds were introduced to attest that any dueling fatality was not the product of ambush and murder and to protect against such ambush. This public witness was in keeping with the notion of the aristocrat, who was 'noble,' that is noteworthy. 'What is implied,' Kiernan writes, 'is a neurotic sense of being always under observation, by a man's peers and by an alien humankind staring from a distance, ready to jeer or mutiny at any hint of weakness.'[64] Hence, there was plausibly less wide divergence of opinion on whether someone violated a dueling norm than on whether someone violated another norm. This characteristic of dueling might also help to explain why duelers who were both unsuccessful could commonly shake hands and let their original conflict pass once their duel failed to kill either of them.[65] The greater motive to duel was not to inflict punishment or vengeance but to maintain personal status. And, since one's own status depended on the status of the class of aristocrats, one had good reason to maintain standards of behavior worthy of aristocrats.[66]

In one context, the role of the functional reinforcement of the dueling norm is elegantly clear. Kiernan notes of the officers in the eighteenth-century Prussian Army of Frederick the Great that they were largely aristocratic landowners 'with more ancestors than acres,' and they depended on their military role for their livelihood. They freely dueled and thereby deterred non-nobles from entering or staying in the officer corps, where they faced the fear of having to duel or being disgraced.[67]

The duel at the center of Ivan Turgenev's *Spring Torrents* displays the social costs and benefits to the individual dueler. Sanin is fond of Miss Gemma,[68] who is expected to marry the older, wealthier Herr Klueber, and who is insulted by Baron Doenhof. Klueber fails to offer a challenge to Doenhof, thereby losing status and face in this ridiculous community of the parasitic and idle bourgeoisie and *émigrés*, and Sanin offers a challenge. Sanin and Doenhof go through the usual ritual, procuring a doctor who is essentially a specialist at overseeing duels (he has a standard fee for the service) and arranging knowledgeable seconds to keep the duelers to the letter of the code. They meet in an isolated clearing in the woods. Sanin fires and misses (as must have been typical). Now Doenhof could coldly, carefully, take aim to kill Sanin for his challenge. But Doenhof fires deliberately into the air, opening himself to another attempt by Sanin. Sanin then can honorably renounce his right to fire again and the duel is over, and Doenhof can finally admit he was churlish to Gemma. Sanin and Doenhof are now both honorably elevated and secured in their status in the community of the frivolous. They have handled the minor dishonor in the best of all possible ways. Of course, Gemma is evidently delighted at Sanin's survival, to Sanin's great pleasure.[69] In this tale, it is only Klueber, with his independent source of status in the world of economic achievement, who might be thought to benefit from violating the norms of dueling for a lady's honor. Even one chance in fourteen of dying to protect his status in Turgenev's unstable resort community was too great a price to pay. Klueber is emblematic of the commercial society that eventually destroyed the incentive to duel for even many aristocrats. With the sweeping success of that society, the norm has virtually died.

Once the duel was established as a norm within a group, it could become a major incentive for behavior even for one who thought it a stupid norm, as a doltish American might think it stupid for a society to drive on the left but would nevertheless do so as an individual while in England. Indeed, Bazerov, one of the sons in *Fathers and Sons*, argues theoretically that dueling is absurd but that 'from the practical standpoint – well, that's another matter altogether.'[70] This subtle observation, distorted by Pavel Petrovich's moralistic retort, is often the sad conclusion one must reach in the face of a convention that is not optimal but that nevertheless governs enough behavior to make it costly to violate it. The church elder Father Zossima in *The Brothers Karamazov* tells of his youthful duel and his realization of its foolishness. But he was unable to break it off, 'it was almost impossible to do that, for it was only after I had faced his shot at a distance of twelve paces that my words could have any meaning for him.'[71] That is to say, he could have broken off the duel, but only at unacceptable cost in lost status in his group of young military officers. Like Turgenev's Sanin, he could act sensibly only after securing his status by braving at least one shot. This is probably all there is behind the pompously worded and otherwise silly conclusion of Von Koren, the opinionated zoologist in Anton Chekhov's 'The duel,' that 'it follows that there is a force, if not higher, at any rate stronger, than us and our philosophy.' That force is merely the quotidian, often corrosive force of incentives, incentives that in this case are the product of an unfortunate convention – not anything grand or mysterious, not even to a Russian.

Father Zossima notes that, 'Although duels were forbidden and severely punished in those days, they were rather in fashion among the military.'[73] Perhaps its being forbidden by the dull, bureaucratic, legalistic government enhanced the appeal of the duel to a group that wished to see itself as distinctly separate and superior. The duel was the aristocrats' nigger or *gueux*, it marked their separateness and distinctiveness by flouting the rest of society for its duller behavior.

If one were choosing whether to enter the society with the dueling norm, one might rightly suppose one's chances of ever having to duel were low and that therefore the odds of dying or being badly hurt were also low. Hence, the cost of joining the society would be very low in so far as joining entailed risks from dueling. At the moment of being challenged or of being in a situation in which one had to challenge, the relative costs would be loss of society versus the risks of the particular duel, the latter no longer discounted by the improbability of getting into a duel. Even then, loss of society might have seemed catastrophic to many aristocrats, who might sooner have risked death than have suffered exclusion.[74]

Collapse of the dueling norm

We are familiar with the duel after it had lost its attachment to the aristocracy, after the thesis of Kiernan no longer fits it. As discussed below, by the late nineteenth century, there was too much general hostility to the duel for it to be as compelling as it evidently once was. Moreover, the aristocratic class that the duel had once helped to define had lost much of its definition in the face of radical economic and political changes. Aleksander Pushkin wrote of one of the most frivolous duels, which killed one participant and grievously damaged the life of the other, and then Pushkin died in a duel of his own, as did the younger writer Mikhail Lermontov soon afterwards. Both of Pushkin's duels seem more squalid than honourable. (Indeed, virtually all the duals of major works in Russian literature seem squalid, including duels from Turgenev, Chekhov, and Dostoevsky discussed here and two from Tolstoy.)[75] Alexander Hamilton may have concluded that he could only lose once he was challenged to duel by Aaron Burr: his career would fail whether he refused or won the duel (as Burr's career did fail despite his winning the duel) and he would die if he lost it. He died perhaps without trying to win and hoping Burr would also not try.[76]

The duel eventually lost its compelling quality when the aristocracy, whose separate status it had served, became weakened, infiltrated, and dissipated.[77] Indeed, as do many norms, the norm of dueling undercut itself by being an implicit source of entrée to aristocratic status for men who were, in Kiernan's felicitous twist, 'not to the manner born.' By challenging an established aristocrat and having the challenge taken up, a parvenu could seem to be included in the class of those set off as distinct and separate by the norm of dueling.[78] The nearly total dissolution of the original functional justification of the aristocratic norm came in the USA, where egalitarian and parvenu visions gave virtually every white man status to challenge any other to duel. The prize of proving one's membership in the class of all white men was not enough to motivate strong attachment to the norm of dueling. The duel finally died perhaps more by ridicule than by law.[79] It had long survived against the law, but it did not long survive widespread ridicule that ill-fit the honor that dueling was supposed to bring or protect. At last we have realized Bacon's clever insight that the way to defeat the hold of the duel was to dissociate it from honor. Clemenceau, with his laughable record of almost no harm done in twenty-two encounters, could hardly be taken seriously. The Russian and other novelists and playwrights who portrayed squalid duels unworthy of any class cannot have helped the norm.

And, finally, the frivolity of the grounds for many duels casts doubt on the practice. For example, one challenge ensued in France when a husband accused another man of looking at his wife through opera glasses while at the opera, another followed a point of musical criticism, another was fought over a cat, and one in Italy followed a debate over the rival merits of the poets Tasso and Ariosto.[80] The mortally wounded loser of the last of these confessed he had never read the poet he defended. A late sixteenth-century writer remarked that seconds, to the number of three, four, or more on each side, would join in a duel *par gayeté de coeur*, from sheer light-heartedness.[81] Prosper Mérimée's fictional duel in 'The Etruscan vase' followed a minor insult when Auguste Saint-Clair, in pain and fury on coming to believe his beloved had had an affair with a troglodyte, carelessly rebuffed the man who'd told him of her supposed affair.[82] For equivalent events of greater severity, half the men of New York would be dead of duels in any given year, even at the poor odds of one in fourteen. Perhaps the apparent aloofness of Frenchmen and the seemingly greater care with which they walk the streets of Paris are the residue of the duel. Bernard de Mandeville noted that refinement of the sense of honor went so far that 'barely looking upon a Man was often taken for an Affront.'[83] If one dared not glance at another, one must also have suppressed overt humor that might be taken amiss by the slow-witted. Dueling may have flourished less from stupidity than stupidity flourished from dueling. Hence, the society of aristocrats must have been impoverished in many ways by the norm of dueling. The duel was finally gutted when its benefits collapsed and when the function it might once have served, of distinguishing the aristocracy, could no longer be served by it.

Understanding the duel may be especially relevant for understanding ethnic and nationalist identification. The duel is about the demarcation of a particular group and about motivating identification with that group in its conflict with other groups. The dueling norm is a norm of honor, as are norms of ethnic purity and nationalism. T. V. Smith argues that 'Whatever social entity can best foster hostile impulse can most easily appropriate the honor motif. The national state has a peculiar advantage here.'[84] That the honor in each of these cases may be determined by interest perhaps sullies it.

The epistemology of norms

One way to understand norms might simply be to suppose that, for idiosyncratic or communal epistemological reasons, people in a relevant community just do believe them to be right. In general, however, it is far more interesting to attempt to construct the epistemology that leads to a particular norm. Moreover, much of the time, a critical element will be such strategic considerations as whether certain others are also regulated by a particular norm. It may actually be in my immediate interest to follow a norm even though it would be better for me if the norm had collapsed or had been displaced by a quite different norm. A full account of a particular norm might explain how it arose and why it survives. In the best of circumstances, this could be done comparatively.

Hereward, one of Sir Walter Scott's blustery soldiers, says that to be called a liar is 'the same as a blow, and a blow degrades him into a slave and a beast of burden, if endured without retaliation.'[85] For him, this is evidently a simple fact that he apprehends directly. That it is stupid beyond measure and that it could not be supposed true outside a peculiar cultural context never occur to him. But if challenging someone to a duel provoked ridicule, contempt, and horror from everyone in the relevant society, one could not easily sustain Hereward's view, and one could not well sustain the view that dueling brought honor. If dueling brought exclusion from society rather than inclusion in it, dueling could hardly be supported.

In a widely known desert island joke, a Jewish man is cast ashore where he remains for five years. One day, the captain of a passing ship notices two impressive buildings on what is supposed to be an uninhabited desert island. He anchors and goes ashore. There are two beautiful synagogues on the beach, about half a mile apart, but no one is to be seen. The captain and his crew enter one of the synagogues, where they find the lone man. Told that the man built the two synagogues himself, the captain is in awe. 'But they're so beautiful. How did you do it?' The man shrugs that, after all, he's been there with nothing else to do for five years. 'But why did you build two?' the captain asks. 'In this one, I worship,' the Jew says. 'That one I wouldn't go near.' This forlorn castaway is so committed to the norm of supporting his branch of Judaism that he cannot escape the conventions of the society in which he grew up even when shipwrecked alone on a desert island.

Hereward and the Jewish castaway seem incredible. That is their fascination; they are not like anyone we can genuinely say we know. Others are too subject to common sense to have their commitments in such extreme contexts. Yet members of groups with strong norms of exclusion seem often to generate such extreme commitments. How do they do this? At least three processes play a role, the first two of which have been noted already. First, a norm of separation and exclusion may evolve to be increasingly strenuous. As fringe members leave, the harder core becomes more nearly the average. The process of out-migration may be much of the explanation of the increasing extremism of, for example, the Lubavitchers in Brooklyn's Crown Heights.

Second, the test of membership may become more demanding as the most stalwart members perform at a level that casts doubt on the commitments of the less stalwart (as in gang challenges). For example, the dueling norm was subject to the excess discussed earlier, in which one could take offense at trivia, one could risk death or murder for a whim. If the demonstration of personal courage and status of membership in the group was the point of the exercise, then dueling for trivial grounds may have given the most effective demonstration.

The third and final process is that, if separation really works, it constrains the group's epistemology, perhaps disastrously. A group may become ignorant at a level that would be appalling in an individual. We would judge an individual who set out to be that ignorant as stupid and plausibly self-destructive. But members of a group that achieves such self-enforced ignorance need not typically intend for it to do so. The group merely produces ignorance as a function of the success of its norm of separation, and that ignorance reinforces the norm. Cults, chiliastic movements, and rigidly fundamentalist sects cause their own ignorance, without which their odd beliefs would not be credible. This is an example of why functional explanation is not inherently subject to the perverse claim that the explained function is somehow good. A clearly self-reinforcing norm can be destructive, both for the affected individuals and, eventually, for the group in which it arises, as in the perverse religious communities at Jonestown and Waco. Functional explanation does not entail a commitment to any of the various brands of functionalism.

The enforcement of norms

If norms are to be significant, they must affect behavior, which typically means they must be enforced. How are norms successfully enforced? There are at least two relatively straightforward ways they can be nearly self-enforcing through incentives created by the norms. Group norms are commonly enforceable through the strong incentive they offer to members of the group: the implicit threat of exclusion from the group. This device is not typically available for universalistic norms, although shunning might be effective in some cases, for example in response to violations of strong parenting or religious norms. Dueling and other norms of exclusion are self-enforcing because they reinforce separation and difference, not because that is necessarily anyone's intention.

A device that seems readily available and attractive for many of the most important universalistic norms (truth-telling, marital fidelity, fair dealing) is directly inherent in the iterated quality of many of the relationships in which these norms have a role. If you and I are to interact repeatedly, my telling you the truth even when it is mildly against my immediate interest to do so may be in my longer-term interest, because it helps secure further valued interaction with you and it contributes to my reputation for honesty.[86] The value of the continued iteration of our interaction may override my momentary prisoner's dilemma interest in defecting from our cooperative relationship. This incentive from hopes for iteration works only in dyadic and very small-number contexts; it typically fails for norms that govern actions on behalf of a large group. Hence, it may work for truth-telling and promise-keeping but not for voting, contributing to large-scale charities, obedience to law, paying taxes without cheating, and many other important but not dyadic concerns.

The norm of serving in the military in time of war may work as a norm of exclusion. One who refuses to serve, even if there is no severe penalty, might still lose substantially from shunning. This would be true, however, only when the general sense of the relevant war is to unite us as a group, merely a whole-nation group. If the war does not motivate many of us, this norm is weakened, as it was in the USA during the Vietnam War, when very many people opposed the war as wrong and many more doubted that it was really their war.

Many universalistic norms typically cannot be motivated by such considerations, however, since they govern relationships that are not ongoing or that are, under some norm, slated for termination. Unlike the norm of truth-telling, the norm of vendetta cannot be maintained through dyadic iteration. But if it also cannot be maintained through exclusion, then it is seemingly less supported by rational constraints than are dyadic universalistic norms or norms of exclusion. Many such norms, however, can be distorted to fit them with interests, so that they then are self-enforcing.[87]

With rapidly rising prosperity, individual hopes for advancement are less tied to group fate. Thus, the hold of the group is likely to be weakened. Oddly, this implies that the introduction of opportunity for great inequality for individuals can break down inequality between groups and can wreck group efforts to achieve for the group.

Functional explanation seems especially apt for interests, that is for motivating individual actions on behalf of collective benefits, especially when there is the possibility of exclusion of those who fail to abide by the norm. The possibility of exclusion is what makes it possible to motivate contributions to collectively provided goods. For example, toll barriers on some public roads can be used to extract payments enough to cover the cost of amortizing and maintaining the roads. The possibility of exclusion is typically part of the nature of norms of difference. But there is a striking and important difference between the standard resolution of the incentive problem in ordinary collective provision of roads and other goods and in the incentive problem in regulation of behavior through norms of exclusion. In the former, there is a state that can mobilize resources to set up mechanisms to enforce individual contributions to the collective good. In the world of norms there is often no independently empowered enforcement authority – enforcement comes directly from the relevant group members. One might think this could be normatively motivated or even that it must be. Obviously, it could be and probably often is. But it is not necessarily normatively motivated. The members, as described and argued above, may have more mundane incentives to enforce the norm by excluding or shunning those who violate it, or merely by being less responsive and welcoming to them.

Non-dyadic universalistic norms typically do not include devices for exclusion. Individual followers of a norm might shun violators from strictly normative motivations. But this means the norm is not self-enforcing merely through individual incentives. Universalistic norms may therefore require strong inculcation or, alternatively, oversight by the state or other strong enforcement agency, such as a hegemonic religious body. In their incentive structure, they have more in common with ordinary collective goods than with typical norms of difference.

Stability and fragility of norms

Walter Pater, the nineteenth-century English essayist, held that 'nothing that has stirred men deeply can ever altogether lose its meaning for us.'[88] Kiernan seems to think this claim applies to the duel. But consider the opposite view, that we may not only no longer feel the force of dead norms, but we may not even understand the force they once had. Perhaps I can still imagine the sensations of anticipation of a duel, but I cannot imagine holding with Sir Walter Scott's Hereward, cited above, that to be called a liar degrades me 'into a slave and a beast of burden' – that is preposterous and not motivating, not even comprehensible, to me. Hence, Pater's view seems to be a theorist's idle thought that has not been brought to ground in experience. He could say such a thing because the words could be strung together, not because he was actually moved by experience to recognize that his view was evidently true.

We are left with the question: Why can a norm motivate in one context and be utterly dead in another?

Let us approach an answer by first considering a simple convention rather than a strong norm. Abiding by a norm can pass from being in our interest to being not in our interest, even to being strongly contrary to our interest just as a coordination can tip from one of the possible points of coordination to another. If the latter actually happened, say, for the driving convention, it would be odd for very many people years later to say, 'Still, it's wrong to drive on the left, we should go back to driving on the right.' People did react that way in the immediate aftermath of the government-sponsored change in the driving convention in Sweden in 1967.[89] Someone who was too slow-witted to change old habits might complain for much longer. But the vast bulk of the population must soon have grown accustomed to the new convention and, if they believed the arguments in favor of the change, they must have considered it morally acceptable. Jane Austen says of Woodhouse, a widowed father whose daughter, who is half his life, wishes to marry, 'He began to think it was to be, and that he could not prevent it – a very promising step of the mind on its way to resignation.'[90] Many Swedes of 1967 and European aristocrats not very long before may have understood Woodhouse's change of heart, step by step. [91]

Now suppose we have a dueling norm and the state effectively intervenes to stop and to punish duels. The self-interest reinforcement of the norm now fails in general, although one might still expect to confirm one's status if one successfully dueled without punishment. Very soon, there will be no duels for the trivial offenses to honor, perhaps there will even be none for very serious offenses. Shunning might soon take the place of dueling for many offenses, although perhaps not for debates over the relative merits of Tasso and Ariosto, which will simply be reduced to the ordinary insignificance they have outside aristocratic circles. There might therefore still be an effective norm of community and exclusion for the aristocratic class, but not one so dramatic or so effective as the duel. Although it might take frequent and severe punishment of duelers to stop the practice initially, it might soon take only infrequent and less severe punishment to keep it stopped. Soon, decades might pass without a single duel or punishment.

Alternatively – and perhaps this is more nearly what happened to the duel in Europe – the duelist might begin to be more the subject of ridicule than of respect or admiration from others. As with forcible suppression, the duelist might therefore see it as no longer in his interest to duel.

Apart from behavior, what will change in either of these developments? Our knowledge and expectations might also dramatically change. Our children might know that the effective response to an offense is disdain, where we once knew the effective response was a challenge to duel. And, reading an 'ought' from an 'is,' they might come to suppose it is *right* to offer only disdain. While we once thought the right way to confirm our status was by dueling, our children might think the right way is to demonstrate a more perfect air of *je ne sais quoi*. Those who have never been governed by the dueling norm may be fascinated by what Bacon called a fantasticall practice. But that is virtually to say that they share none of the motivation of the norm. They share none of it because it gives them no incentive of self-interest.

Notes and references

* Parts of this essay were published in different form, in Russell Hardin, *One For All: The Logic of Group Conflict* (Princeton, NJ: Princeton University Press, 1995). I thank Princeton University Press for permission to reprint here.

1 David K. Lewis, *Convention* (Cambridge, MA: Harvard University Press, 1969); Russell Hardin, *Morality within the Limits of Reason* (Chicago: University of Chicago Press, 1988), pp. 47–53.

2 As should become clear below, this means the norm cannot be given a functional explanation, as many other norms can be.

3 Peter Steinfels, 'Debating intermarriage and Jewish survival,' *New York Times* (October 18, 1992): 1.

4 For the relationship of prisoner's dilemma to coordination and convention in ongoing contexts, see Russell Hardin, *Collective Action* (Baltimore, MD: Johns Hopkins University Press for Resources for the Future, 1982), chs 9–12.

5 Edna Ullmann-Margalit, *The Emergence of Norms* (Oxford: Oxford University Press, 1977).

6 V. G. Kiernan, *The Duel in European History: Honour and the Reign of Aristocracy* (Oxford: Oxford University Press, 1986), p. 277. There is a fine summary of this work in the review by Christopher Hill, 'Touché!', *New York Review of Books* (June 14, 1990): 55–7.

7 Deuteronomy 23: 19.

8 Thomas Aquinas, *Summa Theologiae* II-II. Question 78 ('On the Sin of Usury').

9 Russell Hardin, 'The street-level epistemology of trust,' *Analyse und Kritik* 14 (Winter 1992): 152–76; reprinted *Politics and Society* 21 (December 1993): 505–29.

10 Hardin, *Collective Action*, pp. 153–4.

11 Hardin, *Collective Action*, pp. 173–205.

12 The discussion that follows here is a response to a challenge from Robert K. Merton to make sense of the use of negative terms as markers of self-approbation. Incidentally, despite its very large vocabulary, the spell-checker on my computer does not know the word nigger. Presumably, it is a very bourgeois, perhaps white, spell-checker. Even at this late date, whites have difficulty reinserting nigger into their vocabulary. Ironically, a chief obstacle to reinserting it may be black opposition.

13 John Camper, 'Loyola struggling to handle new racial tensions: Professor's remark sets off firestorm,' *Chicago Tribune*, (April 15, 1990), section 2: 1ff; Jim Bowman, 'Watch more than P's and Q's,' *Chicago Tribune*, (April 21, 1990), section 1: 12. For further discussion, see Michael Davis, 'Wild professors, sensitive students: a preface to academic ethics,' *Social Theory and Practice* 18 (Summer 1992): 117–41.

14 Robert K. Merton, 'Insiders and outsiders: a chapter in the sociology of knowledge,' *American Journal of Sociology* 28 (July 1972): 9–47, at p. 20.

15 Recall that both supporters and opponents of Clarence Thomas's appointment to the US Supreme Court were bothered by the fact that some of the accusations against him were that he made overt and sexually suggestive comments, just as

many blacks, both men and women, commonly do in bantering conversations among themselves.

16 Janet Mancini Billson and Richard Majors, *Cool Pose: The Dilemmas of Black Manhood in America* (Lexington, MA: Lexington Books, 1992).

17 This is a modified version of the account of Jon Elster, *Ulysses and the Sirens* (Cambridge: Cambridge University Press, 1979), p. 28. Also see Russell Hardin, 'Rationality, irrationality, and functionalist explanation,' *Social Science Information* 19 (September 1980): 755–72. In this earlier work I spoke of 'functionalist explanation.' That terminology is a mistake because it tends to invoke the specter of functionalism. Functional explanation does not entail functionalism. In functionalist theories it is supposed that some behaviors are functional for the survival or good of the society. Racism, which is a norm of exclusion, is not likely functional for the survival or good of a society. But it can be given a functional explanation in that it may be supported through its contribution to the interests of racists.

18 This potential benefit may be offset by the potential cost of reduced access to jobs and resources controlled by other groups and by the larger society, as noted below.

19 Sara Rimer, 'Shawn, 17: Running Past Many Obstacles,' *New York Times* (April 25 1993), pp. 1, 47.

20 Kristin Hunter Lattany, 'Off-timing: stepping to the different drummer,' in Gerald Early (ed,) *Lure and Loathing: Essays on Race, Identity, and the Ambivalence of Assimilation* (New York: Penguin, 1993), pp. 163–74, at p. 168. Edmund Morgan, who replaced Leonard Jeffries as head of the Black Studies Department of the City College of New York, reputedly said to a class, 'I fear that I gave up a good deal of my blackness in the course of moving into a mixed world.' One of his students reacted harshly: 'My feeling is that if you have your identity, that's sacred.' (James Traub, 'The hearts and minds of City College,' *New Yorker* June 7, 1993): 42–53, at p. 52).

21 *New York Times* (November 14, 1993): I.8.

22 See further, Robert K. Merton, 'Our sociological vernacular,' *Columbia* (the magazine of Columbia University), November 1981.

23 For example, many aristocrats might have come to grasp the effect of the dueling norm on the exclusion of others from aristocratic status, while many others might never have appreciated the impact of dueling on aristocratic identification. For the first group, Elster's additional conditions were not met; for the latter group they were met.

24 Robert K. Merton, *Social Theory and Social Structure* (New York: Macmillan, 1968 enlarged edition), pp. 114–18; Hardin, 'Rationality, irrationality, and functionalist explanation,' pp. 757–60. Elster's own primary concern with the difference between intentional and non-intentional explanations of behavior may have led him to focus on latent, non-intentional patterns as functionally to be explained.

25 Irving Lewis Allen, *The City in Slang* (Oxford: Oxford University Press, 1993), pp. 217–18.

26 Allen says that 'to name Us with an ironic epithet given to Us by Them . . . implicitly names Them' (Allen, *The City in Slang*, p. 218). It seems unlikely that young blacks who call one another nigger are centrally motivated by the intention to name Them.

27 I came of age during the Civil Rights era in Texas and I have many memories of Toms being quoted, but I have no published source. Similarly, I have memories, possibly exaggerated, of people such as Stokely Carmichael challenging blacks with their racial identity. Carmichael urged abandonment of the term Negro (Stokely Carmichael and Charles V. Hamilton, *Black Power: The Politics of*

Liberation in America (New York: Random House, 1967)). For capsule histories of the changes in self-designations of American blacks, see Tom W. Smith, 'Changing racial labels: from "Colored" to "Negro" to "Black" to "African American,"' *Public Opinion Quarterly* 56 (1992): 496–514.

28 Arthur Hertzberg says that 'anti-Semitism is used by people who want to show they are the truly loyal and pure representatives of their ethnic group or nation' (Hertzberg, 'Is anti-Semitism dying out?', *New York Review of Books* (June 24, 1993): 51–7, at p. 51).

29 The use of the term 'bad nigger,' applied, for example, to a violent criminal, may have separate origins. It may be more nearly a Sartrean or Nietzschean declaration of self. See further, Jack Katz, *Seductions of Crime: Moral and Sensual Attractions in Doing Evil* (New York: Basic Books, 1988), pp. 263–4 and passim.

30 See Edna Ullmann-Margalit and Sidney Morgenbesser, 'Picking and choosing,' *Social Research* 44 (Winter 1977): 757–85.

31 I owe this example to Fritz Stern. See 'Gueux,' *New Encyclopedia Britannica, Micropaedia*, Vol. 4, 15th edition (1978), p. 78.

32 John Howard Griffin, *Black Like Me* (New York: New American Library, 1976 (1961)).

33 Thomas Wolfe, *You Can't Go Home Again* (1940); *Look Homeward, Angel* (New York: Scribner's, 1929).

34 Herman Melville put this concern more generally: 'in the soul of man there lies one insular Tahiti, full of peace and joy, but encompassed by all the horrors of the half known life. God keep thee! Push not off from that isle, thou canst never return!' (Melville, *Moby Dick* (published in 1851 as *The Whale*), any complete edition, ch. 58).

35 Thomas Wolfe, *The Web and the Rock* (New York: Harper, 1939). In his 1988 presidential campaign, George Bush evidently borrowed and distorted Wolfe's 'thousand points of . . . light.'

36 One might nevertheless suppose that, before the Civil Rights Movement, many whites in the south were responsible as individuals for what the larger society did in so far as many of them actively participated in Jim Crow practices. Dwight Macdonald supposed that typical Germans were less culpable of Nazi actions than typical white southerners were of racial exclusion and subjugation. Dwight Macdonald, *The Responsibility of Peoples and Other Essays in Political Criticism* (London: Victor Gollancz, 1957), pp. 19–24.

37 Griffin, *Black Like Me*, p. 153.

38 See further, the discussion of tipping from one norm to another below, under 'Stability and fragility of norms.'

39 There were exceptions, such as the notable bias against Jews and, no doubt, a general bias in favor of Russians.

40 Kiernan, *The Duel in European History*, p. 159.

41 Kiernan, *The Duel in European History*, p. 152.

42 Francis Bacon, *The Charge of Sir Francis Bacon Knight, His Majesties Attourney generall, touching Duells, upon an information in the Star-chamber against Priest and Wright* (London: 1614; New York: Da Capo Press, facsimilie reprint, 1968), pp. 22–3.

43 Adam Smith, *Lectures on Jurisprudence* (Oxford: Oxford University Press, 1978; Indianapolis: Liberty Press, 1982 (from lecture notes dated 1762–3)), p. 123.

44 Bacon, *The Charge of Sir Francis Bacon*, pp. 28–30 (pp. 28 and 29 are misnumbered as 20 and 21).

45 Cited in Kiernan, *The Duel in European History*, p. 282.

46 Bacon, *The Charge of Sir Francis Bacon*, pp. 16–19, 31–2 (the last page is misnumbered as 24).

47 Bacon, *The Charge of Sir Francis Bacon*, pp. 12, 6.

48 Kiernan, *The Duel in European History*, p. 160.

49 Kiernan, *The Duel in European History*, p. 159; also see pp. 16, 111, 329. Kiernan's view of the individual irrationality of dueling might be roughly Bacon's point that the duel was too grievous a response to such trivia as insults.

50 Warren F. Schwartz, Keith Baxter, and David Ryan, 'The duel: can these gentlemen be acting efficiently?', *Journal of Legal Studies* 13 (June 1984): 321–55, at p. 333.

51 Cited in Kiernan, *The Duel in European History*, p. 171. Also see pp. 16, 52, 77. Smith also shared Montesquieu's view of the high cost of failing to duel (Smith, *Lectures in Jurisprudence*, p. 123).

52 Bacon, *The Charge of Sir Francis Bacon*, pp. 9–10.

53 Kiernan, *The Duel in European History*, p. 208, emphasis added. The victim of the duel was Sir Alexander Boswell, son of James Boswell.

54 Kiernan, *The Duel in European History*, p. 27.

55 Kiernan, *The Duel in European History*, pp. 15, 77, 137, 156–7, 213, 328; Smith, *Lectures on Jurisprudence*, p. 123. J. C. D. Clark cites English gentlemen's handbooks of the time that note that failing to duel is, in the words of one of them, 'worse than being buried alive' (Clark, *English Society 1688–1832: Ideology, Social Structure and Political Practice during the Ancien Regime* (Cambridge: Cambridge University Press, 1985), p. 109).

56 Kiernan, *The Duel in European History*, p. 160.

57 Quoted in Robert Irving Warshow, *Alexander Hamilton: First American Businessman* (New York: Greenberg, 1931), p. 216.

58 Kiernan, *The Duel in European History*, pp. 265, 273, 274, 281–2, 101; see also pp. 113–15.

59 As cited in Schwartz *et al.*, 'The duel,' p. 324.

60 Kiernan, *The Duel in European History*, pp. 144, 272, 269, 138. Kiernan's imputation of general concern to vindicate the standards of the class may involve great license. Presumably, the chief, perhaps often even the only, motivation was personal, not collective. The role of the collective, of the class as such, was merely to set contraints on and incentives for individual action. Elsewhere, Kiernan suggests that most duels were 'meaningless scrimmages' (p. 329).

61 Kiernan, *The Duel in European History*, pp. 117, 265, 271, 283.

62 Aristocrats were about 2 percent of the population of France in the early eighteenth century (Roland Mousnier, *The Institutions of France under the Absolute Monarchy 1598-1789* (Chicago: University of Chicago Press, 1979, from 1974 French edition), p. 147).

63 Kiernan, *The Duel in European History*, p. 11.

64 Kiernan, *The Duel in European History*, pp. 63, 317.

65 As happens at the conclusion of the duel in Turgenev's *Spring Torrents* described below. See also Kiernan, *The Duel in European History*, pp. 149–51.

66 Kiernan, *The Duel in European History*, p. 66.

67 Kiernan, *The Duel in European History*, p. 111.

68 Please forgive my sexist use of the first name for the only woman in this story and last names for all the men. That is the convention of Turgenev and his translator. It is also, aptly, the convention for a society governed by a code of (male) honor that includes the duel. Women evidently did duel, but rarely (Kiernan, *The Duel in European History*, pp. 132–3, 203, 327).

69 Ivan Turgenev, *Spring Torrents* (Baltimore, MD: Penguin, 1980 (1872); trans. Leonard Schapiro), pp. 71–7.

70 Ivan Turgenev, *Fathers and Sons*, trans. Rosemary Edmonds (Baltimore, MD: Penguin, 1965 (1861), p. 235.

71 Fyodor Dostoevsky, *The Brothers Karamazov* (Penguin, 1958, in one vol. 1982 (1880)), p. 352.

72 Anton Chekhov, 'The duel,' in Chekhov, *The Duel and Other Stories* (New York: Ecco Press, 1984 (1891); trans. Constance Garnett), p. 133. Earlier, Laevsky, Von Koren's adversary, thinks that dueling is 'stupid and senseless . . . but that it [is] sometimes impossible to get on without it' (p. 126). Again, the impossibility is merely personal costs of defying the norm of the exclusive group of frivolous aristocrats and *arrivistes*.

73 Dostoevsky, *The Brothers Karamazov*, p. 349.

74 Theodore Caplow presents data from many kinds of organizations that suggest a strong tendency for members to distort upward the prestige of their organizations. He calls this tendency the aggrandizement effect. (Theodore Caplow, *Principles of Organization* (New York: Harcourt Brace Jovanovich, 1964), pp. 213–16). We might suppose that tendency afflicted the aristocracy of Europe.

75 Leo Tolstoy, *War and Peace* (London: Everyman, 1911 (1864–69), part 1, chs 73–4. In an apparently petty moment the future pacifist Tolstoy challenged Turgenev to a duel, but later had the sense to back down. Kiernan, *The Duel in European History*, pp. 288–9.

76 Neither Burr nor Hamilton would qualify as an aristocrat by birth. The dueling norm was probably more weakly grounded in their wider community than was the norm of European aristocrats.

77 Kiernan, *The Duel in European History*, p. 326.

78 Kiernan, *The Duel in European History*, p. 112. In our time, the parvenu can buy a coat of arms from the College of Heralds in the UK for a modest sum – less than a thousand pounds in 1984 (p. 326). The trend in the price matches the trend in the value. Alternatively, for $149 one may buy a square foot of land in Caithness in the Scottish Highlands, and thereby become a Laird of Camster (advertisement, *Scientific American*, December 1992, p. 163).

79 This was the view of Algernon West (Kiernan, *The Duel in European History*, p. 218).

80 Kiernan, *The Duel in European History*, pp. 6, 119, 62.

81 Pierre de Bourdielle Brantôme, quoted in Kiernan, *The Duel in European History*, p. 64.

82 Prosper Mérimée, 'The Etruscan vase,' pp. 93–115, in Mérimée, *Carmen and Other Stories*, trans. Nicholas Jotcham (Oxford: Oxford University Press, 1989 (1830)). His adversary had ignored a worse offense in public the evening before.

83 Bernard de Mandeville, *An Inquiry into the Origin of Honour and the Usefulness of Christianity in War* (London: 1836), p. 64 (cited in Kiernan, *The Duel in European History*, p. 75).

84 T. V. Smith, 'Honor,' *Encyclopaedia of the Social Sciences* (New York: Macmillan, 1932), vol. 7, pp. 456–8, at p. 458.

85 Walter Scott, *Count Robert of Paris* (Edinburgh, 1831), ch. 2; quoted in Kiernan *The Duel in European History*, p. 237.

86 Hardin, *Collective Action*. p. 218.

87 See further, Russell Hardin *One For All: The Logic of Group Conflict* (Princeton, NJ: Princeton University Press, 1995), ch. 7.

88 Kiernan, *The Duel in European History*, p. 326.

89 *New York Times* (September 5, 1967): 24.

90 Jane Austen, *Emma* (London: Penguin, 1985, first pub. 1816), ch. 55, p. 464.

91 Tolstoy in his gloomy later years had a grimmer view: 'The people perish, they are accustomed to the process of perishing, customs and attitudes to life have appeared which accord with the process.' Leo Tolstoy, *Resurrection* (London: Penguin, 1966, trans. Rosemary Edmonds; originally published 1899), p. 286.

13 From expressionism and futurism to kitsch

Ethnic and intergenerational conflict, political inaction, and the rise of dictatorship

*Ronald Wintrobe**

Introduction

In this paper, I attempt to use simple tools of economic theory to understand ethnicity, ethnic conflict, and nationalism and their role in destabilizing democracy under the Weimar regime. The paper builds on previous work on ethnicity (Wintrobe 1995), and on political inaction in democratic systems (Howitt and Wintrobe 1993, 1995). The starting point of the analysis is a set of circumstances in which there are gains from trade, as in standard neoclassical theory, but that property rights are not costlessly enforceable. Once the latter fiction is discarded, the situation is that people still wish to exchange, but they always have to worry about being cheated. There are reputation mechanisms for solving this problem (Klein and Leffler 1981, Shapiro 1983), but they tend to be expensive. Similar problems arise in politics, interpreted as political exchange in the absence of legal enforcement (one cannot sue a politician in court for breaking a campaign promise), and within families (parents cannot sue their children for not supporting them in their old age).

In both public and private life, one particularly cost-effective way to provide a foundation for exchange under many circumstances is to invest in ethnic networks or 'ethnic capital.' The central feature of ethnic capital is the peculiarity of blood as a basis for network 'membership.' To the extent that this criterion is used, entry and exit from the network (within a generation) are blocked. I suggest (in the next section) that this gives ethnic networks some advantages as a support for exchange, and partly explains the persistence of ethnicity in modern societies. But if ethnic capital cannot move from one group to another, it also follows that competition among ethnic groups does not equalize returns among them. Consequently differences in returns and therefore in incomes will persist. The result is that successful ethnic groups tend to engender fear and jealousy on the part of outsiders, while members of ethnic groups with low returns tend to become stigmatized. These disparities combined with the zero-sum nature of economic rents imply that there is an inevitable potential for conflict among ethnic groups ('if you can't join them, beat them'), which is not regulated or reduced by market forces.

The third section then looks inside the ethnic group, and in particular at the process of formation of ethnic capital, investments which are largely made by parents for their children. I assume for the purpose of analysis that parents are selfish, and invest in their children in the hope of being repaid in later life. I show that a second peculiar feature of ethnic investments, compared to other kinds of investments in children such as general human capital, is that they are *self-enforcing*, in that the children cannot get the benefits of the capital without exposing themselves to 'ethnic pressure' to repay their parents for their sacrifices. This self-enforcing feature makes ethnic investments very attractive to the parents, but not necessarily to the children. Consequently, parents will tend to overinvest in their children's ethnic capital from the children's point of view. I show the circumstances under which this intergenerational conflict can lead to 'authoritarian' attitudes in the children, as originally described in the classic work on the authoritarian personality syndrome by Adorno *et al.* (1950), and extended in more recent work, notably in Bob Altemeyer's *Right-Wing Authoritarianism* (1981) and *Enemies of Freedom* (1988). The final section applies these concepts to the collapse of Weimar Germany (expressionism) and the emergence of Nazism (kitsch) in the 1930s.

The value of ethnic capital

The starting point for our analysis consists of two assumptions, which will be maintained throughout this paper, except in the next section, where, as noted there, assumption 1 is relaxed. They are:

1   All individuals are rational, in the standard sense of that term in neoclassical economic theory; that is faced with any two alternatives the individual is capable of making a choice between them, and his or her choices are consistent.
2   Property rights or contracts are not costlessly enforceable, and sometimes may not even exist.

The second assumption implies that in any exchange, there is the possibility that one of the parties will cheat or renege on his or her commitments. In markets, this problem was considered by Klein and Leffler (1981) and Shapiro (1983), in the context of markets for high-quality goods. They assumed that, prior to purchase, consumers cannot distinguish high quality from low. What prevents the firm from producing low-quality goods and selling them as if they were high quality? Shapiro showed that there are three conditions required for it to be in the firm's interest not to cheat its customers: (a) the prospect of future sales; (b) the firm's past reputation as a seller of high-quality goods; and (c) the firm's receipt of a price premium on high-quality goods, both to compensate it for its past investments in reputation and to serve as a deterrent to cheating. If the present value of the premiums received from future sales is large enough to overcome the one-time gains from cheating ('milking' its reputation), it will not be in the firm's interest to cheat. In essence, the existence of the price premium provides the consumer with a reason to *trust* the firm. As Klein and Leffler put it, the consumer pays the firm 'protection money' in the form of a price premium to ensure contractual fulfillment. In this way, markets can solve the trust or contractual enforcement problem even in the absence of legally enforceable property rights.

One problem with this solution from the consumer's point of view is that it is expensive. Consumers are forced to pay a premium, the present discounted value of which is at least as large as the gains to the firm from cheating in order to deter the firm from cheating. Consumers willing to pay this premium are not cheated, but they do not get good value for their money: They stay in Holiday Inns, buy Bayer Aspirin, IBM computers, and so on. An alternative solution for the consumer is to establish a trust relationship with a local seller – the local drugstore, computer hack, and so on. The costs of 'signaling' or building trust on a one-on-one basis may be reduced considerably when there is genuine interaction between the parties, as opposed to impersonal market signals. In these cases trust can describe a relationship which is, at the limit, completely private; it exists between a seller and only one buyer – a 'network.' Trust relationships like these are analyzed by Breton and Wintrobe (1982) and Coleman (1990). Breton and Wintrobe pointed out that trust relationships like these are capital. They yield a stream of future returns which are the profits on the exchanges which trust makes possible and which could not otherwise take place.

Trust relationships are also important – indeed, probably much more important – in labor markets. Again, the key is to drop the assumption of costlessly enforceable property rights. One way in which enforceability problems can arise is that employees may try to shirk if monitoring their effort level is not costless to the employer (Shapiro and Stiglitz 1984, Bowles 1985, Bulow and Summers 1986). The central insight of these models is that if markets clear, a worker who is fired for shirking can always get another job at the same wage as the worker is currently earning. In other words, if markets clear, punishment is impossible. Consequently, wages will have to be increased above productivity in order to provide a punishment mechanism. Consequently, jobs are rationed, and those who have them earn rents which are precisely analogous to the premiums earned by producers of high-quality goods in the Shapiro model.

In short, perhaps the most important lesson of these models is that once the assumption of costlessly enforceable property rights is dropped, the existence of economic rents becomes a pervasive feature of industrial economies. The absence of enforceability generates a demand for trust, and *markets do not supply trust except via rents*: the market mechanism deters cheating only if rents are paid which are at least equal to the gains from cheating.

Of course, the same problem of enforceability arises in political markets, in which politicians make promises, especially at election time, and hope to obtain support in exchange for them. What prevents politicians from reneging on the exchange? And what motivates citizens and interest groups to deliver the support that they have promised? Again, the answer suggested here is that both sides of the market will try and look for devices which engender trust (political loyalty) and that these devices imply the distribution of rents. Two institutional mechanisms that engender loyalty in politics are pork-barrel projects and political patronage – the exact analog in political markets to price and wage premiums in economic markets. Thus, only to the extent that a pork-barrel project is genuinely wasteful, or that a patronage job has gone to someone who is genuinely less qualified for it than someone else, do these devices distribute rents, and therefore engender loyalty.

To summarize, rents exist to 'cement' trust relationships in product and labor markets, within firms, and in political processes. They are a pervasive feature of modern industrial society. A typical individual who wants to buy goods and services at reasonable prices and not be cheated, who wants or wishes to keep a 'good' job, and who wishes to get a share of the largesse being distributed by politicians, or even to have his or her views reflected in public policy, therefore has a very complex pattern of network investments to make. For each good or service or political service that the individual wishes to purchase, where there is some prospect of being cheated, he or she may wish to invest in a specific trust relationship. Some goods and services will be bought so infrequently that such investments will not be worth their cost. In many cases, also, the individual has to calculate that investments in these relationships will be lost if he or she moves to another jurisdiction. In these situations, the individual is stuck with the market, and market premiums. In others, the individual may try the networking strategy just discussed. It follows that, in general, the optimal investment strategy (distribution of investments in trust among all the different possible relationships involved) is truly complex. What this individual really wants is a mutual fund. These funds exist, in the form of ethnic networks.

The central feature of ethnic networks is that 'membership' is held to be determined by blood, making it very difficult for outsiders to enter, and often for insiders to truly exit (within a generation), a characteristic that I will refer to as *blocked entry and exit*. This solves one of the problems characteristic of networks – namely, that if the returns turn out to be substantial, others will want to enter, hence lowering the yield on the initial investments of 'insiders.' Moreover, since membership is to some extent at least not subject to choice, part of the difficulties normally encountered in establishing a trust relationship are resolved. Thus, a German (say) who meets another German and contemplates a transaction that requires trust does not have to worry that the other party is only German *temporarily* because the yield on German capital is temporarily high. Of course, the *level* of German-ness exhibited – the extent to which the other person uses German phrases, pretends to like potatoes with whipped cream, goes to German social events, and so on – may be precisely subject to such calculations, but, fundamentally, either he or she is German (or Francophone, or Jewish, or Italian), or not. In part, this is because one's ethnicity is not completely subject to choice, but is also determined by the attitudes of others (as Jews in particular found out under the Nazi regime).

Just as it is difficult if not impossible for an outsider to enter an ethnic group, it may also be difficult if not impossible for insiders to exit. A black man can marry a white woman, live in a white suburb, work for an all-white firm and so on, but he can still find himself greeted by shouts of 'Hey, brother!' when he finds himself in the 'wrong' neighborhood. And he may also find, to his surprise, that while other connections come and go, the permanence of the ethnic connection can sometimes come in handy. This is particularly likely to happen if he discovers that just as insiders would never completely let him go, so outsiders never really let him in, and he is passed over for promotion or turned down in romance because he 'is' black.

To be sure, any man (say) is free to foreswear association with other members of his ethnic group; he can tell his friends and family to get lost, move to another city and refuse to give out his address, never phone his mother again (even on her birthday), change his name to Smith, and so on. Even if he did all these things, however, he will still not be in the same position *vis-à-vis* his ethnic group as an outsider. His ethnic networks will depreciate through lack of use, *but they will not depreciate to zero*. This takes a generation or more. And, should he have a change of heart later on in life and decide to recontact the old network, he will be able to rebuild his capital at less cost than an outsider would incur. It is in this sense that exit from ethnic networks is blocked – an individual is free to reduce his gross investment in this form of capital to zero, but he cannot sell, transfer, or dispose of the 'sunk' capital which has been accumulated through upbringing, socialization, and ascription by others.

Of course, in reality, it is easier to enter and exit some types of ethnic groups than others. Moreover, ethnicity is subject to manipulation, as is its sister concept *nationalism*, usually defined, for example by Rogowski, as 'the striving of members of a culturally distinct group for territorial autonomy' (Rogowski 1985). In the present context, nationalism is naturally interpretable as the claim that the return to ethnic capital can be raised if the group in question were to form a sovereign state, or, more generally, acquire more territory. Gellner (1983) emphasizes that nationalism is essentially deceptive. As he puts it: 'A modern, streamlined, on-wheels high culture celebrates itself in song and dance, which it borrows (stylizing itself in the process) from a folk culture which it fondly believes itself to be perpetuating, defending and affirming' (Gellner 1983: 158). Hechter (1987) suggests ways in which groups can manipulate exit barriers to encourage loyalty, as does Iannaccconne (1992), who explains the often bizarre practices of cults as ways in which the cult tries to lower the marginal rate of substitution of ordinary goods and services to cult members, hence making it more difficult to leave the cult. From our current point of view, what matters is only that people *believe* in ethnicity or the nation state. If they do, the barriers are generated, whether 'real' or not. A more general analysis than that offered here would allow the level of barriers to entry and exit to vary and develop an 'industrial organization' of ethnic groups. In this paper, I will simply assume blocked entry and exit in order to bring out the implications of this assumption.

Indeed, several other characteristics of ethnic networks follow from the property of blocked entry and exit. Thus, ethnic networks are *multipurpose*, and can be used for finding a job or an apartment, a good plumber, a mate, and so on (not necessarily in that order). Ethnic networks also have an *infinite life* – indeed they go on backward as well as forward in time. This means that ethnic networks solve the 'hangman's paradox' often discussed in game-theoretic analyses of the cheating problem. Thus if a game is finite, cheating is guaranteed on the last play (since there is no possible sanction after the end of the game); if the second party (who has the last move) is going to cheat the first party on the last move, the first party should obviously cheat the second on the next-to-last move; hence the game unravels and cheating takes place on the first move. Whatever importance this analysis has in real life, and there are many who believe it to have some, the problem raised is solved by ethnic networks, since blood ties may thin out but never disappear. Because of this longevity, there is always the prospect of punishment if one ethnic member cheats another in the same group, and there is always the prospect that members of one ethnic group will punish the descendants of another for some transgression or other. In these and other ways, ethnic networks often have a superior capacity to sanction transgressors, both by 'insiders' and 'outsiders.' Thus, the Serb leader Slobodan Milosevic was able to raise genuine fears of conquest and occupation by reminding the Serbs of what the Ottomans did to them at the Battle of Kosovo in 1389. The tactic was apparently effective in building his power base (Ramet 1992: 228).

A fourth property of ethnic networks is *(relative) homogeneity of tastes*. Jews like Chinese food, tend to be in favor of human rights, and feel comfortable in big cities. Germans and Japanese people are more willing to work hard compared to Americans. Of course, these ethnic stereotypes are often invalid, but to the extent that tastes do tend to be relatively more homogeneous within ethnic groups than between randomly chosen individuals, collective decision making within the group is made easier, and the capacity of the group for collective action is enhanced. Finally, the costs of forming trust will be lower if signaling and communication is easier, as it often is between members of the same ethnic group (Landa 1981, Breton and Wintrobe 1982).

Finally, ethnic capital investments are *subsidized* through inheritance and upbringing. An individual whose parents are members of an ethnic group will, by the time the individual becomes an adult, have already accumulated a substantial amount of ethnic capital. Some of it is 'in the genes,' some will have been accumulated through education and forced socialization with other members of his or her ethnic group. Of course, at some point the individual is free to choose a different ethnic identity but in that case will have to accumulate all of the costs at his or her own expense. A Frenchman who decides that he really wants to be a Korean can of course try to do so, but his parents are probably unlikely to help him, and he will be throwing away all of those French connections.

There are also, of course, disadvantages to ethnic networks. The most important of these also follows from the central assumption of blocked entry and exit. In the standard economic theory of markets, two broadly conceived assumptions are necessary to ensure the efficiency or (Pareto) optimality of competition: (i) the absence of externalities, 'publicness,' or other factors which would lead to the systematic under- or overpricing of economic costs or benefits; (ii) free entry and exit of capital. As is well known, the second assumption implies that capital will flow out of those industries where its yields are relatively low and into those industries where yields are relatively high. So rents will not persist in long-run equilibrium but will be eliminated as capital flows to those industries where ethnic capital is most valuable, and the supply of goods and services from those industries expands, driving down their prices and reducing economic rents. This mechanism assures the efficiency of competition in economic markets. As discussed earlier, entry to or exit from ethnic networks is blocked. Consequently, if one ethnic group experiences abnormally high returns (e.g. US Jews) and another group abnormally low returns (e.g. US blacks), there is no mechanism whereby the returns to ethnic capital can be equalized across ethnic groups.

To illustrate this point with a simple model, suppose that there are only two ethnic groups, the Grails and the Snails. Assume that all individuals of either type are identical. However, although the individuals are identical, the yield to forming network capital need not be. Suppose that the returns to network capital formation are higher among the Grails than the Snails. The Grails might have a superior capacity to sanction deviant or non-participating members, or they may be able to communicate better with each other, or they may be more isolated from the rest of society and therefore interact with each other more, and so on. Finally, assume that, for either group, there are diminishing returns to aggregate ethnic capital. Let d = the depreciation rate of ethnic capital, and C' = the marginal cost of its formation. The benefits are the increased likelihood of obtaining a rent (p) multiplied by its value (R). The return to ethnic capital is the sum of these rents

$$\sum_i p_i R_i \; \forall i$$

where i denotes all the 'uses' of ethnic capital (jobs, apartments, plumbers, mates, investment counsellors, political patronage, etc.). Each member of the Grails will invest in ethnic capital to the point where the marginal return just equals its cost, that is

$$(\sum_i p_i R_i)_G = C'_G(r + d_G) \tag{1}$$

where G indexes variables for the Grails. The same equation holds for the Snails. Individuals in either group will invest until the *marginal* yields are equal to their costs (and therefore to each other's costs). However, if infra-marginal yields were high for the Grails and low for the Snails, the total amount invested would be high for the Grails and low for the Snails.

In equilibrium the average yield is high for the Grails and low for the Snails. Grails will get more of the good jobs, good apartments, and so on than Snails do. If mobility were possible between groups, Snails would enter the Grail network and average yields would fall there and rise among the Snails. However, blocked entry and exit prevents this mechanism from operating. Returns could be equalized by differential rates of population growth, if the high yield to Grail ethnic capital resulted in high population growth rates there, and the low yield to Snail ethnic capital resulted in low rates of population growth for that group. However, if anything, this mechanism appears to work in reverse: high-income groups appear to have low rates of population growth and low-income groups high rates of growth. Consequently, high yields among some ethnic groups will persist, giving rise to fear, envy, and possibly hatred among other groups who will never share those yields. Low returns among other groups will result in stigmatization, or statistical discrimination (Arrow 1972) as individuals within an ethnic group are judged on the basis of the performance of the average for that group.[1]

In short, the phenomenon of blocked entry and exit explains why market mechanisms do not eliminate ethnic conflict and why competition among ethnic groups has the potential to breed conflict. To some extent, individualism is devalued as the characteristics of the group become more important as determinants of individual welfare. There is also a natural tendency for ethnicity to be linked to territory, as in the 'principle of nationality' that the boundaries of the state should be linked to those of the 'nation' or ethnic group (Hobsbawm 1990). The absence of the market-regulating mechanism implies its replacement by evolutionary or conflict mechanisms, as groups either prosper or decline as a whole. And there is a natural demand for leadership in the management of ethnic capital. In *extreme* form, all of these characteristics – the importance of the group over the individual, the leader and evolutionary principles, and the stress on struggle and the inevitability of conflict – are precisely the characteristics of fascism, in both its Italian and German manifestations. Gregor (1969) describes the intellectual roots of fascism in the thinking of early twentieth-century sociologists like Gumplowicz, Mosca, and Pareto. Thus Mosca maintained that:

> Human beings have a natural inclination towards struggle . . . [but] even when he fights, man remains primarily a social animal. Ordinarily, therefore we see men forming into groups, each group made up of leaders and followers. The individuals who make up a group are conscious of a special brotherhood and oneness with each other and vent their pugnacious instincts on members of other groups.
>
> (Mosca, quoted in Gregor 1969: 42–3)

Similar ideas can be found in the work of Pareto and Gumplowicz, and later in the work of Roberto Michels and, of course, Mussolini (see Gregor for an extensive discussion). Although anti-semitism was not important in the formation of Italian fascism, *ethnocentrism* was, as was the idea that ethnocentric dispositions had a high survival value because they facilitated the survival of the group. The (biological) free-rider problem[2] was not identified as such, but the closely related idea that the masses were incapable of mobilizing themselves but required a vanguard or an elite leadership to mobilize them was a central theme, as, of course it had earlier been in the thought of Lenin, and was to be in Hitler's thinking.[3] For all of these twentieth-century revolutionaries, the majority was the fodder, rather than the conscious agent, of social revolution. Of course, as Linz (in Larsen *et al.* 1980) points out,

> If there is one characteristic of fascism on which all analysts agree it is the central place of nationalism in its ideology, particularly the type of nationalism that goes as far as placing loyalty to the nation ahead of nation to the state.[4]

However, the extremity or the viciousness of *some* ethnic conflicts, such as that under the Nazi regime, or perhaps the contemporary conflict between the Serbians and Croatians, is still, I believe, difficult to account for with a model like this one. To do this, however, I believe it is only necessary to go one step further to the idea that there is some poison *within* the group which is believed to be the central obstacle to fulfilling its goals. Analytically, this requires that we look more deeply inside the ethnic group and investigate in more detail how ethnic capital is formed.

Intra- and intergroup ethnic conflict

So far, I have suggested that ethnic investments can yield a positive return, and have assumed in the last section that individuals accumulate the optimal level of this form of capital. Intergenerational harmony was thus assured, despite the fact that much of the investment in ethnic capital is performed by parents for their children. I also assumed that entry and exit from the network are blocked. In this section, I want to elaborate a more complicated model, in which parents make investments in their children in exchange for control over the behavior of their children in later life, and in which this exchange is 'enforced' by the pressure which can be brought upon the children by other members of the ethnic group.

Thus, suppose that parents invest in the ethnic capital of their children by sending them to ethnic schools, inculcating ethnic customs and rituals, language, and other communication techniques, restricting their socialization while young to other members of the ethnic group, etc. Parents expect to be repaid for these sacrifices through the obedience of the children in later life to norms of the ethnic group, which presumably include support and attention to their parents in their old age, but may also encompass other aspects of their children's behavior: for example, that they will marry within the group and raise children who will continue to participate within it, that they participate in ethnic cultural activities, rites and rituals, respect and/or worship ancestral heroes, take credit as members of the group for the accomplishments of their forefathers, assume the debts of previous generations, and so on. In short, children may repay their parents not only directly with support, but also indirectly by making decisions based on their parents' wishes or utility functions, and by participating in the activities or adhering to the norms of the ethnic group.

But what mechanism can parents count on to enforce the implicit contract between them and their children? The children can't be sued in court if they don't repay. There are obvious reasons for this. One reason is surely that the contract may not be voluntarily entered into by the children, or even if it is, the children may be too young to be deemed capable of 'credible' or enforceable commitments. Another is that the preferred form of repayment can take subtle forms: for example, that the children's career or marriage choices are those that their parents would have liked them to make. With these forms of repayment, it may be difficult for an outsider to ascertain whether repayment has in fact occurred, and to adjudicate disputes between parents and their children over this matter. Yet both parents and children might prefer these forms of repayment to, say, cash repayments.

So how can parents be confident that their children will in fact repay them for the sacrifices they have made on their behalf? Clearly, the problem is a general one, that is it applies to all forms of parental investment, for example, to investments in general human capital such as their children's education or occupational training, and to 'gifts' of land, houses, cash, and so on.

I can think of at least five mechanisms which can act as substitutes for legal enforcement: (a) altruism, (b) bequests, (c) trust, (d) guilt, and (e) shame. Becker (1974, 1976), Frank (1988), and others have argued that altruism is a powerful force in family life, as indeed it no doubt is. In the famous 'rotten kid' theorem, Becker argued that, under certain conditions one-sided altruism, that is the parent loves the child but not *vice versa*, is sufficient to motivate the child's cooperation. However, one problem is that altruism within the family is sometimes insufficient. Becker and Murphy (1988) explicitly acknowledge this and suggest that state intervention (compulsory schooling, pension plans, etc.) often mimics the kinds of contracts that the family would have entered into if legally enforceable contracting were possible. But they do not inquire into the private behavior that ensues where love is insufficient, that is there is no analysis of alternative bases for exchange within the family. Yet, even where love is plentiful, so long as it is not complete, that is the child cares for the parent as much as for him- or herself (Becker's 'full caring'), interaction will sometimes occur between parent and child on the basis of self-interest. For all these reasons, it is necessary to look beyond altruism in discussing family interaction.

Bernheim *et al.* (1985) suggested that, in addition to caring for their children, parents want attention from them, especially when they get older. Children may not mind visiting their parents at first, but after a while they get tired of it, and further visits bring disutility. Parents never tire of seeing their children (at least, never before their children tire of visiting them), and so, at the margin, parents are willing to trade larger bequests for more visits. So the strategic threat to withdraw the bequest is used by parents to enforce their wishes on their children. Amazingly, data exist on the level of attention children give to their parents, in the form of indices of the number of weekly visits paid by children to their parents. Their analysis of the data showed that the larger the potential bequest, the more frequent the visits. Most sadly, perhaps, visits to parents who were poor and became ill dropped off, while those to parents who were rich and became ill increased. Note that the mechanism does not precisely mimic legal enforcement, since with legal enforcement, it would not always be necessary to give all the bargaining power to the parent. Perhaps it is this problem which explains why in some countries (Germany, France) parents are legally proscribed from depriving a child of his or her parents' estate beyond a certain point (e.g. in a two-child German family, each child is entitled to a minimum of one-fourth of the estate).

Both the analysis and the evidence on bequests show that family relations can be illuminated using the model of exchange. However, it still appears that poor parents with no planned bequest have nothing to protect them in their old age. One other possibility is that the parents might simply trust their children to look after them. However, if we rule out the altruistic and economic motives already discussed, and we also assume that the children are rational, then there must be some explanation of why the children would behave in this way. The most obvious motives are shame and guilt. The two are commonly distinguished (e.g. Freud 1929, Kandel and Lazear 1992) on the basis that shame ('external pressure') requires external observability whereas guilt ('internal pressure') does not. Freud interprets much of the advance of civilization to this economy of guilt as a mechanism in enforcing behavioral codes and norms. I will not attempt a comprehensive analysis of the operation of these two motives here, but I will suggest that ethnic capital is an investment vehicle for which they are particularly suited, and discuss their operation in this context.

In brief, the argument is that parents can partly 'bind' their children to the ethnic group by ethnic capital investments in them while young. The children are bound not just because the yield on this form of capital is specific to the ethnic group in question, and cannot be sold or otherwise transferred. The reason is that, in order to obtain the yield on this form of capital, the (grown) children will have to associate with other members of the ethnic group. They, in turn, can be counted on, in the course of normal association, to pressure or shame each other into repaying debts to the parents and to adhere to the other norms of the group. So the 'contract' is 'self-enforcing' from the parents' point of view – the children can only obtain the benefits from this form of capital to the extent that they use ethnic networks, and thereby subject themselves to ethnic pressure to repay their parents for the investments made.

To illustrate, imagine a mythical ethnic group, the Harriets. Two Harriets, Harry and Larry, are discussing a business deal over lunch. Because they are both Harriets, it is easy for them to communicate,[5] and they feel free to ask personal questions. Here are some standard ones (Harry is the interlocutor, Larry is the respondent): 'Of course, Larry, your wife is also a Harriet?' 'How many little Harriet children do you have?' 'Your mother lives with you, or did you put her in a home?' If the answers to questions like these are all negative, the respondent may find the deal coming unstuck, as the interlocutor discovers that he is not maintaining his ethnic capital.

Why does the interlocutor (Harry) want to enforce the norms? Even if they are beneficial to the group, why doesn't Harry free ride, and leave it to other members of the group to police behavior? Although I will not give a comprehensive analysis of this problem here,[6] I will suggest three reasons why other members of the ethnic group can often be counted on to apply the required pressure:

1   Ordinary self-interest: if the respondent didn't honor his implicit contract to repay his parents, there is, *ipso facto*, some reason to believe that he is more likely to renege on his current obligations; hence it is worthwhile to get this information.

2   Guilt: by pressuring other members of the group to honor their obligations, a group member in part fulfils his own, and lessens his sense of guilt.

3   Sanctions for not enforcing the group norm: ethnic groups may have a
    particularly powerful capacity to use sanctions effectively. The reasons
    are implicit in their value as exchange networks discussed earlier:
    subsidized early socialization with other members (hence facilitating
    mutual monitoring), infinite life (therefore implying common ancestry
    and descent, and therefore a long period over which transgressions can
    be punished), multi-purposeness, and so on.

To the extent that members of the ethnic group, for these reasons, can be
counted on to encourage, pressure, or police each other's obedience to
group norms, parents who invest in the ethnic capital of their children
can count on them to repay. Hence ethnic investments are self-enforcing.[7]
In this respect, ethnic networks differ from other forms of parental investment (e.g. general human capital), for which parents may have to rely
entirely on the affection of their children, or on internal pressure (guilt),
to be repaid.

It follows immediately that there will be 'overinvestment' by parents in
the ethnic capital of their children, compared to other types of capital.
Since no other form of capital has this self-enforcing aspect,[8] parents are
guaranteed a return on ethnic capital investments, while for other forms of
investment in their children, they are forced to rely on their children's
affection for them, guilt, or trustworthiness to be repaid for their sacrifices.
Consequently, this biases their investments in the direction of ethnic capital
investments: given two investments of equal yield to their children, parents
will strictly prefer the ethnic over the non-ethnic investment. Indeed, they
will prefer an ethnic investment of lower yield, and the potential differential will be larger, the more militant and committed are members of the
ethnic group (the more that members are willing to act to enforce the
repayments of debt).[9]

Of course, to the extent that the parents love their children, they will take
their children's welfare into account in deciding on their investments. Here,
we have assumed that the parents are entirely selfish, and decide on the
level of investment which is optimal from their point of view alone. It is
worth noting, however, that the overinvestment theorem will still hold in
the case of altruistic parents, though the level of overinvestment will presumably be smaller as the degree of genuine altruism (concern for the
welfare of the child)[10] gets larger.

In any case, at some point the child will reach maturity, and at that point
will find that he or she has involuntarily been made a partner to these
contracts with his or her parents (and perhaps with other relatives). Unless
the child's preferences are identical to those of the parents, the mature child
will find that he or she is 'out of equilibrium' – the child's desired level of
ethnic capital is different from the stock which has been accumulated.
From the overinvestment theorem, it follows that typically the individual
will want to allow some of his or her ethnic capital to depreciate, although

those children whose tastes or opportunities lie heavily in the direction of the ethnic group may want to invest more (the overinvestment theorem only holds on the average). Perhaps it is for this reason that many ethnic groups have institutionalized 'rites of passage' signaling the onset of maturity: at this point the individual, by participating in the ritual, indicates his or her acceptance of the responsibility for the debts that have been incurred on his or her behalf. It is peculiar, and deserves further exploration, that while these rites are common to many ethnic groups, the age at which they take place appears to vary enormously among different groups. Thus, for some Chinese groups, it only takes place just before marriage (hence never at all for those who don't marry), while for Jews, it happens at the age of 13. The strategic aspects are obvious enough: in the Chinese case, the pressure to marry (and perpetuate the group) is increased as the individual who never marries is in effect considered never to have grown up; in the Jewish one, 'maturity' (and the onset of responsibility for debt) is deemed to have taken place at an age when the individual is too young to resist.

Note that the overinvestment theorem obviously neglects possible external effects due to ethnic capital. Thus, if, as De Tocqueville suggested, and as Hechter has re-emphasized (1992), ethnic groups impart useful social values to their members, and these contribute to the creation and maintenance of social order, overinvestment from the viewpoint of the children invested in might easily be an underinvestment from the social point of view. On the other hand, to the extent that ethnic investments create prejudice and hostility among groups, raising tensions, hostility, and leading to wasteful expenses on rent seeking, the level of overinvestment discussed here could easily be an underestimate of the socially optimal level.

To model the effects of parental investment in ethnic capital, let π = the gross yield to ethnic capital to individual i at his or her maturity (subscripts are suppressed for notational simplicity), r = the rate of interest on the debt which must be repaid to the parents, and K = i's stock of ethnic capital. Let p = the level of ethnic peer pressure on i to repay his or her parents for their investments in ethnic capital, so $r = r(p)$. To derive a very simple picture, assume that marginal = average yields and rates of interest, so that π and r are constant (given p). Then the marginal net yield to i's ethnic capital is $\pi - r$, and total net profits are $(\pi - r)K$.[11]

Since ethnic capital is a sunk investment whose value is specific to ethnic networks, and which cannot be sold or transferred, the gross yield on this capital is a quasi-rent (in the sense of Klein *et al.* 1978). Its main value is to permit trade with other members of the ethnic group. Consequently, the yield on this capital (π) will be high when other mechanisms which can enforce trade (such as legal enforcement) are weak, and vice versa. Space prohibits consideration of all of the possibilities, but one interesting case is that where: (a) K is relatively high, (b) π is low, and (c) p is high, so that $\pi - r < 0$. With K high (relative to other forms of capital) the individual is incurring substantial losses. However, exit is difficult because p is high.

What can the individual do? I suggest that individuals in this position are particularly likely to develop prejudices against members of other ethnic groups, and have the potential to engage in conflict with them and to encourage anti-democratic forces in order to raise the yield on ethnic capital. To buttress this assertion, I will try to show that the constellation of returns just described is consistent with the peculiar syndrome described in the classic work by the research team headed by Nevitt Sanford and published by Adorno *et al.* (1950).

The authoritarian personality was a personality structure or constellation of attitudes which was believed to show, as one of the concept's inventors later described it, a *potential* for fascism, a *susceptibility* to anti-Semitic propaganda, and a *readiness* to participate in anti-democratic social movements.[12] The essential technique used in the original work was to discover, on the basis of interviews, attitudes that linked, in a non-obvious way, with general prejudice, anti-Semitism, or fascism, giving rise to the 'E' (Ethnocentrism), 'A-S' (Anti-Semitism) and 'F' (Fascism) scales. As might be expected the scales are highly correlated with one another.

Thus, one item, to which respondents were asked to express agreement or disagreement, was: 'He is indeed contemptible who does not feel an undying love, gratitude, and respect for his parents.' Agreement with this statement was held, because of the way it is expressed, to mask an underlying or unconscious hostility toward the parents. The overt glorification and unconscious hostility towards one's parents (other evidence of which became apparent during the interviews) was held to be a distinguishing feature of the highly ethnocentric person.

A second characteristic was an exaggerated, emotional need to submit to authority, again springing, according to theory, from an underlying hostility to ingroup authorities, originally the parents.[13] Other characteristics were superstition (a tendency to shift responsibility from within the individual to forces outside his or her control), stereotypy (a tendency to think in rigid, oversimplified categories), and a narrow range of consciousness.

Adorno *et al.* found no specific relationship between the scales and socio-economic factors. But they did find that people who scored high on the E scale tended to express similar political and religious preferences to those of their parents. Subsequent work on the correlates of the F scale found a correlation with an emphasis in upbringing on obedience and strict control, and with low education. Although some believe that subsequent work has discredited much of the original psycho-analytical framework, new and similar scales have been developed and intensively tested for their reliability, notably the right wing authoritarianism scale developed by Bob Altemeyer (1981, 1988). The term 'right wing' is not used in the political or economic sense, but in a psychological one: the right wing authoritarian is one who aggressively defends the *established* authorities in his or her life. So, for example, defenders of communism in the former Soviet Union in the late 1980s would tend to score highly on the scale. The scale is a uni-dimensional measure of three attitude clusters: (a) submission to established authority; (b) authoritarian aggression, that is aggression which is believed to be sanctioned by established authorities and which is directed at various persons whose activities are frowned upon; and (c) conventionalism, that is a high degree of adherence to the social conventions which are perceived to be endorsed by society and its established authorities. High scorers on the scale tend to accept government injustices such as illegal wiretapping, believe that 'strong medicine' is necessary to straighten out troublemakers, criminals, and perverts, believe in traditional family structures, obedience and respect for authority, and so on. And they are highly prejudiced against minority groups.

One explanation offered by the Adorno group of authoritarian aggression was that advanced by Fenkel-Brunswik, which postulated that authoritarianism arose in people raised by rigid, threatening, rule-driven and status-conscious parents who had only recently ascended to the middle class and who punished unconventional responses heavily. Altemeyer contends (although not everyone agrees[14]) that there is little evidence for this. He prefers a 'social learning' explanation: people acquire these attitudes from their parents and peer groups during adolescence. Scores are lowered as a result of education, raised from having children, and raised during social crises, especially if a violent left-wing movement appears.

The foregoing is a very brief summary of some of the main themes of the authoritarian personality and subsequent work in that vein. Its purpose is to illuminate my conjecture above that hostility towards other ethnic groups can be predicted on the basis of a particular constellation of returns to ethnic capital: relatively high K and p combined with low net yield or $\pi - r$. Thus, consider the likely attitudes of an individual (a man, say) in such a position who is rational in every respect save one: he must follow the norm of honoring one's parents. So the individual is unlike *Homo economicus* in that he is capable of repressing unpleasant emotions. I assume that the more the parents have invested, the more unpleasant it would be to think negative thoughts about them. Now suppose that the investments are low yielding, and that K and p are high. The individual in this position is awash in debt to his parents and other ethnic group members, but the yield on the capital investments they have sacrificed so hard to give to him is low, too low to cover his debts to them. Because he has substantial ethnic capital he venerates his parents and his forefathers, and they cannot be overtly blamed for the pickle he is in. (But unconsciously, he knows they have plied him with excess ethnic capital.) He has very little space to exercise his own choices in life since in order to repay debts his behavior is largely dictated by his parents' wishes and the norms of the ethnic group. So his political and religious choices are their choices, and his range of consciousness and capacity for conscious choice is narrow. In a sense he is quite rightly superstitious (his behavior *is* largely outside his control, given his adherence to the norm). Thus the authoritarian personality can be made sense of as a response to this constellation of returns to ethnic capital. I do not claim that this is the *only* way this syndrome can arise: no doubt other sets of circumstances can generate it. However, this is one account which springs naturally from the theoretical approach used here.

Why is he prejudiced? To the individual in question, his problem is not that his parents invested too much in his well-being, but that, through no fault of theirs, the yield on this capital is low. Whose fault is that? 'The Jews,' of course, with their tight, high-yielding international network, and their connections with the state and to international markets[15] (the development of which lowers the yield on other ethnic capital). What to do about it? (a) Get rid of them, and (b) engage in other collective actions to raise the yield on ethnic capital. The Nazi ideology of blood and ethnic purity as a means of organizing society was certainly an extreme response, but it is one which fits this pattern. It certainly raised (for a time) the yield on the right kind of ethnic capital. Indeed, it is precisely the extremity of some ethnic conflicts, such as the behavior of the Nazis, and perhaps the contemporary conflict between Serbs and Croatians, that can be explained with the approach suggested here (and are difficult to explain with a strictly rational approach). The fundamental problem in explaining these conflicts is that the ethnic group which is the object of conscious hatred is, to an outside observer, obviously not the real enemy. The present approach does explain why the acts of hatred and destruction toward members of it are inherently unsatisfying and result only in frustration, thus breeding further hatred and violence.[16]

Why can't our individual simply renegotiate his debts with his parents? Since the assets they bequeathed him are low yielding, the simplest solution would appear to be to renegotiate the debts downwards. In this context it is worthwhile to recall the original, psychoanalytical explanation of authoritarian aggression advanced by Fenkel-Brunswik, which postulated that authoritarianism arose in people raised by rigid, threatening, rule-driven and status-conscious parents who had only recently ascended to the middle class and who punished unconventional responses heavily. In our terminology, what this suggests is simply that a contributing factor is the inability to bargain or renegotiate matters within the family; that is, that authoritarian aggression is more likely to arise in family structures where 'transactions costs' are high.

Why can't the individuals affected act collectively to exert political pressure to change the norms or to solve the problems created directly? If the family is unresponsive to their demands, these could still be accommodated through the political system if it were responsive to them. However, under some circumstances, the political system may be unwilling or unable to act. This 'inaction problem' is discussed in detail elsewhere and summarized briefly at the beginning of the next section.

In summary, our individual finds himself in a position of conflict with his parents generated by the difference between the yield on the assets they have bequeathed him and the size of the debts which have to be repaid to them. The conflict could in principle be resolved through renegotiation within the family of the debts owed, or through political action to increase the yield on the assets. When all of these avenues of trade are foreclosed, the individuals involved in such conflicts are likely to develop a tendency towards authoritarian aggression.

Note that the analysis developed here draws on both the classic work of Adorno *et al.* and the more recent work of Altemeyer and others. Like the Adorno group, it emphasizes 'transactions costs' within the family and a repressed hostility towards one's parents as the generating factor of authoritarian attitudes. It differs from theirs in emphasizing ethnic capital, which does not appear in their analysis (or in Altemeyer's), in seeing adolescence as the main period over which these attitudes are crystallized (as does Altemeyer), and in visualizing a role for social learning. Its main contribution is to try to generate these attitudes with the minimum possible departure from rationality (not a typical concern of psychology), and in more precise modeling which makes the drawing of comparative static implications possible (again, not typical in psychology). Thus, although Altemeyer has data on the recent evolution of authoritarianism (it has been going up), the 'social learning' explanation adapted from the work of Bandura which he favours does not lend itself easily to explaining changes in the level of authoritarianism over time or across countries. Of course the theory advanced here could be greatly refined and extended. But the main point is to show that models incorporating variables such as those discussed here – transactions costs within the family and the yield on investments made by parents for their children – are capable of yielding insight into and predictions about psychosocial human behaviour in a way that can complement the research of social psychologists. The next section expands the model in another way by applying it to the historical experience of the decline of the Weimar Republic.

The rise of the Nazi dictatorship

As emphasized earlier, the authoritarian personality syndrome implies only a *potential* for fascism or a *readiness* to participate in anti-democratic social movements. By itself, even if other conditions are appropriate, it does not imply anything about political stability, for there is also the question of the responsiveness of the political system to consider. For example, if the political leadership were to act on or solve the problem of the declining yield to ethnic capital, it is possible that political instability could be avoided. However, under some conditions, the political system may be unable to act, and this inaction can exacerbate the conflicts described so far in a way which generates pressures on the survival of democracy. Peter Howitt and I have elsewhere (Howitt and Wintrobe 1993, 1995; see also Wintrobe 1998: ch. 11) analyzed this problem. To summarize the implications of that analysis, the model of democratic inaction points to the possibility that important problems may not be acted upon in a democracy, essentially when there is a divergence of views on what to do about them, when this divergence is large, when the problem is a divisive one, and when the opposing forces are relatively equally powerful. The allure of dictatorship – essentially, the capacity to overtly repress the opposition to a particular course of action – is never greater than under these conditions.

To apply the analysis of the last section to the rise of Nazism, note first that the simple constellation of intergenerational returns sketched earlier, which I claimed can result in an authoritarian personality syndrome, points to a number of historical factors which can be interpreted as lowering and threatening to lower further the yield on German ethnic capital. To be sure, a number of these factors are often cited in the collapse of the Weimar Republic, but what Coleman (1990) might call the 'microfoundations' of the explanation are usually missing. Here, I claim that the concept of ethnic capital provides the missing link. The collapse in the yield on ethnic capital generated an intergenerational conflict and the paralysis of the political system (what Bracher (1995) refers to as the power vacuum and what I am calling an equilibrium of political inaction) meant that there was no power or authority in the political centre to resolve it. First, the hyperinflation of the 1920s largely destroyed the savings of the German middle class (Kuhnl, in Larsen 1980). In terms of our model, this means that middle-class German parents lacked the power which strategic bequests confers to enforce repayment of their children's debts. And it also implies a considerable reduction in the level of financial assets ultimately passed on to their children, thus reducing their capacity to repay. In this context, perhaps it is worth digressing to note that in Paldam's (1987) study of the causes of dictatorship in Latin American countries, few regimes survived a hyperinflation.

On the other hand, the youth of the 1930s inherited substantial debts, further magnified by the reduction in their capacity to repay caused by the Great Depression. Along with the humiliation of defeat in the First World War, these included the substantial reparations payments imposed on Germany by the Treaty of Versailles. In addition, the so-called 'war guilt' clause of the Treaty required Germany to turn over its war criminals, including the former Emperor, for trial for atrocities, to accept responsibility for causing losses and damages, to cap the German Army at 100,000, and to put an end to the General Staff (Gay 1974: 157). The effect of these provisions was that postwar Germany (the sons) was forced to accept a position of permanent weakness in return for the sins of the fathers in leading Europe into war.

Third, although Germany had surpassed the other European countries in GNP and in population so that by 1913 she had the biggest proportion of world production of any country in Europe, after the war German capital was prevented from investing in African, Asian, and Australian colonies.[17] The Treaty deprived Germany of what few colonies she had, and of other territories such as Alsace-Lorraine, which was returned to France, and Upper Silesia, West Prussia, and Posen, which were turned over to Poland.[18] By depriving Germany of *Lebensraum*, the ratio of ethnic capital to land was raised, hence lowering the yield to ethnic capital.

Fourth, a constellation of factors threatened, or appeared to threaten further, the usefulness of German ethnic capital in the future: 'the Jews,' international socialism, and international capitalism. Thus, the rapid development of markets, modernization, and bureaucratization, and the enormous growth of trusts over this period meant that, on the one hand, impersonal bureaucratic criteria were increasingly replacing ethnic connections and background as criteria by which loans might be granted, promotions decided, and so on. In this sense, the 'fascism as modernization' school can be given a rational interpretation within the context of our model. The threat posed by 'scientific socialism' can, at least in part, be interpreted similarly. On the other hand, the Jewish 'threat' can be interpreted as meaning that underneath the rationalist face (in which jobs, privileges, and promotions were lost) lurked another ethnic group with powerful connections to both international capitalism and international socialism, and which was secretly monopolizing all of the rents which good Germans were being deprived of in the name of one or the other of these abstract principles. The two were nicely combined in the resonating Nazi propaganda theme of the 'chain stores' discussed by the historian Michael Kater, who suggests that 'To the small craftsman and shopkeeper the Jew was the instigator (and owner) of a system of factories and chain stores that threatened their livelihood.'[19] Hannah Arendt (1951) points out that the Jews were historically connected to financing the wars of the European states, a role which the development of modern capital markets had rendered obsolete. She suggests that these connections left them particularly vulnerable when they were believed to be no longer needed. An alternative point of view is that these historical connections made them an especially appropriate target under circumstances when the state and the financial system were essentially the two institutions which had failed most badly and trust in them had collapsed as a result of the war and the Versailles peace settlement, the 1920s hyperinflation, and the weakness or the unwillingness of Weimar to deal with the depression (which hit Germany particularly hard).

Although the evidence on various theses concerning Nazi membership is still muddled (see Larsen *et al.* 1980, Kater 1983) there do seem to be matters on which there is a consensus, and which are relevant to the model proposed here. One concerns the thesis of classes into masses or the 'atomization' of German society originally propounded by Hannah Arendt in her book *The Origins of Totalitarianism* (1951), and which gave rise to a vast literature. To simplify drastically, the basic idea was that totalitarian dictatorships arose because of the rise in the twentieth century of 'atomized' masses, that is individuals with few or no social ties, who are unorganized in interest groups. In democracies, these interest groups serve as intermediary links between individuals and political parties (as Tocqueville emphasized), and help to promote responsive government and democratic stability. In modern guise, a related thesis has been put forward by Putnam (1993), who argues that differences in 'social capital' (essentially, the density of interest group association) among the various regions of Italy account for the variations in effective government to be found there. (He also argues that these differences are amazingly stable, but that that controversial contention does not concern us here.)

If the thesis that it was the atomization of the German people which effectively left them vulnerable to the Nazi propaganda machine and accounted for the rise of Hitler were true, it would suggest that there are serious problems with the present model, which is based on the idea that it is those with *high* levels of ethnic capital (K is a form of social capital) who are likely to engage in authoritarian aggression. However, Bernt Hagtvet (1987) showed that in the German case at least

1   there was no paucity of intermediary links between individuals and political parties; on the contrary, Weimar Germany appeared to be densely permeated by a network of intermediary organization

2

the Nazis' most conspicuous success came in the regions with the greatest cohesion. In other words, it was not the people with the fewest social ties who were most receptive to mass appeals, as Kornhauser asserted, but those most thoroughly integrated.[20]

3   The interest groups themselves facilitated the rise of Nazism. For example, 'when the rural producers joined the Nazi party, they did so as members of precisely the same intermediary network which, in theory, is presumed to establish a social defense against extremism.'[21]

On this line of analysis, the mass society theorists simply confused cause and effect; the mass society was not the cause of the Nazi's rise to power, but an outcome of it (see e.g. Broszat (1981) on the systematic destruction of alternative centres of power once the Nazis took over). Moreover, the model developed here suggests an alternative interpretation of much of the 'atomization' literature which is consistent with the evidence presented by Hagtvet and others: it was not that the level of social or ethnic capital was low, but that it was *low yielding*. This would naturally give rise either to atomization as people would drift away from networks which yielded little return, or to a demand for radical new leadership.

The second piece of evidence which is now, I believe, well established is that the Nazis were disproportionately young. Merkl summarizes the evidence comparing fascist movements in a large number of countries. He concludes: 'the evidence for generational revolt as the one great motivating force all these diverse fascist movements have in common appears to be strong and persuasive indeed.'[22] Thus, for example, about one-half of the 1933 Nazis and the vast majority of the stormtroopers were born after 1901. His interpretation is that 'The generational conflict, in a nutshell, pitted the war and postwar Nazi youth against the prewar generations dominating the SPD and the "reactionary" conservative and liberal parties.'[23] Peter Gay's well-known book *Weimar Culture* describes the central theme of Expressionist culture as the son's revolt against the father.[24] And he notes:

> from 1918 to 1924 . . . Expressionism dominated politics as much as painting or the stage . . . [but] between 1929 and 1933, the years of disastrously rising unemployment, government by decree, decay of middle-class parties and resumption of violence, culture became less the critic than the mirror of events; the newspaper and film industries ground out right-wing propaganda, the best among architects, novelists or playwrights were subdued or silent, and the country was inundated by the rising tide of *Kitsch*, much of it politically inspired.[25]

Whence the title of this paper.

Finally, it is worth emphasizing that, on the interpretation developed here, the only irrational element is prejudice and especially anti-Semitism. The revolt against the parents and the desire to raise the yield on ethnicity can be made sense of in perfectly rational terms as a response to the decline in the yield on ethnic capital instigated by defeat, inflation, and the secularism and the weakness of the Weimar Republic in dealing with the depression and organized violence. Moreover, the Nazi movement appealed to the young in many other ways, in its futuristic outlook (the 1,000-year Reich), in its programs which promised to deal with problems which no other party could (unemployment, reparations), and in the structure of the party, which by its fluidity and dynamism offered unusual scope and opportunity to those among the young who were willing to swear allegiance to its goals.[26] The totalitarian solution is appealing not least because of its claim, as Bracher puts it 'that there is total trust and complete agreement, that the people and the leader, rulers and ruled, the party and the state are identical' (Bracher 1995: 73). Consequently, what Gay for example refers to as the 'strange connexion' among the young of revolutionary mutiny and blind obedience towards the Führer (Gay 1974: 31) is not, on this interpretation, irrational but a simple instance of what Coleman might call a transfer of authority from one group to the other, motivated, on the present analysis, by the fall in the yield on ethnic or trust capital. What *is* irrational, on the present approach, is the projection of blame onto minority groups for problems which even the elimination of these groups will obviously not do much, if anything, to resolve. I explain this with a single 'irrational' element: the children could not break with the norm of honoring their parents. Even this irrational element combines with a rational one: they, perhaps correctly, saw the success of these groups as the precise mirror image of the failure of their own. There are other, related types of explanations, perhaps most famously that advanced by Sartre (1960), who saw in the hatred of the 'other' (prejudice towards minorities) a projection of the hatred of self. I do not dismiss these at all, but am concerned here to depart as minimally as possible from purely rational styles of explanation, and to be parsimonious: the single departure from rationality used here suffices for a consistent explanation.

Notes

* Much of the material in this paper appears in Chapter 12 of my book, *The Political Economy of Dictatorship* (New York: Cambridge University Press, 1998). I wish to thank Bob Altemeyer, Albert Breton, Joel Fried, Gianluigi Galeotti, Michele Grillo, Michael Keating, Theo Offerman, Hilton Root, Pierre Salmon, Nathan Sussman, and Robert Young for helpful discussions. I am grateful to the Lynde and Harry Bradley Foundation for financial assistance.
1 Borjas (1992) presents highly suggestive evidence of the persistence of differential earnings capacity among ethnic groups across generations.
2 See Becker (1976) for a good exposition.
3 See Huxley (1994: ch. 5) for an insightful description of Hitler's views of the masses and the use of propaganda to deal with them.
4 Juan Linz, 'Political space and fascism as a latecomer,' in Larsen *et al.* (1980: 161).
5 I would argue that two members of an ethnic group do not necessarily like or trust one another, but do find it easier to communicate with one another, thus making it easier to establish whether or not they can trust or like each other.
6 A more general analysis would derive the level of enforcement from the characteristics of the ethnic group, and from its environment; I hope to do this in another paper. Here, I will just assume general obedience to the norm, and suggest why this could be the case. On some conditions for the persistence of codes, see Wintrobe (1983).
7 Indeed, the self-enforcing nature of ethnic capital provides a further reason for the persistence of ethnicity.
8 The statement in the text is obviously too strong; other parental gifts, interpreted here as loans, may be partially self-enforcing (e.g, the gift of a house next door to one's parents keeps the children next door) and therefore encourages attention, so long as the house is illiquid.
9 To demonstrate this point, let p = the level of ethnic pressure which the parents can anticipate can be brought to bear on the next generation (i.e. p = the estimated probability that the children will be forced to repay their debts by pressure from their fellow ethnics), t = the extent to which parents trust their children to repay out of a sense of moral obligation (guilt) in the absence of pressure, and A_k = the probability that the children will want to repay out of a sense of affection or altruism towards their parents. Suppose the parents invest $\$X$ in their children, which yields $\$X(1 + \pi_e)$ in the case of ethnic capital, and $\$X(1 + \pi_g)$ in the case of general human capital. Suppose for simplicity that the

fraction k of it must be repaid in either case. Then the parents will be indifferent between two investments, one ethnic and one general, where $kX(1 + \pi_e)(t + A_k + p) = kX(1 + \pi_g)(t + A_k)$. The required ratio between the yield on general vs. that on ethnic capital is $(1 + p_c)/(t + A_k) = (1 + p_g)/(t + A_k + p)$ that is investments in general human capital will be 'artificially' discounted by the factor $1/(1 + p)$.

10 Note that for altruism to reduce overinvestment, the altruism must take the form of concern for the child's own welfare or utility, and not for the child's consumption pattern, that is the parent's utility function must have the form $U_p = U_p(c_p, U_k)$, where p = parent, k = kid, c = a vector of consumption goods, and not $U_p = U_p(c_p, c_k)$. Increased altruism of the latter variety can lead to *more* ethnic investment if the parent believes that ethnic capital is particularly good for the kid.

11 A more complete model would also specify the sanction f for non-repayment, so that, at maturity, an individual would have the choice between repayment, and earning $\pi - r$, and non-repayment, yielding expected profits of $(1 - p)\pi - p(\pi - f)$.

12 Sanford (1973: 142).

13 Sanford (1973: 144).

14 Brewster-Smith, in his introduction to Altemeyer (1988), suggests that the evidence is more favorable to the psychoanalytic theory than Altemeyer admits.

15 Arendt (1951: Part One, Antisemitism) discusses these factors in the context of anti-Semitism in the nineteenth century.

16 In other respects, the implications of the present approach accord with those which might be predicted from completely rational models: ethnic conflict would appear more likely, *ceteris paribus*, the greater the difference in wages or other factor returns between groups, the smaller the complementarity between their factors (hence the less they 'need' each other), and the more similar they are in terms of tastes or resource utilization (hence the more they are in direct competition with each other for scarce resources.)

17 Kuhnl, in Larsen *et al.* (1980: 127–8).

18 Gay (1974: 157).

19 Kater (1983: 26).

20 Bernt Hagtvet, 'The theory of the mass society and the collapse of the Weimar Republic: a re-examination,' in Larsen *et al.* (1980: 90).

21 Hagtvet, in Larsen *et al.*, op. cit. p. 91.

22 Peter H. Merkl, 'Comparing fascist movements', in Larsen *et al.* (1980).

23 Merkl, op.cit., p. 772.

24 Gay (1974: 119).

25 Gay (1974: 126).

26 For details on the Nazi party structure, see Breton and Wintrobe (1986).

References

Adorno, Theodor W., Fenkel-Brunswik, Else, Levinson, Daniel, and Sanford, R. Nevitt, (1950) *The Authoritarian Personality*, New York: Harper.

Altemeyer, Robert (1981) *Right-Wing Authoritarianism*, Winnipeg: University of Manitoba Press.

Altemeyer, Robert (1988) *Enemies of Freedom*, San Francisco: Jousey-Bass.

Arendt, Hannah (1951) *The Origins of Totalitarianism*, New York: Harcourt, Brace, Jovanovic (2nd edition, 1973).

Arrow, K. J. (1972) 'Models of job discrimination,' in A. H. Pascal (ed.) *Racial Discrimination in Economic Life*, Lexington, MA: Heath.

Becker, Gary (1974) 'A theory of social interactions,' *Journal of Political Economy*, 82: 1063–109.

Becker, Gary (1976) 'Altruism, egoism, and genetic fitness,' *Journal of Economic Literature* 14: 817–26.

Becker, Gary and Murphy, Kevin (1988) 'The family and the state,' *Journal of Law and Economics*, 31: 1–19.

Bernheim, B. Douglas, Shleifer, A., and Summers, L. H. (1985) 'The strategic bequest motive,' *Journal of Political Economy* 93: 1045–76.

Borjas, George J. (1992) 'Ethnic capital and intergenerational mobility,' *Quarterly Journal of Economics* 107: 123–50.

Bowles, Samuel (1985) 'The production process in a competitive economy: Walrasian, neo-Hobbesian, and Marxian models,' *American Economic Review*, 75(March): 16–36.

Bracher, Karl Dietrich (1995) *Turning Points in Modern Times: Essays on German and European History*, Cambridge, MA: Harvard University Press.

Breton, Albert and Wintrobe, Ronald (1982) *The Logic of Bureaucratic Conduct*, New York: Cambridge University Press.

Breton, Albert (1986) 'The bureaucracy of murder revisited,' *Journal of Political Economy* 94: 905–26.

Broszat, Martin (1981) *The Hitler State: The Foundation and Development of the Internal Structure of the Third Reich*, London: Longman.

Bulow, Jeremy and Summers, Lawrence (1991) 'A theory of dual labor markets with applications to industrial policy, discrimination, and Keynesian unemployment,' *Journal of Labor Economics* 4: 376–414.

Coleman, James (1990) *Foundations of Social Theory*, Cambridge, MA: Harvard University Press.

Freud, Sigmund (1991) *Civilization and its Discontents*. Original edition 1929; reprinted in the Penguin Freud Library Vol. 12, *Civilization, Society and Religion*, 1991.

Frank, Robert H. (1988) *Passion Within Reason*, New York: W. W. Norton.

Gay, Peter (1974) *Weimar Culture*, London: Penguin.

Gellner, Ernest (1983) *Nations and Nationalism*, Ithaca, NY: Cornell University Press.

Gregor, A. James (1969) *The Ideology of Fascism*, New York: Free Press.

Hechter, Michael (1987) *Principles of Group Solidarity*, Berkeley, CA: University of California Press.

Hechter, Michael, Friedman, Debra, and Kanazawa, Satoshi (1992) 'The attainment of global order in heterogeneous societies,' Paper delivered at the 1992 meetings of the Public Choice Society.

Hobsbawm, E. (1990) *Nations and Nationalism Since 1780*, Cambridge: Canto.

Howitt, Peter and Wintrobe, Ronald (1993) 'Equilibrium political inaction in a democracy,' in A. Breton, G. Galeotti, P. Salmon, and R. Wintrobe (eds) *Preferences and Democracy*, Dordrecht: Kluwer.

Howitt, Peter and Wintrobe, Ronald (1995) 'The political economy of inaction,' *Journal of Public Economics* 56: 329–53.

Huxley, Aldous (1994) *Brave New World Revisited*, London: Flamingo.

Iannacconne, Laurence R. (1992) 'Sacrifice and stigma: reducing free riding in cults, communes and other collectives', *Journal of Political Economy* 100(2): 271–91.

Kandel, Eugene, and Lazear, Edward (1992) 'Peer pressure and partnerships,' *Journal of Political Economy* 100: 801–18.

Kater, Michael (1983) *The Nazi Party: A Social Profile of Members and Leaders, 1919–1945*, Cambridge, MA: Harvard University Press.

Klein, Benjamin and Leffler, Keith B. (1981) 'The role of market forces in assuring contractual performance,' *Journal of Political Economy* 89: 615–41.

Klein, Benjamin, Crawford, R. G., and Alchian, A. (1978) 'Vertical integration, appropriable rents, and the competitive contracting process,' *Journal of Law and Economics* 21: 297–326.

Landa, J. (1981) 'A theory of the ethnically homogenous middleman group: an institutional alternative to contract law,' *Journal of Legal Studies* 10: 49–62.

Larsen, S. U., Hagtvet, B., and Myklebust, J. P. (1980) *Who Were the Fascists? Social Roots of European Fascism*, Norway: Universitetsforlaget.

Paldam, Martin (1987) 'Inflation and political instability in eight Latin American countries,' *Public Choice* 52: 143–68.

Putnam, Robert (1993) *Making Democracy Work*, Princeton, NJ: Princeton University Press.

Ramet, Sabrina (1992) *Nationalism and Federalism in Yugoslavia 1962–91*, 2nd edition, Bloomington, IN: Indiana University Press.

Rogowski, Ronald (1985) 'Causes and varieties of nationalism: a rationalist account,' in Edward A. Tiryakin and Ronald Rogowski (eds) *New Nationalisms of the Developed West: Toward Explanation*, Boston: Allen & Unwin.

Sanford, Nevitt (1973) 'The authoritarian personality in contemporary perspective,' in *Handbook of Political Psychology*, San Francisco: Jossey-Bass.

Sartre, Jean-Paul (1960) *Anti-Semite and Jew*, New York: Grove Press; New York: Schoken Books, 1965.

Shapiro, Carl (1983) 'Premiums for high quality products as returns to reputations,' *Quarterly Journal of Economics* 98: 659–79.

Shapiro, Carl, and Stiglitz, Joseph (1984) 'Equilibrium unemployment as a worker discipline device,' *American Economic Review* 74: 433–44.

Wintrobe, Ronald (1983) 'Taxing altruism,' *Economic Inquiry* XXI: 255–69.

Wintrobe, Ronald (1995) 'Some economics of ethnic capital and conflict,' in A. Breton, G. Galeotti, P. Salmon, and R. Wintrobe (eds) *Nationalism and Rationality*, Cambridge: Cambridge University Press.

Wintrobe, Ronald (1998) *The Political Economy of Dictatorship*, New York: Cambridge University Press.

14 Multiple equilibria, critical masses, and institutional change

The *coup d'état* problem

Ulrich Witt

Introduction

The individualistic, economic, approach to political behavior developed over the past three decades in public choice theory is based on the idea that political agents, like their economic counterparts, have a limited set of alternatives from which they choose the one most preferred according to their subjective preferences. The heuristic potential of this approach is documented by the impressive growth of interest in, and the soaring number of contributions to, public choice theory. In part, this success is due to extremely simple assumptions about the agents' preferences – usually derived from presupposing naïve self-interest. Provided the political agents' constraints can be theoretically reconstructed in a sufficiently realistic way, the simple presupposition allows empirically meaningful hypotheses about what happens in domestic as well as foreign affairs to be derived. An important aspect of individual constraints in the political domain is the fact that in general the interactions are strategic ones. Right from the beginning of public choice theory reference to game-theoretic arguments has therefore been a common stance. However, something that went largely unnoticed in the recourse to game theory was the fact that, in more recent times, game theory turned away the notion of unique strategic equilibria in predicting the outcome of interactions.[1]

The notion of unique equilibrium points in the games describing political conflict is, indeed, by no means a self-evident assumption. As will be argued in this paper, the existence of multiple equilibria is a crucial ingredient for understanding what has so far been neglected in the public choice approach: the relevance of evolutionary phenomena for politics. If game-theoretic models are to make sense in a meaningful theory of evolution, the existence of multiple equilibria is a generic prerequisite: only when a development is not predetermined in the sense of converging to a unique equilibrium is it possible to account for the idea of an open future – which is a constitutive part of the concept of evolution. The gist of the idea can be expressed in simple bifurcation models with two locally stable equilibrium points (or attractors). Even though these models do not reach the degree of complexity which would be necessary to actually capture the non-anticipatable nature of evolutionary processes, they already suffice to gain valuable insights into characteristic evolutionary phenomena such as critical masses (Schelling 1978) and the paramount role of frequency dependency effects (Witt 1992).

Whenever such effects appear, far richer developments can be imagined and explained than is the case for global, asymptotically stable systems. In so far as public choice theory argues on the basis of models which ignore actual frequency dependency effects the conclusions drawn are likely to be misleading. In what follows this will be discussed for the case of constitutional (in)stability – an important empirical question as well as a crucial condition if recent attempts at legitimizing constitutional government are to work. The second section contains a brief summary of the argument launched by the 'new contractarianism' (Scott 1976) and points out that the idea of legitimizing constitutional order and the state by hypothetical public consent actually implies a critical mass phenomenon. The third section appraises the role of protective state authorities (police, military) for constitutional (in)stability under the above-mentioned self-interest conjecture. By leaning towards either constitutional loyalty or opportunistic usurpation of power – the two possible equilibria once again giving rise to a critical mass problem – protective authorities may cause a constitutional dilemma. The fourth section discusses the prerequisites for constitutional instability (i.e. for a *coup d'état*) on the basis of more realistic assumptions. Because the contractarians have no understanding of the evolutionary nature of the political process – implying the possibility of ending up in opposing states of affairs – it is argued that their view disregards the richness of actual political developments and ignores the risks involved for society. The final section offers some tentative conclusions.

The social contract as a critical mass problem

An old problem in social philosophy is the question of whether and how the state, and the coercive power which it commands, can be legitimized. In more recent times, the problem has gained renewed attention through work by Rawls (1971), Nozick (1974), and Buchanan (1975). These writers revive the idea, earlier ventilated by Locke, Rousseau, and Hobbes, of lending legitimacy to the state and its coercive authorities by deriving conditions for a hypothetical social contract. In an anarchic state of nature, it is argued, self-interest suggests that the members of society agree to grant coercive power to the state so that everybody is compelled to comply with law and order. Without coercive authority the state would be incapable of overcoming, and later on withstanding, the anarchic 'law of the strongest.' Yet, given the productive inefficiency and the obstacles to a division of labor that are associated with anarchy, this cannot be in the interest of the members of society – hence their supposed consent to a social contract by which the coercive state is established.

The argument has been developed in particular detail by Nozick (1974: ch. 2). To him it is a significant fact of human life that the individual is vulnerable to the opportunistic behavior of other members of society. Under anarchic conditions, physical force is thus used opportunistically; agreements cannot be sustained. Nozick clearly recognizes that, because of their inherent instability, voluntary alliances cannot provide a remedy. He submits, however, that agents may specialize in providing protective services so that, in geographically distinct areas, protective agencies can be imagined to emerge spontaneously. These agencies offer to monitor and, if necessary, enforce compliance with private contracts for everyone ready to pay for these services. Investigation, prosecution of infringements of individual rights, and restitution enforcement presuppose, of course, that the agencies are in command of coercive power beyond what is available to opposing parties, that is single members or subgroups of society.

The argument can be put more rigorously by assuming that the state of anarchy is represented by a symmetric prisoner's dilemma game. This is indeed the usual way of expressing the self-interest presupposition of the public choice approach in the present context (Schmidt-Trenz 1989, Okada and Kliemt 1991). In the simplest form, the players – the members of society – indexed $i = 1, \ldots, n$ have just two strategies c and d in this game. Strategy c means behaving peacefully and honoring private agreements, in short 'cooperating,' and d means violating private agreements opportunistically, in short 'defecting.' In the state of anarchy nobody complies with private agreements and everybody fights against everybody else, that is everybody chooses d because it dominates c – the odd implication of the prisoner's dilemma. Nozick's idea of how to overcome the dilemma can be expressed as follows. An entrepreneur, or for that matter, an agent of collective action, initiates a 'club,' which may be joined on a voluntary basis by each member of society on paying a membership fee and on submitting to the statutes of the club. Statutes prohibit any form of defection in interactions with other club members and commit the club to punishing members who violate the statutes. To keep things simple, let us assume that club members identify themselves unequivocally in interactions with other club members. Membership fees are used to establish and support an enforcement authority, the protective agency, endowed with superior coercive power to enforce the statutes.

For simplicity, let interactions in society take place in sequences of pairwise random encounters, that is they involve just two randomly matched individuals i and j, $i \neq j$. If n is large, the individuals can be assumed to interact without recall. The option of joining the club expands the set of strategies of each member of society. Strategies c and d of the prisoner's dilemma are still available. In addition, there is an alternative strategy z of joining the club and playing contingent on who is met. Strategy z can be described as follows. After having paid their fees, club members can meet a member or a non-member. In the latter case, self-interest suggests defecting – more precisely choosing the contingent strategy d' which reads: 'pay membership fees and defect.' This is so because d' dominates the alternatively available contingent strategy c' – which reads 'pay membership fees and cooperate' – and which would be exploited by non-members who always defect. If, however, one club member happens to encounter another, he or she will choose c', that is cooperation, because he or she can expect cooperation from his or her counterpart who would be punished by the protective agency in case of defection. This means that in this case strategy c' dominates d'. (The very idea of the 'protective agency' would be invalid, should the protective agency fail to make this dominance relation credible.)

Hence, while those members of society who do not belong to the club are limited to strategies c and d and, due to the logic of the prisoner's dilemma, trapped into d, joining the club is equivalent to always choosing the compound strategy z:

$$z_i = \{c'_i \text{ if } j \text{ belongs to the club and } d'_i \text{ otherwise}\} \tag{1}$$

After joining, a cooperation gain can be realized whenever another club member is met in the pairwise random interaction. In this case, club members are better off than under conditions of anarchy. If, however, a non-member is encountered the situation is even worse than under anarchy. In addition to the unpleasant outcome of anarchic mutual defection, the payoff is reduced further by the club membership fees which have been paid in vain, so to speak. The crucial question thus arises as to whether, and if so, under what conditions, the members of society should be willing to join the club (adopt strategy z).

In order to answer this question it is useful to write down the payoffs an agent i can obtain conditional on the strategy chosen by his or her counterpart j and to determine the likelihood of the respective payoffs. As usual, payoffs are denoted in terms of a Neumann–Morgenstern utility function as

$$u_i = u_i(s_i, s_j) \quad s_{i,j} \in \{c, d, z\} \tag{2}$$

A prisoner's dilemma is characterized by an order relation

$$u_i(d_i, c_j) > u_i(c_i, c_j) > u_i(d_i, d_j) > u_i(c_i, d_j) \tag{3}$$

over the payoffs. The above considerations on the club members' payoffs imply

$$u_i(c_i, c_j) > u_i(c'_i, c'_j) > u_i(d_i, d_j) > u_i(d'_i, d_j) \tag{4}$$

The payoff a club member can realize depends on the probability p of encountering another member. Let there be $m(t)$ club members at a time t where the new option of joining the club has become feasible and the individuals in society have made up their minds whether or not to join. The probability p can then be equated to the relative frequency $m(t)/n$ of club members in society. Accordingly, the probability of meeting a non-member is $(1 - p)$. Since t is a future point of time, $m(t)$, and thus p, is not yet known for sure. Let P be the individual's subjective estimate of p and, given a symmetric game, be the same for all individuals. Accordingly, the payoff $E(u'_i)$ to be expected in case of joining the club is conditional on P as follows:

$$E(u'_i|P) = Pu_i(c'_ic'_j) + (1 - P)u_i(d'_id_j) \tag{5}$$

Analogously, for the case of not joining,

$$E(u_i|P) = (1 - P)u_i(d_id_j) + Pu_i(d_id'_j) = u_i(d_id_j) \tag{6}$$

results since, from a non-member's perspective, there is no difference defecting against club members or non-members.

As a corollary of the self-interest conjecture the individuals are assumed to choose the strategies which they subjectively expect to yield the largest payoff (utility). Given this decision hypothesis, a necessary and sufficient condition for joining the club is

$$E(u'_i| P) - E(u_i|P) > 0 \tag{7}$$

Solving for P, a threshold value P^* is found which gives rise to the decision rule:

join the club once $P > P^*$, otherwise do not join   (8)

The critical relative frequency can be calculated as

$$P^* = \alpha/(\alpha + \beta) \tag{9}$$

Here $\alpha = u_i(d_id_j) - u_i(d'_id'_j)$ measures the loss accruing in interactions with non-members from having paid the fee and $\beta = u_i(c'_ic'_j) - u_i (d_id'_j)$ is a measure for the cooperation gain. Because of (3) and (4), $0 < P^* < 1$. Furthermore, the smaller α and/or the larger β, the smaller P^*.

The implication of decision rule (8), if generally followed, is thus that either all or none of the members of society will want to join the club and install the protective agency, depending on whether or not the subjective estimate of the relative frequency of people joining exceeds the critical value P^*. The formal criterion of the critical relative frequency model leaves open what kind of development(s) may be able to bring about the transition. In a minimal explanation, a cumulation of random fluctuations (a phenomenon known in physics as a 'fluctuation catastrophe') may simply be assumed to occur in the subjective estimates so that $p(t)$ exceeds P^*. Alternatively, agents of collective action may be supposed to effect the transition. Through their agitation they may be able to persuade more than the critical mass $m^* = \alpha n/(\alpha + \beta)$ of members of society of the possibility of P^* being exceeded (in which case the assumption of independent subjective estimates that had implicitly been assumed above is abandoned). Note that the prediction would be self-fulfilling. Once the critical mass is exceeded, all the rest of the population would choose to also join so that a 'club' including all members of society would emerge – the constitutional state. The membership fee would simply be a kind of lump-sum tax which everyone is willing to pay for the services of the protective agency. So far, the formalization of Nozick's argument seems to support the basic view of modern contractarianism. However, one important presumption on which the 'calculus of consent' outlined rests has not yet been discussed: the question of whether the protective agency will indeed perform the way that has implicitly been assumed. In the next section this presumption will be discussed – with the consequence of potentially dramatically different conclusions.

Constitutional (in)stability as a problem of multiple equilibria

As has been shown, the notion of a fictitious social contract by which the state, endowed with coercive power, can be legitimized crucially depends on the existence of an efficient protective agency. Only if that agency can prevent defection or, at least, curb it to a tolerable rate, does it pay for the members of society to accept the lump-sum tax. In order for that effect to be achieved the protective agency would have to be endowed with coercive power superior to that commanded by other individuals or groups. However, an agency endowed with unequaled physical power creates a new problem: how can the agency be constrained to a constitutional use of its power? How can usurpation of power by agency personnel in pursuit of their own private interest be prevented? In view of the general self-interest conjecture it would appear only logical for agency personnel to be tempted to (mis-)use their power to capture a share of the cooperation gains which society can realize through overcoming anarchy. By doing so, the cooperation gain accruing to the average member of society would necessarily be reduced – an obvious constitutional hazard. If anticipated by the members of society, such a hazard may deter the individuals from consenting to the social contract. A protective agency that needs superior power to be effective thus causes a dilemma that renders the contractarians' very concept problematic.

The dilemma has probably failed to arouse much interest in the recent revival of contractarianism because in recent decades the armed forces and other empowered branches of the administration in most of the Western democracies have been loyal. However, the countless *putsches* that have overthrown constitutional orders and have led to the usurpation of power all over the world, not only in the 'dark' ages but also in modern times, are evidence that the problem is a real one. Given the diversity of historical experience, a natural question which arises is when those in control of the coercive means, that is the personnel of a state's protective authority, can be expected to be loyal and when not. To examine this important question in more detail, yet at a sufficiently simple level, a stylized model of the personnel's choices will first be developed and the conditions inducing loyalty will then be discussed in the light of this model.

For expository convenience let us assume that the behavior of the protective authority is a phenomenon of collective action in which all the personnel of the authority affect the collective performance equally. More specifically, assume that, with respect to the question concerned, each single agent in the authority has the same two strategies, either to support usurpation (strategy s) or to reject it (strategy r). An agent choosing s may be called 'putschist,' one choosing r 'loyalist.' The payoffs, again measured in utility terms on a constant ratio scale, depend on whether a *putsch* does or does not take place successfully, the events being denoted o (overthrow) and l (loyal regime) respectively. Thus, four payoffs conditional on the respective events can obtain from the two strategies: $u(s|o)$, $u(s|l)$, $u(r|o)$, and $u(r|l)$.

A crucial hypothesis is the one concerning the individual agent's order relation over the payoffs. Consider first – the standard assumption of public choice theory – an 'opportunistic' agent who appreciates the opportunity, implied by the usurpation of power, to appropriate for him or herself, at least for the short run, some of society's gains from cooperation. This does not necessarily mean that the motivation is crudely materialistic. There has hardly been a *putsch* in history in which the gains from usurpation have not been claimed to be associated with some 'supreme values' (Bernholz 1991). With respect to the constitutional dilemma it makes no difference how usurpers obtain utility from spending the usurpation gain. Hence, the agent's ordering is assumed to be

$$u(s|o) > u(r|l) > u(r|o) = u(s|l) \tag{10}$$

By equating $u(r|o) = u(s|l)$ the assumption is expressed that personnel who go against the authority's prevailing policy will always be persecuted and lose their offices or even their lives. Given (10), the agent's choice of strategy depends on which of the events, o or l, the agent expects to occur.

Let F denote the fraction of supporters of usurpation in the authority at a given point of time. In general, it can be presumed that a *putsch* must at least be supported by more than a minimal fraction F^m of personnel for it to be successful. This threshold fraction of supporters depends on historical and cultural factors as well as on military technology and will therefore vary over time and place. For simplicity, F^m will be treated here as an exogenous parameter the value of which at the given time is common knowledge to all agents in the authority. By contrast, the value of F is unknown, but the agents are assumed to have subjective guesses as to whether F exceeds F^m at the time. This can be expressed by probability estimates w as follows:

$$\Pr(F > F^m) = w \quad \text{and} \quad \Pr(F \leq F^m) = 1 - w \tag{11}$$

If, for convenience, the probability assessment is taken to be identical for all personnel, each agent associates subjective probability w with the occurrence of o and the tail probability with the occurence of l. Lacking more specific information about F except that it must lie between 0 and 1, it seems plausible to assume that, in the agents' assessment, w increases as F^m decreases. This means that the agents perceive a functional relationship ϕ,

$$w = \phi(F^m) \quad \phi' < 0 \tag{12}$$

If the agents held that F is a uniformly distributed random variable on the interval $(0,1)$, ϕ would be a linear function given by the tail of the uniform distribution function at point F^m, that is $w = 1 - F^m$. More generally, if F were believed to be randomly distributed with a distribution function $H_F(F^m) = \Pr(F \leqslant F^m)$, function (12) would take the form

$$w = 1 - H_F(F^m) \tag{13}$$

Returning to the agent's decision problem, the subjectively expected utilities $E(U^s)$ of supporting, and $E(U^r)$ of rejecting, usurpation at the given time depend on w in the following manner:

$$E(U^s|w) = wu(s|o) + (1 - w)u(s|l) \tag{14}$$

and

$$E(U^r|w) = wu(r|o) + (1 - w)u(r|l) \tag{15}$$

Assuming subjectively expected utility maximization once again the necessary and sufficient condition for advocating usurpation at the given time is

$$E(U^s|w) - E(U^r|w) > 0 \tag{16}$$

Solving for w yields a threshold value

$$w^* = \gamma/(\gamma + \delta) \tag{17}$$

such that usurpation is supported once $w > w^*$. Here $\gamma = u(r|l) - u(s|l)$ measures the opportunity costs of non-loyal behavior in case that the regime remains loyal, and $\delta = u(s|o) - u(r|o)$ is a measure for the opportunity costs of loyalty in case that an overthrow takes place. Because of (10), $\gamma < \delta$, and hence $0 < w^* < 1/2$. Substituting according to (12) leads to

$$F^{m*} = \Phi[\gamma/(\gamma + \delta)] \tag{18}$$

with Φ denoting the inverse function of ϕ, if it exists. In the simple case of F uniformly distributed between 0 and 1 one obtains $F^{m*} = 1 - \gamma/(\gamma + \delta)$. As is easily seen, the smaller γ and/or the greater δ, the greater F^{m*} will be. (This result holds generically for non-degenerate forms of (13).)

The solution implies that, given the subjective probability w and its functional dependence on F^m, the agent's 'opportunistic' decision on whether or not to become a putschist solely depends on whether the current value of F^m falls below the critical value F^{m*} which is determined by weighing the benefits against the costs of advocating usurpation. Once $F^m < F^{m*}$ the agent will become a putschist, because that agent holds that enough putschists will turn out to be present to exceed the necessary minimal fraction. The agent will remain loyal as long as $F^m \geqslant F^{m*}$ because of the subjective prediction that the minimal fraction will not be surpassed. Thus, the agents just 'wait for their turn,' that is for the opportunity of the minimal necessary support fraction being brought down sufficiently by historical accident. Note that under the chosen assumption their predictions are self-fulfilling: once $F^m < F^{m*}$, F does jump to 1 so that $F > F^m$, while $F = 0$ as long as $F^m \geqslant F^{m*}$.

The present problem and its solution thus turn out to be structurally quite similar to what underlies the collective consent problem in the previous section. In both cases there is an abrupt transition from one kind of behavior to its opposite (joining the club or not; advocating usurpation or not) once a critical relative frequency of supporters for one or other alternative is exceeded. Furthermore, here and there the subjective estimates of what others are doing are self-confirming. Yet, there is also a difference as, in the present model, unlike in the one in the previous section, there is no counterpart to an agent of collective action. While crusading for an organizational basis to overcome anarchy is crucial and appears to be an indispensable service of agents of collective action, the conspiratorial nature of an overthrow is clearly at odds with any open agitation. It is not an agent of collective action but historical accident which pushes F^m up and down over time, and serves as the triggering factor in much the same way as in the model suggested by Kuran (1989) to explain revolutions.

Moreover, the fact that overcoming anarchy and overthrowing constitutional order seem to be structurally similar phenomena has quite different implications for the contractarian program. To demonstrate that a transition from the dilemma of anarchy can be made by gathering a critical mass of supporters for a constitutional solution confirms the validity of that program. The possible transition from loyal performance of the protective authority to usurpation, in contrast, seems to lend an alarming relevance to the argument of the constitutional hazard and thus throws doubts on the contractarian program. The latter result has, of course, been derived on the basis of several specific assumptions which may be controversial, among them the hypothesis that all the personnel of the authority have indeed an 'opportunistic' preference order which values the gains from usurpation more than those from being loyal. Before definite conclusions are drawn the robustness of the results when the assumptions are changed should therefore be examined.

Abrupt institutional change: the *coup d'état* case

How does the result obtained in the previous section change, if assumptions are introduced that seem to favor the likelihood of the protective authority behaving constitutionally? Does, for instance, a preference for loyal behavior exclude the proneness to *putsches*? Does a low time preference or a long time horizon eliminate opportunism, or do hetero-geneous attitudes among the authority's personnel curb the constitutional hazard? Since different assumptions in these respects may be taken to represent different conditions in different states, the discussion may help in understanding why susceptibility of power to usurpation is a variable phenomenon.

An inclination in favor of (or against) constitutional performance may be introduced into the model in two ways: as a personal attribute reflected by a particular preference ordering different from the one in (10); or as a feature of the subjective probability assessment (11) that expresses a belief about a distribution phenomenon of the agents, namely about a bias of the agency's personnel for or against supporting usurpation. Consider, in order to discuss the personal attribute variant first, the ordering

$$u(r|l) \geqslant u(s|o) > u(r|o) = u(s|l) \tag{19}$$

Compared to (10), the agent now no longer evaluates private appropriation of gains from usurping power more highly than loyalty, that is using power within the institutional constraints, though it might still be possible to make those gains.

Inspection of the payoffs shows that, nevertheless, the basic structure resembling that of a convention game is maintained. A threshold value $w^{*\prime}$, $1/2 < w^{*\prime} < 1$, results on the basis of (19). Since γ is greater than before and δ smaller, yet still positive, the resulting critical value $F^{m*\prime} < F^{m*}$, where F^{m*} indicates the value previously obtained on the basis of (10). This result means that historical accident, which is viewed here as pushing F^m up and down, has to be more 'favorable' to the putschists now, that is bring down F^m more than before if the overthrow is to take place. Hence, an overthrow remains a probable event although the personnel of the authority may prefer to stay loyal: under reasonable assumptions about (12), for example under all non-degenerated forms of distribution functions in (13), $F^{m*\prime} > 0$.

The reason for this perhaps baffling result is easy to find. According to (19) loyalty is only preferred subject to the condition that the loyal regime prevails. If it fails, 'howling with the wolf' is preferred. Expression (19) may thus be considered to denote a limited form of opportunism. Only an unconditioned preference for loyalty in the form

$$u(r|l) \geqslant u(r|o) > u(s|o) = u(s|l) \tag{20}$$

would produce the kind of self-commitment that could render usurpation impossible. Since the motivation for the orderings (10) and (19) has been the empirical observation that putschists tend to be merciless to loyalists when an overthrow occurs – and, in fact, have to be if they want to achieve their conspiratorial aims – (20) would indeed be a preference ordering from which heroes emerge. Are protective authorities populated by potential heroes?

What results if the bias in favor of, or against, constitutional perform-ance is modeled as a feature of the subjective expectations of the agents?

More formally, this can be expressed by the shape, or skewness, of the density function of F, where F, the share of supporters of usurpation, is now interpreted as a random variable. Under the uniform distribution previously alluded to, the probability density is evenly distributed over all values of F, which means that no particular inclination for or against constitutional loyalty is presupposed. Imagine now a skew distribution in which the probability density is strongly concentrated at small (large) values of F indicating a corresponding bias toward (against) loyalty as conjectured in the agents' subjective assessment. When solving (16) for w and substituting the solution for the right-hand side of (13), a critical value $F^{m*''}$, $0 < F^{m*''} < 1$, results which is smaller (greater) than the threshold value $F^{m*} = 1 - \gamma/(\gamma + \delta)$ obtained for the uniform distribution.[2] Hence, the effect of this way of modeling a bias toward loyalty is qualitatively the same as the one obtained for a preference ordering (19). This should come as no surprise in view of the underlying assumption of opportunistic preferences.

A similar result obtains from a variation of the time preference, or the time horizon, of the personnel. The larger the part of society's gains from cooperation that is siphoned off after usurpation of power by the personnel of the protective authority the smaller is the incentive for the members of society to keep to cooperative behavior or to stay within the community. Even though the protective authority commands the coercive means, these may not suffice to suppress a fallback to anarchic non-cooperative behavior in all parts of the state territory. Similarly, these means may not suffice to cut off emigration. Accordingly, revenues from usurpation can be anticipated to decline over time and thus affect the payoffs of the personnel's alternative strategies differently. Within the static framework of the present analysis, this can be accounted for by assuming that the utility terms $u(\cdot)$ represent the present values of a finite or infinite stream of future payoffs discounted on the basis of the personnel's time preference rate. With decreasing time preference and/or increasing time horizon, $u(s|o)$ should then decline and $u(r|l)$ increase, and vice versa. If these changes are sufficiently strong, the ordering (10) will be reversed into (19) with an effect that has already been discussed.

The simple model explored above is based on the concept of a representative individual – a useful concept for reconstructing a calculus of self-interest. In an evolutionary perspective, however, that concept impedes the understanding of certain phenomena which are described as instances of selection (where selection operates on the variety of behaviors, see Witt 1992). In order to capture variety, a model would be required that focuses on a population of individuals and allows for polymorphic equilibria. The present modeling approach can be extended to accommodate this. However, a first simple approximation of the implications of a variety of preferences, personal biases, and/or subjective assessments can already be derived in the simpler framework used so far.

Consider, for instance, an authority in which 'opportunists,' with a preference ordering according to (10), and 'semi-opportunists,' with a preference ordering according to (19), co-exist. Since the fraction of supporters in the two groups can be assumed to differ, the subjective guesses of w, previously given by (11), now depend on two F-values and an additional variable, the relative frequencies f and g, $f = 1 - g$, of the two types in the personnel. Moreover, two critical values of minimal support result from (16) where, as shown above, $F^{m*'} < F^{m*}$. This means that a *putsch* is likely to be initiated by the 'opportunists.' Depending on whether or not the latter have correctly estimated f, the *putsch* will or will not succeed. The predictions are no longer necessarily self-fulfilling. Yet, if the estimate of f is sufficiently accurate, or if $F^m < F^{m*'}$, then the implications analyzed above are unchanged.

Analysis becomes more complicated if 'opportunists,' 'semi-opportunists,' and 'heroes' (i.e. agents with a preference ordering (20)) co-exist in the authority. In this case a rather complex payoff structure results due to the fact that putting 'heroes' out of action may have high costs for putschists; the greater the relative frequency $1-f-g$ of 'heroes' the higher the costs. Under the previously chosen assumptions, $1-f-g > 1 - F^m$ would even make it impossible for a *putsch* to succeed. Since the relative frequencies are not known, and are difficult to discover except by attempting a *putsch*, the mere conjecture of a large share of 'heroes' may suffice to deter 'opportunists' from trying their luck. On the other hand, an underestimation of the share of 'heroes' could give rise to *putsches*, even bloody ones, that fail.

In the light of these discussions, how can the empirical differences in proneness to *putsches* be explained, differences that can be observed between North American and Latin American states, say, or between Greece, Turkey, and other European states? One may focus on factors that induce $F^{m*} < F^m$ assuming basically the same values of F^m for the different states; or one may search for systematic differences in F^m between the states presuming approximately the same conditions for the personnel in the different protective authorities; or one may try to combine the two approaches. As indicated above, explanations building on different F^{m*}-values would have to argue with different self-assessments, different time preferences and/or time horizons, or, most importantly, differences in the composition of 'opportunists,' 'semi-opportunists,' and 'heroes,' within the different protective authorities. Would there, for instance, be more 'heroes' in North American than in Latin American authorities – and if so, why? Or would North American personnel only assess loyalty as being more probable? Obviously, the traditional utility maximization approach, which lacks material hypotheses on preferences and their formation, reaches its limits here.

Conclusions

In this paper it has been argued that multiple equilibria are a crucial feature of evolution significant also for understanding the conditions and contingencies of societal evolution. A theoretical problem – the contractarians' argument for legitimizing the state's coercive power – has been used to exemplify the relevance of this concept of evolutionary analysis in a political context. Unlike the contractarians' own view, it has been shown that their basic argument – that anarchy can be overcome by collective consent to a social contract – presupposes the existence of multiple equilibria and, as a consequence, critical mass phenomena. The idea that anarchy may be overcome by social contract requires the state's protective agency to credibly guarantee law and order. In order to achieve this the agency has to be endowed with superior power. Precisely this, however, creates a dilemma: it may be difficult to prevent the agency from usurping its power in the private interest of its personnel. If it is assumed that the constitutional hazard involved here is anticipated by the members of society, their supposed consent to the social contract may be difficult to justify. The possibility of a usurpation hazard may thus do harm to the contractarian approach. As the further investigations in the paper have shown, this hazard – the proneness to *putsches* – is indeed difficult to exclude theoretically, except in a world with 'heroes,' who are reluctant to submit to the self-interested opportunism usually presupposed in public choice theory.

Public choice theory has paid little attention so far to evolutionary thought. No wonder, therefore, that it has failed to recognize the relevance of multiple equilibria for its domain. From an empirical and historical point of view, however, the existence of the multiple equilibria as analysed above is quite obvious. Usurpation of state power is a serious problem in many states – though certainly not in all (in spite of the fact that, as is the case with North American and Latin American states, written constitutions do not differ significantly). What makes the difference in constitutional reality is a complex network of factors which could only be alluded to here. A particularly important empirical point, left open in this paper, is the question of whether the minimal fraction of personnel needed for a successful *coup d'état* may differ systematically between countries. One might speculate, for example, that countries with an effective division of control over coercive means, for example between different layers of a federal state which command their own armed forces or police troops, may be able to establish a system of checks and balances. Such a system may drive up the minimal fraction of personnel necessary to successfully carry out a *putsch* to high or even very high percentages of the entire forces. A closer analysis of the impact of institutional conditions like, for example, command structures and military technology, deserves further in-depth interdisciplinary examination along the lines suggested above.

Notes

1 The problem of multiple equilibria has now gained considerable attention in game theory, though it seems to be regarded more as an unpleasant complication in determining the outcome than as a challenge to rethink the nature of strategic interactions (see e.g. Harsanyi and Selten 1988, Samuelson 1993).

2 To sketch the proof for this assertion, start from the uniform distribution which has a linear distribution function $H(F)$. Shifting the probability density to the left induces a non-linear distribution function H' (F) such that for any $F^m \in [0, 1]$, H' $(F^m) \geq H(F^m)$. Shifting it to the right induces $H''(F^m) \leq H(F^m)$ respectively. When substituting the right-hand side of (13) for w^* and solving for F^{m*} in (18), the inverse of the distribution functions enters. This implies a reversal of the inequality sign such that $F^{m*'} < F^{m*}$ for the left skew density and $F^{m*''} > F^{m*}$ for the right skew density.

References

Bernholz, P. (1991) 'The constitution of totalitarianism,' *Journal of Institutional and Theoretical Economics* 147: 435–40.

Buchanan, J. M. (1975) *The Limits of Liberty. Between Anarchy and Leviathan*, Chicago: University of Chicago Press.

Harsanyi, J. C. and Selten, R. (1988) *A General Theory of Equilibrium Selection in Games*, Cambridge, MA: MIT Press.

Kuran, T. (1989) 'Sparks and prairie fires: a theory of unanticipated political revolution,' *Public Choice* 61: 41–74.

Nozick, R. (1974) *Anarchy, State, and Utopia*, New York: Basic Books.

Okada, A. and Kliemt, H. (1991) 'Anarchy and agreement – a game theoretic analysis of some aspects of contractarianism,' in R. Selten (ed.) *Game Equilibrium Models II*, Berlin: Springer Verlag, pp. 164–87.

Rawls, J. (1971) *A Theory of Justice*, Cambridge, MA: Harvard University Press.

Samuelson, L. (1993) 'Recent advances in evolutionary economics: comments,' *Economics Letters* 42: 313–19.

Schelling, T. C. (1978) *Micromotives and Macrobehavior*, New York: Norton.

Schmidt-Trenz, H. J. (1989) 'The state of nature in the shadow of contract formation,' *Public Choice* 62: 237–61.

Scott, G. H. (1976) 'The new contractarians,' *Journal of Political Economy* 84: 673–90.

Witt, U. (1992) 'Evolutionary concepts in economics,' *Eastern Economic Journal* 18: 405–19.

Index

accountability 154
adaptation to environmental changes,
    allowing time for 33–44
Adorno, Theodor *et al.* 261, 274–5, 277
advertising 65, 72, 74, 120
agrarian society 180–6, 190–4, 206,
    222; transition from 191, 206, 211
Alchian, Armen 5, 7, 16–17, 273
Altemeyer, Bob 261, 274–5, 277
altruism 118, 269–72
American Constitution 107–8; *see also*
    United States Congress
American Economic Association 55
analytical techniques, limitations
    of 90–2
anarchy 143
anti-Semitism 281; *see also* Jews
Aquinas, St Thomas 91, 229
Arendt, Hannah 202, 279
aristocracy 242–50
Armenians 198
arms race 72
Arrow, Kenneth 6
asymmetric information 24, 31–2, 36,
    38, 43
'atomized' masses 279–80
Austen, Jane 254
Austrian economists 88, 121
authoritarian attitudes and
    personality 261, 274–80 *passim*
authority relationships 16–18
automobile accidents, law governing
    174

Bacon, Sir Francis 242–4, 249, 255
Bagehot, Walter 107–8
Balkan states 196
Barry, B. 36
Bartolini, S. 137

Barzel, Yoram 53–4
Bastiat, Frederik 145
Baxter, Keith 244
Becker, Gary 7, 48, 118–19, 270
benevolent despotism 104–5, 109,
    116–17, 120
Berman, Harold 148
Beveridge, William 118–19
bi-positional goods 65–7, 70
bifurcation models 286
bilateral monopoly 71, 75
Bilson, Janet Mancini 233
Birdzell, I. 148
black Americans 227, 232–41, 266
Böhm, Franz 142, 144
Borcherding, Thomas 106
Bosnia 95
bourgeois revolution 215, 220
bourgeoisie, the 238, 242
Bowles, Samuel 5–6, 48–9; *co-editor
    and co-author of Chapters 1 and 2*
Boyer, Robert 8
Bracher, Karl Dietrich 278, 281
Braverman, Harry 5
Brennan, Geoffrey 106, 111
Breton, Albert 7–8, 115–16, 121, 129,
    134, 262; *author of Chapter 7*
Brezhnev, Leonid 210
bribery 51
British Leyland 50
Brontë, Charlotte 119
Broszat, Martin 280
The Brothers Karamazov 247
Buchanan, James 6, 51, 106, 111–12,
    118–19
Bülow, Bernhard von 245
Bundestag, the 137
bureaucracy 212–13, 241
Burr, Aaron 248–9
business executives, decision-making by
    4

calculus of consent 6, 111, 118, 291
Cameron of Lochiel 212
Canada 108, 123, 173, 231
capital structure of firms 60
capitalism 4, 14–15, 77–8, 214
capitalist firms 16, 65, 72–6
causality (political and economic) 91
central banks 155
centralisation by the state 135–6, 138, 206–7
Chamberlain, Edward Hastings 5
Charlottetown Consensus 123
cheating 261–5
checks and balances 107–9, 114–16, 123–4, 139, 298
Chekhov, Anton 248
Cheung, Steven 108
children: economic relationships with parents 118–19, 186, 260–1, 269–73, 278, 281–2
China 96, 273
choice *among* rules and *within* rules 141, 145–6
Civil Rights Movement 239, 241
class distinctions *see* social class
class struggle 220–1
Clemenceau, Georges 245, 249
'closed' processes *see* decision-making
coalitions 171–3
Coase, Ronald 5, 16
Cockburn, Judge 244
coercion: forms of 107, 180–1; by the state or a protective authority 106–7, 109, 287–8, 291, 296, 298; in voluntary exchange 13–15, 23–4
Coker, David 170
Coleman, James 262, 278, 281
command economies 16, 88–90
'common good' and 'common will', doctrines of 104–5
communal or community norms 225–7, 230; *see also* norms of exclusion
communication, forms of 187–8
competition: asymmetry in 18, 146–7; benefits from 145; coexisting with cooperation 122; concept of 120; of currencies 155–6; dynamic 123; entrepreneurial 121–2; intergovernmental 109, 121, 124, 148–57; perfect and imperfect 120–1; political 130–2, 139, 148; role of 141–3; *see also* market competition
competitive equilibrium 13–15
competitive federalism 155–8

competitive government 109, 121, 124
competitive order 143, 145, 147
compulsion *see* coercion
condominium associations 53–4
Congressional government 107–8
consecutive experimenting 153
consent of citizens 116
constitution, European 155
constitutional choices 141, 145–6
constitutional economics 141–2, 148
constitutional efficiency 111–12
constitutional hazard 287–8, 295, 298
constitutional safeguards 154
consumer interests 147
contested exchange 18–24
contingent renewal 18–23
contractarianism 287, 291, 294, 298
conventions 226, 244, 248, 254, 275
cooperation: coexisting with competition 122; in decision-making *see* decision-making; gains from 289, 291–2, 296
cooperatives *see* workers' cooperatives
countervailing power 123
coup d'état problem 287–8; *see also* putsches
Cox, Gary 170
Crain, W. Mark 170
Crawford, R.G. 273
'creative destruction' 122
critical mass 287, 294, 298
cube law of voting 136
cults 251, 265
cultural convergence 203
cultural differentiation and diversity 183–5, 195
culture: high and low 183, 187–90, 195, 207–8, 213, 217; relationship to the state 190; standardisation of 188–90
currencies, competing 155–6
Czech nationalism 200, 216

Dahl, Robert 24, 113–15, 124
Darwin, Charles (and Darwinism) 123, 199–200, 206
de Maistre, Joseph 85
de Mandeville, Bernard 249
deadweight losses 110, 113
decision-making processes: cooperative 55; design of 51; modification of 56; 'open' and 'closed' 53–5, 59; in

public and quasi-public organizations 55; *see also* centralisation
defection from groups 227–8, 289
defense, national 65, 72, 173
democracy: criteria for 103–4, 113–16; economic 25; Madisonian 114–16, 124; *see also* representative democracy
democratic inaction, model of 278
democratization 90
Demsetz, Harold 5, 16–17
Denmark 214
deregulation 157
dialects 207, 216
diaspora nations 198
discriminatory treatment 147, 157
disintegrated nationalism 215
distinctiveness of behaviour 238–9
divestiture decisions by firms 56
division of powers *see* separation of powers
Dostoevsky, F.M. 248
Douglass, Frederick 233
Dow, Gregory 59
Downs, Anthony 6, 121, 129–33
drug use 236
dueling 228, 232, 242–55
Dunn, John 7, 87; *author of Chapter 6*
Duverger's law 172
dyadic norms 230–1, 252
Dye, Thomas R. 151
dynamic competition 123

Eaton, Curtis 119
economic growth 188, 190
economics: and politics, division between 1–8, *see also* political economy; of politics 103; *see also* public choice
Edlin, Aaron 50
education 65, 72–3, 78, 186–7, 190
education titles, devaluation of 72
Edwards, Richard 5
efficiency: concepts of 103–4, 109–13, 124; of governments 106
efficiency wage 32
egalitarian societies 188–9
elections 105–6, 114–16, 130, 137–8
electoral systems 136–7, 172
Elster, Jon 237
employment relationships 19–25, 74–6
employment rent 20, 22–4
enforcement: of contracts 15–19, 21,

24, 115, 261–3, 269; of norms *see* norms; of property rights 119–20; *see also* sanctions
enforcement rent 20–4
Enlightenment, the 192, 202
entrepreneurial activity 121–3
environmental policies 154
equilibria: competitive 13–15; multiple 10, 286, 298
ethnic capital 8, 260–81 *passim*
ethnic groups: assimilation of 225; conflict between 241, 260–1, 267–8, 274–6; definition of 231; identification with 250; marriage between 227
ethnic networks 260, 263; entry to and exit from 263–7; *see also* ethnic capital
ethnic stereotypes 265
Eucken, Walter 142, 144
Euclid 191
European central bank 155–7
European constitution 155
European history (of nationalism) 192–213, 222
European integration 141–2, 156, 158
evolutionary processes 123, 143, 286–7, 296
exchange: concept of 1–4; politics of 5; voluntary 13–15
exit: as a market sanction 30–6, 41–3; from a political jurisdiction 106–7, 150–2
exogenous enforcement, axiom of 15
expenditure and revenue decisions, connection between 113, 124
experimenting in markets 153
Expressionism 281
expropriation 93
extermination of populations 198, 201
externalities 69, 173
extremism 251

families: coercion by 107; relationships within *see* children
famine 91
fascism 268, 274, 277, 279, 281; *see also* Nazism
fashion 65, 72, 74
Fathers and Sons 247
federalism 150–2, 173–4; 'centralist' and 'competitive' 155–8
feedback 237
feudalism 212–13, 215, 217–18

Fiat 50
figures of speech 235–6
Finland 198
First World War 197, 278
Fitzgerald, F. Scott 189
'fluctuation catastrophe' 290
folk culture 199, 208, 217, 265
founders of firms or institutions 52–3
France 172, 217, 245, 249, 270
Frank, Robert H. 270
Franzini, Maurizio 6; *co-editor, author of Chapter 3 and co-author of Chapter 1*
Frederick the Great 246
free-rider problems 6, 36, 38, 43, 53, 75–6, 268, 271
French Revolution 212, 217
frequency dependency effects 287
Freud, Sigmund 271
Fuller, L.L. 4

Galbraith, John Kenneth 123
Galeotti, Gianluigi 7, 115, 129, 134, 137; *author of Chapter 8*
game theory 90, 119, 147, 286
gang challenges 251
Gauthier, David 13
Gay, Peter 281
Gellner, Ernest 8, 264; *author of Chapter 11*
George II, King 245
German language 207
Germany 137–8, 145, 155, 196, 198, 201, 216, 245–6, 265, 268, 270, 278–9
Ghana 96
Gintis, Herbert 5–6; *co-author of Chapter 2*
Golden, Miriam 50
government: goods and services supplied by 116–17, 124; limiting the power of 152; models of 103–9; responsiveness to citizens 154; *see also* competition: intergovernmental
government policy 24, 50, 85, 97
government procurement 52
Granovetter, Mark 17
Greece 198
Greene, Graham 184
Griffin, John Howard 240–1
Grossman, Sanford 16, 58
groups: benefits of membership 229; demarcation between 250; strength of identification with 234–5
Gueux les, 239–40

guilt 271
gymnastics 200

Habsburg empire 208, 210
Hagtvet, Bernt 280
Hamilton, Alexander 245, 248–9
'hangman's paradox' 265
Hansman, Henry 55
Hardin, Russell 8; *author of Chapter 12*
harmonization of constitutional provisions 153
Harsanyi, John C. 23–4
Hart, H.L. 4
Hart, Oliver 5, 16–17, 58
Hayek, F.A. 6, 143–6, 152
Hechter, Michael 265, 273
Hemingway, Ernest 189
Hereward 250–1, 253
heuristic analysis 286
hierarchical orientation of society 180–1
Hirsch, Fred 63
Hirschman, Albert 6, 33–6, 42, 78
Hitler 198, 268
Hobbes, Thomas 17, 91, 143
Hobsbawm, Eric 211
Hochman, Harold 118
Homans, George 2
home, comforts of 240–1
honor 242–50 *passim*
Hotelling, Harold 121
House of Commons 108
House of Representatives, US 170
Howitt, Peter 278
Hroch, Miroslav 211–12, 214–15, 217, 219–22
Hunt, Shaun 235–6
Hunter Lattany, Kristin 235
hyperinflation 278–9

Iannacconne, Laurence R. 265
ideology 136, 169, 182
ignorance within groups 251
imitators of innovation 122–3
'incentive problem' 142, 151
incentives for behaviour 238
income *see* redistribution of income and wealth
income insurance 118–19
incomplete contracts, theory of 5–6, 18
industrial revolution 215
industrial societies 191–4, 206, 220–1; cultural convergence of 203

industrialisation 194, 214–15, 219, 222; stages of 204–5
inequality 64
inertia 36–44
influence costs 6, 46, 51, 54–7, 59 60
information networks 168
innovation 121–2, 186, 188; in government 123
'insurrectional nationalism' 215
interaction, general theories of 1–2, 7
interest groups 105, 280; *see also* pressure groups
involuntary unemployment 22
Ireland 207
irredentism 192, 195–7, 206, 208, 211
Israel 217
Italy 89, 138, 184, 196, 216, 268, 280
Itoh, Hideshi 55

Japan 50, 265
Jews 107, 168, 198, 227, 229, 250–1, 264–6, 273
job loss, cost of 20; *see also* employment rent
just price theory 91
justice: concept of 14; economic 92; 'formal' and 'substantive' 209; laws of 144; perceptions of 93; 'supply' of 116

Kampuchea 89
Kant, Immanuel 201, 230
Kaplan, Abraham 14
Kater, Michael 279
Kiernan, V.G. 244, 246, 248–9, 253
Kiewiet, Roderick 174
Klein, Benjamin 261–2, 273
'knowledge problem' 142–3, 151–2
Kohn, Hans 219
Krueger, Anne 50
Kuran, T. 294
Kuwait 95

labor economics 94
labor extraction function 20
labor markets 16, 24, 262
labor unions *see* trade unions
Lagrangian multipliers 79–80
Landes, William M. 105
language 232–3
Lasswell, Harold 14
Latin America 278
Lazear, Edward 55
learning, competition as a form of 143

Leffler, Keith B. 261–2
legitimization of the state 287
Leipzig 245
lending 229
Lenin 268
Lermontov, Mikhail 248
Lerner, Abba 2
Levi-Strauss, Claude 4
'leviathan' models of government 106
Lewis, David 226
Lewis Allen, Irving 238
liberalism 25, 144; *see also* Ordo-Liberalism
Lindahl equilibrium 71
Lindblom, Charles E. 4
Linz, Juan 268
literacy 182, 193, 213
Lithuanian nation 216
lobbying 147, 167
local government, competitive 121
logrolling 111
long side of the market 22
Lotman, Yuri 184
loyalty: to the nation 268; political 169–71, 263; of the state's protective agencies 291–7
Lubavitchers, the 251
luxury cars 64

Maastricht Treaty 157
McAfee, Preston 56
McCubbins, Matthew 170
Machiavelli, Nicolò 7
McMillan, John 56
Madison, James 114–16, 124
Mair, P. 137
majority rule 172
Majors, Richard 2331
Makhzen 181
Malinowski, Bronislaw 3, 217
Mansfield (Texas) 240–1
Marglin, Stephen 5
mark (currency) 156
market competition 16, 31–2, 143–50
market processes: legitimacy of 92–4; limitations of 93; nature of 91–2
market socialism 76
marketization 90
markets: 'long' and 'short' sides of 18, 22–4; non-clearing 18, 22
marriage, interethnic 227
Marx, Karl (and Marxism) 7, 16–17, 182, 204, 209–14, 218–22, 228
Meech Lake Accord 123

Mérimée, Prosper 249
Meyer, Margaret *et al.* 56
Michels, Robert 138, 268
Michels' disease 130
Mickiewicz, Adam 242
middle classes 278
migration, costs of 149–50
Milgrom, Paul 6, 48, 55–7; *co-author of Chapter 4*; *see also* Meyer, Margaret *et al.*
military service 252
Mill, John Stuart 2, 114, 129, 133
Milosevic, Slobodan 265
minorities, treatment of 106, 132
Mitsui (company) 50
monetary organization in Europe 156–7
'monolithic' government 105–6, 109, 116–17, 120
monopolies: establishment of 145; governments seen as 106; *see also* bilateral monopoly
monopoly rents 51
monopoly rights 144
Montesquieu, Charles-Louis 244
Moore, J. 16
Muller, Max 245
multi-positional goods 65–70 *passim*, 75
Murphy, Kevin 118–19, 270
Mussolini, Benito 216, 268
Myanmar 89

'nation', meaning of 185, 195
nation-building 207–8, 215–18
nation states 179, 191, 217
national sovereignty 156, 158
national unity 216
nationalism 8, 106, 179, 186, 221 *passim*, 231, 250, 260, 264, 268; four types of 215; virulent style of 200–1
nations, 'historic' and 'non-historic' 208, 216
natural selection 123, 200
Nazism 198, 201–2, 210, 231, 264, 268, 271, 276–81
Nelson, Richard 123
Netherlands, the 239
Neumann–Morgenstern utility function 289
New Mexico 53
Nietzsche, F.W. 200–1, 206
'nigger', use of word 232, 238–9
Nobel Lecture 111

norms: categorization of 225–8; enforcement of 240–1, 245–6, 251–2; epistemology of 250–1; of exclusion and difference 8, 225–35, 241, 251 3; origin and development of 238–40; of partiality 228; self-reinforcing 230–1, 251–3; universalistic 226–8, 230–1, 252–3
North, D.C. 32
Nozick, Robert 14, 288, 291

oligarchy, iron law of 138
Olsen, Mancur 6–7
'open' processes *see* decision-making processes
opportunism 5–6, 31–9, 42–3
optimal taxation 110
optimal wages 19
Ordnungsrahmen and *Ordnungspolitik* 154
Ordo-Liberalism 142, 144–5
Ordover, Janusz 49
'organicist' theory of government 104, 106, 109, 117, 120
Ottoman empire 208, 210, 217, 265

Pagano, Ugo 6, 8, 60; *co-editor, author of Chapter 5 and co-author of Chapter 1*
Paldam, Martin 278
Palmer, Matthew 107
Panagopoulos, Epaminondas 107
pan-positional goods 65–71 *passim*
parallel experimenting 153
parents *see* children
Pareto efficiency 6, 23–4, 49, 113, 266, 268
Parliamentary government 108–9, 114
Parsons, Talcott 14
party leaders 170–3
party lists (of election candidates) 137
party organization 129–30, 134–6, 138, 168–73, 280
pastoralists 193–4
Pater, Walter 253
pay-determination processes 54–5, 59
pay policy 48, 56
peasant culture 207, 216
Pepsi Cola 203
perfect and imperfect competition 120–1
Perotti, Enrico C. 59
perquisites, employees' 47
Philip II of Spain 239

pluralism in society 185
'poetry of unreason' 201
Poland and the Polish nation 185, 198, 242
policy coordination 154
political activity within the firm 1, 46–7
political economy 2, 85–8, 95
political exchange 129–30
political limitations on economic options 88–91, 94–6
political markets 31–2, 35, 44, 111, 151, 262–3
political organization, theory of 174
political parties: as coalitions of special interests 171; competition between 130–2; loyalty to 169–71, 263; role of 115, 135–6; weak and strong 139; *see also* party leaders; party lists; party organization
politics, economic approach to 130
pollution 173
Popper, Karl A. 114
positional goods 6, 63–79; acquisition of 78; conflictual consumption of 71; examples of 72–8; pricing of and markets for 69–72
Posner, Richard A. 105
power: accountability of 25; allocation of 78; concept of 24; as a positional good 6, 63–6
'power problem' 142, 151
power relations 14–15, 23–5
preferences 6, 78–9, 117–18, 286, 294–5
pressure groups, function of 167–8; *see also* interest groups
prestige 63–4
price mechanism 13
price premium for high-quality goods 262
price-setting decisions 55
principal–agent relationships 15, 174
prisoner's dilemma 147, 227–8, 230–1, 252, 288–9; iterated 230
private goods 63–70
private and public spheres 18, 25
production possibility frontier 49
productive potential 180, 186
profits and taxation, distinction between 14
promotion processes, modelling of 57–9
property rights 71, 91–3, 119–20, 132, 134
proportional representation 136–7, 172

protective agencies 288–97
public choice theory 7, 103, 109, 111, 114, 145, 286–7, 292, 298
public economics 103, 109
public goods 6, 63–7, 69–71, 107, 110, 130
purchasing power 24
Pushkin, Alexander 248
Putnam, Robert 280
putsches, proneness to 291–8

quasi-rents 31–2, 48, 273
quorum rules 55

racism 241
rank in society 180–4, 188–9, 212
raps and rappers 232–5, 238, 240
rational choice 7, 130–1, 225, 238
Rawls, John 14, 112
recontracting 35–44
'recuperable deterioration' 33
redistribution of income and wealth 110, 116–19
Reformation, the 192–3, 213
religious coercion 22, 107
Renaissance, the 213
Renan, Ernest 217
rent-seeking behaviour 50–1, 145, 147; in condominium associations 54; at federal and nation state levels 157; in firms 55, 60; by interest groups 105; in politics 138, 152; in the public sector 52
rents 31–2, 266–7, 279; of entrepreneurship 122; equalizing the distribution of 56; gained by employees as perquisites 47; gained by managers 50; governments creation of 105–6; necessary to maintain quality of supplies 59; sources of 48, 262–3; *see also* employment rent; enforcement rent
representative democracy 129–30, 133–4
reservation wage 20–1
revelation, theory of 183, 186
Riker, William 172
rites of passage 273
Roberts, John 6, 55–7; *co-author of Chapter 4; see also* Meyer, Margaret *et al.*
Robertson, D.H. 16
Robinson, Joan 5, 90
Rogowski, Ronald 264

Röpke, W. 144
Rosenberg, N. 148
Rotemberg, Julio 59
'rotten kids' theorem 270
Rottenberg, Simon 108
Rousseau, Jean-Jacques 85
Rubin, Gayle 4
Russia and the Russian empire 96, 184, 198, 208–10, 217, 247–9; *see also* Soviet Union
Ryan, David 244

Sahlins, Marshall 8
St Joan 213
Samuelson, Paul 121, 123
sanctions against opportunism 14–15, 18–19, 24, 31–44, 272; *see also* enforcement
Sanford, Nevitt 274
Sartre, Jean-Paul 201, 382
Sass, Tim R. 53–4
scarcity (natural and social) 65, 78–9
Schumpeter, Joseph 121–2, 129–33
Schwartz, Warren F. 244
scientific revolution 192
Scotland 212, 244
secession from federation 150
Second World War 198
security, national 65, 72, 173
self-enforcing contracts 271–2
self-enforcing norms *see* norms
self-interest 7, 225, 238, 270–1, 286–90, 296; of governing groups 105; of individuals 107; of managers and union officials 50
semi-positional goods 64, 68–9, 67–8
semi-public goods 64–71 *passim*
separation of powers 107–8, 114–16, 192
Serbs 236, 265, 268, 276
shame 270–1
Shapiro, Carl 5, 32, 49, 261
Shaw, Bernard 213
Shepsle, Kenneth A. 169
'shifting involvements' 65, 72, 78
shirking: by politicians 138, 171; by workers 16, 32, 48, 262
short-side power 23–5
shunning 252, 254
Simon, Herbert 5
slang 232–5
slaves and slave traders 76–7, 236
'small' nations 214–15, 219

Smith, Adam 31, 120, 130, 142, 144, 212, 242
Smith, T.V. 250
'snowballing' of power and wealth 193–4
social capital 280
social class 65, 72, 76–8, 218–22, 231, 243–4; defined in terms of positional goods 76
social contracts 1, 287, 291, 298
social insurance 118
social learning 275, 277
social norms *see also* communal or community norms
social order 143, 182, 244, 273
social status *see* status in society
social welfare functions 110
socialism 76, 88–9, 144, 214, 218
soft budget constraints 89
Sokol organisation 200
Solon 242
sovereignty: of citizens 154; national 156, 158
Soviet Union 203, 211, 241, 274; *see also* Russia
Spain 239
Spier, Kathryn 59
Spinoza, Baruch 191, 210
Spring Torrents 247
Stalin 198, 210
Stanford University 55
status in society 64–6, 72–4, 77, 180–4, 189, 212, 243, 248
status symbols 73–4
Stigler, George 48, 132, 137
Stiglitz, Joseph 5, 32, 50, 106–7, 110
Sweden 254
Switzerland 150

takeovers, corporate 46
taxation: as distinct from profits 14; efficiency of 110–11; reform of 110
technical efficiency 49, 59
Terborgh, John 123
territorial movements 219
Thompson, E.P. 8
Tiebout, Charles 121
Tocqueville, Alexis de 204, 212, 273, 280
toll roads 253
Tolstoy, Leo 248
trade barriers 97, 157
trade unions 50, 75; coercion by 107; officials of 50

transactions cost analysis 5, 7, 15,
    110–11, 167–8, 171, 173–4, 276–7
transnational institutions 89
Trobriand Islanders 8
trust, relationships of 262–4
truth-telling 226, 228, 230–1, 252
Tullock, Gordon 6, 50, 111–12, 118
Turgenev, Ivan 247–8
Turkish–Greek War 198
tyranny 114–16, 124

Ukraine 214
Ullmann-Margalit, Edna 228
unanimously-agreed-upon rules 111–12
unemployment 22–3
unions *see* trade unions
United States Congress 169–70; *see
    also* Congressional government
United States President and Presidential
    elections 138, 171–2
universal suffrage 114
Uruguay Round 90
usurpation of power 291–8
utility functions 79, 104, 289

value-maximizing institutions 46–7,
    52–3, 59
Vanberg, Viktor 7; *author of Chapter 9*
'veil of ignorance' principle 112
vendetta 242, 252
Venice in the Renaissance 108
Versailles, Treaty of 278–9
Vietnam War 252
'vital organisations' 39–42
'voice' 33–6, 43
voluntary exchange 13–15

wages, 'optimal' 19

Walras, Leon (and Walrasian model) 2,
    13–15, 21
wasted votes 172
wealth: relationship to class 77; *see also*
    redistribution
Weber, Max 93
Weimar regime and period 260–1,
    277–81
welfare economics 2, 65–6, 68, 103,
    109–13
Wells, Robin 60
White, William 119
Wicksell, Knut 111–12
Wicksell-Lindahl efficiency 112–13,
    115, 124
Williamson, Oliver 5, 31, 56, 59
Wilson, Edward 123
Winter, Sidney 123
Wintrobe, Ronald 8, 121, 262, 278;
    author of Chapter 13
Witt, Ulrich 8; *author of Chapter 14*
Wittman, Donald 7, 32, 111; *author of
    Chapter 10*
Wolfe, Thomas 240
work: assignment of 75; nature of
    186–8; variable intensity of 19–21;
    see also shirking by workers
workers' control 49, 55–6, 59
workers' cooperatives 65, 76
Wright, Jim 170

youth culture 203
Yugoslavia 198, 217

Zaire 98
zero-sum enterprise, politics as 117
zero-sum goods 63–4; *see also*
    positional goods